CHURCH BUILDERS OF THE NINETEENTH CENTURY

CHURCH BUILDERS OF THE NINETEENTH CENTURY

*A Study of the Gothic Revival
in England*

BY

BASIL F. L. CLARKE, M.A.

WITH A PREFACE BY

SIR CHARLES NICHOLSON, Bart., F.R.I.B.A.

A Reprint
with new Preface, Corrections and Annotations
by the author

DAVID & CHARLES REPRINTS

7153 4454 4

This book was first published by the SPCK in 1938
This edition published in 1969

© 1969 Basil F. L. Clarke

Printed in Great Britain by
Redwood Press Limited Trowbridge Wiltshire
for David & Charles (Publishers) Limited
South Devon House Railway Station
Newton Abbot Devon

PREFACE TO THE 1969 EDITION

No one likes to re-read what he has written, once it is in print; but after thirty years it is possible to come back to it, read it as though it were the work of someone else, and reassess it in an unprejudiced way.

As I look over this book, I am surprised that I ever attempted to write it at all: my only excuse was, as I said in the preface, that no one had written much on the subject since Eastlake, and I thought that I might as well have a try. I had no special qualification, except that I was interested, and other people did not seem to be. My interest in the nineteenth century was first aroused at the age of fifteen, when I took Bumpus's *London Churches Ancient and Modern* out of the local library—with the result that when I went out on church crawls, I visited the nineteenth-century churches as well as the old ones, and found them all alike interesting. It did not occur to me that there was anything odd about this; but as late as the 30s there were many to whom such an interest seemed strange. 'There's nothing to look at in my church', the vicar would say, 'it isn't old, you know—just a Victorian monstrosity.' Percy Dearmer was blaming the nineteenth-century hymn tune for all our troubles in the Church, and progressive clergymen were as eager to purge their sanctuaries of Victorian work as they were to get rid of *Hymns A and M*. The English altar must come in together with the *English Hymnal* and the *Folk Mass*: coloured marbles must be hidden with curtains and bricks covered with limewash. There were, of course, many people who appreciated the achievements of the nineteenth century; but there were also many, who ought to have known better, who knew as little about them as Batty Langley knew about the Middle Ages. A well-known Oxford clergyman, who once gave me a lift from the cemetery to the city, told me in the course of the drive that all the houses in North Oxford were designed by Ruskin, and seemed rather cross when I showed signs of doubting it. In the face of such ignorance, it was less surprising that a young man should have thought that he knew enough to try to write a book on the subject.

Anyhow, I made the attempt, and the book, when it came out, was surprisingly well received. I can see its faults now. I did not altogether avoid the temptation to present the Victorians as comic. They were, of course—but so are all human beings, and it is not fair to make too much of that aspect of them. I was too much inclined to think of the whole thing as an ascending graph of progress, and to belittle some of the earlier churches, which have in fact more sincerity and life about them than many of the later ones. Nor did I avoid the temptation to quote too much from other books, desiring to show how much I had read, rather than express opinions of my own.

There are two chapters in particular which I now regard as unsatisfactory. That on Sir Gilbert Scott relies too much on his *Recollections*, which are very amusing, but which do not really give a fair picture of him. It ends by saying that he had no recognisable style of his own, which is quite untrue. He could be uncharacteristic, but there was a distinctive Scott style, as I ought to have known perfectly well.

The chapter on Restorations might have been written by one of the more aggressive early members of the SPAB: it picks out the worst features of the restoration movement, and says hardly anything about what was valuable and necessary.

The list of architects at the end includes some who were hardly worth including, and leaves out some of more importance.

And, of course, there are many mistakes, of which some are derived from my sources, and some are my own. I have added a list of these.

But the book remains as it was. I am naturally pleased that it has been thought worth while to reprint it. My wish, that a better book on the subject would be written, has been fulfilled several times: but I hope that there may still be some people to whom this modest pioneer effort may still be of use.

It has been necessary to note a number of churches that have been destroyed since 1938.

B.F.L.C.

PREFACE

IT has always been the custom for persons of taste to venerate their ancestors, to despise their predecessors, to accord faint praise to some of their contemporaries, and to patronise the rising generation. But things move so quickly nowadays that those of us who recollect the likes and dislikes of the Victorian Age are able to take as a matter of course the creation of a " Georgian Group " and even to sympathise with the new born appreciation of the stuccoed villas that still lie hidden beneath the shadow of the blocks of flats in St. John's Wood.

Perhaps, therefore, the day is not far off when the Victorian Church builders will come into their own again. They were often absurd, being but human beings like ourselves, but at any rate they were not "soft". Names such as Cockerell and Penrose are now suggestive of dignified and courtly frequenters of the Athenæum, but their owners had excavated and drawn Greek temples in days when the searcher for knowledge had to carry a blunderbuss to keep off the brigands. One is hardly surprised at anything Pugin did, but even he must have sometimes found it unpleasant to start his day's work at six o'clock in the morning as was customary in his father's office, and must sometimes have found it chilly to travel through the Midlands in his gig and across the Channel in his lugger. One pictures the great Sir Gilbert Scott as the typical prosperous practitioner, but one is apt to forget his twenty-four mile tramps to sketch St. Albans Abbey before Lord Grimthorpe destroyed it, and the hectic days of his partnership with Moffat.

There are still some among us who have personal recollections of some of the old school of church builders, of Shaw, Bodley, Pearson, Sedding, Micklethwaite and the rest, and who have known the keenness and the intolerance, the friendships and the rivalries, of the generation that was still young when Queen Victoria died, the discussions at the " Art Workers' Guild " in the 'nineties, the atmosphere savouring of the Latin quarter in some of the architects' offices in those days, the old fashioned builders who have now for the most part been supplanted by companies.

Although the mediæval architects were not all saints, and although a man may easily be a good artist and at the same time a loose fish, the Church builders of the nineteenth century were for the most part men who were prepared to sacrifice a good deal for their religious principles and in many cases they regarded their work as an integral part of their religion. Pugin of course was demonstrative in this respect—(can it be the case that Charles Dickens tried his hand at polemics when he located Mr. Pecksniff in the neighbourhood of Salisbury ? Even the best natured people are apt to say unkind things about enthusiasts if they don't sympathise with the enthusiasms, and Pugin's house at Farley certainly has a Dragon Inn close to it). But many of the other nineteenth-century Church builders held quite as strong convictions as Pugin did though they talked less about them. And few of them made large fortunes ; even Sir Gilbert Scott died a far poorer man than many a successful lawyer or prosperous tradesman.

The Victorian architects are often regarded as mere copyists. This is quite unjust, but if it were true it cannot be denied that they aimed high even if they missed their mark. It is surely more worthy to draw inspiration from the Parthenon or York Minster than from an eighteenth-century proprietary chapel. But the fact is that there was very little actual copying done—even the Camden movement was a process of experiment in search of something appropriate to the age, and the desired result was very nearly attained by the middle of the century in Carpenter's Church in Munster Square.

We may find it difficult to understand the convictions and prejudices of the Victorian age ; this book may help us think more kindly of those who have gone before, to whose labours we probably owe a good deal more than we are apt to realise.

CHARLES NICHOLSON.

July 25, 1938.

AUTHOR'S PREFACE

It is customary now to visit old churches. Antiquarians, of course, do it: so do religious people. Ordinary educated people know enough about architecture to make a visit worth while. But very few trouble to look at modern churches. Some holiday-makers, indeed, who are determined to visit something, visit modern churches because they do not know enough to be able to distinguish them from old ones: they murmur, " Beautiful old building ", or write " Peace, perfect peace " in the visitors' book. But if they are told that the church which they admire is new, they consider themselves defrauded. Old churches are worth looking at: new ones are not.

The religious visitor who wants to say his prayers will, of course, be ready to say them in any kind of building. But the antiquarian who loves churches because they are old passes by a modern church with scorn. Church-building, as far as he is concerned, came to an end in the sixteenth century. Modern churches may be all very well for holding services in, and the clergy connected with them undoubtedly do good work: but they are not the real thing.

Is this unsympathetic attitude partly due to the lack of books ? There still seems to be an insatiable appetite for books on the pre-Reformation period. They are continually being produced. Some of them are good, and illustrated with magnificent photographs such as could not have been taken even a few years ago. Some of them are common-place, and merely follow in the footsteps of Rickman along the path of Norman, E.E., Dec., Perp. and Debased. In any case they give the impression that there was no Church-building worth considering after a certain date. The date is now put rather later than it was : but even now very few books go beyond the early part of the eighteenth century.

I have long felt that a book was needed on the subject of nineteenth-century church architecture. Eastlake's *History of the Gothic Revival* was published in 1871, and the average visitor of churches is not at all likely to possess it. Sir Kenneth Clark's *Gothic Revival* is quite recent : but it does not deal particularly with churches, and is mainly a study of the history of Taste, interested more in the ideals which produced neo-Gothic buildings than in the buildings themselves.

This book is a modest attempt to fill a gap. I hope that a better book will soon be written : but I have, I think, collected together the main facts, and a certain amount of miscellaneous information which is not otherwise easily accessible.

I have visited a large number of the churches which I mention, and for the most part know what I think of them. But in many cases I have preferred to give contemporary criticisms rather than my own. It interests me to know what people thought of the churches when they were first built : and it is hard to resist quoting criticisms so vigorously and attractively phrased, in comparison with which any remarks expressed in twentieth-century language would seem flavourless and uninteresting.

I have done my best to ensure accuracy in the notes on churches that I have not been able to visit : but I should be glad to be told of any mistakes.

My thanks are due to Sir Charles Nicholson for the preface, to Mr. E. J. Carter, Librarian of the R.I.B.A., for his kind assistance and permission to reproduce illustrations from books and prints in the R.I.B.A. Library, to the various people who have read the proofs and made suggestions, and to the clergy who have answered my enquiries and given me information.

BASIL F. L. CLARKE.

CONTENTS

CHAP.   PAGE

PREFACE TO THE 1969 EDITION v

PREFACE BY SIR CHARLES NICHOLSON . . . vii

AUTHOR'S PREFACE ix

CORRECTIONS AND ANNOTATIONS (1969) . . . xv

I. INTRODUCTION: THE SEVENTEENTH AND EIGHTEENTH CENTURIES 1

II. CHURCH-BUILDING: THE COMMISSIONERS' CHURCHES 20

III. ARCHITECTURAL STYLES: GRECIAN, GOTHIC AND OTHERS 30

IV. GOTHIC IS CHRISTIAN ARCHITECTURE: THE LIFE OF PUGIN 45

V. ECCLESIOLOGY AND THE *ECCLESIOLOGIST*—THE CAMDENIANS AND SYMBOLISM 72

VI. SOME CHURCHES AND THEIR ARCHITECTS . . 107

VII. FOREIGN INFLUENCE: RUSKIN AND THE ECCLESIOLOGISTS: SOME MORE ARCHITECTS . . . 128

VIII. SIR GILBERT SCOTT, *VIR PROBUS, ARCHITECTUS PERITISSIMUS* 160

IX. LATER NINETEENTH-CENTURY CHURCHES: SOME MORE ARCHITECTS 173

X. NEW PARISHES: PARISH LIFE: THE RAISING OF MONEY 216

XI. RESTORATIONS 227

EPILOGUE 248

APPENDIX I: SOME NINETEENTH-CENTURY ARCHITECTS AND THEIR CHURCHES 250

APPENDIX II: SOME TOWNS AND THEIR CHURCHES . . 265

INDEX 271

LIST OF ILLUSTRATIONS

PLATE

I. PUGIN . . . . . . *facing page* 10

II. ST. PETER'S, HAMMERSMITH . . ,, ,, 11

III. ST. GEORGE'S, RAMSGATE . . ,, ,, 26

IV. ST. MICHAEL'S, STOCKWELL . . ,, ,, 27

V. CONTRASTED CHAPELS, FROM PUGIN'S *CON-TRASTS*
BISHOP SKIRLAW'S CHAPEL
ST. PANCRAS CHAPEL . . . *facing page* 42

VI. ST. AUGUSTINE'S, RAMSGATE . . ,, ,, 43

VII. HOOK CHURCH
BROCKHAM GREEN CHURCH . . ,, ,, 58

VIII. ST. STEPHEN'S, WESTMINSTER . . ,, ,, 59

IX. ST. MARY MAGDALENE'S, MUNSTER SQUARE
facing page 74

X. ALL SAINTS', MARGARET STREET . ,, ,, 75

XI. ST. ALBAN'S, HOLBORN . . . ,, ,, 90

XII. ST. CLEMENT'S, CITY ROAD . . ,, ,, 91

XIII. GEORGE EDMUND STREET
SIR GEORGE GILBERT SCOTT . . ,, ,, 106

XIV. ST. JAMES THE LESS, WESTMINSTER . ,, ,, 107

XV. ST. JOHN'S, TORQUAY . . . ,, ,, 122

XVI. GEORGE FREDERICK BODLEY
WILLIAM BURGES . . . . ,, ,, 123

PLATE

XVII.   SKELTON CHURCH . . . .

XVIII.   THE TRANSFIGURATION, LEWISHAM . ⎫ *between*
                                         ⎪ *pages*
XIX.   ST. GEORGE'S, CAMPDEN HILL . ⎬ 130–131
                                         ⎪
XX.   ALL SOULS', HALEY HILL . . ⎭

XXI.   PRIVETT CHURCH . . . . *facing page* 138

XXII.   HOLY TRINITY, SLOANE STREET . ,, ,, 139

XXIII.   ST. PETER'S, VAUXHALL
           ST. ALBAN'S, BIRMINGHAM . . ,, ,, 154

XXIV.   ST. MICHAEL'S, CROYDON
           COMPLETED DESIGN
           THE EAST END. . . . ,, ,, 155

XXV.   ST. MICHAEL'S, BRIGHTON . . ,, ,, 170

XXVI.   ST. AUGUSTINE'S, PENDLEBURY . . ,, ,, 171

XXVII.   ECCLESTON CHURCH
           EXTERIOR, INTERIOR . . . ,, ,, 186

XXVIII.   HOAR CROSS CHURCH . . . ,, ,, 187

XXIX.   ST. AGNES', KENNINGTON . . ,, ,, 202

XXX.   STOKE D'ABERNON CHURCH IN 1829 ,, ,, 203

XXXI.   STOKE D'ABERNON CHURCH TO-DAY ,, ,, 218

XXXII.   ST. MICHAEL'S, CORNHILL . . ,, ,, 219

*The illustrations so far as possible have been taken from
the original sketches, which represent the architects'
conceptions better than modern photographs would do.*

CORRECTIONS AND ANNOTATIONS 1969

p 3, l 12: *for* 1708 *read* 1711.
   l 13: *for* fifty-two *read* fifty.

p 6, lines 23–24: This really refers to ornament: 'ye outward ornaments to be sollid, proporsionable according to the rulles, masculine and unaffected.'

p 11, l 5: the hymn is by Charles Wesley.

p 15, l 9: *for* Rious *read* Riou. The book is *The Grecian Orders of Architecture*, 1768.

p 25, l 13: True, but St Pancras was not a Commissioners' church.

p 31, l 25: Taylor's name was Thomas.

p 36, l 5: John Peter Gandy changed his name to Deering on inheriting an estate in 1827.
   l 8: Not now.

p 37, 1st paragraph: The church was, in fact, partly Victorianised, though this has been undone as much as possible.

p 40, l 24: St George's, Birmingham, is demolished.

p 41, l 1: St Peter's, Saffron Hill, is demolished.

p 41, l 3: St Mary's, Haggerston, was completely destroyed by a bomb.

p 42, l 7: Both these churches have gone.

p 43, l 20: Christchurch has been demolished.

p 43, l 25: *for* south-west *read* south-east. Holy Trinity has been demolished.

p 61, last paragraph: St George's was bombed and completely reconstructed after the War.

p 75, l 16: *for* Thorpe *read* Thorp.

p 78, l 31: *for* Evangelicanism *read* Evangelicalism.

p 84, l 10: *for* Woking *read* Worthing.

p 105, l 13: J. F. Turner became Bishop of Grafton and Armidale. *For* S. Gray *read* W. Gray. There was many other clerical architects.

p 108, 2nd paragraph: I now feel that this is only partly true: I find some of the early Camdenian churches very attractive.

p 111, 3rd paragraph: More true in 1938 than now.

p 113, l 3: Elsted is demolished.

     l 4: St Andrew's, Croydon, is by Woodyer.

     l 5: Wadesmill should be Thundridge.

     l 9: St Mark's, Old Street, is demolished.

     l 11: Holdenhurst is an alteration of a previous church.

p 115, l 35: It has now been redecorated.

p 116, last line: St Stephen's was rebuilt later, and is now demolished.

p 117, l 8: His Cathedral was not built.

     l 20: *for* Dawkes *read* Daukes.

     bottom line: *Add* 'to a reduced scale.' The spire was not built.

p 122, 2nd paragraph: St Matthias' was restored after bomb damage, and its interior arrangements were much altered.

     3rd paragraph: St Alban's was rebuilt after bombing, and only its general shape and proportions recall Butterfield's church.

     3rd line from bottom: Helidon is a restoration. Omit All Saints', Highgate.

p 123, lines 2–3: St Clement's and St Mary's are demolished.

     lines 4–5: St Thomas's is demolished.

     l 6: Poulton is a rebuilding.

     l 8: St Barnabas' is demolished.

     l 9: *for* J.T. *read* J.P.

p 148, 2nd paragraph: St John's was bombed, and carefully restored by H. S. Goodhart-Rendel.

p 154, 1st 4 lines: This does very much less than justice to the Cathedral.

p 155, l 13: What does this mean? They are not such fun, but they are more practicable.

     last paragraph: St Saviour's is demolished.

p 156, 6th paragraph: The chancel of All Hallows' was built by Giles Gilbert Scott in this century.

     last paragraph: St Michael's is demolished, and The Transfiguration is a deaf and dumb centre.

p 158, 1st paragraph: St Andrew's is demolished.

     l 15: St Thomas's is demolished.

p 159, l 7: *for* 1850 *read* 1852.

last paragraph: The following have been demolished: St Luke's, Nutford Place; St Benet's, Stepney; St Paul's, Clerkenwell; St Mary's, Hoxton; St Stephen's, Spitalfields; St Mary's, Carlisle; Christchurch, Weymouth.

p 163, footnote: This is inaccurate. Pugin was addressing the ultra-Protestants, and accusing them of inconsistency. He extracted Catholic doctrines from the first English Prayer Book, and said, 'You must either acknowledge all the contents of this book to be true . . . or you must acknowledge Cranmer and his colleagues to be' . . . etc.

p 172, last paragraph: As I have already said, I now entirely disagree.

p 178, lines 3–4: It would be nearer the truth now to say that almost everyone agrees that they were. It will soon be time for the pendulum to swing back again.

p 183, l 6: *for* not *read* but.

p 192, l 18: St Luke's has been demolished.

l 19: and so has St John's.

p 193, lines 10–11: St John's and St Barnabas' have been demolished.

lines 13–14: St Jude's has been demolished.

lines 14–15: So has St Mary's, Bourdon Street.

l 20: *read* 'addition to nave.' St John's, Great Marlborough Street, has been demolished.

p 198, l 6: Laverstoke in Hampshire is by Pearson, but its date is 1892–5.

l 7: *for* Ferrilby *read* Ferriby.

second paragraph: Holy Trinity has been demolished.

p 199, 7th line from bottom: St John's, Red Lion Square, is demolished.

p 202, l 23: *read* 'The church was consecrated in 1880, and the tower and spire'. . . .

p 203, l 20: The baptistery was added by his son. All the verbs in this paragraph must be put into the past tense.

p 207, l 27: 'One of my cheap churches,' wrote Pearson.

p 208, l 18: This church is in the parish of Chilcomb, on the edge of Winchester.

lines 24–5: St Matthew's is by M. H. Holding.

p 209, l 8: *for* Bloxham *read* Bloxam.

p 213, l 29: The church is at Selsley.

p 214, lines 21f: St Agnes', Kennington and All Hallows', Southwark, have both gone.

p 241, l 14: *for* Pritchard *read* Prichard (and elsewhere).

p 245, footnote 1: This will do for a footnote, but it ought to distinguish between the different members of the Smith family.

p 249, last paragraph: This seemed to amuse one reviewer, but I do not apologise for it.

APPENDIX 1. This list could be enormously extended, but I confine myself to comments on what is already there.

p 250: BARRY, C. and E. M. The dates of Charles were 1823–1906. It was he who was partner with Banks.

p 251: BLACKBURNE's name was Edward Lushington. Both of the churches mentioned have been demolished.

BLORE. The first three churches mentioned no longer exist.

BODLEY. St Michael's, Folkestone, is demolished, St George's, Nottingham, has only a chancel by Bodley. Omit Horninglow. *For* Bowdon *read* Bowden. Souldern was the exact rebuilding of an old tower.

p 252: BRANDON. St Peter's, Great Windmill Street, is demolished.

p 253: CLUTTON. St John's, Limehouse, is demolished.

COLSON. His date of birth was 1820.

CUTTS. Their Christian names were John Edward Knight and John Priston, and their dates 1847–1938 and 1854–1935. St Luke's was bombed, and rebuilt to a different design, and St Matthew's is demolished.

DAWKES should be DAUKES. *For* Pritchard *read* Pritchett. St Stephen's has been demolished.

DERICK. The church at Manchester is Birch in Rusholme.

p 254: DOLLMAN. St Stephen's, Haggerston, and All Saints', Stoke Newington, are no more.

FLOCKTON's name was Thomas James; he died in 1899.

FRANCIS. Horace was partner with his brother Frederick John, 1818–96. I only know of one church, St Mary's, Kilburn, in Hampstead.

p 255: GOUGH, A. D. St Matthew's and St Philip's, Islington, have been demolished.

GOUGH, H. R. Killamarsh and Kippax are restorations.

GWILT. The church at Lee only lasted a few years.

HADFIELD. *For* Matlock, Bath *read* Matlock Bath.

HAKEWILL. Wolverton is Norman. John Henry's dates were 1811–80, and Edward Charles's 1812–72.

HANSOM. Archibald Dunn, trained by Charles Hansom, joined Joseph's son Edward.

p 256: HAWKINS. His name was Major Rohde, and his dates were 1820–84. The first two churches mentioned have disappeared.

HAYWARD, C. F. St Andrew's, Haverstock Hill, has been demolished.

HAYWARD, J. His name was John and his dates were 1808–91.

HEALEY, Thomas, 1809–63. Partner with James Mallinson. His sons continued the practice.

INWOOD. St Peter's, Regent Square, is demolished.

JACKSON, T. G. Was a pupil of Scott.

JOHNSON, J. St Paul's, Camden Town, is demolished. *For* St Edmund's *read* St Edward's.

p 257: JOHNSON, R. J. 1832–92.

KEMPTHORNE's dates were 1809–73.

LAMB. St Philip's, Clerkenwell, is demolished.

LEE. Whitechapel Parish Church is demolished.

p 258: MOUNTFORD's name was Ernest William.

NASH, E. His master was James Field.

NICHOLL's name was Samuel Joseph. His work at St Walburge's, Preston, was an apse added to the church designed by Joseph Hansom.

PEARSON died in 1897.

p 259: PRYNNE. *For* Windyer *read* Windeyer.

p 260: RICKMAN. This list of his churches is quite inadequate.

ST AUBYN's master was Thomas Fulljames.

SCOLES. *For* Nickoll *read* Nicholl.

p 261: SCOTT, Sir G. G. St Andrew's, Westminster, and St Matthew's, City Road, are demolished.

SEDDON. *For* Adamstown *read* Adamsdown.

p 262: SHAW, R. N. The Notting Hill church is no longer used as such.

SHELLARD's name was Edward Hugh.

SMIRKE. Markham Clinton and West Markham are the same place.

SMITH, W. B. St Mary's, Caterham, *omit* 'additions'.

STREET. *Omit* Bracknell.

p 263: TEULON. *For* Potter *read* Porter. St Paul's, Hampstead, St. Paul's, Bermondsey, and St Thomas's, Agar Town, are demolished.

WHITE. *For* Squirrell *read* Squirhill.

p 264: WILLIAMS's name was Stephen William.

WITHERS. St Anselm's, Streatham, is demolished.

WOODYER's dates were 1816–96.

APPENDIX 2. There is no need to repeat the names of the churches that have already been mentioned as demolished.

FULHAM, St Etheldreda. Skipworth's church was bombed, and rebuilt to a different design.

HACKNEY. The parish church was bombed and demolished.

HAMPSTEAD. Manning's initials were M.P.

BIRMINGHAM. St Patrick's is to be demolished.

LEEDS. St Andrew's is demolished. St Chad's is by Lord Grimthorpe and W. H. Crossland, enlarged by J. and J. H. Gibbons.

OXFORD. Drinkwater's initials were H.G.W.

CHAPTER I

1. CHURCH-BUILDING

IT has often been pointed out that in the Middle Ages the parish church was the centre not only for worship, but also for all kinds of activities that were not religious at all. " The fabric," as Dr. Cox said, " served in many respects . . . the purposes for which a clubroom or institute is nowadays used, as well as for the Divine Offices for which it was primarily built and hallowed." [1] It was also used for civic purposes, for the transaction of business, and sometimes for the storing of goods. There was no clear dividing line between sacred and secular : all the activities and interests of the people were centred in the church.

We can hardly imagine a church being used for eating and drinking, marketing and dancing ; but these things were taken for granted in former days. The church was a place of worship : it was also a place for almost everything else. It was used not only by the religiously minded, but by everybody.

Then came the Reformation ; and after that all the varied and interesting uses of the church came to an end. Not all at once. In the seventeenth century application was made to Archbishop Laud to allow the holding of Ales in church, according to the old custom. And the nave of St. Paul's Cathedral, as we have often been told, was used for secular purposes. But neither Puritans nor High Churchmen approved, and the old customs died. The church was no longer a theatre or a market or a parish hall or a storehouse or a law-court : it was a place. of worship. And the result was, naturally enough, that men lost interest in it. Religion before the Reformation may have been superstitious and in need of purification ; but it was bound by innumerable links

[1] *The English Parish Church*, p. 13.

to common life, and the natural and the supernatural, earth
and Heaven, were firmly united. When they became dis-
united, religion did not become more spiritual: it became—to
the ordinary people, if not to the theologians—less interesting.
And churches too became less interesting.

Mr. A. R. Powys says [1] that in modern churches " the
desire for worship is singly represented, and there is little
evidence that profane life is married to religious ; they do not
fully express the people's beliefs and fears, struggles and joys ;
and this being so, they are at best but noble forms consecrated
to the spiritual need of a race which depends for breath on
things almost wholly material ".

The need for worship is not strongly felt by the average
man, and a church which is simply a place of worship makes
no particular appeal to him. In the Middle Ages he subscribed to the building of his church because he had an interest
in it. After the Reformation a church was built for him and
he was expected to go to it : not at any time and for any
purpose, but at particular times for the hearing of the Word
and partaking of the Sacraments.

This was taken for granted.

Mr. Molesworth, in his *Penny Sunday Reader*, which was
presumably widely read in the early nineteenth century, said,
" This is our parish church! How many subjects of the
deepest interest do these words call forth! In this lowly
building God is worshipped. It is *consecrated* to Him. It
must not be set apart for *any secular purposes*. Here we offer
up the sacrifice of prayer and praise." " Reader," he continues, " whosoever thou mayest be, if thy soul hath caught
one spark of the pure fire of Christian devotion, if thy bosom
hath been penetrated by one ray of the free light of Christian
charity, wilt thou refrain thy lips, or withhold thine heart,
from the prayer which we offer for blessings on these holy
uses to which the parish church is dedicated ? "

But most souls are not aflame with Christian devotion, and
do not burn to erect places for the offering of the sacrifice of
prayer and praise. So that church-building became the business of those who were religious, or who considered religion to

[1] *The English Parish Church*, pp. 161–162.

be a good thing for other people. It became the concern of the ecclesiastical or civil authorities, or of the wealthy, and the average man had very little to do with it. Churches had to be built for him.

In the eighteenth century a certain number of churches were built in the towns. London had grown considerably, and it was computed at the beginning of the century that 200,000 people in the suburbs were without church accommodation. These had to be supplied, and the procedure is interesting. Action was taken not by the parishes, but by Parliament.

An Act of Parliament was passed in 1708 for the erection of fifty-two new churches in London. The House of Commons stated that " neither the long, expensive war in which we are engaged, nor the pressure of heavy debts under which we labour, shall hinder us from granting to your Majesty whatever is necessary to accomplish so excellent a design ". Following the precedent set after the Great Fire, they imposed a duty of one shilling on every cauldron of coals, and by this means raised £350,000. But, as Sir Roger de Coverley said, Church-work is slow: enthusiasm waned, and in fact only twelve churches were actually erected. And, in spite of the still continuing growth of the town, only a few were added to the number later in the century.

Some new churches were erected in other large towns. The new parish church of S. Philip, Birmingham, was begun in 1710 and consecrated in 1715 ; St. Paul's, Sheffield, was begun in 1720; and Holy Trinity, Leeds, was built in 1722–1727. The money for the building of churches was raised by rates—for every parish until 1868 was bound to keep its parish church in repair—and by briefs. Briefs were Royal Letters Patent addressed to the churchwardens of the whole country, or of some particular county, requesting contributions for some object. Thus in 1732 a brief was issued for the raising of money to rebuild St. Mary's, Monmouth. It stated that " part thereof has already fallen down, and that part which remains now standing is so small that it is not sufficient to contain half the inhabitants of the said parish, and is also ruinous in the foundations, walls and roof thereof ".

B

But briefs were not a very successful way of raising money. There were too many of them, and much of the money collected was often absorbed by the expenses of collection.

Other methods were also used. When St. Mary's, Battersea, was rebuilt, £1900 was raised by the issue of subscription bonds at 4 per cent., and £945 by the lease of pews.

In the country many churches were rebuilt, but very few new ones erected. The church accommodation of the villages was already large enough—very often, in view of the fewer uses to which the church was put, far too large. If there was rebuilding, the church was usually reduced in size. The elegant and graceful new building was designed to provide sufficient seats for the congregation, and had no room for anything else. Sometimes the old church was in decay and had to be rebuilt; often it was rebuilt simply in order to harmonize with the large house of the place. But unless it was dilapidated, or unless the local squire or nobleman wanted to improve it, the old building was left alone and satisfactorily supplied the needs of the people.

If new centres of population grew up in the country, they were left unsupplied with places of worship, unless chapels were built by the Nonconformists. In Cornwall, where an unusually large number of old chapelries had been disused at the time of the Reformation, nothing was done for the communities of miners and others until the coming of the Methodists. Methodism succeeded in interesting the ordinary people in religion; and the result was that they were eager to build chapels. But for the time being the members of the Church were not similarly inspired, and new churches were not built.

2. Styles of Architecture

What did the churches of the seventeenth and eighteenth centuries look like? Sir Christopher Wren's churches are of various plans: square with a domed roof, square with a Greek cross arrangement of columns, or planned in the old way with nave and aisles. Some unusual churches were built in the eighteenth century: All Saints', Newcastle, is elliptical; St. Chad's, Shrewsbury, is circular; Stony Middleton, Derbyshire, is octagonal; Long Ditton (by Sir Robert Taylor) was cruciform with only four windows, one at the end of each limb of the cross. But most architects adhered to tradition, and designed churches with nave and aisles. Naves were designed to contain seats, and for no other purpose, pulpits were made more prominent, and galleries were often introduced. The most important alteration was the reduction of the chancel to very small dimensions: usually the chancel was merely a recess to contain the altar. It is not altogether true to say that the sermon was now regarded as more important than the Sacraments; but, as Sir Christopher Wren wrote, " In our reformed religion it would seem vain to make a parish church larger than that all that are present can both see and hear. . . . It is enough if they (the Romanists) hear the murmur of the Mass and see the Elevation of the Host, but ours are fitted as auditories."

The style was Renaissance. We should remember that in the Middle Ages there was no " style " of architecture, to be adopted and used for a particular purpose. We say that the old churches are in the Gothic style, and simple people imagine that they are in that style because they are churches. Certainly the building of the Middle Ages was " church-conscious ", and was chiefly developed in church building; but churches were not built in a style of their own. Castles, halls and houses were built in the same way. And the manner of building was not something to which a name could be given: it was inspired by a definite architectural vision which carries it far beyond the natural; and yet it was the way in which it was natural to build. The manner changed as years went by; but the changes came from within, not from without. They were not the result of imitation of any other fashion.

In the sixteenth century certain features began to be imported. England, like every other European country, was affected by the Renaissance, and Englishmen began to take an interest in the cultures of ancient Greece and Rome. Little Renaissance details began to creep into architecture, and took their place rather incongruously against a background in the traditional manner. Then the traditional manner became less and less apparent—though it may never have quite disappeared —and the Renaissance element became stronger.

But in England Renaissance architecture—at any rate to begin with—was seldom copy-book architecture. There was always a tendency for it to become so ; but English architects on the whole managed to avoid the tendency.

Vitruvius had given an account of the Classic—at least, the Roman—orders which was regarded by many as being final, and many of the architects of the Renaissance adhered rigidly to his rules. This kind of regulated Classic building is often known as Palladian, after the architect Palladio (1518–1580), whose architecture, as Mr. H. Heathcote Statham has said, " was of a conventional and scholastic type, and too much subject to arbitrary rules. He himself was undoubtedly an architect of genius, and perhaps the real reason why his name has been thought synonymous with dullness and convention-ality in architecture is that many have adopted his rules without possessing his genius." [1]

But English architecture of the sixteenth and the seventeenth centuries on the whole avoided that reproach. Inigo Jones was the first architect in this country to grasp the meaning of the Renaissance and to show its possibilities; but his work—of which there is unfortunately very little—was the product of genius, and certainly not of a " conventional and scholastic type ". He believed that architecture should be " solid, proportional according to the rules, masculine and unaffected ".

Sir Christopher Wren (1632–1723) " adopted the formal Italian school of the Renaissance "; but he, too, was a genius, and was able to use conventional forms in an unlimited number of new and interesting ways. His younger contemporaries, Hawksmoor and Vanbrugh and Gibbs, used the stock features, but used them with great effect.

By the end of the seventeenth century the old manner of building had become superseded. It did not disappear—there are some seventeenth-century buildings in the traditional manner which are hardly distinguishable from similar ones of the preceding century—but it was considered somewhat rustic and unsophisticated. And it gained a name. It was called Gothic.

It is not certain who first applied the name. Sir Christopher Wren is supposed to have originated it ; but it was current

[1] *A Short Critical History of Architecture*, pp. 460–461.

before his time. A footnote to the introduction to the *Essays on Gothic Architecture* by Milner, Bentham and Grose (1802 : 2nd edition) says that it " originates with Italian writers of the fourteenth and fifteenth centuries ; who applied the expression of ' La maniera Gotica ' in contempt to all the works of art of the Middle Ages ".

Wren in fact " was of opinion that what we now vulgarly call the Gothic ought properly and truly to be named *Saracenic Architecture*, refined by the Christians, which first of all began in the East after the fall of the Greek Empire, by the prodigious success of those people that adhered to Mahomet's doctrine, who, out of zeal to their religion, built mosques, caravansaras and sepulchres, wherever they came. . . . The holy wars gave the Christians who had been there an idea of the Saracen works, which were afterwards, by them, imitated in the West."

To John Evelyn the diarist the cathedrals of the Middle Ages were " congestions of heavy, dark, melancholy, monkish piles, without any just proportion, use, or beauty ". This is the account of the Gothic style given by Wren's son in his *Parentalia* : " It was after the irruption of swarms of those truculent people from the north, the Moors and Arabs from the south and east, overrunning the civilized world, that wherever they fixed themselves they soon began to debauch this noble and useful art ; when, instead of those beautiful orders, so majestical and proper for their stations, becoming variety, and other ornamental accessories, they set up those slender and misshapen pillars, or rather bundles of staves, and other incongruous props, to support incumbent weights and ponderous arched roofs, without entablatures."

He compares unfavourably, in several exceedingly long sentences, Henry VII's Chapel, with its " sharp angles, jetties, narrow lights, lame statues, lace, and other cut work and crinkle-crankle ", with St. Paul's and with Wren's other work at Oxford, Cambridge and Greenwich.

And he says, " The universal and unreasonable thickness of the walls, clumsy buttresses, towers, sharp-pointed arches, doors, and other apertures without proportion ; nonsensical insertions of various marbles impertinently placed ; turrets and pinnacles thick set with monkies and chimeras, and abundance of busy work, and other incongruities, dissipate and break the angles of the sight, and so confound it, that one cannot consider it with any steadiness, where to begin or end ; taking off from that noble air and grandeur, bold and graceful manner, which the ancients had so judiciously established. . . . Vast and gigantic buildings indeed ! But not worthy the name of architecture." [1]

It was a "fantastical and licentious manner of building " not worthy of the serious attention of men of taste. ("Licentious ", of course, has no moral significance. The seventeenth-century critics, unlike those of the nineteenth, did not confuse bad building with bad morals.)

Of course the word Gothic is inaccurate : mediaeval building had nothing to do with the Goths. But it continued to be used ; and, finally, like the word Christian, came to be regarded not as a term of reproach, but as a symbol of everything that is noble and glorious.

The fact that the old manner of building had a name is a sure sign that it was a thing of the past. We use the name "Victorian " because the Victorian age is past. In the nine-teenth century everything was Victorian : now the Queen is dead, and the fashions of her reign have departed. Victorian-ism has not disappeared ; but it is a thing of the past, and it is dying out. Many of the pictures and ornaments in poor houses are Victorian. But educated people, we consider, have no business to approve of Victorianism. It is a dying fashion, fit only for those who are unable to appreciate anything better.

Something of the same kind was implied when the old styles were given the name of Gothic. Unimportant people might cling to the old tradition ; but those who knew what was right could afford to despise such fantasticalness and licentiousness.

Sir Christopher Wren occasionally used Gothic—probably the parishioners of some of the City parishes insisted on their churches being rebuilt as they had been before—but his Gothic churches are not very interesting, and he used the style without enthusiasm.

The Classic City churches of Wren are renowned for their

[1] Wren, *Parentalia*, p. 306.

beauty and variety.   But the churches built by other architects
in the early years of the eighteenth century are also well
designed and extremely attractive.

The churches of Nicholas Hawksmoor (St. Mary Woolnoth ;
St. Anne's, Limehouse ; St. Alphege, Greenwich ; St. George's
in the East ; St. George's, Bloomsbury, and Christchurch,
Spitalfields) are all imposing.   Of Christchurch, Spitalfields,
Mr. Goodhart Rendell says, " It remains doubtful whether of
its date and kind there is any finer church than this in Europe ".[1]

St. Martin-in-the-Fields and St. Mary-le-Strand, by James
Gibbs, are noble and beautiful buildings.   Gibbs also designed
All Saints', Derby (now the Cathedral), which was rebuilt in
1725.   To this church Mr. F. C. Eeles has applied the words
" a mystery above all price which may not be spoken against ".
This is something of an exaggeration ; but it is pleasant to
read it.

Most of the smaller churches of this time—and indeed
throughout the century—when they have escaped nineteenth-
century interference, are delightful.   They are well proportioned and their craftsmanship is excellent.   Some have
few definitely Classical details, except for the cornice and a
doorway ; others are more elaborate.   But they all display
an almost unfailing good taste.   They have been almost
unnoticed in the past : guide-books will devote pages to older
buildings, and pass over eighteenth-century churches with a
mere statement of their date.   If they say anything more
it is abusive : the word " hideous " almost invariably accom-
panies the word " Georgian ".   It is curious that so many
writers and educated Church-people who love and appreciate the old Gothic churches should fail to grasp " the
peculiar charm and appropriateness of these later productions,
which reflect so admirably the individualism and churchmanship of their times ".[2]   Churches such as Blandford, or
Charlton Marshall, or North Runcton, or Avington, or Tong
(Yorkshire), or even Chislehampton, have so obvious a charm
that it is difficult to imagine how anyone could fail to respond
to it.   Even if it is assumed that eighteenth-century church-

[1] H. S. Goodhart Rendell, *Nicholas Hawksmoor*, p. 27.
[2] J. C. Cox and C. B. Ford, *The Parish Churches of England*, p. 64.

manship was dull and apathetic, it by no means follows that
eighteenth-century churches are poor buildings. A certain
type of Churchman can never look at an eighteenth-century
church without remembering Bishop Hoadly and Bishop Watson
of Llandaff—and his judgement is clouded by what he remem-
bers of Church history.   But when he sees a Norfolk fifteenth-
century church he forgets the worldliness of the time in
which it was built; and in the nave of Durham he never
thinks of the wickedness of Bishop Flambard, who built it.

Poor churches were built in the eighteenth century, as they
have been at every other time; but the majority are not poor :
they are very attractive.

A few Gothic churches were built at the same time—such as
St. Nicholas', Warwick (1779–1780), Hartwell (1756), Tetbury
(begun in 1771) and Preston-on-Stour (1752–1757).   They
are curious and interesting, but abnormal.   Gothic was not
the natural style for a church at the time—or for any other
building.   But the few churches, and a much larger number
of houses, bear witness to a certain amount of interest in the
style.

The interest was not technical or professional : it was mainly
literary, and it was confined to people of leisure or wealth.
The literary interest was apt to be of a melancholy nature.
It was the habit of poets throughout the century, and of a
certain number of religious writers (certainly not all !), to sit
(or to picture themselves sitting : it is hardly likely that they
actually did so) in churchyards or in the neighbourhood of
ruined abbeys by moonlight, and to be impressed by awful
sentiments.   The richer works are stiff with horror : owls
hoot and flit, and skulls leer among the desolate ruins.   Sometimes the melancholy has a religious tone ; but the horror is
not spared in any case.   Hervey, in his *Meditations among the
Tombs*, contemplates a skull and says, " Instead of the sweet
and winning aspect, that wore perpetually an attractive smile,
grins horribly a naked, ghastly skull.   The eye that outshone
the diamond's brilliancy, and glanced its lovely lightning into
the most guarded heart—alas !   Where is it ?   Where shall we
find the rolling sparkler ? "

Sacred Gems from the British Poets contains the lines

PLATE I

[National Portrait Gallery.

PUGIN

(Artist unknown)

PLATE II

ST. PETER'S, HAMMERSMITH

By Edward Lapidge

An unambitious Commissioners' Church in the Grecian style

" Cease, mortal, then to boast thy transient charms,
A prey to worms ; in vain the glass reflects
A well proportioned harmony of parts,
Since thou must rot in earth a hideous corpse."

The Hymn-book of the Countess of Huntingdon's Connexion
even sang,

" With solemn delight I survey
The corpse when the spirit is fled,
In love with the beautiful clay,
And longing to lie in its stead."

But to this kind of melancholy meditations the Gothic building
in the background was merely scenery. A ruined Classical
building would have harboured similar owls and produced the
same effect. Most English ruins are naturally Gothic ; but
that was an accident. Anyone who was in need of emotional
stimulation would seek a Gothic ruin, or a churchyard with
an unruined but dilapidated church ; but that meant no interest
in the Gothic style. He would not desire to restore the
buildings or to revive their style (unless, indeed, he wished for
a new ruin). Admiration of that kind was a literary fashion
and led nowhere. But it was extraordinarily popular.

Towards the end of the century numbers of novels were
produced of the type that thrilled Catherine Morland and
Isabella. (" ' I will read you their names directly. . . . Castle
of Wolfenbach, Clermont, Mysterious Warnings, Necromancer
of the Black Forest, Midnight Bell, Orphan of the Rhine, and
Horrid Mysteries. Those will last us some time.' ' Yes,
pretty well ; but are they all horrid, are you sure they are all
horrid ? ' ") [1] They were very crude and feeble, and their
horrors were of an obvious nature ; but they must have been
a relief after the rather cold literary fashions of the eighteenth
century. They seem to have had the effect—if Jane Austen
can be trusted—of associating ancient buildings, especially
abbeys, with sentiments of terror. The novels of Sir Walter
Scott are usually given the credit for first calling attention to
the romance of ancient buildings. But that had been done
before. Sir Walter Scott's achievement was to associate
comparatively sane and historical romance with Gothic

[1] Jane Austen, *Northanger Abbey*, p. 40 (Oxford Edition).

buildings in place of the wild absurdities of the horrid novelists.

The first of the horrid novels was the *Castle of Otranto : A Gothic Story*, by Horace Walpole, who was the first eminent man in the eighteenth century to attempt Gothic building on a large scale. In 1747 he bought Strawberry Hill in Middlesex ; three years later he began to Gothicize the house.

There had been small Gothic works before that. Some sham ruins had been erected. Batty Langley (whose name became a by-word) produced in 1742 a book called *Gothic Architecture improved by Rules and Proportions in many Grand Designs of Columns, Doors, Windows, Chimney-pieces, Arcades, Colonades, Porticos, Umbrellos, Temples and Pavilions, &c.* It is an imposing title : but " arcades and colonades "—and even " umbrellos and temples "—are on a comparatively small scale. A Gothic house of the size of Strawberry Hill was a novelty. It was admired at the time. Gray the poet (who was also an antiquarian) said that there was " a purity and propriety of Gothicism in it that I have not seen elsewhere ".

C. L. Eastlake, in his *History of the Gothic Revival in England*, has treated Strawberry Hill in rather a pedantic manner. It is, he says, " just what one would expect from a man who possessed a vague admiration for Gothic without the knowledge necessary for a proper adaptation of its features ".[1] But what is a " proper adaptation " ? Walpole did not try to produce an exact, copy book imitation of a mediaeval house, for there were none like it to imitate : he was an amateur archaeologist with a taste for amusing and fanciful effects. Speaking of his rooms, he said, " Every true Goth must perceive that they are more the works of fancy than imitation ".[2] The designs were a congeries of inexact copyings from mediaeval work, mixed according to taste, which seemed to the Victorian critics to be almost profanity, but which we find rather attractive.

The fashion for Gothic houses soon spread, and culminated in the extraordinary Fonthill Abbey, built for William Beckford by James Wyatt. Wyatt's work was generally admired, and his epitaph expressed the opinions of many when it spoke of

[1] *History of the Gothic Revival*, p. 47.
[2] Quoted in Kenneth Clark, *The Gothic Revival*, p. 73.

his professional ability, the combined result of superior genius, science and energy. But he was usually known in the nineteenth century as the vandal, the Destroyer, or even as the unspeakable Wyatt. Fonthill—which never was an abbey—was an enormous erection of the most romantically Gothic type. It was a nine days' wonder: it collapsed in 1825, and has now disappeared.

Wyatt was also a restorer, and his restoring activities roused the wrath of an opponent whose language was a foretaste of that of some of the nineteenth-century devotees of Gothic architecture. John Carter wrote during nearly thirty years a series of articles abusing and attacking Wyatt. He would not admit that any ancient building needed restoration, and was horrified at Wyatt's interferences. " Nothing but devotion to Novelty and hatred of Antiquity," he cried, " governs all these undertakings." At times he rose to prophetic fervour, and threatened Wyatt with divine judgement. Wyatt's reputation is only now beginning to recover from these attacks.[1]

It is worth noticing that there was no religious motive in the interest in the Gothic style during the eighteenth century. If religious writers mention Gothic buildings, it is merely that they may stand in the background while they inspect skulls and moralize on Death. There are abbeys in the horrid novels; but abbeys were Popish, and there was no likelihood of reviving Popery. As a style of modern building it was hardly taken seriously. It was a style for gazebos and furniture : rich men could build great houses like Strawberry Hill and Fonthill. But it was not a religious style. Strawberry Hill had a chapel, but it was a sham. (It is merely a rather ironical chance that the house is now a Roman Catholic College.) Fonthill had an oratory, with gilt fan vaulting and elaborate golden lamp, a statue of St. Anthony and massive candelabra. The *New Monthly Magazine* (June 1844) said that no descrip-

---

[1] This vilifying of Wyatt has become a habit. Mr. Edward Foord, in a handbook to Hereford, refers to him as the " unspeakable " Wyatt, and says that the artist will " pray for Oriental fecundity of malediction " upon him. But as a matter of fact Wyatt did very little serious harm to the cathedrals of England. He did more or less unsatisfactory work at Lichfield, Salisbury, Hereford and Durham ; and good work at Westminster Abbey.

tion could convey an idea of the effect of this " solemn recess ",
or of the awful sensations which it inspired.   It was proper
that it should convey awful sensations, but that was all it was
there for.   Except in a few cases, churches were built in the
admirable, unsentimental style which we have mentioned ;
and the exceptions prove the rule.   Ancient Gothic was awful
—at any rate, if it was on a large scale or suitably dilapidated.
Modern Gothic was an amusing hobby—like the Chinese style,
with which it seems to have been sometimes confused.   But
Gothic as a universal style for churches was undreamed of.

But there were a few who took Gothic seriously, and who
attempted to understand the old buildings.   When we see an
old church, we instinctively ask, " When was it built ? " ;   and
knowledge of the subject is now so widespread that many can
answer at once—at any rate with reasonable accuracy.   Almost
anyone can see that Durham Cathedral is older than York, or
that St. George's Chapel, Windsor, is of a different century
from Salisbury.   But in the eighteenth century only a tiny
minority had any knowledge at all of the subject, and that was
slowly and laboriously acquired.   The wildest guesses were
made as to where and how Gothic began.   Bishop Warburton
in his notes on Pope's Epistles said, " When the Goths had
conquered Spain, and the genial warmth of the climate and
the religion of the old inhabitants had ripened their wits and
inflamed their mistaken piety (both kept in exercise by the
neighbourhood of the Saracens, through emulation of their
service and aversion to their superstition), they struck out a
new species of architecture, unknown to Greece and Rome ;
upon original principles, and ideas much nobler than what
had given birth even to classical magnificence.   For this
northern people having been accustomed, during the gloom
of Paganism, to worship the Deity in groves (a practice common
to all nations), when their new religion required covered
edifices, they ingeniously projected to make them resemble
groves as nearly as the distance of architecture would permit ;
at once indulging their old prejudices and providing for their
present conveniences by a cool receptacle in a sultry climate ;
and with what skill and success they executed the project, by
the assistance of Saracen architects, whose exotic style of

building very luckily suited their purpose, appears from hence, that no attentive observer ever viewed a regular avenue of well-grown trees, intermixing their branches overhead, but it presently put him in mind of the long visto through the Gothic cathedral; or even entered one of the larger and more elegant edifices of this kind, but it presented to his imagination an avenue of trees; and this alone is what can be truly called the Gothic style of building."

A certain Mr. Rious, in his book on architecture, said, " Such buildings have been called Modern Gothic, but their true appellation is Arabic, Saracenic or Mooresque. This manner was introduced into Europe through Spain."

The Rev. J. Milner, in his *Treatise on the Ecclesiastical Architecture of England during the Middle Ages*, quotes some curious opinions.

Mr. Murphy, in his *Introductory Discourse on the Principles of Gothic Architecture*, had concluded that it came from the Pyramids. Mr. Smirke, junior, found its origin in Italy. Sir James Hall, Bart., derived it from basket-work. Sir James published the results of his researches in an *Essay on the Origin, History, and Principles of Gothic Architecture* (1813). " I have been enabled," he says, " to reduce even the most intricate forms of this elaborate style to the same simple origin, and to account for every feature belonging to it from an imitation of wicker-work." Some early churches, such as Durham and Glastonbury, were originally of wicker: these, he surmises, were venerated and imitated. There is a frontispiece of a wicker church erected by the author; " not intended to represent a primitive place of worship, but rather a bower, such as the Freemasons might be supposed to construct as an exercise of taste and invention, or as a model of any new and ornamental device which it was intended to submit to the approbation of the brotherhood ".

The picture shows a complete and extraordinary Gothic structure with a spire like that of St. Nicholas', Newcastle. The upright posts have taken root and begun to bud: this is the origin of crockets. Cusps are derived from the peeling off of the bark. Various illustrations show how Gothic tracery, spires, vaulting, etc., can be satisfactorily reproduced in wicker-work, and may therefore safely be said to have been derived from it.

The most comprehensive opinion was that of Mr. Payne Knight, who, on page 162 of his *Enquiry into the Principles of Taste*, said, " The style of architecture, which we call the cathedral or monastic Gothic, is manifestly a corruption of the sacred architecture of the Greeks and Romans, which is formed out of a combination of Egyptian, Persian and Hindoo ".

There was no idea of the dates at which the various styles prevailed. Some ascribed Gothic to the Goths, some to the Danes. And the confusion was worse confounded by the varying use of names. According to Milner, some called all ancient architecture Gothic, others used " Norman " for the pointed style. But no one, except by accident, gave true names to the styles or had any idea of how to date them.

But there were some who made serious researches : among others, the brothers Warton and the poet Gray. In 1771 James Bentham published his *History and Antiquities of the Conventual Church of Ely*, which contained some valuable work. He proves that stone churches were known before the Conquest, and that " architecture was carried in that age to some considerable degree of perfection ". The Normans improved on the old architecture. They were " moderate and abstemious, and delicate withal in their diet ; fond of stately and sumptuous houses ; affected pomp and magnificence in their mien and dress, and likewise in their buildings, public as well as private ". The criterion of their building is chiefly " its massiveness and enlarged dimensions, in which it far exceeded the Saxon ". There had been some Norman building before the Conquest. He gives an accurate account of the characteristics of Norman work.

Then " in Henry the Third's reign the circular arch and massive column seem wholly to have been laid aside, and the pointed arch and the slender pillar substituted in their room ". In the latter part of Edward the First's reign there was a change in the vaulting, the columns and formation of the windows.

In the reigns of Henry the Seventh and Eighth " the windows were less pointed and more open ; a better taste for statuary began to appear ; and indeed a greater care seems to have been bestowed on all the ornamental parts, to give them a lighter and higher finishing ". He calls architecture with pointed arches Modern Architecture.

Grose's *Antiquities of England and Wales* appeared between 1773 and 1787. In 1786 Carter's *Specimens of Ancient Sculpture and Painting* was published; in 1795 his *Ancient Architecture of England*; and in 1798 the *History of Gothic and Saxon Architecture in England, Exemplified by Descriptions of the Cathedrals, etc.*, by Bentham and Brown Willis.

In 1800 came *Essays on Gothic Architecture*, by Milner, Bentham and Grose. This contained, among other things, a reprint of part of the *History and Antiquities of Ely*. The illustrations were quite good.

The *Gentleman's Magazine* over a long period of years contained letters and articles on mediaeval architecture.

The best of the illustrated works were those of John Britton, who was responsible for *The Beauties of Wiltshire* (1800), *The Beauties of England and Wales* (1800–1816), a description of St. Mary Redcliffe, Bristol (1813), *Architectural Antiquities of Great Britain* (1805–1814), and *The Cathedral Antiquities of Great Britain* (1814–1835). The careful engravings in the last two works familiarized people with the real appearance of old buildings, and the text is careful and painstaking.

It was possible at last for ordinary people to know something about mediaeval architecture. Only one thing remained to be settled: the question of names for the style as a whole and for the different periods of it.

Warton's suggestions were as follows:

He says that the Normans used the Saxon style: " The style which succeeded to this was not the absolute *Gothic*, or Gothic simply so called, but a sort of *Gothic* SAXON, in which the pure *Saxon* began to receive some tincture of the *Saracen* fashion. . . . In this style, to mention no more, is Salisbury Cathedral. . . . The ABSOLUTE *Gothic*, or that which is free from all Saxon mixture, began with ramified windows of an enlarged dimension. . . . Of this fashion the body of Winchester Cathedral . . . will afford the justest idea. But a taste for a more ornamental style had for some time before begun to discover itself. This appears from the choir of St. Mary's

Church at Warwick, begun, at least, before Wykeham's improvements at Winchester, and remarkable for a freedom and elegance unknown before. . . . The ORNAMENTAL *Gothic* at length reached its confirmation about 1441, in the chapel of . . . King's College at Cambridge. . . . Afterwards what I would call the FLORID *Gothic* arose, the first appearance of which was in the chapel of St. George at Windsor." It also occurs in Henry VII's Chapel, Westminster, and in the vault of Gloucester.

This is very inaccurate, and his suggested names are of no value. The introduction to the *Essays on Gothic Architecture* has a footnote in which it is proposed to substitute " English " for Gothic, " because it was here brought to its highest state of perfection ". It points out, somewhat obviously, that " the architecture used by the Saxons is very properly called Saxon. The improvements introduced after the Norman Conquest justify the application of Norman to the edifices of the period. The language, properly called English, was then formed ; and an architecture, founded on the Norman and Saxon, but extremely different from both, was invented by English artists ; it is, surely, equally just and proper to distinguish this style by the honourable appellation of English."

But unfortunately this was not the truth. Gothic architecture is not particularly English : some old writers called it the German style ; it would be nearer the truth to call it French.

Milner used " the pointed style " of " that light and elegant species of architecture which properly began in the reign of our first Tudors "; and the architecture of the Saxons and Normans he called " the architecture of the Middle Ages ".

Finally the names suggested by Rickman in his *Attempt to Discriminate the Styles of English Architecture* (1819) were adopted. In future, Saxon and Norman architecture were distinguished and called by their obvious names, and the style of the thirteenth century was called Early English.

This was not a very satisfactory name. Mr. Beresford Hope, who refers to " Rickman's awkward nomenclature ", says [1]

[1] Beresford Hope, *The English Cathedral of the Nineteenth Century*, p. 35.

that the term " recalls us to the time when Gothic architecture was studied in this country in a purely insular spirit. . . . Rickman honestly believed, in the simplicity of his heart, that all Gothic architecture was good or bad in proportion as it approached the English standard, and with him Early English meant Early Gothic." Rickman called the style of the fourteenth century Decorated ; and that of the late fourteenth, and of the fifteenth and sixteenth centuries Perpendicular. Rickman's names were disliked in the mid-nineteenth century, and were soon considered to have been superseded. The more non-committal First, Second and Third Pointed were preferred. Some spoke of the successive styles as Lancet, Decorated and Florid; Professor Willis suggested Early, Complete and After-Gothic. It was thought by some that Ascetic and Spiritual ought to be " recognized aliases " for Romanesque and Gothic. But Rickman's names took a new lease of life, and are still commonly used. Everyone recognizes their inadequacy; but they are well known, and the use of them saves trouble.

So that by the beginning of the nineteenth century mediaeval architecture was quite well understood, and it was possible —theoretically—to use the styles if necessary in designing new buildings. But, as we saw, very few buildings were erected.

The Church of England was not fully alive to its responsibilities or prepared to supply the needs of its members. But the population was increasing, London was growing, and new towns were rising in the North. The people were not prepared to build churches for themselves. And the learned gentlemen who studied old buildings, and the architects who profited by their researches and made experiments in the Gothic style, were not sufficiently interested to build churches for them.

c

CHAPTER II

CHURCH-BUILDING : THE COMMISSIONERS' CHURCHES

WHEN at last Churchmen began to awaken to the condition of things, they were horrified by what they saw. The religious literature of the early years of the nineteenth century is full of demands that something should be done. Big populations had grown up in the preceding years, and the Church had done nothing to supply their spiritual needs. English people had been alarmed by the French Revolution. What might happen if anything of the kind occurred here—to the Constitution and to the Established Church ? Crowds of rough, working people, ignorant of religion and influenced by seditious teaching, would be capable of anything. What was to hold them in check ?

There is more than a hint in much that was written at the time of the belief that religion would serve as an effective policeman for the lower orders, and restrain them from violence. With the aid of religion the public peace would be secure. The more rigid Churchmen also hoped that Church extension would check the spread of Dissent, which was considered to be much less on the side of law and order than the Establishment. But no motives are entirely unmixed ; and no doubt in the main there was a genuine desire that the poor and ignorant should share in religious privileges which were valued by those who were fortunate enough to have them already. And that meant that new churches would have to be built. Proprietary chapels such as were common at the time would be of no use, for they were " built and conducted wholly as pecuniary and commercial speculations. The first object of the proprietor is to get the highest rent for pews ; and the poor are excluded." [1] Even the *Christian Observer*, the Evangelical organ, condemned the proprietary chapel.

[1] Letter from Mr. Yates to Lord Liverpool : " The Church in Danger."

The condition of the towns and the remedy for it were eloquently described in the *British Critic* [1] some years later (1836). The towns were places of " ungodliness, profligacy, intemperance, improvidence, turbulence, filth, riot, sullenness, ferocity, desperation, disease : the unmitigated and intolerable penury which is ever at the heels of vice and low debauchery ; the destruction of physical, mental, moral and spiritual health ; the murder of soul and body ; the atmosphere of pollution spreading and propagating itself without a check ".

" A larger supply, then, of churches, and clergymen attached to them, in connexion with the Establishment, is emphatically *the* need of our country, and most of all, of our towns. Without putting our trust, more than Dr. Chalmers, in any magic of masonry, we may yet say that the very architecture—the building standing visibly before the eyes of men—must produce its solemn effect. The edifice of public worship, as it raises its sacred head, has its eloquence and power. There is a moral attraction in its walls. . . . True it is, as some have in substance objected, that churches are not visitors ; that churches are not household ministrations ; that churches are not schools, or saving-banks, or lending libraries, or other parochial institutions, or the living beings by whom those institutions are to be managed. No : but churches will have faithful ministers attached to them ; and faithful ministers will bring all these things in their train. Plant but a church, and all the loveliest flowers of Christianity will grow around it. Erect a house of prayer, and other institutions will arise and shine with their attendant lustre like satellites about a luminary of the noblest magnitude."

Harriet Martineau was nearer the truth when she said, " Churches come of Religion, but Religion does not come of churches."

However, something clearly had to be done. Statements about the need of church accommodation were made again and again in the early nineteenth century. They were made with great persistence, and at last they produced some result.

[1] The *British Critic* was founded in 1793 by Jones of Nayland. For a time it was edited by Newman, and then handed over to Thomas Mozley. It became the organ of the Romanizing party, and came to an end in 1843.

In 1811 it was pointed out to the Prime Minister (Spencer Perceval) that in St. Pancras and St. Marylebone there was church accommodation for only one-ninth of the population. In 1814 Dr. Howley was appointed Bishop of London. Soon after his appointment he received a letter from a number of laymen which called his attention to the state of affairs. In many places only one-tenth of the Church population could be accommodated in the existing buildings; this was " one great cause of the apparent defection from the Church, and of the increase of Sectarianism and Methodism ". The work of the National Society would suffer if children were unable to carry out what they had been taught. The war was now at an end. " Let us show our thanks by immediately dedicating to God's honour a number of free churches and chapels, sufficient to supply the wants of all God's faithful worshippers in the Established Church of England." The proposal, it was considered, was more influential as coming from laymen than from the clergy. They asked the Bishop's sanction for the calling of a meeting " chiefly of clergy, nobles and other excellent laymen " to draw up a plan to be submitted to the Bishop, and afterwards to the Regent and the Archbishop. The letter had the approval and support of eminent laymen such as Joshua Watson and Charles Daubeny.

It was favourably received, but the proposed meeting was not held. It was not possible to do much at the time, for the war was not yet over. The writers of the letter had been too optimistic. And as long as the war continued, money was not available. The *British Critic* complained some years later that " the nation would not devote one ten-thousandth of its annual expenditure to the service of God. . . . Two pence out of every £100 employed annually in this great struggle would have built a lasting temple to their Maker's praise . . . but they would not."

But in 1815 the war ended, and in that year the matter was taken up again. The Rev. Richard Yates, Chaplain of Chelsea Hospital, addressed to the Prime Minister (Lord Liverpool) a pamphlet entitled *The Church in Danger*, and John Bowdler sent a letter signed by about 150 laymen. The facts were repeated, and it was stated that Parliament alone could supply the remedy.   Parliament at the time could not; but two years later some progress was made.   The Prime Minister was willing to help, and advised application to the Archbishop and the Bishop of London.

Early in 1818 the Prince Regent mentioned the lack of church accommodation in his speech from the throne; and in February the Church Building Society was constituted.   The Duke of York, who was now devoting much of his time to philanthropy, and was a strong supporter of the National Protestant Church, gave his support to the scheme.   (His patronage, and that of the Regent, lent lustre to the undertaking, but could not have had much religious value.)

The Society received gifts from the King, the clergy, the nobility and the Universities of Oxford and Cambridge; but its policy was to encourage the subscribing of money by the people in the places that were in need of churches.   This was considered by some to be Methodistical, and unworthy of a National Church; but it was undoubtedly a wise plan.   No more than a quarter of the sum to be raised in each case was supplied by the Society: the rest had to be found.

The records of the meetings of the Society—which is of course still in existence—prove that a great deal of work was being done.   In March 1837 grants were made for the enlargement of the church at Charminster, Dorset; building a chapel at North Barcombe, Sussex; restoring the chapel at South Runcton, Norfolk; enlarging the gallery in the church at Walterstone, Hereford; building a church at Skipton, Yorks; enlarging, by rebuilding, the church at Flaunden, Herts; building a church at Monk Bretton, Yorks; repairing the church at Barrington, Cambridgeshire; enlarging the chapel at Bourton, in the parish of Gillingham, Dorset; repairing and increasing the accommodation in the church of St. Martin, Colchester; building a gallery in the church of St. James, Taunton, Somerset; building a chapel at Uxbridge Moor, in the parish of Hillingdon, Middlesex; enlarging, by rebuilding, the church of Haynford, Norfolk; building a church at Abram, in the parish of Wigan, Lancashire; building a chapel at South Hetton, in the township of Haswell, Durham; building a chapel at Gray's Inn Lane, in the parish of St. Andrew, Holborn, London; restoring the church at Orsett, Essex, damaged by fire; and enlarging by rebuilding, the church at Cheadle, Stafford.

At the next meeting, in April 1837, grants were made for the building of a chapel at Tynemouth, Northumberland; increasing the accommodation in the church of St. Martin-at-Oak, Norwich; enlarging, by rebuilding, the chapel at Walmsley, in the township of Turton and parish of Bolton-le-Moors; building a chapel at East Bourne, Sussex; building a chapel at Handsworth in Staffordshire; restoring the ruined chapel at South Runcton, Norfolk; building a chapel at Catshill, in the parish of Bromsgrove, Worcestershire; building a chapel at Llanerchrochwell, in the parish of Guilsfield, Montgomeryshire;[1] building a chapel at Colwyn, in the parish of Llandrillo, Denbighshire; building a chapel on the Beacon Hill, in the parish of Walcot, Bath; enlarging, by rebuilding, the church at East Farleigh, Kent; building a chapel at Ovenden, in the parish of Halifax; building a chapel at Middleton, in the parish of Wirksworth, Derbyshire; enlarging the chapel at Wibsey Low Moor, Yorkshire; and enlarging the church at Yoxford, Suffolk.

Soon after the formation of the Society a proposal was made that a million pounds should be voted by Parliament for the building of churches, and spent under the supervision of Commissioners. A Bill was brought before Parliament; there was little opposition, and the Church Building Act was passed. The Commissioners appointed Christopher Wordsworth, Richard Mant, Archdeacon Cambridge and Joshua Watson to carry out the proposals. Six years later another £500,000 was granted, and in 1828 the Church Building Society was incorporated by Parliament. The same Act abolished Church Briefs, and provided for the better collection of voluntary contributions.

The churches built as the result of the Act were officially known as the Commissioners' Churches; the general public called them Waterloo Churches. After twelve years, 134 had been built, and fifty more were in process of building. The total number was 214. They stand four-square in the middle of Lancashire and Yorkshire and Midland towns and

[1] This was never built.

London suburbs, and are all very large and capacious. It is hardly true to say that they have no merit beside capacious-ness : it is certainly not true to say that " there are probably no churches which are more of a puzzle and a despair to architects and clergymen than the churches built in the early part of the nineteenth century. Unmitigated ugliness and hopeless inconvenience are their chief characteristics." [1] They are very much less ugly and inconvenient than many later nineteenth-century churches. But they are certainly not attractive, many were far too expensive, and some have never been particularly useful. There were objections at the time to the enormous expense of some of them—the new Church of St. Pancras cost £76,677 7s. 8d.—and it was also considered that they failed to fulfil the purpose for which they were built. The Bishop of Chester said that a provision for the Church by the government would excite no spiritual feeling whatever in any breast. The *British Critic* a few years later expressed the view that the whole scheme had been a failure. It said:

" That odious vulgarity of supposing that parliamentary grants for the building of vast showy churches to hold 2000 or 3000 people were the legitimate and effectual way to ' turn the disobedient to the wisdom of the just and make ready a people prepared for the Lord ' has certainly prevailed more in the suburbs of the metropolis than in any of the less enlightened ' provinces '. To be sure, even in the sight of Westminster and St. Paul's the folly is now exploded. It is found by painful experience that the vast Ionic and Corinthian temples built twenty years ago, though inviting the multitude with all the eloquence of porticos, cupolas and handsome iron palisades, are, after all, frequented almost exclusively by persons who could well have afforded to build the churches out of their own pockets. Somehow or other, parliamentary money has not done the church much good ; it has proved like that kind of food which puffs up more than it nourishes ; it has been blessed neither in the giver nor in the receiver. But what is still more conclusive with some minds, it is no longer forth-coming. Accordingly in London itself, our prelates are now

[1] J. H. Overton, *The English Church in the Nineteenth Century*, p. 155.

obliged, in a nobler cause than Peter the Hermit's, to raise the banner of the cross—the cross of personal self-denial, in order to build churches for a vast and miserable population, whom parliament itself and the wealthiest corporation in the world have driven from localities where churches were plenty, and are now to spare."

The reference is to Bishop Blomfield, who was appointed to London in 1828 and who raised the banner of self-denial most persistently and effectively.

In his charge in the year 1834 he said, " In the eastern and north-eastern districts of the metropolis there are ten parishes containing together a population of 353,460 persons. In these parishes there are eighteen churches and chapels, served by twenty-four incumbents and curates : the average being not quite one church or chapel for every 19,000 souls, and one clergyman for every 14,000."

In 1836 he proposed the formation of a Church Building and Endowment Fund.   Churches were to be built in Islington, Bethnal Green, St. Pancras, Paddington and Westminster. Church-building, he said, " was a work of prudence no less than charity " ; and its object was to " reclaim hundreds of thousands of the poor from practical heathenism, and to give increased efficiency and therefore stability to the Church ". A meeting was called, and the cause was urged on property-owners, the City Companies, merchants, bankers and trades-men.   The Bishop was disappointed at the result of the appeal : but by the end of the year £100,000 had been subscribed, and further sums promised. Efforts to appeal to the people themselves do not seem to have been successful. In Bethnal Green a zealous worker tried to raise a contribution of sixpence a head.   The reply was, " They would give him a shilling to hang the Bishop, but not sixpence for the work ".   Nor were they appreciative of the churches. When the foundation-stone of the first church was laid, " the whole party were abused in the most violent language, and an infuriated ox was driven among the school-children who were assembled to sing a hymn ".   However, passions cooled during the next few years, for when the foundation-stone of the tenth church was laid, a working-man was heard to say " I will not believe any-

PLATE III

ST. GEORGE'S, RAMSGATE

By H. E. Kendall

Pre-Ecclesiological Gothic of the better type

PLATE IV

ST. MICHAEL'S, STOCKWELL

By W. Rogers

A cheap church in the Early English style

thing they say against the Bishops again. Look at those children." [1] The great benefactor of Bethnal Green was William Cotton of Leytonstone; and the Bishop himself contributed £18,000 towards the cause, and consecrated nearly 200 churches.

The *British Magazine* in 1836 published the following figures with regard to Birmingham :

Population of Birmingham, 1831	. .	142,206
Increase of 19 per cent. .	. .	27,018
		169,224
Church accommodation for	. . .	61,932
Persons for whom there is no accommodation		107,292

New churches were accordingly built in Birmingham; and the same thing happened in other parts of the country. Attention was called to the lack of church accommodation, someone took the lead, and the want was to some extent supplied. Large numbers of churches were built by Church enterprise in the industrial districts of the North, in which " the parliamentary principle of Church extension was not in favour "; and in country places many new districts were formed, each with its new church.

It was a race against time, and it was necessary to build as many churches as possible as cheaply as possible. Various helpful suggestions were made. A writer to the *British Magazine* (July 1836) suggested the cheap mode of building which the French call *pisé*—earth, rammed as hard as possible in a frame, with a total exclusion of water, and vegetable and animal substance, which hardens in a week to a sort of most tenacious and unbreakable stone excluding heat and cold. One church was to be " executed in a good substantial and workman-like manner for the sum of £460 ".

The Rev. William Carus Wilson wrote a book called *Helps to the Building of Churches and Parsonage Houses ; containing Plans, Elevations, Specifications, etc.* In it he says, " It is much to be regretted that the money expended on many of our modern churches, and the statements even in some influential

---

[1] *Church Quarterly Review*, January 1885.

quarters of the necessary expenses of the erection of a church, have been calculated to discourage persons from the under-taking. . . . A church, destitute of architectural propriety, is in no case recommended ; but the maintenance of that propriety is quite compatible with the strictest economy."

He gives one example of cheapness—not, indeed, in building, but in the equipment of a church—which he regards as creditable, but which seems to carry the principle of economy rather far. He mentions " A very neat portable font " lately given to a new church, " which answers every purpose, not requiring even the expense of a stand ; as it might be placed when not wanted on the communion table, from which the ceremony might be performed. The price is fourteen shillings ; and it is to be had at Sharpur's, Pall Mall East, London."

The Communion plate was got at Messrs. Rodgers, Sheffield, and the price was as follows :

					£	s.
Sheffield plate chalice .	.	.	.	.	1	11
Do. salver .	.	.	.	.	1	12
Best hard Britannia metal flagon .	.	.	.	0	16
					£3	19

Mr. Carus Wilson would have agreed with Dr. Dale, who said in 1879 that the Evangelicals' business was to bring men to God. " It did not occur to them that heavy galleries and high-backed pews were ugly, if only they were crowded with men and women eager to listen to the Gospel. . . ." The Evangelical " fears rather than welcomes the awe and solemnity which are produced by the wonderful work of the architects of the Middle Ages ". Sir Charles Barry found the Evangelical clergy· " very fluent preachers, with great ideas of erecting churches for nothing ".

Many other similar books were produced containing a selection of cheap designs ; and in due course many of the designs were carried out. They are not beautiful, but they fulfilled their purpose.

There is a school—if it can be called a school—of writers

who would have us believe that light only dawned on the Church of England at the time of the Oxford Movement : just as there are other writers who are still sure that light dawned on a Popish and enslaved Christendom when Martin Luther nailed his theses to the door at Wittenburg. Many are convinced that the Church of England before 1833 was a welter of Bishops who examined Ordination candidates during cricket matches, of drunken parsons who staged cock-fights in their churches, and of laymen who slept in cushioned pews with fireplaces. Churches were neglected : dank grass surrounded them, and ivy pushed its way through their rotting rafters. Then came Keble's Assize Sermon, Dr. Pusey, Sir Gilbert Scott—and everything sprang into new life : churches were restored, new ones were built, and the Church of England began to be active.

There is truth in that : but not a great deal. The religious literature of the early nineteenth century, before the Oxford Movement, gives the impression of a very serious Church, conscious of its shortcomings, but determined to find a remedy for them. There is certainly nothing about Apostolic Succession, and very little about Worship ; but churchmen were convinced of the seriousness of their calling. Our outlook and methods are not theirs ; but we are not safe in assuming that they were always wrong and that we are right. We are inclined to smile at the solemn and wordy style of the religious articles in their magazines, which are sandwiched between heavy slabs of information on miscellaneous subjects—Popery in Ireland, the habits of volcanoes, and ruined cities of Asia ; we may smile at the architecture of some of their churches. But we should take them seriously. They lived in a difficult and bewildering age, and they had enormous problems to deal with. At any rate they attempted to deal with them. What they wrote is banished to the top shelves of libraries and to the cheapest of second-hand bookstalls ; but hundreds of parish churches, from Lancashire to London, stand as the practical result of what they did.

CHAPTER III

IT is obvious that it was more important that churches should be erected than that they should be designed in any particular style. The Commissioners in their first report (1821) said nothing about style : later they mentioned Roman, Grecian and Gothic, and specially recommended Gothic. For Gothic could be built of brick and was cheap ; but Classic churches should have porticoes, which must be of stone, and were exceedingly expensive. Mr. John Bowdler looked to the Church Building Society to " correct a vicious taste and encourage a plainer and less expensive method ". But the list of suggestions which the Society drew up, though it encouraged cheapness, had little to say of taste.

The site of a church should be central, but quiet : it should have a paved way round it. If there were a crypt, it could be used for the storing of coals or of the parish fire-engine. Chimneys might be concealed in pinnacles. Windows ought not to resemble modern sashes ; but, whether Grecian or Gothic, the glass should be in small panes, and not costly. The minister should be placed " near an east wall, or in a semi-circular recess under a half dome ". Cast-iron pillars could support the galleries in a chapel ; but " in large churches they might want grandeur ". Ornament should be neat and simple, yet venerable. The Gothic or the Grecian style might be used.

Lord Grenville thought it of importance that " that mode should be adopted which was best calculated to inspire devotion, and which was characteristic of the Established Church, and that there should be a decent decoration ". But what was that mode ?

The vagueness as to the styles, and the uncertainty of architects in using them, were a source of annoyance to critics at the time. There was some dissatisfaction, as we saw, with the scheme, and doubt as to the usefulness of the churches : there was still more dissatisfaction with their architecture. The architects had the opportunity, and the money was forthcoming ; but it was generally considered that the opportunity was missed.

I have seen one nineteenth-century book (*Church and Chapel Architecture, from the earliest period to the present time, with an account of the Hebrew Church : to which are added one thousand authenticated mouldings, selected from the best examples which this country contains.* By Andrew Trimen, architect), whose author seems to be satisfied. The nineteenth century, he says, " opened with bright prospects for architecture ; men of genius and science were animated by the patronage of the sovereign to project and carry out designs for the improvement of the edifices of the country ". He mentions the Act of 1818—as the result of which " an impulse has been given to the study of architectural science, which promises to make this country celebrated as the era when the glorious fanes of the Middle Ages shall be imitated by those whose talents and acquirements have already contributed to the intelligence of the age ". The age, he says, is " the most enlightened and eventful period in the history of the known world ".

Of all the architects he is inclined to award the palm to Mr. Taylor, who designed churches at Ripon, Quarry Hill (Leeds), Attercliffe, Hanging Heaton and Dewsbury Moor : Mr. Taylor's greatest masterpiece is Pudsey Church near Bradford. (Mr. Trimen gives a table in which are coordinated the names of architectural writers, architects, eminent, and edifices. It begins with the Tower of Babel and the Pyramids, with Moses as the first architectural writer, and Beseleel as the first eminent architect. It goes no further than Ware, Perronet and Soufflot ; and Somerset House is the last edifice. Surely it should have ended with Mr. Taylor and Pudsey Church.) [1]

[1] Mr. Trimen's book deserves to be remembered for its suggested derivation of the word " chapel ". " Chap " or " chop " means to exchange, diverge or divide. *Chap*-EL is God's *chap* ; an offset or branch from the church ; a chapel of ease ; a diversion for convenience or relief in the worship of God.

With regard to the mixture of styles, the imperturbable Andrew Trimen is satisfied to remark that " in England, and in many parts of the Continent, the revival of religion, and latterly the efforts of the dissenting denominations, conducted on the voluntary system, have thrown back our modern church and chapel architecture into that utilitarian medley, which may be supposed to have prevailed among the persecuted christians of the first three centuries ".

But few writers, then or later, agreed with him. The *British Critic* of 1839, looking back at the recently erected churches, can only say, " The present age has no vernacular style of architecture. . . . Architecture is become a language. We learn a number of styles as we do a number of dead languages.

" The exact scholar . . . though he trusts he can pass off his work on the present generation, knows full well that anyone to whom that style was natural would perceive a great uncouthness and probably detect some downright solecisms : just as a Browne medallist knows that his Greek ode may pass muster at Cambridge, but would have sounded barbarous, and perhaps have been unintelligible, at Thebes. This is the utmost that even the best architectural scholars can now accomplish : as for the mass of builders, theirs is a kind of *lingua franca*, or rather a macaronic style, a mere jumble of languages. . . . There is hardly any age, realm or religious system but what contributes somewhat to a modern church. You can see included under one expansive roof of slate a vast and heavy pile, whose proportions are perhaps those of a heathen temple ; from one end of the roof rises a tower, emulating in its lightness, but not in its height, the aërial tracery of Mechlin or Antwerp. From the other end of the building seems to bud, as it were, an incipient chancel. The windows are of all ages and all shapes, from lancet to the most florid ; round, pointed and square. The buttresses, battlements and pinnacles, etc., are selected at random from four different centuries. . . . The building becomes a type of the religion of the day, and the present state of the Church : at once sectarian, eclectic and comprehensive.

" Profaneness and vulgarity are at the bottom of all these absurdities, which promise therefore to enjoy no brief ascenlancy. . . . It appears to us most strangely inconsistent, that he very same persons who are most precise and rigorous in :nforcing the canons and denouncing the anathemas of ' society ', should strenuously advocate a vulgar, lax, slovenly, higgledy-piggledy order of things, as soon as they leave their own houses and come into the House of God."

But the Grecian churches—as distinct from the Gothic— were, as far as they could be, fairly consistent in style. They were the product of a short-lived attempt that was being made at the time to revive pure Greek architecture.

Greek architecture was the parent of Roman, which was a more flexible, less refined, and more practical version of it. Renaissance architecture was (sometimes) a more flexible and practical version of Roman. But, as we said, there is very little that is definitely Classical in many eighteenth-century churches and houses. There is a symmetrical arrangement, and an orthodox cornice or doorway; but nothing much else. As a reaction from this reduced Classic style, the cry " Back to Greece " was raised at the beginning of the century. The remains of Greek architecture were better known than they had been before, and various works on the subject gave examples which could easily be reproduced.

Stuart and Revett's *Antiquities of Athens*, in four volumes, was issued between 1762 and 1816, and a second edition in 1825–30. Richard Chandler's *Antiquities of Ionia*, in three volumes, was issued between 1769 and 1840. These books gave examples which could be copied : it only remained to adapt them to modern churches. Revett's church at Ayot St. Lawrence was perhaps the first Grecian church in England.[1] This had been built in 1778 : the need for new churches produced a large crop of Grecian efforts.

Of one of the new churches (St. Pancras) it was said that " it is designed according to the plan of the ancient temples, with slight alterations in accordance with the requirements of Christian churches ".

[1] The cost of this church was over £6000. It bears an inscription which says (in Latin), that " Nicholas Revett, a native of Suffolk, having dwelt many years at Rome, Athens and Smyrna, designed, erected and adorned this church, after the examples of ancient architecture yet to be seen in Greece and Asia Minor".

Unfortunately for the architects, the required alterations were more than slight. A Greek temple, unlike a Christian church, was not designed for congregational worship: the central building, the *naos* or *cella*, was comparatively small. In a small temple there were porticoes of columns at one or at each end; in a large one there was a colonnade round all the sides, sometimes a double one at the ends and a single one at the sides; in very large examples a double one all round. The temple was to be seen from the outside: the interior was unimportant.

But in a Christian church the interior is obviously important; and the Commissioners' churches of the early nineteenth century had to have a large accommodation. So that in the planning of the buildings the architects had to desert their Greek originals. They retained, in fact, the large rectangular body which had been the rule in the eighteenth century, with its galleries and pews, and a double row of windows at the sides. (Even in the plainest examples there had been a certain amount of Classic detail. Now this often disappeared altogether—at any rate externally—and the body of the church became almost forbiddingly plain.) But a galleried body with a double row of windows behind the portico was more than a slight alteration.

And custom demanded a tower. This, of course, was quite unnecessary; but it seems to have been regarded as something which must not be omitted. And Greek temples certainly never had towers.

With regard to the porticoes, no adaptation was necessary. They were useless; but if the building was to be Greek, of course there must be a portico. And so, at great expense, the porticoes were built.

It was optimistic of architects to imagine that porticoes which were designed to stand in Athens in the days of Pericles would look equally impressive in an English street. The wonder is that they appear as dignified as they do. It was optimistic to expect that details which were designed for the Greek sunlight could be reproduced with good effect in London or Edinburgh. But they attempted it. With naïve enthusiasm and absurd pedantry, they did their best, and some of the

secular buildings are very fine.   But the churches are seldom
inspiring.   The most famous of them is St. Pancras Church,
London, which has been called " the culminating feat of the
Classic style in this country ".   It was designed by W. and
H. W. Inwood.   The Act for its erection was passed in 1816 ;
it was begun in 1819 and consecrated in 1822.   The church is
modelled on the Erechtheum at Athens, which is an unusual
building, combining three temples in one, and having three
porticoes of different design—two Ionic, and one composed of
caryatides (female figures serving instead of columns).   One
of the Ionic porticoes is reproduced at St. Pancras, and rather
poor copies of the caryatid portico have been placed on either
side.   Each of the figures has a ewer, and an inverted torch,
the symbol of death.   Mozley, in his *Reminiscences*, says that
the exterior is " sadly too monumental.   Indeed, the church,
with its imposing entrances to the sepulchral crypt, is a
curious memorial of the idea of Church endowment prevailing
at that time—burial fees."   The eastern apse is an original
feature.

The part of the church that has been most severely criticized
is the tower, which is a copy of the Temple of the Winds—or
rather two copies : one, on a smaller scale, is placed above the
larger.   As a matter of fact, the tower is not ungraceful ; but
its position is unfortunate.   It rises directly above the portico,
and undoubtedly spoils its effect.   In St. Martin-in-the-Fields,
Gibbs combined a tower with a portico ; but there the portico
seems to stand in front of the tower, and the tower is large and
dignified.   In the Greek churches of the early nineteenth
century the towers are small and rise from the top of the
portico.   The St. Pancras tower is a better specimen than most,
but no tower in that position could be a success.

Of the interior, Fergusson, in his *History of Modern Architecture*, says that its arrangements are " appropriate to a
Protestant church of the first class ".

One of the Grecian churches in London—St. Matthew's,
Brixton, by Porden—has its tower at the east end, and the
Doric portico stands unimpeded in its rather gloomy grandeur.
Two of the better churches are St. Peter's, Walworth, and
Holy Trinity, Marylebone, by Sir John Soane.   These two
D

churches are practically identical; but Holy Trinity has been given a not particularly successful chancel by Somers Clarke. The vestibule and west end of St. Mark's, North Audley Street, are unaltered and interesting work by J. P. Deering (otherwise known as Gandy). Christchurch, Lisson Grove, by Hardwick, has an interior which might be quite grand; but it has suffered (as have most of these churches) from inept attempts at decoration, and is at present very shabby. Camden Town Church, by the Inwoods, is worth a visit. All Souls', Langham Place, at the end of Regent Street, was designed by John Nash, and was the cause of a great deal of ribaldry. A question was asked in Parliament about it: Mr. Henry Grey Bennet asked to be told the name of the architect. " There was certainly something very extraordinary in that work— something so sublime as to be beyond comprehension. Persons shrugged up their shoulders and exclaimed, ' Who is doing this work ? ' He wished to know who was the architect, what it was to cost and who was to pay for it ? Indeed, he must say he would give a trifle to have this church pulled down." [1] A cartoon appeared rather later showing Nash impaled on his spire: the legend was " NASHIONAL TASTE ! ! ! "

Nash was the favourite architect of George IV, and was responsible for Regent Street, Regent's Park, and a large number of streets in the neighbourhood. He had large ideas and was an excellent town-planner, but was careless in details. All Souls' has a curious spire which rises from the middle of a circular Ionic portico: it is quite unorthodox, but well suited to its position, and the new B.B.C. House which stands beside it has been designed to harmonize with it. Nash is taken more seriously now than in his lifetime.

Nash's Regent Street has been destroyed, together with two churches that used to stand there: Hanover Chapel, by Professor Cockerell, and St. Philip's, by Repton—both of which were good buildings. Hanover Chapel was of the Ionic order externally, with two square towers and a dome.

St. Mark's, North Audley Street, St. Luke's, West Norwood, by Bedford, and St. Peter's, Eaton Square, by Hakewill, have been remodelled internally in an elaborate and unattractive style.

[1] Quoted in J. Summerson, *John Nash*, p. 227.

Egham Church, Surrey, was built in 1817 on the site of an old church, and consecrated in 1820. Of it Mrs. Esdaile says,[1] " It would be hard to find a more perfect expression of the Greek Revival, as applied to ecclesiastical architecture. The ceiling, the walls, the very pews are stencilled in Greek or Pompeian patterns ; even the doors are simplified from those of the Erechtheum, and the monuments by Flaxman and Baily within the chancel rails are purely, and in their way quite exquisitely, classical. Only the floral cushion at the altar-rails, woolwork of the Regency as fresh in colour and design as it was a century ago, shows the least trace of any other taste."

One account of it says that " Egham Church and parish has had a not inconsiderable share in brightening the world ". But that refers to the Church life, and not to the church itself. The building is interesting but depressing, and looks rather forlorn. It is out of place in a way that an eighteenth-century church never is. But it has one merit. According to the same account, " Its acoustics are perfect and greatly encourage the congregations to be hearty and full-throated in their worship ". That is a virtue possessed by many such churches. They are not suited to services of a Full Cathedral type; but for congregational worship they are excellent. They are not divided up by heavy arcades, and the altar is not remote from the people in a long and raised chancel. The type of worship for which they were built was not inspiring. We need not take too seriously Eastlake's description [2] of " the portentous beadle; the muffin-capped charity boys; the wizen-faced pew-opener eager for stray shillings; the earnest penitent who is inspecting the bottom of his hat ; the patent warming-apparatus ; the velvet cushions which profane the altar; the hassocks which no one kneels on; the poor box which is always empty; the complicated discord of the words of the Psalter as revised by Tate and Brady ; and the overwhelming dulness of the sermon ". Public worship was not always as bad as that. But it was dull, and there was very little in it of the family spirit which liturgi-cally-minded clergy are now trying to foster. But the un-

[1] Katharine A. Esdaile, *English Monumental Sculpture since the Renaissance*, p. 104.
[2] *The Gothic Revival*, p. 117.

ambitious interiors of some of the early nineteenth-century
Classical churches, simply because they are not ambitious,
lend themselves very well to family worship : far better than
many Victorian buildings which sacrifice convenience to
correctness, and are arranged to suit the requirements of a poor
and out-of-date liturgical tradition.   The fine and expensive
porticoes are a home of soot and a resting-place for sparrows ;
but the interiors, which were despised by superior people
almost as soon as they were built, are admirable for congregational worship.   And in not a few cases they have been
transformed, with a minimum of alteration, into homely and
delightful places, in which the family spirit can flourish as
easily as in any modern basilica or church hall in any new
housing estate.

The Gothic styles had by this time been studied rather more
carefully.   Pugin and Willson's *Specimens of Gothic Architecture* was designed for the practical architect who wanted
measured drawings of old details.   We mentioned the accurate
books of the preceding years.   But they had contained only
descriptions and engravings of buildings as a whole.   Pugin
and Willson supplied plans and sections and elevations for
those who wished to design in the Gothic style, and made it
possible for those who were not willing to make careful studies
for themselves—and very few were—to achieve some kind of
accuracy without much effort.

But the Gothic churches of the period are strangely depressing.   The portico of a Grecian church, in however bleak a
street, and however dirty, has dignity ; but the west front of a
contemporary Gothic church looks grubby and mean.   The
truth is, that the architects were half-hearted.   Most of them
would design in the Classic or the Gothic style ; but they
preferred the former, and were more at ease in it.   Wyatt, in
spite of Fonthill Abbey and his other Gothic works, had been
a Classical architect ; and so were many of his successors.
Barry, who afterwards designed the Houses of Parliament,
was called on to design some Gothic churches.   But his
sympathies were then Classic, and his son says, " To this style
(Gothic) he had never paid sufficient attention.   He had now
to become a student ; and he threw himself into the new study

with characteristic diligence and perseverance. His first essays were not very successful, though certainly not below the average of the time ; he used to think and speak of them afterwards with a humorous kind of indignation ; he carefully destroyed every drawing relating to them, and would have still more gladly destroyed the originals." [1]

Savage's Classical church of St. James's, Bermondsey, is an impressive building ; his Gothic church of All Saints', Upper Norwood, is depressing. St. Luke's, Chelsea, by the same architect, is much better than most of its kind. Its style is Perpendicular. It was expensive, and it has some quite elaborate detail and a genuine stone-groined roof. The *Gentleman's Magazine* admired it, and it is still possible to find points in it to admire. But it has a curiously frail appearance, which suggests a model or a pencil sketch rather than a solid stone building.

Perpendicular—or the transition from Decorated to Perpendicular—was generally adopted for the more ambitious buildings, and the details of many of them are reasonably accurate. But they are very dull. In the seventeenth and eighteenth centuries Gothic had been regarded as fantastical and licentious ; and some of the eighteenth-century buildings might answer to the description. But nothing could be less licentious than a Gothic Commissioners' church, and there is no fantasy about it at all. Architects knew enough about Gothic to bind themselves by some of its precedents ; but they were not well acquainted with the style, and used it timidly and unnaturally. And they never reproduced the mediaeval proportions and arrangements. This was quite natural, for the old churches were, after all, pre-Reformation and Popish, and their plan and arrangement were suitable only to the Popish ritual. Barry " felt strongly that the forms of mediaeval art, beautiful though they are, do not always adapt themselves thoroughly to the needs of a service which is essentially one of ' Common Prayer '. Deep chancels, high rood-screens, and (in less degree) pillared aisles, seemed to him to belong to the worship and institutions of the past rather than the present. Time-honoured as they were, he would have in some degree put them aside, and,

[1] Rev. A. Barry, *Memoir of Sir Charles Barry*, pp. 68–69.

accepting Gothic as the style for church architecture, he would have preferred those forms of it which secured uninterrupted space and gave a perfect sense of unity in the congregation, even at the cost of sacrificing features beautiful in themselves, and perhaps of interfering with the ' dim religious light ' of impressiveness and solemnity." [1]

But at the best the combination of mediaeval details, expurgated of Popery, with an un-mediaeval plan, was a compromise. The plan was the usual one—a rectangular body with galleries, and no chancel. It could be rendered in the Gothic style, but it was apt to look uneasy in its Gothic dress ; and the Gothic details appeared rather forlorn in their new positions.

One of the obvious objections to buildings of this type is their rigid regularity of plan. That was suitable and necessary in a Classic building, but by no means so in a Gothic one. But the architects of the time in their Gothic churches kept strictly to an exact balance of parts. A critic of St. Paul's, Stalybridge (designed by Mr. Tattersall), remarked that " the exterior presents the usual fault of all the angles made by the tower and chancel with the nave being filled up, one at least of the fill-ups being made merely for the sake of uniformity ". Many porches and other features of churches at the time were merely for the sake of uniformity.

Typical churches of this type are St. George's, Birmingham, by Rickman ; St. Peter's, Brighton, by Barry ; St. Luke's, Liverpool, by Foster, and St. George's, Sheffield, by Woodhead and Hurst. The last has quite good arcades.

Leeds Parish Church was rebuilt by R. D. Chantrell—another architect who had designed in the Classic style. He said, " Having erected many churches in the North of England before I rebuilt the parish church of Leeds for Dean Hook, I worked without system, merely adapting ancient features to masses, to which I could give no just proportion ". The church has its good points, but the interior is very confused. The gallery fronts have an extraordinary profusion of heavy Gothic ornament. The cost of the church was almost £26,000. It was considered to have " an air of rude grandeur ".

London has the churches of Barry (St. Paul's, Balls Pond ;

---

[1] *Op. cit.*, p. 78.

Holy Trinity, Cloudesley Square; St. Peter's, Saffron Hill, and St. John's, Upper Holloway),[1] St. Michael's, Highgate, by Lewis Vulliamy, and many others. St. Mary's, Haggerston, designed by Nash, and displaying " the versatility of the architect's mind ", is the only building that has some claim to be considered licentious, at any rate as regards its tower.

A few churches were built in the Early English style, and sometimes, when they are on a small scale, these are less unsuccessful than the Perpendicular ones. But Early English on a large scale was a failure. The large Early English churches, with enormous lancet windows which gape depressingly in their high walls, are extremely poor and repellent.

According to Mr. A. J. B. Beresford Hope,[2] " the Lancet style enjoyed extensive popularity with the fabricators of cheap churches on account of the happy reputation which it enjoyed of surviving more starvation than any other. It was emphatically the cheap style, and in the hands into which it fell it as often emphatically proved itself to be the nasty one."

There is a large number of churches which are in a mixed Gothic style. They have lancet windows, and roofs of fifteenth-century pattern; or they have Perpendicular windows in the body of the church and lancets in the tower. St. John's, Park, Sheffield, designed by Matthew Hadfield, has lancet windows, and a Norman west doorway and sanctuary arch.

In many churches the architects not only mix their details, but also combine them with others that belong to no style or period: they are in the style which the *British Critic* called Macaronic. St. Mary's, Somers Town, London, originally known as Seymour Street or Mr. Judkin's Chapel (Mr. Judkin's " merits as a divine were not eclipsed by his talents as a poet and an artist "), received a great deal of merited abuse. The *Gentleman's Magazine* said that " the windows, being destitute of tracery, remind the spectator of the ' Gothic and Chinese design ' which may be seen in many a tea garden and summer house in the environs of this building ".

[1] Sir Gilbert Scott said that Barry's churches, " with all their faults and their strange commissioners' ritualisms, were for their period wonderfully advanced works ".

[2] Beresford Hope, *The English Cathedral of the Nineteenth Century*, p. 35.

Another critic said that in the design " are assembled so ingeniously all the various absurdities of modern Gothic, that, not having seen the original, we can hardly believe it to be a sober fact ". The tower buttresses and pinnacles " look like a procession of paupers dragging *honoris causâ* the parish fire-engine round the town, a mere exhibition of profitless labour ".

St. Mary-the-Less, Lambeth, and St. Chrysostom's, Peckham, are two South London specimens of the Macaronic style.

Christchurch, Cheltenham, by R. W. C. Jearred, has a tall nave and transepts of vaguely Early English appearance. The west front has porches with elaborate gables flanking a large pinnacled tower. It was remarked that " all this splendid frontage, according to the most approved watering-place principles, *desinit in piscem* ".

But this kind of church is much more interesting and amusing than many of those whose details are more orthodox.

A few architects attempted to use other styles. Some made experiments in the Norman style, which was no longer included under the title of Gothic. A book of a few years later considered that " the Anglo-Norman style possesses many peculiarities and elements of beauty, that ought to recommend its occasional adoption ; and although it may not be altogether applicable for a place of worship whose dimensions are so large as to require aisles, since the bold and massive character of the piers or pillars must always necessarily interfere with the convenient arrangement of the interior of the building, yet from its great simplicity it is peculiarly adapted for small rural churches ; which ought not in this style to be designed of very lofty proportions ".[1]

St. Mary's, Cardiff, is quite a favourable specimen of a Norman town church. But I do not remember ever having seen a really successful adaptation of the Norman style.

Some sensible suggestions were made by John Shaw in his " Letter on Ecclesiastical Architecture, as applicable to Modern Churches " ; addressed to the Right Rev. the Lord Bishop of London.

He says that Lombardic architecture " contains in an eminent degree the qualities now so important. These appear to be,

[1] James Barr, *Anglican Church Architecture* (1842), p. 77.

PLATE V

Contrasted Chapels, from Pugin's *Contrasts*
Top: Bishop Skirlaw's Chapel
Bottom: St. Pancras Chapel   By W. Inwood
(Now known as St. Mary's, Somers Town)

PLATE VI

St. Augustine's, Ramsgate

By A. W. N. Pugin

The Church in which he attempted to express his ideals

first, economy ; secondly, facility of execution ; thirdly, strict simplicity combined with high capability of ornament ; fourthly, durability ; fifthly, beauty." He advocates the use of two stories of pillars and arches in the interior, of which the lower one supports the galleries. Brick should be used both inside and out, and it should not be disguised.

The necessity of providing " the most ample accommodation at the least possible expense " involves galleries, which violate " the perpendicular line, the prevailing principle and genius of the Early English and Tudor architecture ". So he suggests galleries " supported on a series of semicircular arches, of fourteen-inch brickwork, resting on slender iron columns, ten feet apart. . . . The front of the gallery is proposed to be constructed of nine-inch brickwork ; over the lower arches is a semicircular range of arches, upon the system of the ancient triforium ; these support the clerestory. . . . I think it will be allowed that much effect is produced by the repetition of the double tier of arches, and the simplicity of its lines."

Several churches of Italian type were built in London during Bishop Blomfield's episcopate. Christ Church, Watney Street, by Shaw, has a handsome interior in which the problem of galleries is satisfactorily dealt with in the way suggested. Christ Church, Streatham Hill, by J. W. Wild, is another effective building, with a tall, semi-detached bell tower at the south-west. Holy Trinity, West Greenwich, is another church by Wild. It was considered to be, externally, " a very picturesque, graceful, and Catholic building ".

But, on the whole, churches in a foreign style were not appreciated by Churchmen. It was said that " our jealousy for the indigenous English orders tempts us to predict that no foreign growth will ever answer here ". Appreciation of English Gothic was growing. People looked wistfully at the old churches, and their opinion deepened into a certainty that " these venerable structures, from the many interesting associations that are connected with them, as well as on account of their sacred character and beauty, afford indeed the only appropriate models for edifices to be consecrated to the service of the Anglo-Catholic Church ".[1]

[1] *Anglican Church Architecture*, p. 8.

Greek temples were foreign and pagan ; Italian churches were foreign ; so were French, German and any other churches but our own. We are Christian and English : there are therefore no other models suitable to us than the churches built by our forefathers. It hardly seems a very strong argument : but for many years after this few dared to question it.

CHAPTER IV

GOTHIC IS CHRISTIAN ARCHITECTURE: THE LIFE OF PUGIN

THERE were several reasons for the adoption of Gothic. Some had designed in the Gothic style because it was romantic, others because it was cheap. Some felt it to be essentially English: that was one of the reasons why it was adopted for the new Houses of Parliament. But there was another reason— the most impressive of all: it was Christian. The prophets of the Gothic style began to preach with fervour that there was no other style but Gothic possible for a Christian architect who wished to build a Christian church, or who wished to build any kind of building in a Christian country.

Attempts had been made before to find a religious sanction for styles of architecture—John Wood of Bath in the eighteenth century wrote a book to prove that the orders of classical architecture were involved in the divine instructions given to the Jews—but never had it been done with such vehemence and sincerity as in this case.

The leaders of the Oxford Movement were not leaders in this matter. Newman's ideas of church-building were utilitarian.[1] He admired Gothic, but gave only a cautious blessing to the Revival. He said (in his *Discourses on the Scope and Nature of University Education*), " it is surely quite within the bounds of possibility that, as the *renaissance* of three centuries ago carried away its own day, in spite of the Church, into excesses in literature and art ; so a revival of an almost-forgotten architecture, which is at present taking place in our own country, in France, and in Germany, may in some way or other run away with us into this or that error, unless we keep a watch over its course ".

Keble disliked his Georgian church at Hursley, and had it rebuilt in the Decorated style ; but he was not particularly

[1] T. Mozley, *Reminiscences*, Vol. 1, p. 345.

interested in Gothic architecture. Hurrell Froude is said to
have " applied his thoughts to architecture with a power and
originality which at the time were not common " ; but his dull
essay on the subject in his *Remains* is in the eighteenth-century
manner. The Revival soon became associated with the
Oxford Movement and gave the outward and visible signs
which we associate with it ; but the best-known leader and
prophet of the Gothic-Is-Christian-Architecture movement
was not an Anglican but a Roman Catholic. That is to say,
he became one ; but he was not a typical Roman, and his views
were such as we now associate as a matter of course with the
Anglican Church.

Augustus Welby Northmore Pugin was the son of Auguste
Charles Pugin, who had been a refugee from France at the time
of the revolution and became draughtsman to John Nash.
He designed very few buildings, but was a clever artist, and
produced several books of drawings of architectural subjects
primarily intended to help Nash in his Gothic work. Nash had
to meet the demand for Gothic buildings, but knew nothing of
the style, and disliked it. *Specimens of Gothic Architecture* has
already been mentioned. Other works. were *The Edifices of
London, Examples of Gothic Architecture, Ornamental Timber
Gables*, and a book of drawings of the Pavilion at Brighton,
which Nash designed in the Indian style for the Prince Regent.
Pugin married Catherine Welby, " the Belle of Islington ", and
their son was born in 1812.

Augustus studied in his father's office, in Store Street,
Bedford Square, which seems to have been a most unpleasant
place. Mrs. Pugin established a régime which was, according
to Benjamin Ferrey, who went through it, " severe and
restrictive in the extreme, unrelieved by any of those relaxations
essential to the healthy education of youth ".[1] " The cold,
cheerless and unvarying round of duty, though enlivened by the
cheerful manner and kind attention of the elder Pugin, was
wretched and discouraging." [2]

Religious exercises added to the boredom of the pupils.
The elder Pugin was not religious. " If he ever formally

[1] B. Ferrey, *Recollections of Pugin*, p. 26.   [2] *Ibid.*, p. 28.

conformed to the Church of England, it is not on record that he illustrated his new profession with any extraordinary exhibition of zeal." The obituary of Ferrey in the *Builder* (September 4, 1880) says that Pugin was a Protestant. But whatever he was, he left religious observances to his wife.

On Sundays Mrs. Pugin would take her unfortunate son and some of the pupils to the Scotch Presbyterian church in Hatton Garden to hear Edward Irving, who would preach for hours.

But there were occasional relaxations. Ferrey would relate " in his graphic and animated manner " how the pupils would play jokes on their master. And they were often taken on tours. Young Pugin went with them and his father on tour in France, and " the surpassing grandeur of many of the continental churches seems to have thrown him quite into raptures ".[1] But he was very critical of the Italianate altars and the debased forms of vestments that he saw.

Soon afterwards he produced designs for plate and for the furniture of Windsor Castle. The furniture designs are in the Strawberry Hill style, and show no understanding of the nature of Gothic. For a while he was interested in the theatre, and painted scenery—which, according to Fergusson, was his true work in life—and then developed a love of the sea which never left him. " He usually wore a sailor's jacket, loose pilot trousers, a low-crowned hat, a black silk handkerchief thrown negligently round his neck, and shapeless footwear carelessly tied. His form and attire suggested the seaman rather than a man of art." [2] He would spend long periods at sea in a small boat, and at one time he owned, and sometimes commanded, a merchant smack trading with Holland. The whole of his short life was dominated by two passions—for the sea and for Christian—that is to say, Gothic—architecture. They were to him the only things worth living for, and he divided his time between the two. Sometimes he combined them, and made designs while sailing. In 1831 he married; in 1832 his father died; and in 1833 his wife also died. He married a second wife; she also died, and he married a third time.

In 1834 he joined the Church of Rome. It was said that his

[1] B. Ferrey, *Recollections of Pugin*, p. 40.   [2] *Catholic Encyclopedia.*

conversion was due more to architectural than to theological considerations. Pugin denied that. He said that the Roman Church was " the only one in which the grand and sublime style of architecture can ever be restored " ; but he declared that the real reason for the change was that he was convinced that the Roman Catholic Church was the only true one. That is what all converts say ; but who can satisfactorily analyse his own motives ? In any case, Pugin could never keep religion and Gothic architecture distinct : he could never think of Christianity without thinking of Gothic architecture.

But he was disappointed. The English Church seemed to be unsympathetic ; but the Roman Church was far more so. On the whole it had no love of Christian architecture at all. There were no grand churches, taste in church furniture and vestments was low, and when new churches were erected they had to be built as cheaply as possible. Some regarded Italian fashions as the hall-mark of true Catholicism. " Newman and Faber, after their conversion, both deserted Gothic for the Italian architecture of the Renaissance and modern Rome." [1] A few leading Romans, such as Dr. Rock, the Rev. Henry Weedall, President of St. Mary's College, Oscott, and Lord Shrewsbury, were friendly to Pugin. But by most of the Romans he was regarded as a rather dangerous and very difficult person. Certainly he was very difficult. His enthusiasms were never qualified, and his language was never anything but vehement. " After all, my dear sir," he once said, " what's the use of decent vestments with such priests as we have got ? a lot of blessed fellows ! Why, sir, when they wear my chasubles, they don't look like priests, and, what's worse, the chasubles don't look like chasubles." [2] " Since Christ Himself hung abandoned and bleeding on the Cross of Calvary, never has so sad a spectacle been exhibited to the afflicted Christian as is presented in many modern Catholic chapels, where the adorable Victim is offered up by the Priests of God's Church, disguised in miserable dresses intended for

[1] Wilfrid Ward, *William George Ward and The Oxford Movement*, p. 154. But Mr. E. S. Purcell, in the Appendix to Ferrey's *Recollections*, denies that the converts as a whole were hostile to the Gothic revival.
[2] Quoted in Ferrey, p. 112.

the sacred vestments, surrounded by a scoffing auditory of Protestant sight-seekers who have paid a few shillings a head to grin at mysteries which they do not understand, and to hear the performances of an infidel troop of mercenary musicians, hired to sing symbols of faith they disbelieve, and salutations to that Holy Sacrament they mock and deny." [1] The English Romanists had their customs which they saw no particular reason to change : who was this upstart convert who ridiculed and insulted them ? Pugin dreamed of glamorous mediaeval cities with beautiful buildings, and noble men and women in the streets. He pictured noble cathedrals with soaring spires, crockets and crosses, and figures of saints in their niches. In imagination he entered their portals and gazed at the twinkling points of light and the rich colours of the glass. There were altars and rich screens and metal-work and tiles and tapestries, and priests in beautiful vestments and acolytes in albs. The organ played and the choir sang, and hearts were uplifted in praise to God. But it was all a dream. The Roman Church in fact was content to worship in Italianate chapels, the priests were content to wear Italianate vestments, and the music of the Mass was operatic, with a solo by Madame Somebody. The very altar was profaned. " Cut papers of various colours, pretty ribbon, china pots, darling little gimcrack artificial flowers and all sorts of trumpery are suffered to be introduced, not only into the vicinity of the seat of the most Holy Mysteries, but actually in the presence of the Blessed Sacrament itself." [2] It is not to be wondered at that Pugin finally went mad.

After his conversion Pugin bought some land near Salisbury and built himself a house, which he called St. Marie's Grange. Here in 1836 he published at his own expense his famous book called *Contrasts ; or, a Parallel between the noble edifices of the fourteenth and fifteenth centuries,*[3] *and similar Buildings of the present day : showing the present decay of Taste.* The object of the book was to prove, as he said later, that :

[1] Pugin, *Apology*, pp. 22–23.
[2] " Remarks on the Present State of Ecclesiastical Architecture in England," *Dublin Review*, May 1842.
[3] In the second edition " Middle Ages " was substituted for " fourteenth and fifteenth centuries ", and some of the more violent passages were modified.

" 1. Everything grand, edifying and noble in art is the result of feelings produced by the Catholic religion on the human mind.

" 2. That destruction of art, irreverence towards religion, contempt of ecclesiastical persons and authority, and a complete loss of all the nobler perceptions of mankind have been the result of Protestantism, wherever it has been established.

" 3. That the degraded state of the arts in this country is purely owing to the absence of Catholic feeling among its professors, the loss of ecclesiastical patronage, and the apathy with which a Protestant Nation must necessarily treat the higher branches of Art."

He says that the test of architectural beauty consists in the fitness of the design to the purpose for which it was intended, and the correspondence of the style of a building with its use. Pagan buildings set forth pagan beliefs ; Christian churches set forth by their plan and design the Christian faith. Only the Christian mind can conceive buildings which shall produce such effects : pagan buildings can only set forth paganism. In the first edition Protestantism is blamed for the decay of art ; the later editions say that paganism and Protestantism both arose from the same cause—the decay of faith that attacked the Church. In any case, one of the blows to the progress of architecture was the suppression of the monasteries ; then came the establishment of the Reformed religion, and the old architecture perished with the old Faith.

The last two chapters deal with the degraded state of ancient ecclesiastical buildings at the time. What is to happen to them finally ? Pugin hopes that so many may return to Catholic unity that they may protect these glorious piles from further profanation, and, in the real spirit of former years, restore them to their original glory and worship.

But the main point of the book is not the letterpress, but the pictures which illustrate it.

He proved his theses in a simple way : by setting side by side a drawing of an ancient building and of a modern one. Certainly the flesh cannot fail to creep at the contrast. Here is a complete mediaeval town, with its churches and abbeys and cross and bridge chapel ; there is the same town in 1840 with no cross, a toll bridge, a few mutilated churches, several chapels, a ruined abbey, gasworks, lunatic asylum, viaduct and warehouses. (Pugin designed a Gothic viaduct; but could even he have designed gasworks in the Decorated style?) We see the Guildhall, London, George Dance, Esqr., Archt., contrasted with an Hotel de Ville: All Souls, Langham Place, John Nash, Esqr., Archt., with Redcliffe Church, Bristol; Hereford Cathedral 1830 with Dyrham Abbey in 1430; St. Pancras Chapel, Inwood, Esqr., Archt., with Bishop Skirlaw's Chapel, Yorkshire; Chapel Royal, Brighton, with St. George's Chapel, Winsor (*sic*); the monument of the Earl of Malmsbury in Salisbury Cathedral, Chantrey 1823 Invt. et fecit, with that of Admiral Gervase Alard, Winchelsea Church; King's Cross, Battle Bridge, S. Geary, Archt., with the cross at Chichester; the conduit, St. Anne's, Soho, with West Cheap Conduit, Thomas Ilam, 1479; the gateway of King's College, Strand, Sir Rd. Smirke, Archt., with Christ's College, Oxford; the western doorway of St. Mary Overies, Southwark, destroyed in 1838, with the new doorway; Ely House, Dover Street, 1836, with Ely Palace, Holborn, 1536; the Angel Inn, Oxford, with the Angel Inn, Grantham; a modern Poor House, built on the " panopticon " system, with an Antient Poor House; and a monument to " the Right Reverend Father in God, John Clutterbuck, D.D., aetatis suae 73. Also of Caroline and Lydia his two wives " with a monument of a mediaeval prelate.

Pugin hoped that he had " conducted the comparison with the greatest candour "; but of course he had done nothing of the kind. Ferrey, with great moderation, says that the illustrations were certainly not all selected with fairness. The *British Critic* said that the book " betrays an utter want of either soundness or fairness in its pretence at argument ". " We need scarcely inform such of our readers as chance to have seen Mr. Pugin's attempts at controversy, that he has performed his undertaking more in the spirit of the pleader than the judge. . . . He has chosen some of the most magnificent works of English antiquity, coupled them with some of the most meagre, cold and tasteless of modern times, and then left the reader to imply *ex uno disce omnes*. If Mr. Pugin would like to see an illustration of his method of reasoning in

E

an instance where he will not be disposed to admit its fairness,
we would recommend to his perusal a series of Irish tales,
published some years back, painting in the darkest colours the
working of Popery in that ill-fated island. . . . In truth,
though architecture is much affected by religious feeling, it is
not the proper school of theology. . . . The churchman may
indeed reverence the monuments of his forefathers' piety,
and with discretion may emulate the zeal which raised such
mighty works ; but if he attempts to make them the foundation
of his faith and his arguments, he runs great risk of being
betrayed into that portion of error which alloys the best and
noblest works of man. . . . The *written* part of his work is
childish both in style and argument ; in fact, it is scarcely worth
reading. . . . Mr. Pugin ought never to write, when he can
draw so infinitely better. . . . This world is a system of
compensations : *non omnis fert omnia tellus* ; Homer was blind,
and Mr. Pugin cannot argue. Nature has made him a first-
rate architect, but amerced him of logic."

That is true : Pugin was incapable of arguing, nor was he
capable of disentangling architecture and theology—or morals.
In all the contrasts there is the implied contrast between the
characters of the people of the Middle Ages and those of the
nineteenth century. The mediaeval people are kind and good
(Pugin had not the privilege of reading the works of Dr.
Coulton), the contemporary people are hard and brutal. They
appear against the background of their own buildings, and the
inference is obvious : the good and kind men of the past
built good buildings ; and the men of the cold, hard, utilitarian
nineteenth century built bad buildings. Buildings were like
their creators. In fact the men of the past were often cruel,
and the worshippers who used the old churches were blood-
thirsty, dirty and ignorant. But not in the dreamland of Pugin.
Those beautiful churches were built and used by men who held
the Catholic faith and had beautiful characters. They must
have been. Good architecture results from good morals. It
was a curious doctrine. But it proved much to the taste of
the nineteenth century, and was adopted with enthusiasm by
Anglicans.

Ferrey says that " the general current of public opinion was

certainly very favourable to the ' Contrasts ', and on the whole
the book was well spoken of by the Press. It gave, as might be
expected, some offence, but at the same time it caused much
amusement by the pungent character of its remarks." He
quotes some lines by Mr. M'Cann, an Irishman, which he calls
" droll and clever ". The first two verses are as follows :

> " Oh ! have you seen the work just out
>   By Pugin, the great builder ?
> ' Architect'ral Contrasts ' he's made out
>   Poor Protestants to bewilder.
> The Catholic Church, she never knew—
>   Till Mr. Pugin taught her,
> That orthodoxy had to do
>   At all with bricks and mortar.
>
> But now it's clear to one and all,
>   Since he's published his lecture,
> No Church is Catholic at all
>   Without Gothic architecture.
> In fact, he quite turns up his nose
>   At any style that's racent,
> The Gracian, too, he plainly shows
>   Is wicked and ondacent." [1]

The rest of the poem is no less droll.

From 1836 onwards Pugin was helping Barry in his work on
the Houses of Parliament. Barry was not well acquainted with
Gothic detail, and Pugin supplied almost all of it. He was kept
in the background ; but there is no doubt that he was responsible for most of the details of the work. At the same time
he was producing designs with great rapidity for numbers of
new churches, chapels and houses, and for Gothic ironwork,
glass, tiles and all kinds of furniture. He worked unceasingly
and without help : he is reported to have said, " Clerk, my dear
sir, clerk ? I never employ one ; I should kill him in a week."

In 1837 he became Professor of Ecclesiastical Antiquities at
St. Mary's College, Oscott, and in 1841 he produced *True
Principles of Pointed or Christian Architecture*—a reprint of two
of his lectures at the College. The object of the book was to
set forth the two great rules of design : " 1st, that there should
be no features about a building which are not necessary for
convenience, construction, or propriety ; 2nd, that all ornament should consist of enrichment of the essential construction

---

[1] Ferrey, p. 115.

of the building ".   " The neglect of these rules," he says, " is
the cause of all the bad architecture of the present time.
Architectural features are continually tacked on buildings with
which they have no connexion, merely for the sake of what is
termed effect."   It is in pointed architecture alone that these
great principles have been carried out.[1]   Classic architecture
abounds in shams.   Buttresses, the distinguishing feature of
pointed architecture, are essential for strength and beauty ;
in the Gothic style they are not concealed, but beautified,
while St. Paul's hides its buttresses, and also has a false dome.

The second section concerns metal work—in which, he says,
the design should also be fitted to the materials, as it always
was in the Middle Ages.

The next lecture has some remarks on decoration in wood,
and on propriety in architecture.   Propriety means that the
external and internal appearance of an edifice should be illustrative of and in accordance with the purpose for which it is
destined.   First, there is Ecclesiastical Propriety.   Religion, he
says, should be, and was, the leading motive in the minds of
church builders.   The old church buildings " all show that
they are dedicated to the one true faith, raised by men actuated
by one great motive, the truly Catholic principle of dedicating
the best they possessed to God ".   But churches are now built
without the least regard to tradition, to mystical reasons, or
even propriety.   No deception should be allowed in a church :
tricks and falsehoods may deceive men, but not God.   Pagan
emblems and architecture cannot express Christianity.   But
Gothic architecture is just right.

[1] What would Pugin have thought of the following passage from
Lord Grimthorpe's book on St. Albans Cathedral and its Restoration ?   " These sham critics of ' shams ' most likely do not know that
every detached shaft of every Gothic wall arcade is a sham, and would
probably break, if it were not ; and yet that deceives everybody who
does not know the secrets of construction, and that the shaft does not
hold up the cap, but the cap holds it.   Every stuck-on cornice is a
sham ; for every cornice professes to be, if it is not, a projecting piece
of wall, or timber on it, carrying the beams of the roof or ceiling, or a
parapet ; which it very seldom does carry, and had better not.   The
great majority of buttresses are shams, only built to look strong and
give shadows.   The finest cathedral fronts which have not two
towers, and some that have, are shams, not at all corresponding to the
roof behind them ; and those that do correspond to aisle roofs of a
high slope always look inferior to gabled or horizontal ones."   (*St.
Albans Cathedral and its Restoration*, p. 65.)

What, indeed, is more appropriate for the ancient worship than an old English parish church, with its heaven-pointing spire—the beautiful and instructive emblem of a Christian's brightest hopes—with its solemn-sounding bells to summon the people to the offices of the church? " Then the southern porch, destined for the performance of many rites—the spacious nave and aisles for the faithful ; the oaken canopy covered with images of the heavenly host, and painted with quaint and appropriate devices ; the impressive doom or judgement pictured over the great chancel arch ; the fretted screen and roodloft ; the mystical separation between the sacrifice and the people, with the emblem of redemption carried on high and surrounded with glory ; the great altar, rich in hangings, placed far from irreverent gaze ; and with the brilliant eastern window terminating this long perspective." [1]

Then there is Collegiate Propriety, which means that colleges should be of Catholic and Christian architecture.

And finally Domestic Propriety—that is to say, that houses should be English, not Italian or Greek or Oriental, as they were in the days of Catholic, Merry England.

In 1843 he produced *An Apology for the Revival of Christian Architecture in England*. There is, he says, no consistent national style : private judgement has run wild, and any number of foreign styles are used capriciously. " Styles are now *adopted* instead of *generated*, and ornament and design *adapted to*, instead of *originated by* the edifices themselves." Even Gothic is adopted " not on consistent principle as the expression of the Christian Faith, but as a style to be put on and off at pleasure, to be used when the architect felt so disposed, to please those who admire old things, or because it is MELANCHOLY, and *therefore fit for religious buildings* ! ! ! " [2]

Pointed architecture is not to be defended on the grounds of abstract beauty alone : it must be taken in reference to the purpose for which it was intended. " The belief and manners of every people are embodied in the edifices they raised." " Will the architecture of our times, even supposing it solid enough to last, hand down to posterity any certain clue or guide to the system under which it was erected ? Surely not ; it

---

[1] *True Principles*, p. 42.　　　　[2] *Apology*, p. 2.

is not the expression of existing opinions and circumstances, but a confused jumble of styles and symbols borrowed from all nations and periods."

He violently attacks the Royal Academy and the Universities : " a man who paganizes *in the Universities* deserves no quarter." Modern paganism is beneath contempt : ancient pagan principles were the perfect expressions of imperfect systems. They were the summit of human skill, expended on human inventions. But Christian art has a merit and perfection impossible in pre-Christian days. How can Englishmen, professing the Christian creed, reject their own architecture in favour of pagan styles ? " If we worshipped Jupiter, or were votaries of Juggernaut, we should raise a temple or erect a pagoda . . . but, in the name of common sense, while we profess the creed of Christians, whilst we glory in being Englishmen, let us have an architecture the arrangement and details of which will alike remind us of our faith and our country—an architecture whose beauties we may claim as our own, whose symbols have originated in our religion and our customs." [1]

Some have objected that Christian architecture did not develop for many years after Christ. Of course not : the Church was persecuted and had no chance to pay attention to such things. " But modern men are constantly referring to the Church in her suffering state, described by our Lord under the similitude of a grain of mustard seed, while they refuse to recognize her, when, as the greatest of all trees, she extended, triumphant in beauty and luxuriant foliage, over the earth." When the great, powerful Church found a voice in the material arts, it was in the pointed styles. Why do the material arts now speak with so uncertain a sound ? Because they do not speak the voice of the Church, and the Church's voice is paralysed by paganism. " When pagan ideas triumphed over Christian principles, *inconsistency* for the first time was developed in architectural design. Previous to that period, architecture had always been a correct type of the various systems in which it was employed ; but from the moment that Christians adopted this fatal mistake, of reviving classic

[1] *Apology*, p. 6.

design, the principles of architecture have been plunged into miserable confusion." Inconsistency is the cause of all modern failures. What chances have been lost in the railways and in cemeteries !

What of the future ? Pugin wants students to study Gothic, and at the same time to be imbued with the mysteries of the Faith. They must know something of Church history and of the lives of the saints, and also of the annals of our country, its constitution, laws, privileges, dignities, and literature ; and of the rubrics, customs and ceremonies of the Church. " Local interest would be restored, and English architecture assume a distinct and dignified position in the history of art ; *for we do not wish to produce mere servile imitators of former excellence of any kind, but men imbued with the consistent spirit of the ancient architects, who would work on their principles, and carry them out as the old men would have done, had they been placed in similar circumstances, and with similar wants to ourselves.*"

With regard to Church architecture, the position of the Church of Rome is perfectly clear : it has kept the old Faith, and therefore wants exactly the old arrangement, symbols and ornaments. (But it does not always get them.) The position of the Church of England is not so clear. But it is evident that a church belonging to that body should have the following features—the old arrangement of nave and chancel ; a tower for bells, surmounted by a spire ; a nave without galleries or large pews ; a font in the old position with a cover ; pulpit, lectern and litany-desk (not a reading-pew) ; a screen ; a stone altar with ornaments ; and decoration with sacred symbols, imagery and stained glass. So that the Anglican Church can work exclusively on the principles of Christian architecture, and renounce all pagan adaptations with sorrow.

Sepulchral memorials should of course be Christian, and not pagan, and all civil architecture should be Gothic, inasmuch as our wants and purposes are almost identical with those of our English forefathers : the climate is the same as in the past, and we are governed by nearly the same laws and the same system of political economy.

After some remarks on the use of modern inventions and on

sculpture, Pugin ends the essay on a high note. He hopes that, as the true principles of architecture are understood, England will once more attain to architectural excellence. This country has been more fortunate than the Continent. We have the remains of Catholic piety of the past, which raise the thoughts to religion. " The cross, that emblem of a Christian's hopes, still surmounts spire and gable ; in flaming red it waves from the masts of our navy, over the towers of the sovereign's palace, and is blazoned on London's shield. And who can look on the cross-crowned spire, and listen to the chime of distant bells, or stand beneath lofty vault of cathedral choir, or gaze on long and lessening aisles, or kneel by ancient tomb, and yet *protest* against aught but that monstrous and unnatural system that has mutilated their beauty, and marred their fair design ? "

In the same year *The Present State of Ecclesiastical Architecture in England* was published; in 1844 the *Glossary of Ecclesiastical Ornament and Costume*; in 1849 *Floriated Ornament : A Series of Thirty-One designs*; and in 1851 *A Treatise on Chancel Screens and Lofts*.

The last of these is a most violent and intemperate book. It has the kind of attacks which one would expect on churches which resemble concert-halls or show-rooms. " There is no legitimate halting-place between Catholic doctrine and positive infidelity, and I am quite certain there is none between a church built on Christian traditional symbolism, and Covent Garden Theatre." The very *vitals* of Catholic architecture are assailed by the opponents of screens. Screens are concerned with discipline and faith ; their disuse is due to the decay of reverence ; faith in the Holy Eucharist could not survive their destruction. " Those who oppose the revival and continuance of open screens are not only enemies of Catholic traditions and practices, but the grounds of their objections militate as strongly against every symbolic form and arrangement in ecclesiastical architecture, and, therefore, till they retract their opposition, they are practically insulting the traditions of the Church, impeding the restoration of reverence and solemnity, and injuring the progress of religion." He has some kindly words to say about the Anglican Church. " *Real Protestants*

PLATE VII

HOOK CHURCH, SURREY
A cheap church condemned by the *Ecclesiologist*.   It has since been rebuilt

BROCKHAM GREEN CHURCH
By Benjamin Ferrey

PLATE VIII

ST. STEPHEN'S, WESTMINSTER
By Benjamin Ferrey

have always built rooms for their worship. . . . But the separated Church of England, though Protestant in position, in name, and in practice, has retained so much of traditions in her service, and is linked by so many ties to older and better times, that she naturally turns back to them with affection and reverence, and seeks, as far as her maimed rites and fettered position will permit, to restore the departed glory of the sanctuary."

The book ends with four chapters on Ambonoclasts, Calvinist, Pagan, Revolutionary and Modern. He shows that pagan and revolutionary ambonoclasts were apt to come to a bad end. Of the modern ambonoclast he writes, " This character is of comparatively recent creation—none of this species having been seen about in this country previous to the consecration of St. George's Church. About that time two or three made their appearance, and, though not by any means in a flourishing condition, they have somewhat increased." [1]

" Modern ambonoclasts have a perpetual habit of abusing the finest works of Catholic antiquity and art, and exulting in the admiration of everything debased, and modern, and trumpery ; an inordinate propensity for candles and candlesticks, which they arrange in every possible variety ; they require great excitement in the way of lively, jocular and amatory tunes at divine service," etc., etc.

The best part of the book is the appendix of drawings of screens. Pugin could draw, as the *British Critic* said, so much better than he could argue.

There were many lesser book and pamphlets.

Towards the end of his life Pugin became more and more obsessed with his one idea. In 1846 he built a house for William George Ward, " and gradually, during their necessary intercourse in this connexion, he came at last to realize the terrible deficiencies of his client. Comfort was preferred to beauty of form ; lancet windows were tabooed ; plenty of light and fresh air were insisted on at the cost of any degree of infringement of

[1] Cf. the *Rambler* on the subject of the rood screen at St. George's, Southwark : " Of its merits as a composition we are perhaps hardly unbiassed judges, our aversion to screens, both theologically and architecturally, being very strong." The screen was removed to the west end of the church.

the rules of art. Pugin grew depressed and then angry."
In 1849 he is said to have expressed himself unable to eat
puddings unless they were Gothic in form, and made a design
for a Gothic pudding. When Ward attacked rood screens,
Pugin wrote, " I can only say that the less we have to do with
each other in future the better, for I must plainly tell you that
I consider you a greater enemy to true Christianity than the
most rabid Exeter Hall fanatic ".[1]

In 1851 he assisted in the preparation of the Great Exhibition.
He was shocked by the building, and " rather disgusted at the
notion of enclosing everything under the shelter of a huge
GREEN-HOUSE ". He " considered the construction of the
building rather an instance of retrogression than advance-
ment ".[2] He arranged the mediaeval court; but the strain
was too great. His mind was already unbalanced; finally he
became completely insane; and in 1852 he died.

Pugin's churches are seldom satisfactory. A writer in the
Saturday Review (quoted in the *Ecclesiologist*, New Series,
No. CXIV) considered that " Pugin . . . was unconscious of
the defects of the practical side of his work. He was always
creating at high fever heat, till the archetype took possession
of his excitable imagination, and till the joyous pen-sketch or
etching, done in noble contempt of scale, revealed the dominant
idea of which the actual fabric was but the feeble counterpart.
The working drawings dashed off to suit the paymaster to the
left, and Mr. Myers [3] to the right—and still more, the buildings
in which those drawings resulted—revealed the hard battle
with necessities. Yet Pugin, if he saw the discrepancy, kept
up an heroic if not defiant heart, and hustled out of the patent
incongruities, till the premonitions of a premature termination
of his active life led to a sad and sudden sobering."

It is certain that towards the end of his life he admitted
failure. He had " passed his life in thinking of fine things,
studying fine things, designing fine things and realizing very
poor ones ".

" I have never had the chance of producing a single fine

---

[1] W. Ward, *William George Ward and the Oxford Movement*, pp.
154–155.
[2] Ferrey, p. 257.
[3] The builder who erected most of Pugin's works.

ecclesiastical building, except my own church, where I am both
paymaster and architect; but everything else, either for want
of adequate funds or injudicious interference and control, or
some other contingency, is more or less a failure. In the process of canonization there is always a devil's advocate, and I am
satisfied that there is the same personage in the erection of
every church, who contrives to mar the result. Sometimes he
appears in the character of a furious committee-man, sometimes as a prejudiced ecclesiastic, sometimes in the form of a
liberal benefactor, sometimes as a screw, but there he is in
some character or other, thrusting in his claw and spoiling the
job." [1]

But though the blame may have lain to some extent on clergy
and building committees with limited funds, Pugin cannot be
excused. He could dream and he could draw; but his
designs could not bear the transition from paper into brick and
stone.

St. George's Cathedral, Lambeth, was planned as a soaring
building with an enormous central tower, and an apse with
long windows. The design was too expensive, and St.
George's was reduced to more reasonable dimensions. It was
built, and opened in 1848. It has a long nave, with wide aisles
of the same height, a short chancel with chapels, and the base
of a large tower and spire which have never been completed.
We do not regret the non-execution of the first design : such
grandeur as it seems to have in Pugin's drawings would
probably have disappeared from it if it had been actually built.
But surely in the modified and simplified design Pugin could
have done himself justice ? St. George's is simple enough in
plan, and its details are obvious fourteenth century : surely it
could not go wrong. But it has. We can see it in the frontispiece of Pugin's *Apology* rising splendid in its Gothic majesty,
with the setting sun behind it. But now we see it standing
forlornly in a rather gloomy street in South London, with its
prickly pinnacles and grimy brick walls. We do not approve
of Ruskin's hysterical rhetorical questions : " Was it want of
money that made you put that blunt, overloaded, laborious

[1] *Some Remarks on the Articles which have appeared in the
"Rambler," relative to Ecclesiastical Architecture and Decoration.*

ogee door in the side of it? Was it for lack of funds that you sunk the tracery of the parapet in its clumsy zig-zags? Was it in parsimony that you buried its paltry pinnacles in that eruption of diseased crockets?" But we agree with East-lake's more temperate fault-finding. "There is a want of vitality about the building. The pinnacles which crown the buttresses are cold and heavy. The carved work, though executed with care and even delicacy here and there, is spirit-less, except in the treatment of animal form. Crockets and ball-flower ornaments are needlessly multiplied. The tracery of the windows is correct and aims at variety, and the doorways are arched with orthodox mouldings, but there is scarcely a single feature in the exterior which arrests attention by the beauty of its form or the aptness of its place." [1] We must admit that St. George's is a failure. St. Chad's Cathedral, Birmingham, has some good points, and succeeds, in spite of its small scale, in being impressive. But the furniture is on the whole better than the building.

St. Marie's, Derby, stands opposite to the Anglican church of St. Alkmund, itself a product of the Gothic Revival. St. Marie's is in the Perpendicular style, with a western tower and an eastern apse. It has been restored and redecorated, and has a bright interior. But there is nothing interesting in it. Mr. Trappes-Lomax in his life of Pugin makes a curious comment, " Its proximity to Gibbs' Protestant cathedral offers a contrast which shows more plainly than pages of description the service which Pugin rendered to English ecclesiastical architecture ".[2] That is presumably not intended as irony. It is a common failing in English Romanists to represent their geese as swans. But there are times when the attempt to do so becomes absurd. All Saints' Cathedral is a magnificent Renaissance swan; and St. Marie's, in spite of its sincerity, is but a Gothic goose.

Pugin's model church was St. Augustine's, Ramsgate, which stands close to the house which he built for himself on West Cliff. It was begun in 1846 and left incomplete when Pugin died. Of this church Sir Kenneth Clark says, " The masonry is solid

[1] Eastlake, *Gothic Revival*, p. 155.
[2] M. Trappes-Lomax, *Pugin*, p. 102.

and the whole building has no obvious faults, but it has none of those qualities which may often be found in the simplest traditional parish church, none of the repose, much less the thrill of great architecture. The exterior is undistinguished, the interior crowded, the masses are unco-ordinated, the proportions are bad. Pugin lacked the essential quality of a great builder—he did not think in volume; his wonderful dreams were wasted because he did not think in three dimensions." [1]

The *Ecclesiologist* (January 1846) objected to the designs which had been published in the *Dublin Review*: " Mr. Pugin, clever and enthusiastic as he is, has not answered the expectations which were formed of him. . . . The rocks upon which artistically he has split are quickness and versatility. . . . He has been too apt, by the magical use of shades and felicitous etching, imaginary diaper, and picturesque-looking mediaeval figures most dexterously put in just in the right place and the right posture, to produce an unreal appearance of perfection in his engravings of his own buildings." " These buildings are . . . to speak generally, all represented, whether yet commenced or not, as in a state of ideal perfection ; to which humanly speaking there is very little probability of their attaining, excepting in a few cases, for an indefinite period. . . . This is scarcely dealing as he should with his readers ; for not only does he represent the buildings as in a state of perfection, but he gives the impression of their being larger and more stately than they turn out on examination to be.

" Of such pictorial architecture, perhaps the most striking example is the ' Benedictine Priory of Saint Gregory's at Downside, near Bath.' Here we are presented with a bird's-eye view of an immense monastery with four quadrangles and a huge church, crowned by three lofty spires, stately indeed to look upon ; but when will it be finished ? How far is this priory an example of the present state of architecture in England in 1842, any more than the gorgeous palaces which form the backgrounds of Mr. Martin's pictures ? The safe generalities of the letter-press leave this question very doubtful. Such a proceeding on Mr. Pugin's part is calculated to throw an unreal halo, not only around his own reputation, but (are we un-

[1] Clark, *The Gothic Revival*, pp. 169–170.

charitable in the sentiment ?) round that of the communion to whose services he has devoted himself."

The unreal halo was the trouble.

Pugin was a romantic character.   He dressed in extraordinary garments ; he worked " with no tools but a rule and rough pencil, amidst a continuous rattle of marvellous stories, slashing criticisms, and shouts of laughter ".[1]   He made beautiful drawings while sailing a small boat on a rough sea.   He worked with uncanny energy, and " did in a few years the work of a lifetime ".   He designed for himself mysterious Gothic houses. In all this he was eccentric—but surely it was not genuinely mediaeval ?   The Middle Ages were not particularly romantic.

His picture of them was, of course, fictitious.   There was certainly beauty then ; but the beautiful cities had terrible slums, and the beautiful churches were used in ways that would have shocked Pugin.   He is related to have burst into tears when Wiseman brought some ladies east of the screen at St. Barnabas', Nottingham.   He was an extremely sensitive person, and could not have stood the life of the Middle Ages for a week. His ideas on the subject were phantasy—a refuge from the intolerable boredom of life at Store Street, Bedford Square. Unfortunately the phantasy lasted : it became an obsession, and ended in insanity.

He understood the architecture of the Middle Ages up to a point.   He was right in his insistence on the importance of construction in Gothic work.   Mr. Bernard Miller has said,[2] " The Gothic builders reverenced construction ; they built up, as it were, a personality around the anatomy of building. Structure, truthfully in evidence and never concealed became the touchstone of Gothic building."   The Gothic style arose from the necessities of construction.   But it was a new thing. The article goes on to say that after the dark ages " it became necessary to establish tradition once again and to build up a new foundation and theory of architecture to meet the changing conditions of the time.   The result was an entirely new departure, quite free from imitation of earlier traditional forms

[1] Barry, *Memoir of Sir C. Barry,* footnote to p. 196.
[2] " Modern Church Architecture.   The English Contribution." *Church Quarterly Review,* July–September 1936.

and details which had lost their significance. In this way . . . they became the modernists of their day. It has been said that ' it is traditional to be modern '. What was the subconscious attitude of the mediaeval builders to tradition ? Whatever it was, it was certainly not imitative. It was retrospective, but only in the evolutionary sense. Beyond this, they interpreted tradition, paradoxically though it may seem, as a forward looking movement, continuously advancing towards the creation of an architecture charmingly and reasonably fashioned to the life and requirements of the time."

He is speaking of modern churches which are not in the least " traditional ", but which are certainly built on the same principles as those of the mediaeval builders. There is no reason why the adoption of these principles should lead to the copying of their works. In this matter Pugin was mistaken. He was aware that the essential nature of Gothic lies in construction, and not in decoration and detail. But at the same time he insisted on Gothic decoration and detail at all costs, and his buildings have those, and not much of the other. Were they, to his mind, after all, the more important ? When he becomes eloquent and prophetic, he forgets True Principles : he gives us highly coloured visions of flowing tracery and roodscreens and painted glass and reredoses. The True Principles are mixed up with the vision of a mediaeval England, chivalrous, Catholic, moral, merry and altogether wonderful—and he cannot separate them from it.

It seems curious to us that anyone could have thought seriously of restoring the life and the architecture of the Middle Ages in the early years of Queen Victoria. Rich men in the late eighteenth century had played with mediaevalism, and amused themselves with sham castles and ruined abbeys ; but they were simply romantic, and had no thought of taking it seriously. Nothing enraged Pugin more than that. Eighteenth-century Gothic was an abomination to him, and eighteenth-century restorations roused him to fury. Carter was Wyatt's implacable enemy while he lived, Pugin continued the anti-Wyatt campaign, and it has been conscientiously waged by writers until the present time. Might not Pugin have said, " Wyatt was a pioneer : all honour to him " ? He

might; but he did not. He visited Hereford and wrote
" Horror ! dismay ! the villain Wyatt had been there, the west
front was his. Need I say more ? No ! All that is vile,
cunning and rascally is included in the term Wyatt." He
visited Lichfield and wrote, " This monster of architectural
depravity—this pest of cathedral architecture—has been here.
Need I say more ? "

But what was there in Wyatt to arouse such unreasoning
wrath in Pugin ? It was not so much the absence of correct
Gothic detail in his work—though that was serious enough—
as the absence of everything which would make it, in the eyes
of Pugin, " the real thing ". It was Protestant architecture,
and it sometimes included shams : the vault of the nave of
Hereford, for instance, though it looks like stone, is of plaster.
Wyatt's policy, too, was to remove screens and to open a
building from end to end : he was an ambonoclast. And so
he was the vile, cunning and rascally Wyatt. In fact, there was
nothing seriously wrong with Wyatt, except for his slovenly
and unbusiness-like habits ; [1] but Pugin did not worry too
much about that. He deduced his character from his
buildings.

What would his attitude to Wyatt have been if Wyatt had
been a Roman Catholic ? As we have seen, Pugin changed or
modified his early ideas on the subject of the connexion of
Protestantism and bad architecture. There are signs that
before his death he looked with a more kindly eye on the Church
of England. He prepared material for, but never published,
*An Apology for the separated Church of England since the reign
of the Eighth Henry. Written with every feeling of Christian
charity for her Children, and honour of the glorious men she
continued to produce in evil times. By A. Welby Pugin Many
years a Catholic-minded son of the Anglican Church, and still an
affectionate and loving brother and servant of the true sons of
England's Church.* It ended, " Let us then always speak and
think with gratitude of the old bridge that has brought us over,[2]
and lend a pious help to restore her time-worn piers, wasted by
the torrents of dissent and infidelity, and, what is worse, internal

[1] See A. Dale, *James Wyatt*, Chap. 15.
[2] Is this the first instance of the expression " the bridge Church " ?

decay by rotten stones, but which God in His mercy, beyond our human understanding, appears yet to sustain, and to make it the marvel of some of the most zealous men that have appeared since the ancient glory of the Church in pious early times. *Pax omnibus.* Amen." That is rather faint praise; but he is alleged to have said, " The rest of my life must be one of penitence to seek forgiveness for the wrongs I have done to the Anglican Church ".[1] He had said that pointed architecture could only be restored in the Roman Church; but for the last ten years of his life he saw his principles taken up by Anglicans with far more enthusiasm than by Romans. Italianate taste was deeply rooted in the Roman Church; but the Church of England was not closely attached to Classic modes, and everything was ready for a Gothic revival. The article in the *Dublin Review* of February 1842, on " The Present State of Ecclesiastical Architecture in England ", praises the Anglican clergy for their following of the true principles of architecture. Mr. Purcell cannot have been speaking only of the Roman Church when he said,[2] " Look around on the churches and public edifices now being raised in England, and whatsoever is grand and solid in construction, or Christian in principle, and whatsoever is in keeping with the traditions of the ancient architectural glory of England, is a proud and eloquent monument to him who was the first to raise his voice against the abominations of an adopted paganism, against the base imitation of a corrupt style, foreign to our soil, to our climate, and to our national character ". Pugin's convictions were modified, and he saw that it was paganism and unbelief, invading the Roman as well as the Reformed Churches, that was responsible for the decay of Christian architecture. He was a loyal son of the Roman Church—but he was not appreciated there. He dared to attack abuses, and an attempt was made to place his " Earnest Address on the Establishment of the Hierarchy " on the Index. If he had lived a few years later, he would almost certainly have remained an Anglican, and have been a pioneer of " British Museum " architecture and ceremonial. His association of true architecture with Roman Catholicism

[1] Ferrey, p. 271.
[2] *Writings and Character of A. W. N. Pugin,* Appendix to Ferrey.

F

was a mistake.   If Wyatt had been a Roman, he would still have attacked him.

But the main objection to Wyatt and his fellows was the objection to shams.   But in this matter Pugin was mistaken. He had a right to object to plaster vaulting and to ornament which concealed construction ; but he mixed his architectural objections with morals.   He was partly right in his belief that architectural style should result from the necessities of construction—though it is hard to see why Gothic should necessarily result.   He said that " every building that is treated naturally, without disguise or concealment, cannot fail to look well " ; and there is something in that.[1]   He hated shams.   Ferrey says [2] that " perhaps the greatest service has been done, through the agency of this work, by Pugin's unsparing exposure of the system of SHAMS in architectural design.   Every kind of unreality is pointed out and denounced."   An article in *The Times* said, " He it was who first exposed the shams and concealments of modern architecture, and contrasted it with the heartiness and sincerity of mediaeval work.   He showed the fair outside of a modern building having no relation to its construction except that of a screen to hide its clumsy makeshifts.   He then showed how the first principle of mediaeval work, was to expose construction and not to hide it, but to adorn it ; a modern building for example conceals its flying buttresses with a dead wall ; an ancient one exposes them and derives a principal charm from these contrivances being seen." But the article also said, " It was he who first showed us that our architecture offended not only against the law of beauty but also against the laws of morality ".

Did it ?   According to Pugin, an honest, noble, Christian, Catholic man would build an honest, noble, Christian, Catholic building ; a bad, pagan, un-Catholic man would build a bad, pagan, un-Catholic building.   False construction proved the false character of the builders, true construction their truthfulness—or at least the falsehood or truthfulness of the religion

---

[1] Mr. Geoffrey Scott in *The Architecture of Humanism* calls this " the Mechanical Fallacy ".   He says that the appearance is all-important : it is not necessary that the columns which we see should bear the weight ; it is enough if they seem to do so.

[2] Ferrey, p. 146.

which they professed. This is the " Ethical Fallacy " : the idea that good buildings can only be built by good men, and that bad men—or even ordinary, unspiritual men—will build bad buildings. But what does " good " mean ? St. Francis was a good man, and the cathedrals of the thirteenth century are good buildings ; George IV was a bad man, and the churches built in his reign—according to Pugin—are bad. But the words " good " and " bad " are obviously used in two different senses. A good building is one that is soundly built and pleasing to the eye ; a good man is one who successfully attempts to do his duty to God and man. But there is no connexion between the two meanings ; and there is no reason why a bad man should not design a " good " building. There is only too much evidence that good men can design bad buildings.

Pugin would have agreed with an absurd passage in a later book by an Anglican clergyman who, speaking of St. Paul's, said,[1] " In all this there is humiliation and disgrace. Our greatest cathedral pleads with us to take from it the lie which defiles it on its right hand and on its left. It stands in our midst, as it were, silently but constantly imploring us to take from it its reproach—to grant to it consistency and truth—to give to it its right, however long delayed, to be absolutely true, like the brave Apostle whose fearless name it bears. Would it not be worthy of a nation that loveth the truth to make the great cathedral true ? "

Sir Kenneth Clark says that " Pugin laid the two foundation stones of that strange system which dominates nineteenth-century art criticism, and is immortalized in *The Seven Lamps of Architecture* : the value of a building depends on the moral worth of its creator ; and a building has a moral value independent of, and more important than, its aesthetic value ".[2] It is certainly a curious theory ; but Pugin believed it, and he and his followers, and Ruskin, succeeded in getting almost everyone else to believe it.[3]

[1] H. H. Bishop, *Pictorial Architecture of the British Isles*, p. 87.
[2] Clark, *Gothic Revival*, p. 190.
[3] It is not necessary to give quotations in illustration of this. But cf. *Pagan or Christian ?* by W. J. Cockburn Muir, p. vii : " Though you are doubtless bent upon not believing it, it is bound up closely with our Religiousness, and our structures afford an infallible indica-

Pugin was a prophet. We may consider that he was a false prophet : but it is impossible not to be half convinced when we read his writings. We are carried away by his conviction and by the spate of words. We admire his unfailing optimism : he even had hopes of rebuilding St. Peter's, Rome, in a better style, and gained support from two prelates who were in immediate attendance on the Pope. We are impressed by his drawings, though we know that many of them are only dreams, and those that were carried out do not look like that.

But when we have put down the books, we realize that he was wrong. He was dreaming of something impossible. Mr. Trappes-Lomax says [1] that " all that Pugin could do was to discover ' true principles ' and use them to uphold an unsound edifice. As Herr Bruno Taut says, ' The work of the architect lies in the interpretation of a new social order '. Pugin's error lay in not realizing that the social order was new. To his mind, the ' pagans ' were but an invasion ; as it were merely an iridescent scum on the clear pool of social life. Clear away the scum, and, like a pool freed from a film of oil, the underlying mediaeval life would once more thrust up its natural growths into the air—St. Mary Redcliffe, Salisbury. . . . But there was no underlying mediaeval life. There was nothing, as it were, in which his work could strike deep roots. This is not to say that masterly Gothic work was not done, is not being done, nor will be done ; only that Gothic could never again become the permanent and normal mode of expression. And that was what Pugin desired."

And he had faith that it would happen. In the *Apology* he wrote of the pagans, " Their works will hardly be endured for the time they have to run, and the remembrance of them will be the laughing-stock of posterity ; and when the ancient glories of our native land are restored, and this generation of pretenders have passed away, men will be amazed that a period could have

---

tion of our moral status ". The author also says, on pp. 130–131, speaking of the reign of Charles II and St. Paul's, " There is a singular coincidence between the unbridled immorality of this reign, and the building which we are taught to admire as the perfection of the modified Classic Architecture ".

[1] M. Trappes-Lomax, *Pugin*, p. 327.

existed when they were permitted to disfigure and destroy, unchecked and unreproved ".

Could he ever have believed that the twentieth century would admire the works of Nash, and photograph and describe the buildings of Wyatt ?

CHAPTER V

PUGIN was a prophet without honour in his own country; but principles similar to his were adopted with enthusiasm by Anglicans. They were not borrowed from Pugin: they formed themselves independently in the minds of men of High-Church views. They were not, of course, carried to the same conclusion to which Pugin had carried them. Pugin had considered that Gothic architecture led logically to the Roman Catholic Church. Malcontents who disliked the new-fangled Gothic craze agreed with Pugin. He and they were sure that Gothic architecture and Popery were connected, and they were grateful to him for putting the case so clearly. As Eastlake says, " The extreme Protestant party was still a strong one. They saw mischief lurking in every pointed niche, and heresy peeping from behind every Gothic pillar. They regarded the mediaevalists with suspicion, and identified their cause with Romish hierarchy, with the Inquisition and Smith-field." [1] Mr. A. L. Drummond, in *The Church Architecture of Protestantism*,[2] says that Eastlake " reads his own generation's suspicion of Gothic into the Protestant consciousness of the period preceding the Oxford Movement ". But that is surely a mistake. By Eastlake's time Protestants were happily erecting Gothic buildings. In the 1820's Gothic had been used under Evangelical auspices without any fear of Popery; but Eastlake is writing of the 1830's. By that time Gothic had acquired a new meaning. There was a world of difference between Gothic as set forth in the churches of James Savage and Gothic as explained by Pugin. One of *Weale's Quarterly Papers* says that " the only ' faithful ' Gothic structures now erecting are the Romish churches and chapels ". That remark must have represented a great deal of Protestant opinion.

[1] *Gothic Revival*, p. 266.   [2] P. 66 note.

But high Anglicans disagreed both with Pugin and with the Protestants. Pugin was essentially right; but wrong in his opinion that Christian architecture had no place in and could not flourish in the Church of England. (Later, as we have seen, Pugin himself changed his mind and began to agree.) The Protestants were right in connecting faithful Gothic with Catholicism; but they were wrong in identifying Catholicism with Popery. They began to stress the half-forgotten truth that Catholicism is not the same as Romanism, and to proclaim that the Anglican Church is a true part of the Church Catholic.

Certain things had been discarded at the Reformation; but many things had been kept. It was the intention of the Reformers to continue the use of such ceremonies as were not dark or dumb. Chancels were to remain as they had done in times past, and the rubrics ordered, or did not forbid, many of the old usages. Certainly many things had not been used for years; but, even so, there was post-Reformation precedent for their use—in the seventeenth century, and even in the eighteenth. They were part of the heritage of the Church of England; and so was Gothic architecture. Dissenters and separatists had left the Church, and had no right to the Church style. But it belonged rightfully to the Church of England, the old Church of the country—and it belonged to her more certainly than to the Romanists.

Gilbert Scott, after his conversion to pure Gothic architecture, of which we shall speak later, argued that Popery was responsible for the decay of the Gothic style. It would appear at first sight, he says, that the Romanists as such have a just claim to the entire possession of Pointed architecture. It is certainly true that " this wonderful phase of art made its appearance just at the era of the most absolute sway of the Roman usurpation, that it declined from about the time when that sway began to be shaken, and that it became extinct nearly at the period of the Reformation. But," he adds, " it arose rather in spite of, than as a consequence of, that usurped domination and its accompanying errors." In the first place, Gothic was not the architecture of the usurping party, but of the nations which suffered from it. It was the style of the northern nations, while in Italy it is rarely found in a pure form.

Secondly, the time of Gothic architecture, although one of Papal domination, was also a time of the revival of piety and learning. The time of its decline was a time of decay in religion and of ecclesiastical corruption.

Thirdly, its extinction was directly due to the influence of Rome, for the indulgences for the rebuilding of St. Peter's were the immediate cause of the Reformation.

Lastly, the paganization of art spread through the Roman Catholic countries, but took a long time to take root in ours. The modern Roman Church was not interested in the recovery of Gothic until the secession of Pugin. Even according to Pugin, the final abandonment of Gothic for Pagan art took place in the Papal Court itself.[1]

So the Anglican Church was the heir to Gothic architecture. And that was a very serious matter. It was not a question of imitating Gothic details when architects felt inclined to do so. The Gothic style was a sacred heritage and trust—like the Prayer Book, or even the Creed. You could not make selections from the Creed or the Prayer Book, or use them according to taste. You might revive interest in certain parts, such as the clause " The Holy Catholic Church ", or the Ornaments Rubric. But you could not drop anything or make innovations.

It was the work of Churchmen to revive their Mother Church in her belief and worship ; it was also their work to revive the Christian style of architecture. The two things went together, for only by building churches in the style that the Christian faith had produced, planned and fitted in the old way, could the Faith be set forth and the rubrics of the Prayer Book be faithfully obeyed.

[1] Our old friend Andrew Trimen seems to regard Gothic architecture as certainly Popish, but at the same time the morning star of the approaching Reformation. He says, " Long and tedious was the night through which the nations of Europe toiled in darkness, being forbidden the light of revelation, and the word of God. . . . Yet for several centuries before the morning dawned, and the nations of Europe began to struggle into day, the ambition of a supreme and universal Church conceived the idea, and felt the importance, of impressing the public mind with awe, by the imposing grandeur of ecclesiastical structures. Architectural science, as most essential to the magnificence and splendour of the Church, was the first to rear its head amidst the pervading gloom, and to give omen that the ages of darkness were passing away—that the night was far spent and the day was at hand."

PLATE IX

St. Mary Magdalene's, Munster Square
By R. C. Carpenter
A successful carrying out of Camdenian ideals

PLATE X

ALL SAINTS', MARGARET STREET
By William Butterfield
The Ecclesiological Society's model Church

Barry had come to the conclusion that the exact reproduction of old churches was not suitable for the carrying out of the Prayer-Book services : the High Churchmen came to the opposite conclusion. The English rite required long chancels, choir stalls, returned stalls for the clergy, fonts and altars raised on steps, frontals, altar crosses—above all, it required the Gothic style. Churches should be built exactly in the old way : and only then could the rubrics of the Prayer Book be faithfully obeyed.

This was the new ideal ; and as the result of it there arose also a new society and a new word.

The Society was the Cambridge Camden Society. In 1839 J. M. Neale and Benjamin Webb, who were then undergraduates at Trinity, formed a plan for the founding of a society for the study of Gothic architecture and of ritual arrangements. The Rev. T. Thorpe, their tutor, became President, and the name of the old antiquary Camden suggested the rather clumsy title. The object of the Society was to " promote the study of Ecclesiastical Architecture and the restoration of mutilated architectural remains ". It would visit and describe churches, and make a collection of brass rubbings. The Camdenian ideals were set forth in pamphlets : *Hints for the Practical Study of Ecclesiastical Antiquities* (1839) ; *A Few Words to Church Builders* and *A Few Words to Church-wardens on Churches and Church Ornaments* (1841) ; and *Church Enlargement and Church Arrangement* (1842). Smaller publications were *Twenty-three Reasons for Getting Rid of Church Pues*, and *Hints to Workmen Engaged on Churches*. These works made it quite clear that the Society was not merely an antiquarian society : it had ideals of a new and unusual kind.

The new word was ecclesiology, which seems to have been invented by a writer in the *British Critic*. There was some dispute about the word : ecclesia*l*ogy was suggested as being more accurate ; but ecclesiology won. It is not very easy to say exactly what the word means. The *British Critic* said (January 1837), " We mean by *ecclesialogy* a science which may treat of the proper construction and operations of the Church, or Communion, or Society of Christians ; and which may regard men as they are members of that society, whether members of the Christian Church in the widest acceptation of the term, or members of some branch or communion of that Church, located in some separate kingdom, and governed according to its internal forms of constitution and discipline ". But if the word was ever used in that sense, it very soon ceased to be.

The *Oxford Dictionary* says that it means " the science of Church building and decoration ".   The *Century Dictionary* says also that it " treats of all the details of church furniture, ornament, etc., and their symbolism, and is cultivated especially by the High-Church party in the Church of England ".   That is more adequate.

Mr. Beresford Hope (" the Nestor of Ecclesiology ") said in 1879 that ecclesiology was the science of worship, carried out in all its material developments.   " It embraced within its scope the buildings which were erected for worship, and all the accessories and adjuncts pertaining to such buildings, as well as the service of worship itself.   It was the vehicle whereby many arts were made subservient to one great end, and the greatness of the end demanded the employment of the highest art. . . . The science of ecclesiology, too, included one of the most recondite branches of archaeology, viz., liturgiology.   It also included the study of church music, hymnody, organs, etc."

First of all ecclesiology meant the study of Gothic churches.   That was done ceaselessly.   Ecclesiologists had field days, in which they visited churches and discovered piscinae and aumbreys, and knocked away the plaster and brickwork that concealed the carving upon fonts.   They sketched with enthusiasm, and many books were published of carefully executed engravings of the various parts of a church.

J. H. Parker's *Glossary*, the *Companion to the Glossary*, and *Introduction to the Study of Gothic Architecture* are well known. An extremely popular book was M. H. Bloxam's *Principles of Gothic Architecture elucidated by Question and Answer*.   This was first issued in 1829 ; there was a new edition in 1835.   In the sixth edition the catechetical form was abandoned.   (The inquirer had certainly asked some rather improbable questions.) Seventeen thousand copies had been sold in England when the tenth edition of 1859 was exhausted. A new and enlarged edition was issued in 1882. Another popular book was Brandon's *Parish Churches.* The *Analysis of Gothic Architecture* was practical rather than historical: it gave over 700 examples of doors, windows, etc. *Open Roofs of the Middle Ages* gave thirty-five examples.

The young ladies of England were instructed in the subject by *Aunt Elinor's Lectures on Architecture.* But Aunt Elinor was unsatisfactory, inasmuch as she included descriptions and plates of the Pagan orders, and omitted to mention any of the books of the Cambridge Camden Society.

These books, and many others like them, provided some of the materials for ecclesiology. The more churches were examined the better, for, as Professor Willis said, " When principles are to be recovered by the examination of examples alone, which is the case with Middle Age religious architecture, of which no precepts are preserved, the greater number of examples that can be compared the better ; and we are by no means to confine ourselves to the most excellent, for we may often detect the rules of successful practice by comparing the attempts of unskilful artists or the experiments of experienced ones with those specimens in which the desired effect has been obtained in the highest degree ".

So as many churches as possible had to be visited and described and drawn, and their several parts assimilated, if they were considered worthy, into new and synthetic Gothic churches, worthily furnished. But though that was part of ecclesiology it was not the whole of it. That was the outward part without the inward spiritual grace. You might know everything that could be known about Gothic churches and their furniture, but you were not yet a true ecclesiologist. An ecclesiologist must know something of Church history, antiquities, masonry, carpentry, music, mechanics, geology, glass, embroidery, tapestry, etc. ; but, " after all, these things will be of little avail by themselves. As Cicero says that none but a good man can be a good orator, much more may I say so of the ecclesiologist." So said Palaeophilus to Practicus in

Hierologus, or The Church Tourists [1] (by J. M. Neale). Ecclesiology meant understanding the Christian Faith and the rubrics of the Prayer Book, and embodying them in a building which should show them forth. The science of church-building as the ecclesiologists understood it was not architectural science : it was the unveiling of the inner mystical meaning of old churches and the infusion of the same meaning into new churches. Its relation to the science of church-building in the more obvious sense was almost that of astrology to astronomy. Astronomy is the serious scientific study of the stars ; astrology attempts to find a mystic significance in them. Astrology would not be considered a science by most educated people ; nor, probably, would ecclesiology. But when the Camdenians began to preach it, it was taken seriously, at any rate by good Churchmen, and it was regarded as a sure sign of unspirituality, and even of heresy, if anyone were unable to appreciate it.

This is not made clear in the statement of the objects of the Society. Anyone could study architectural remains or make rubbings of brasses—even heretics and schismatics. But it is clear from the Society's writings that only a good Churchman could appreciate the inwardness of it all, or build new churches as they should be built. Only a good churchman could be an ecclesiologist.

One of the chief ecclesiological dogmas was the superiority of fourteenth-century Gothic (Middle Pointed) over the Gothic of all other periods. It is not difficult to see how this came about. The ecclesiologists were beginning to realize the Catholic nature of the Church of England at a time when very few Churchmen did so. During the eighteenth century, as they saw it, the Church had been Latitudinarian ; in the early nineteenth century it was infected with Evangelicanism, Liberalism and various Neologies. And if theology and architecture were inseparable, it followed that the architecture of the unorthodox must be bad. Therefore " from the beginning of the reign of George I to the year 1820, not one satisfactory church was built ".

But the Church of the early nineteenth century was un-

[1] A curious little book, which was considered to be " well calculated to stimulate many an errant-knight to essay his first church tour ".

orthodox too, and that tainted all its church-building, Grecian and Gothic. But so far hardly any churches had been designed in the fourteenth-century style. There were modern Norman churches, and Early English churches and Perpendicular churches; but none with flowing tracery and ball-flower ornament. " Decorated " suggested to the ecclesiologists rich ancient churches such as Heckington and Hawton, which had been built by undeniable Catholics and were all that a church ought to be. " Norman ", " Early English " and " Perpendicular " recalled the lamentable modern churches which had been lately built by Evangelicals and Liberals.

Let heretics keep to their own styles—which were either undeveloped or decadent, and therefore suitable to them. An ecclesiologist would use the only style which had not been degraded by modern use—the pure, true, noble and Catholic style of the fourteenth century.

It would be generally agreed now that fourteenth-century Decorated work is not Gothic at its best. It has plenty of facile ornament and superficial prettiness; but it is often poor in comparison with what came before and what came after it. But to the ecclesiologists it seemed very beautiful, and they laid down the dogma that Christian architecture reached perfection in the early days of Late Middle Pointed.

But these new ideals and doctrines had to be spread.

In 1841 the Society began to publish a magazine called the *Ecclesiologist*, which was intended to " convey both interesting and useful information to all connected with, or in any way engaged in church-building or the study of ecclesiastical architecture and antiquities " ; to criticize new churches and to suggest (where it can be done without unwarrantable interference or presumption) alterations or improvements in their arrangement or decoration ; to describe restorations ; to point out churches in need of repair ; to review antiquarian books ; to afford a convenient medium of communication between architects and ecclesiologists ; " and to afford facilities for proposing and obtaining answers to questions on any points of taste or architectural propriety upon which the clergy may wish to consult the Society ". It was hoped that the new magazine would strengthen the connexion and co-operation between the

Society and the other kindred societies which were already flourishing under happy auspices in two of our principal cities. The Society did not wish to obtrude itself : the object of its members was to render it subservient to the good of the Church, to which the Society deemed it no small privilege to be the humblest handmaid.

The *Ecclesiologist* lasted until 1868, and on the whole continued on the same lines on which it had begun. In its later years its articles were of rather more general interest than they had been at the beginning : it included, for instance, more on the subject of hymns.[1] Some of the more crude points of view of the first numbers were somewhat modified. But in most ways it ended as it had begun. It would require great bravery and perseverance to read through all the volumes. Many of the articles are immensely long and decidedly turgid. Probably they were easier to read at the time when they were written ; but we are not at home with the literary style of the Victorians. The sentences are too long, and there are too many commas and capital letters. When the writers become controversial it is sometimes hard to see whether they mean what they say, or whether they are being elaborately ironical. And, above all, we are repelled by the sanctimoniousness of it all. No doubt the writers were in earnest, and honestly believed all that they said. But to us it seems goody-goody. The conversion of a debased church into an ecclesiologically satisfactory one is recounted in the same style as the conversion of a drunkard or a swearer into a good Christian. And we are as irritated by the one as we are by the other.

A few selections from the first volume will be enough to show the ecclesiological point of view, which was maintained with boring persistence during the lifetime of the *Ecclesiologist*.

The first article of the first number is most extraordinary ; very short and most absurd. The Cambridge Camden Society has been asked to furnish designs for the Lord Bishop of New Zealand for his cathedral and for parish churches. The cathedral is to be built as our fathers built. For the parish churches the Society will furnish working models of capitals,

[1] It is interesting to read its tepid review of *Hymns Ancient and Modern*. (December 1861.)

sections of mouldings, ornamented pier, door and window arches in the Norman style. It is surprising to find the ecclesiologists recommending Norman, which they did not approve as a style for English churches. But " as the work will be chiefly done by native artists, it seems natural to teach them first that style which first prevailed in our own country ; while its rudeness and massiveness, and the grotesque character of its sculpture, will probably render it easier to be understood and appreciated by them ". It was probably hoped that in course of time the natives would duly develop a First and Second Pointed style (and stop there). This synthetic Norman church will be the only model provided, " because the churches will be, at first, 200 miles apart ". The Bishop's chaplain is to be a member of the Cambridge Camden Society, and will see that everything is as it should be. The other members of the Society, when they see the model church, will say " with respect to the temples about to be erected in so distant a land, ' Peace be within thy walls and plenteousness within thy palaces ' ".

Then there is a criticism of the new church of St. Paul, Cambridge. As first written this caused serious offence. Half-converted Camdenians, including the Vice-President, addressed a remonstrance to the Committee. The object of the article, they say, appeared to be " to throw ridicule not only on that church, but on every similar attempt to supply the religious destitution of the overgrown population. . . . We fear from this and other indications, that there exists in some quarters a desire to convert the Society into an engine of polemical theology, instead of an instrument for promoting the study and the practice of Ecclesiastical Architecture."

The Committee, of course, defended themselves. They had no intention of ridiculing efforts for good ; but it must not be supposed that they are simply concerned with taste. " They have acted and spoken as Churchmen no less than as antiquaries, desirous to make taste subservient (as it may be to a high degree) to the promotion of sound religion, and under the strong conviction that the arrangements to which they have invited attention have far too great an influence to be sacrificed." It is not right that a congregation should be brought together into " a place where the sacraments can scarcely be decently and rubrically administered, and which possibly presents to the unlearned parishioner no mark of distinction from some neighbouring conventicle ; and they do not esteem it a trifling oversight, if such distinctions are needlessly disregarded ". In the case of the new Cambridge church, " they cannot conceal their belief that a church might have been built for the same sum, whose style of architecture and plan of internal arrangement should have been after some approved ancient model, and that resources adequate to furnish more costly materials would have been forthcoming if such a plan had been pursued ". They deny the accusation of mixing ecclesiology with polemical theology, and declare that their objects are co-extensive with the whole Church of England : they have never recognized the existence of any party in the Church, and they attack architectural, not doctrinal errors. Nevertheless, to avoid offence, they will reissue the first number of the *Ecclesiologist* with another article substituted for the offending one.

This new article is very interesting as a setting forth of ecclesiological principles.

" The most important requisite in erecting a church is that it be built in such a way that the Rubricks and Canons of the Church of England may be consistently observed, and the Sacraments rubrically and decently administered. But how can the Chancel ' remain as it hath done in times past ', when there is no Chancel whatever ? How can the Minister ' baptize *publickly* at the stone Font ', such Font standing ' in the ancient usual place ', when, if it did stand so, he would be so enclosed by galleries, that most surely he would not be seen or heard ? . . . And how can that due reverence be paid to the Communion-table which ' was in this Church for many years after the Reformation ', if . . . the Vestry (with its nameless appurtenances) is close by, and a door opens almost on the Altar rails ? "

Every church ought to have a chancel. And a building, to be church-like, need not be expensive. This one is expensive, and at the same time poor in architecture. " A church which costs little need not be a cheap church, and a church which costs a great deal may be one. A cheap church is one which makes the greatest show for the least money. Now herein lies the fault of modern church builders. They *will* have the ornamental part of the church, at whatever cost to the church itself. But that day is nearly gone by ; and we may hope that the sun of Ecclesiastical Architecture, after suffering a long eclipse, is again beginning to shine ; that a generation more pious, if not more rich, than ourselves, may rival our ancestors in their glorious minsters, their long-drawn vistas of stone vaultings, pier behind pier and bay behind bay, their carved rood-screens glittering with gold and eloquent with figures, their capitals flowers, wanting only life to be equal to Nature's ; nay, that they will even emulate those glorious conceptions, the one the most sublime, the other the most beautiful that ever entered into the human mind, the West Front of Peterborough, and the Angel's Choir at Lincoln."

And why had the new Cambridge church a tower ? A chancel was necessary ; a tower was not.

" But if ornamental appendages are bad when anything real is given up for their sake, much more are they so when they are imitations of that which they really are not. Stucco, and paint, and composition, and graining, are not out of place in the theatre or the ballroom ; but in GOD's House everything should be *real*. Plainness need not be inconsistent with reverence : pretence is, and must be. Our readers will see that we refer to the mouldings of the pier-arches which are *cast in plaister* ; to the pieces of wood in the roof which, appearing to be purlins and principals, have in fact little to do with its support ; to the varnish which is intended to make deal look like oak ; and other imitations of the same kind."

The whole of this criticism sets out most clearly the ideals of the ecclesiologists : the unspeakable importance of rubrics, the necessity of chancels, the wickedness of ornament without a rubrical plan (and the Puginesque daydream of the wonderful results of combining the two), and the hypocrisy of a building which shows any materials that are not *real*.

The other criticisms of new churches are shorter, but on the same lines.

Among other things, we learn that the font in the new church at Brookfield, Kentish Town, should be octagonal, not hexa-

G

gonal (we shall see why later on).   The triple lancets at its
west end have no authority.

Christchurch, Streatham, is in the Romanesque style of
Southern Europe.   " Why were our own ecclesiastical styles
deserted for forms which are at best imperfectly developed ? "

Llangorwen Church is a church as it should be.   It has a
long chancel and perfect fittings—a carved eagle and Litany
desk, and an altar of Bath stone with an arcaded reredos
behind it.

Christchurch, Woking, has a chancel, even though a small
one.   But St. Simon and St. Jude, on whose day the foundation
stone was laid, is a more suitable dedication for a small church
than Christchurch.

No one, unless they were told, could imagine that St. Paul's,
Hook, was a church.

The side elevation of St. Andrew the Great, Cambridge,
presents a tolerably ecclesiastical appearance.

In All Saints', Spitalfields, the drawing-room appearance of a
mere nave with galleries, the piers of which do not reach the
roof, is most detestable.   The font is not large enough for
immersion, and is made of composition.

Cam, Gloucestershire, had a north aisle, which is less in
character with ancient buildings than one on the south.   But
the plan has been altered in compliance with the suggestions of
the Society.

Radipole Church has no string course under the lancets.
Ancient lancets usually had strings, so as to combine the
horizontal with the vertical, that the *predominance of the latter
over the former, as exhibited by contrast,* and not vertical ascend-
ancy alone, should produce that peculiar effect which is so
characteristic of Christian compared with pagan architecture.

Most people, they say, have already laughed at the church at
Friar's Mount, Shoreditch.   It is in the Romanesque style ;
and all new Romanesque churches, except in New Zealand,
were apt to be objects of ridicule to ecclesiologists.

There are also reviews of books.   Some are approved of :
but Petit's *Church Architecture* (which is a curiously scrappy
book with very poor sketches) [1] comes in for some severe

---

[1] But Scott called Petit's sketches " truly marvellous ".

handling. Petit adopts "a merely utilitarian view of the subject; there being no reference whatever to any higher standard than that of mere *taste* in church-building, which is treated as a matter of trade, convenience, caprice or of arbitrary arrangement, instead of one that has ever involved and been influenced by the most unvarying and exalted principles ". He deals too much with foreign examples, and has the temerity to suggest the adoption of Italian, French and German forms. True, he advocates the imitation of our own old churches; but he admits that circumstances may occur which render it inexpedient or impossible to follow exactly their proportions or arrangements. "These are principles which we believe to be necessarily subversive of correct church-building, and which we therefore will persist in condemning as most pernicious in themselves, and most derogatory to GOD's glory." Nay, more: Mr. Petit suggests that architects "should study to produce a perfect model, with but little reference to any details of style, and at the least possible expense consistent with durability"; then he may add ornament. He should have said that the architect ought to work "in faith, humility, devotion, and with a deep sense of awe and responsibility, as men once worked". Indeed, this unfortunate writer has disregarded ecclesiological principles in almost every possible way. He says that Italian buildings are suitable to some English landscapes: he mentions Amiens and Strassburg, and says nothing of Beverley, Ely, Salisbury and Westminster; he says that the modern Italian style harmonizes with houses (that they should do so "may be the wish of an artist, but is certainly not that of one who has high views on the *exclusive* sanctity of a church"); he has a predilection for flat roofs and horizontal lines; he wishes for new styles when "we are already in possession of models most perfectly adapted to our purposes"; he believes in picturesqueness; he prefers no chancel to a small one; and he would experiment with unorthodox plans.

He receives a little faint praise; but it is very faint.[1]

[1] The *Christian Remembrancer* in September 1842 published an article which was pro-Petit and anti-ecclesiologist. It denied that Gothic was the only Christian architecture. We should not confine ourselves to it because we cannot do it satisfactorily, and we may in the future invent a better style. The *Christian Remembrancer* was generally anti-ecclesiologist.

Some light relief is provided by A Sketch—which records a conversation between the Rev. Mr. Herbert, incumbent of Sedgwell, Wilts, Mrs. Herbert, Miss Herbert and Miss Newmarsh. The Rector has received an application from the Cambridge Camden Society for information with respect to his church. Miss Newmarsh, the devil's advocate, has heard of the Society. " It is professedly set on foot for the restoration of ' Fonts, Altars, Crosses, and other rubbish ', but in reality, I fear, with a far worse design." The Rector gently corrects her ; and after morning service, which was never omitted at Sedgwell, the party remains in the church, and discovers the answers to the questions. " What is the dedication of the church ? " " What is the ground plan ? " " What is the length of chancel and nave ? " Miss Newmarsh can see no use in chancels. In Mr. A's chapel at B—— there was none : the pulpit stood just before the rails, there were Commandments, and " nice galleries all round, as comfortable as possible ". Mr. Herbert explains the use of chancels ; but his argument is not given. " Is the chancel higher than the nave ? " " How many steps are there to the altar ? " " Is there any peculiarity in the south-west or north-west windows of the chancel ? " " Is there any screen ? " Pensfold is requested to ask Master Jones to bring his tools : and the painted base of a screen is at once discovered hidden behind pews.

The sketch ends rather abruptly ; but we are told that the answers to the questions afforded satisfaction to the Society.

Here are a few more selected ecclesiological sentiments from the first volume of the *Ecclesiologist* :

" Fresh from his Mechanics' Institute, his Railroad Station, his Socialist Hall, he (the architect) has the presumption and arrogance to attempt a church. Let it be remembered what a church is—a building set apart for the highest purposes, adapted to the administration of solemn rites, symbolical in every part."

" Conceive King's College Chapel to have been in the Early Decorated style, with very lofty gables " (and how much more beautiful it would be).

" If you intend to build *churches*, dismiss every mercenary or selfish thought, be content to labour as in God's service, without care for your personal fame, without thought of your personal services."

The workman should have not only a knowledge of his art, but also " a sense that he is working for GOD's honour and not only for man, together with that holiness of life and thought which, while it is necessary for all their fellow-workers in their several degrees, is to none more becoming than to those in whose occupation HE, Whose House they are adorning, did not disdain while on earth to employ His Sacred Hands ".

" The names of the Gothic styles are singularly incongruous, and it would be well if some terms could be adopted which would express the character of Rise, Perfection and Decline, which severally characterize them."

" Cordially as we detest brick . . . we would rather build a church doorway of it, because it professes to be what it is, than of Parker's cement, because it professes to be what it is not."

Here are nearly all the articles of the ecclesiological creed ; but one of them is not very much in evidence. That is the doctrine of Symbolism. There are references to it in the early numbers of the *Ecclesiologist*, but the subject is not exhaustively explained. However, the deficiency was soon made good.

In the year 1843 the two leading Camdenians, J. M. Neale and Benjamin Webb, produced a translation of the first book of the *Rationale Divinorum Officiorum*, by Willielmus Durandus, who was Bishop of Mende in the thirteenth century.[1] They gave the book an introduction and notes ; the introduction, which is very long, sets out the doctrines of the ecclesiologists so clearly that it is worth while dealing with it in some detail.

It begins by deploring the fact that no architect has arisen who can build a really church-like church. What is needful ? Not merely accuracy, or reality, as Pugin taught ; but an architect who is Catholic at heart. The best buildings are built by the best men, such as William of Wykeham and Bishop Poore. " We have every reason to believe, from God's Word, from Catholic consent, and even from philosophical principles, that such must always be the case."

[1] The Rev. J. Dudley in his book on *Naology* applied to the translators the text, " of such the condemnation is just ".

Architecture has become " too much of a profession . . . instead of being the study of the devout ecclesiastic. . . . We are not prepared to say that none but monks should design churches, or that it is impossible for a professional architect to build with the devotion and faith of an earlier time. But we do protest against the merely business-like spirit of the modern profession, and demand from them a more elevated and directly religious habit of mind."

An architect should be a Churchman ; and a church architect should design only churches. " To think that any Churchman should allow himself to build a conventicle, and even some-times to prostitute the speaking architecture of the Church to the service of Her bitterest enemies. . . . Conceive a Churchman designing a triple window, admitted emblem of the MOST HOLY TRINITY, for a congregation of Socinians ! "

It cannot be expected, as things are, that church architects should never design secular buildings ; but how can men who design workhouses and prisons and assembly rooms, and give the dregs of their time to church-building, expect to be filled from above with the Spirit of Wisdom ?

And the architect should design in one style only. He should know enough of earlier styles to be able to restore earlier churches ; but for his own style he should choose fourteenth-century Decorated, " in which alone he will express his architectural ideas ".

The idea that pious monks and bishops designed the churches of the Middle Ages must be due simply to ignorance ; but the authors take it for granted that " the deeply religious habits of the builders of old, the hours, the cloister, the discipline, the obedience, resulted in their matchless works ; while the worldliness, vanity, dissipation and patronage of our own architects issue in unvarying and hopeless failure ".

But there is something in old buildings besides Catholic life and discipline : there is Symbolism or Sacramentality— " the material fabric symbolizes, embodies, figures, represents, expresses, answers to, some abstract meaning ".

This may be wrongly understood : Mr. Lewis, for instance, imagined that all church architecture was intentionally sym-bolical. But that was not the case. (The truth was that architects with a Catholic ethos worked on the materials which they had, and progressively developed from them a transcript of that ethos in Christian architecture.   Mind subdued matter, until we see in Christian architecture the projection of the mind of the Church.)   The Cambridge Camden Society has recognized the principle, the Oxford Architectural Society has not. Nor has Mr. Rickman (" as might have been expected from a separatist ").   And Mr. Coddington of Ware is one of the chief opposers of the whole system.   They then proceed to examine the arguments which may lead us to suppose that the principle of sacramentality really exists.

There is the argument *a priori*, which is as follows : The early Christians used many symbols, such as the cross, the lamb, the fish, the ark and the dove.   The Fathers saw an allegorical meaning in numbers : one meant the unity of God ; two, the two natures of Christ ; three, the Trinity ; four, the evangelists ; six, the attributes of the Deity ; seven, the gifts of the Spirit ; eight, regeneration ; twelve, the Apostles or (tropologically) the whole Church.   The 380 (*sic*) servants of Abraham correspond to the number of the Fathers of Nicaea.   Undoubtedly the Catholic Church has ever evinced a great attachment to symbolism.

Then there is the argument from analogy.   The symbolism of the Jews was one of the most striking features of their religion.   We find symbolism also in the New Testament, and even among heretics and heathen.   Nature, too, has her symbolism.   " Shall we wonder that the Catholick Church is in all Her art and splendour sacramental of the Blessed TRINITY, when Nature herself is so ?   Shall there be a trinity of effect in every picture, a trinity of tone in every note, a trinity of power in every mind, a trinity of essence in every substance— and shall there not be a trinity in the arrangements and details of Church art ? "

It is well known that music is symbolical.   Haydn says that the trombone is deep red, the trumpet scarlet, the clarionet orange, etc.   Flowers, too, are symbolical : the rose is for beauty, the violet for modesty, the sunflower for faithfulness, etc.   So was our Lord's teaching, so are the Sacraments.

This does not seem very clear.   But there are other arguments.   There are weighty philosophical reasons.

" The fact that anything exists adapted to a certain end or use is alone enough to presuppose the end or use ; who can see a ποίημα without distinguishing its relation to the want or necessity which brought about ποίησις ?   In short, the ἐργόν, whatever it may be, not only answers to that which called it forth, but, in some sort, represents materially, or symbolizes, the abstract volition or operation of the mind which originated it.   Show us a pitcher, a skewer . . . : do not the cavity of the one, and the piercing point of the other, at once set forth and symbolize the τέλος which was answered in their production ? "   (If this means anything, it can only mean that a skewer symbolizes skewering, and a pitcher symbolizes holding water.   That is true, but scarcely worth saying.)   A theatre is " the emblem of the purpose for which it was planned " : so is a church, which is planned for the ritual of the church services. That is also obviously true ; but ten pages of philosophic argument are not needed to prove it.   And it has nothing to do with the Holy Trinity, or with the showing forth of the four evangelists or regeneration.

Then there is the analytical argument.   A stranger would see at once that the cruciform plan is the usual plan of our old churches.   (As a matter of fact, it is not.)   He would inquire " Why ? "   And on learning that the churches were designed for the religion of the Cross, he would at once see the appropriateness of the plan.   He would see the altar raised on three steps and, the doctrine of the Trinity having been explained to him, he would understand the reason.   And so on.

Then there is the inductive argument.   There is evidence in early writers of the symbolical arrangement of churches. Eusebius, for example, describes a church whose great portico symbolized God the Father, and the two side porticoes the two other Persons of the Holy Trinity.   (Would not this apply to St. Pancras ?)   And there is a great deal of evidence in other authors.   " Is it possible to conceive that the Church which invented so deeply symbolical a system of worship should have rested content with an unsymbolical building for its practice ? "

The argument is now complete. Actual examples of symbolism are then given.

There are the symbols of the Trinity : the triple division of

PLATE XI

ST. ALBAN'S, HOLBORN

By William Butterfield

As first built

PLATE XII

ST. CLEMENT'S, CITY ROAD
By William Butterfield

Norman churches into nave, chancel and sanctuary; the arrangement of arcade, triforium and clerestory; the altar steps; the three towers of large churches; and triple windows, which should be placed at the east of a church, and not at the west.

Regeneration is symbolized by octagonal fonts; the Atonement by a cruciform plan and by gable crosses; and the Communion of Saints by monuments and lady chapel. Windows symbolize the Light of the World; a circle above a triple window typifies the crown of the King of Kings; a hood mould above all three lancets means the unity of the Godhead. A two-light window symbolizes the two Natures of Christ, or the mission of the disciples two by two. The complex designs of the Decorated style are hard to explain; but it will be noticed that the numbers three and six often occur in them, which numbers, of course, symbolize the Trinity.

Doors symbolize Christ as the Door, and the entrance through much tribulation into the Kingdom of God. They are placed near the west end because we enter the Church Triumphant through the Church Militant. The screen symbolizes the division between these two parts of the Church. The curious tracery of the screen typifies the obscure manner in which heavenly things are set forth while we look at them from the Church Militant. The straitness of the entrance into the Kingdom is set forth by the excessive narrowness of Norman chancel arches. Corbels represent the heavenly host; gargoyles, evil spirits.

Objections are then considered. How, for instance, can the nave and aisles symbolize the three equal Persons of the Trinity, when the nave is wider and higher than the aisles? The answer is that Symbolism must not be pressed too far. How is one to account for churches with only a nave, or with only one aisle? But it is not necessary that everything should be symbolized: the things that are there symbolize something; we need not worry about the things that are not.

The development of Symbolism is then traced, and then follows the general conclusion.

There is a description of a Protestant place of worship. It has galleries and a prominent pulpit and very few free seats.

There are neat cast-iron pillars to hold up the galleries, and still neater pillars in the galleries to hold up the roof. There is a fashionable congregation, and there are clerk, beadle and pew-openers. This symbolizes " spiritual pride, luxury, self-sufficiency and bigotry ".

Compare that with a Catholic Church !

" Far away, and long ere we catch our first view of the city itself, the three spires of its cathedral, rising high above its din and turmoil, preach to us of the most Holy and Undivided Trinity." The transepts tell of the Atonement, the chapels of the Communion of Saints. "Lessons of holy wisdom are written in the delicate tracery of the windows : the unity of many members is shadowed forth by the multiplex arcade : the duty of letting our light shine before men, by the pierced and flowered parapet that crowns the whole.

" We enter . . ." and are met with a luxuriance of Symbolism. Everything symbolizes something : the font symbolizes Baptism, and is of stone because Christ is the Rock. And so on. " Verily, as we think of the oneness of its design, we may say ' *Jerusalem edificatur ut civitas cujus participatio ejus in idipsum.*' "

After this we feel that we have had enough. We do not feel inclined to read through the whole of Durandus, for we know what we shall find. And we do find it. He speaks of the church and its parts, of the altar, of pictures and images, of bells, of cemeteries and other places, sacred and religious; of the dedication of a church, of the consecration of an altar, of consecrations and unctions, and of the Sacraments of the Church. Durandus happily rambles on, and quotation is difficult, for rich and varied examples of Symbolism occur in every few lines.

" The arrangement of a material church resembleth that of the human body : the chancel, or place where the altar is, representeth the head : the transepts, the hands and arms, and the remainder—towards the west—the rest of the body. The sacrament of the altar representeth the vows of the heart. Furthermore, according to Richard de Sancto Victore, the arrangement of a church typifieth the three states in the Church : of virgins, of the continent, of the married."

" Furthermore, the church consisteth of four walls, that is, built on the doctrine of the Four Evangelists."

" Again, in the temple of God, the foundation is faith, which is conversant with unseen things : the roof, charity, ' which covereth a multitude of sins '. . . . The four side walls, the four cardinal virtues, justice, fortitude, temperance, prudence. . . . The windows are hospitality with cheerfulness, and tenderness with charity."

" The towers are the preachers and prelates of the Church, which are her bulwark and defence. . . . The pinnacles of the towers signify the life or the mind of a prelate which aspireth heavenwards. The cock at the summit of the church is a type of preachers."

" The glass windows in a church are Holy Scriptures, which expel the wind and the rain, that is all things hurtful, but transmit the light of the true Sun, that is, God, into the hearts of the faithful. These are wider within than without, because the mystical sense is the more ample, and precedeth the literal meaning."

" The piers of the church are bishops and doctors : who specially sustain the Church of God by their doctrine. . . . The bases of the columns are the apostolic bishops, who support the frame of the whole church. The capitals of the piers are the opinions of the bishops and doctors. . . . The ornaments of the capitals are the words of Sacred Scripture, to the meditation and observance of which we are bound."

" The chancel, that is, the head of the church, being lower than its body, signifieth how great humility there should be in the clergy, or in prelates." (A footnote says that " the fact that in many unaltered and unmutilated churches the chancel is lower than the nave, appears to have been unnoticed by ecclesiologists ". Ecclesiologists liked their chancels to be raised.)

" The seats in the choir admonish us that the body must sometimes be refreshed."

" The tiles of the roof which keep off the rain are the soldiers, who preserve the Church from paynim, and from enemies."

" Some say that the ostrich, as being a forgetful bird, ' leaveth her eggs in the dust ' ; but at length, when she beholdeth a certain star, returneth unto them, and cheereth them by her presence. Therefore the eggs of ostriches are hung in churches to signify that man, being left of God on account of his sins, if at length he be illuminated by the divine Light, remembereth his faults and returneth to Him, Who by looking on him with His mercy cherisheth him." In spite of its valuable Symbolism, the ecclesiologists do not seem to have adopted this custom.

" Bells do signify preachers. . . . Also the cavity of the bell denoteth the mouth of the preacher. . . . The hardness of the metal signifieth fortitude in the mind of the preacher. . . . The clapper or iron, which by striking on either side maketh the sound, doth denote the tongue of the preacher. . . . The wood of the frame upon which the bell hangeth doth signify the wood of our Lord's Cross. The rope hanging from this, by which the bell is struck, is humility, or the life of the preacher."

" Commonly also they be rung three times at nocturns. First with a *squilla* or hand-bell, which by its sharp sound signifieth Paul preaching acutely. The second ringing signifieth Barnabas joined to his company. The third intimateth that, when the ' Jews put from them the word of God, the Apostles turned themselves to the Gentiles ', whom also they instructed in the faith of the Trinity by the doctrine of the four Evangelists. Whence also some do use *four* bells."

The explanations of the ceremonies of dedication, consecrations and unctions, are slightly less far-fetched, for ceremonial is often intentionally symbolical, and with respect to many of the ceremonies Durandus is no doubt right.

The editors then give a translation of the first and second chapters of the *Mystical Mirror of the Church* by Hugo de Sancto Victore. These contain much of the same information. There are also appendices : on Chancels and on Orientation ; the Design of the Analogium, Ambo, or Rood-loft, and the Reading of the Gospel from it ; the Sign of the Cross, the Four Colours used in Church hangings, etc. ; of Bells being not rung three days before Easter ; and on the Dedication of a Church.

The *Ecclesiologist* often returned to the subject of Symbolism.

The prohibition of Western triplets seems to have been considered a matter of great importance. It was justified by principles of beauty, by principles of Symbolism and by principles of propriety.

In 1850 J. M. Neale read a paper on " Symbolism ", in which he mentioned the names of writers of the Western Church who dealt with the subject. They were : Gregory of Tours, Alcuin, Amalarius, St. Theodulph, Hrabanus Maurus, St. Paschasius Ratbertus, Hincmar, Remy of Auxerre, St. Abbo, Fulbert of Chartres, St. Bernon, John de Bayeux, St. Peter Damian, St. Ulric of Cluny, John, author of Micrologus, Etienne de Baugé, Ives of Chartres, Honorius, Marbodus, Earnulph, Guibert, St. Bruno of Aste, Hildebert, Hugh of St. Victor, Rupert, Radulphus, Richardus de Sancto Victore, Robert Paululus, Pierre de Celle, Cencio, Peter of Blois, St. Antony of Padua, William Bishop of Paris, Guisbert, St. Bonaventura, John Peckham, Doctor Robert Holkot, Herman de Schild, Michael Ayguan, John du Bourg, William Lindwood, Henry Gorcomius, Jerome Savonarola, Antony Margaletta, St. Thomas a Villa Nova, Maldonatus, Stephen Durantus, Nicolas de Thou, Lancelot Andrewes, Augustine de Ferrara, Francois de Harlai, J. B. Thiers, Gabriel de Henao and Joseph Pierre de Houtre.

That sounds final. But, in spite of everything, it is not clear exactly what the ecclesiologists meant by Symbolism. Obviously a church building ought to be suitably planned for church worship ; if it is, apparently the ecclesiologists would say that it symbolized it. A font is used for Baptism and an altar for Communion ; they say that a font symbolizes Baptism and an altar symbolizes Communion. If " symbolize " had been used only in that sense, the meaning would have been curious, but clear. But it has another meaning : that the object, by its shape or form or position, sets forth a number of ideas which people with Catholic hearts, strong imaginations and an extensive acquaintance with Holy Scripture can appreciate. The nave of a church symbolizes, in the first sense, the accommodation of a congregation ; in the second sense it symbolizes the Ark of Salvation or the Church Militant. It does not look like the Ark (unless one imagines the Ark turned upside down, in which case its keel would distinctly recall the pointed roof of a Gothic church) or like the Church Militant; but it symbolizes them (or anything else) because it was built by pure and Catholic-hearted Christians.

But Gothic was not the style for churches only: it was used at the time for any other kind of building. Does a Gothic hall or castle also symbolize something? In the first sense it does: it symbolizes eating or defence. But in the second sense? The ecclesiologists would probably have said No. But why not? The hall and the castle were built at the same time, in the same style and by the same kind of men as the churches. But they were not churches, and therefore not symbolical. The argument does not seem very strong.

The most arbitrary decision of the ecclesiologists was that Symbolism was to be found at its best in the Gothic style, and especially in the churches of the fourteenth century. Their long list of quotations from the Fathers on the subject of Symbolism is very impressive. But the Fathers were certainly not referring to Gothic churches. Why did they quote the examples of Symbolism that the Fathers found in their Basilican churches, and then deny that it was really—or fully—to be found there? Even Durandus wrote before the Decorated style was known, and therefore, as they admit, did not know as much about Symbolism as they did.

Of course it is possible to find Symbolism anywhere. It is found by some in the Great Pyramid; Father Ronald Knox, using the methods of the Pyramidists, has found it in Westminster Cathedral. We could find it in plenty in the Grecian Commissioners' churches. The three porticoes of St. Pancras represent the Trinity; the six pillars of the western portico, being a multiple of three, have the same meaning. And why should not the neat pillars which support the gallery of a Protestant church, the gallery itself, and the pillars above it, also symbolize the Trinity? The absence of a chancel symbolizes the rending of the veil of the Temple, and that we are all one body in Christ; the flat roof symbolizes (as Scott Holland said of the dome of St. Paul's) the coming down of God to man in revelation. In fact, the regularity of a Classical church lends itself far better to symbolical interpretation. Gothic is

seldom regular, and it has so many different forms that classifica-
tion is impossible.   There is no one type of a Gothic church.
You may say that a Gothic church has a chancel with an eastern
triplet, transepts and an octagonal font.   But what of the
churches with four light windows, no transepts and a circular
font ?   The ecclesiologists' argument amounts to this : that
when a symbolical feature is there, it is ; when it is absent it is
not.   And, anyhow, by reason of the convenient fact that any
number can be symbolical, symbolism of some kind can be
found in any features that happen to be there.

In 1849 the *Ecclesiologist* admitted that some of J. M. Neale's
early attempts to find Symbolism had been far-fetched.   " But
when we reflect how many years (comparatively) have elapsed
since that work was published, and how young and ardent its
translator-authors were, and when we weigh the fascinating
interest of the new field of thought that it opened out to them,
we can only be astonished that they were not more often led
to seek resemblances where their more matured judgements
would tell them that none could wisely be found."   But this
applied only to details : no fault was to be found with Symbolism as a whole.

It seems strange that such pious dreamings could have
convinced anyone, but they did.   The followers of Mr.
Coddington of Ware remained unconvinced ; but the clergy
were carried away with enthusiasm.   An incalculable amount
of harm was done to old churches in the attempt to make them
correct in architecture and truly symbolical.   In many cases
genuine old features were destroyed to make room for more
symbolical ones : east windows of three lights were inserted in
place of old windows of five lights, and octagonal fonts
substituted for ancient specimens that did not symbolize
Regeneration.

We may have dealt at rather excessive length with this
curious subject ; but we have been flogging a horse that is by
no means dead.   There are still some who believe it all, and
will explain that a chancel out of line with the nave symbolizes
the inclination of Our Lord's head on the cross.[1]   But such
teaching has little influence on modern church-building.   In

[1] Pugin did not believe this.

the 1840's it was otherwise. An additional and burdensome weight was laid on the architects, and many of them submitted. They had to design churches that were not only correct in their imitation of the Gothic styles—or rather, style, for they were now only allowed one, the Decorated—but were also correct in their Symbolism. The ecclesiologists were supreme.

But though the principles of the Society lasted, it was not to be expected that the Society itself would escape attack. By 1843 there were 700 members,[1] the Society had the patronage of two archbishops, sixteen bishops, and thirty-one peers and members of Parliament. But in spite of this, it was hardly likely that people would swallow the new doctrines without a murmur. Nor did they. Even now, after a hundred years, it is not clear to the average man that there is any particular difference between High Anglicanism and the Church of Rome : in the 1840's it was not clear at all. The Camdenian doctrines were obviously Popery, and they were vigorously attacked as such. The redoubtable Mr. Close, afterwards Dean of Carlisle, produced a book called *Church Architecture, Scripturally Considered, from the Earliest Ages to the Present Time*. In it he said that " ALL TEMPLES, ALTARS, CHURCHES, AND RELIGIOUS CEREMONIES, ARE THE BADGES AND PROOFS OF THE FALLEN, GUILTY STATE OF MAN ". He reviewed the progress of church architecture from the time of Abel onwards, and spoke of the *remarkable unwillingness on the part of God* to allow a permanent temple to be erected. For Christians, " THAT TEMPLE IS THE LIVING BODIES AND SOULS OF HIS REDEEMED AND SANCTIFIED PEOPLE : HIS CHURCH ! THE ONLY CHURCH OF THE NEW TESTAMENT ! " In the fourth century " ecclesiastical buildings were multiplied, in which scenes were enacted alike disgraceful to Christianity, morality, and reason. In fact, the large piles which were raised towards the middle and close of this century, might more justly be considered as vast mausoleums, in which truth, scripture, light, salvation, and common sense were entombed together." In short, " Superstition and Church Architecture were coeval from the beginning ".

[1] Disraeli's *Coningsby* (1844) says that Henry Sydney, when he first went up to Cambridge, was " full of church architecture, national sports, restoration of the order of peasantry ".

On November 5, 1844, Mr. Close preached a sermon in Cheltenham Parish Church which must have been well worth hearing. Its title was " *The ' Restoration of Churches' is the Restoration of Popery : proved and illustrated from the Authentic Publications of the ' Cambridge Camden Society' "*—a title which has a genuine seventeenth- or eighteenth-century ring. It proved that " such *Restoration of churches not only tends to,* but *actually Is* POPERY " ; and the variations of type must represent considerable variety and emphasis of speech.

" It will," he said, " be my object, then, on the present occasion, to show that as Romanism is taught *Analytically* at Oxford, it is taught *Artistically* at Cambridge—that it is inculcated theoretically, in tracts, at one University, and it is *sculptured, painted,* and *graven* at the other." " No well-instructed Protestant, or enlightened English Churchman *could* discover such sympathies as these with their great hereditary, antagonistic power—POPERY ! " Eastlake says that Mr. Close " proved a determined though not very formidable antagonist " ; but his opinions must have been those of a large number of churchmen. The ecclesiologists, of course, replied. Mr. Arnold made some remarks on *Church Architecture Scripturally Considered,* in which he revealed the fact that Mr. Close had set up a stone altar in Christchurch, Cheltenham, in 1840 or 1841. The *Ecclesiologist* replied with an accusation of heresy. " We respectfully but positively decline to argue any religious questions, and above all, those questions with him, until he shall have cleared himself from a report which appeared in the public journals during the summer of 1844, and remains, so far as we can learn, uncontradicted ; namely, that he did at a public meeting speak in laudatory terms of certain avowed Nestorian heretics. If the report be correct, we cannot but decline all religious controversy, and especially upon that great article of our faith, the Incarnation, with one who may be thought to share in the anathema of St. Cyril and the condemnation of the third general council."

But the *Ecclesiologist* did argue—in two very long articles in two numbers. They lamented the unfairness of Mr. Close's attacks.

He had misrepresented them by saying, " Neither can we stop here to record many of their GROSS SUPERSTITIONS ;

H

they believe in ' miracles wrought by Church-wells ', and ' in the *hidden virtues attached to the angelic harmony of Church-bells* ' . . . they have invented an instrument called an *Orientator,* by which to take the bearing of churches."

The first two accusations, they said, were not true ; and the Orientator was a compass.

The reply ended, " THOU SHALT NOT BEAR FALSE WITNESS AGAINST THY NEIGHBOUR ".

But many agreed with Mr. Close. Heresy does not alarm Englishmen particularly, but Popery does.

The Cambridge Camden Society was obviously Popish, as Miss Newmarsh had seen very clearly. Had it not erected a stone altar in St. Sepulchre's Church, Cambridge ? And, in any case, Gothic architecture and chancels and ritual and Symbolism were Popish.

The ecclesiologists had to stand many attacks, at this time and later. Professor Lee, the Rector of Barley, considered that the Cambridge Camden Society " will in all probability lead to great and violent political commotions, and it may be to distress and bloodshed ". The *Eclectic Review* said in January 1849, " This party has actually done *something* for the increase of our knowledge in this direction, much alloyed with exaggerated pedantic emphasis on specialities, and general Puseyistical religious leaven. It *claims* to have done much more—to have been, in fact, originative of that tone in thought and feeling, of which it has been only an accidental embodiment. For as we have already estimated, this general transition of taste is altogether a much larger matter ; belongs to the spirit of the age, not to that of the Universities, or the Tractarian portion of the Establishment. This party, indeed, has been characterized as much by its petty pedantry, its arrogance, and ill-considered positiveness of assertion, as by its love of ancient art. Hence no slight feeling of hostility was, at one time, roused against it among some of the professional architects ; a feeling evidenced very strongly in some articles which appeared in ' *Weale's Quarterly Papers* '." Mr. R. D. Chantrell called the *Ecclesiologist* " a mischievous tissue of imbecility and fanaticism ".

Sometimes dislike expressed itself in violent action. The

story of the riots which took place a few years later in some of
the London churches is well known; but perhaps few have
heard of the running amok of the Bishop of Manchester
(Bishop Prince Lee) at St. John's, Higher Broughton. A
Third Pointed chancel, properly arranged, had been added to
that church. When the Bishop entered, he gave an exhibition
of maniacal fury. He cast down cushions and altar cloths;
he screwed off carved ornaments and dashed them on the
pavement. On being informed that the chancel had been built
by Mr. Bayne, he replied, "Mr. Bayne? *Saint* Bayne, I
suppose you mean. . . . The man must either have been a
knave or a fool." He also expressed a wish that the boys
might break the stained-glass windows of the church. Well
might the *Ecclesiologist* say, "Had our cause not been that of
the Catholic Church in its external manifestation, we should
most assuredly been shipwrecked ".[1]

They defended themselves, and in any case they were sure
of divine protection. But in 1845 the Camden Society severed
its connexion with the *Ecclesiologist*. In 1846 it was considered advisable for the Society to change its name to the
Ecclesiological (late Cambridge Camden) Society, and to
transfer itself from Cambridge to London. The Society in
its new form continued to issue the *Ecclesiologist*.

Advice was given to the new society by George Wightwick,
architect, writing in *Weale's Quarterly Paper on Architecture*
(Lady Day, 1845). He hoped that it would make use of all
retrospective operations only as the means of prospective
improvement; that it would emulate Sir Christopher Wren in
adapting to the present the materials of preceding times.
"What St. Stephen's, Walbrook, is to the Pantheon, such, we
conceive, should be the new Protestant Church to the Abbey
of Westminster." The new society ought also to systematize
Norman and Gothic details, forming a series of GOTHIC
ORDERS. "What Sir Wm. Chambers accomplished, in giving
us a grammar of Greco-Roman Architecture, might be afforded

---

[1] Even after ecclesiological principles were quite firmly established,
there were violent attacks. The *Builder* of January 10, 1857, has some
amusing remarks by Mr. Thomas Goodchild on "useless papistical
piscinas, obsolete screens, and disease-engendering sedilia ". But he
does not explain the last phrase.

by the Cambridge society in respect to the required modern Anglo-Gothic." He discussed a suggested design for a Protestant church, without internal pillars, and considered to be both picturesque and convenient.[1] " This design was made, in the first instance, without regard to any particular style. The Norman is adopted, not only because the *most* fitting, but on account of its being the *only* fitting style." Mr. Wightwick could not believe that the Camdenians had anything like the same amount of enthusiastic admiration for the old Roman Catholic temples which he himself entertained. Poor Camdenians !

The ideals of the Society continued unchanged. But in future it had no particular connexion with Cambridge, and the Committee consisted of others beside Cambridge men.

Soon after, the Cambridge Architectural Society was founded.

The *Ecclesiologist* gave details of the secessions, as follows :

	Seceded from the Society.	Remained in the Society.
Members, not members of the University	7	125
Undergraduates	13	129
B.A.	13	124
M.A.	67	267
Of higher standing than M.A. .	21	35
	121	680

In January 1845 the progress of the Society was reviewed. " Whenever people have told us we *could* not do such or such a thing, we have all the more set ourselves to do it, and have done it by the word TRY. It has cleansed churches, rescued fonts, restored the altar without ' setting up altars ', transformed sectarian churchwardens into active and loyal servants of the sanctuary, reconciled parishes, and abolished pues. It involves, in fact, the whole character and history of the *Ecclesiologist* and the Cambridge Camden Society. They now part company : the mother sends her child to seek his fortune ;

---

[1] But even the Protestant Church was to be symbolical. It was to be cruciform, as signifying our faith in Christ crucified ; triplet features were to symbolize Trinitarian belief whenever possible. The sentiment of Infinity was to be expressed as much as possible by the adoption of some old style, or the invention of a new one.

may they go on their parallel ways, working, it is hoped, to the same end, so far as that has God's favour. . . . Yes, we will TRY again : if this word has already given us hope, our new motto shall give us confidence, *Surge igitur et fac, et erit Dominus tecum.* FAC may well be taken as the developement of TRY."

Other societies of a similar kind were unmoved. The Oxford Society continued without much disturbance. It was " engaged in the same objects, actuated by the same motives, and using, in a great measure, the same means ". But it was less interested in Symbolism, and was, according to *Weale's Quarterly Paper,* " not practical, but at any rate respectable ". There were societies at Bristol, Northampton, Lichfield and Exeter, among other places, which continued to proclaim, as Weale expressed it, " an eleventh Commandment issued from heaven itself declaring, Thou shalt worship only Gothicism ". They were all Camdenian in their views. The Committee of the Exeter Diocesan Architectural Society declared that they " willingly sanction, and, as far as their calling will permit, heartily abet every effort to make men good ritualists, sound Churchmen, and true men ; and they think that they need not be careful, after that, nor will have long to wait to find also, good, sound and true architects ".

Ecclesiology spread even to Ireland. Pugin had not been optimistic. He had written, " I see no progress of ecclesiastical ideas in Ireland. I think if possible they grow worse. It is quite useless to attempt to build true churches, for the clergy have not the least idea of using them properly."

But the outlook in the Anglican Church seemed to be more promising. The St. Patrick's Society for the study of ecclesiology was founded in Dublin. According to the *Ecclesiologist,* " External religion has fallen very low in Ireland—more cause then for us to look with an eager eye upon the labours of those earnest and real men who have undertaken this work of faith and love. They are, we know, no triflers or half-hearted labourers, and we, therefore, venture, if we may reverently do so, to prophesy success to their endeavours."

So ecclesiology spread.[1] It spread to America, and the *New*

---

[1] One of the best features of ecclesiology was that it formed a bond of union between churchmen of other countries. The ecclesiologists were

York Ecclesiologist began to be issued.   It was most orthodox.
No. VI had an article called " Why do so Few Church Edifices
Satisfy ? "   The answer was, " Want, not of art, but of devo-
tion ".   The English *Ecclesiologist*, however, did not like some
of the American dedications : it objected to Grace, Zion,
Bethesda, Holy Communion, Our SAVIOUR, Redemption,
Church of the Reformation, Centurion, Monumental, Bethel
and Hobart.

Ecclesiology spread to the Colonies : to India, Newfoundland, Canada, Ceylon and Australia, a new type of Gothic, the
Speluncar, being devised for hot climates.   It spread even
among Nonconformists in England.   The ecclesiologists at
first could not bear the thought of the Christian style being
used for schismatic places of worship.   When a new meeting-
house in the Gothic style was designed for Manchester in 1847
they said, " It will, according to the temperament of various
persons, be either set down as a hopeful sign, an indication of
the general leavening of the whole mass of society, or as a piece
of mere unreal pageantry, a proof of deadness of heart, and
obtuseness of sense, a hollow and sickening thing, like the
laughter of idiocy, or a drunken revel in a charnel house ".

In 1848, " The Unitarians of Leeds, *horribile dictu*, are
building a meeting-house in florid Middle Pointed ".

But Dissenting Gothic could not be checked.   Some years
later Mr. F. J. Jobson, a Methodist, produced a book called
Chapel and School Architecture, which is entirely based on
Pugin.   He concludes that Gothic is Christian architecture,
and that it is also the most economical style of chapel-building
that can be employed.

But we are not concerned with chapel architecture.[1] . What
concerns us is that the ecclesiologists were supreme in the
English Church.   As Sir Kenneth Clark says,[2] " For fifty

---

in close contact with the work that was going on in France, Germany
and Belgium ; they followed with interest the progress of the restorations of Cologne Cathedral and of Notre Dame ; they made suggestions
which the Continental architects were sometimes willing to adopt.
Even in Lutheran Denmark a Church History Society was formed
which was in communion with the English ecclesiologists.

[1] *The Church Architecture of Protestantism*, by A. L. Drummond,
gives an extremely full account of the subject.

[2] *Gothic Revival*, p. 226.

years almost every new Anglican church was built according to their instructions ; that is to say, in a manner opposed to utility, economy or good sense—a very wonderful achievement in the mid-nineteenth century ".

Churches of course continued to be built by architects, and not by saintly bishops. There were some clerical architects in the nineteenth century. Newman's church at Littlemore was " in the main the work of priestly architects ". The Rev. J. L. Petit—who persisted in regarding " aesthetical beauty as the *primum mobile* of Christian architecture ", and was unsound on the question of Middle Pointed—designed a church at Dolgelly. St. Maurice's, Ellingham, was designed by the Rev. Mr. Turner. The Rev. S. Gray planned St. Michael and All Angels, Swanmore, Isle of Wight, the design being carried out by Mr. R. J. Jones. The eccentric church of Booton, Norfolk, was designed by the Rev. Whitwell Elwin. Prebendary Hingeston-Randolph restored St. Columb Minor and other churches. But on the whole the clergy confined themselves to studying ecclesiology, raising money, and making suggestions.

Architects continued to regard their work as a profession, and to take questions of trade into consideration, and probably did not trouble to make themselves acquainted with every detail of Durandus. The conversion of the architects was not altogether easy. " We have in our communion hardly a man who can be pointed out as one who labours religiously . . . who attends at the prayers which our Church still offers up daily in all cities and in many towns, who fasts or rejoices as his Church directs at the different seasons of the Christian year, and who attempts not to design a church, except after rigid abstinence and humble prostration of mind."

The ecclesiologists found the architects rather a problem. " Some of the architects snapped their fingers . . . some . . . felt irritated to the last degree at this ecclesiological espionage and self-constituted paternal government." Still, many of them built churches with chancels and without galleries, and they eschewed Norman and Perpendicular. They looked to the noble edifices of our own land, averting their eyes, at any rate for some years, from the contemplation of Continental examples.

So there came into existence the Anglican parish church as

we know it to-day, which is, to all intents and purposes, a
Camdenian church.   It is certainly not like the parish church
of the Middle Ages.   Many old churches have been made to
look Camdenian ; but they were not like that originally.
Church-people are apt to resent any departure from the
standard of what they imagine to be orthodox arrangement.
But what they wish to keep is the expression of the ideals of a
small, pietistic society founded by undergraduates at Cambridge
at the beginning of the reign of Queen Victoria.   So powerful
is the influence of faith, even if it be mistaken, and so irresistible
is the force of obstinacy.

PLATE XIII

George Edmund Street

PLATE XIV

ST. JAMES THE LESS, WESTMINSTER
By G. E. Street

CHAPTER VI

FROM this time onwards very nearly all new churches were built in the Gothic style. That is not surprising, considering the enormous moral pressure that was brought to bear on clergy and architects. There are very few un-Gothic churches after about 1845. There is an Italianate church at Wilton, near Salisbury, by T. H. Wyatt. For the adornment of this church Sidney Herbert brought from South Italy a quantity of mosaics, an altar, some twisted mosaic columns and some large twisted columns of marble. As the bishop forbade a stone altar, the materials were worked into the pulpit. The other materials were used wherever possible. The church has been called " the production of a powerful and ingenious idio-syncrasy ".

Professor Cockerell was regarded by the *Ecclesiologist* as a rather dangerous man. He viewed art " as something fought for and won by the human intellect (one might almost say, without irreverence) from GOD and against nature, instead of being something given to man by the Spirit of Wisdom. In short, the scriptural notion of art, as shown in the case of Bezaleel, is never recognized ". When this temerarious man built the church of St. Bartholomew, Moor Lane, to take the place of St. Bartholomew by the Exchange, and reproduced the old church, which had been built by Wren, the ecclesiologists were furious. " Mr. Cockerell is a scholar and a gentleman ; he has proved . . . that he can feel for and, to some extent, with Christian art. Why, then, insult it in this way ? . . . ' If ye were blind, ye should have no sin ; but now ye say, we see ; therefore your sin remaineth '."

When Mr. Allom built a church in London " in that faint and debased imitation of the Wrennian type which was in vogue thirty years ago ", they said, " Let us suggest Hindostanee or Burmese, or Japanese for his paulo-post-future church ".

Some architects continued at first unrepentantly to build un-ecclesiological churches, without chancels, only accidentally symbolical, and incorrect in style ; but there is nothing much to be said about their productions, for they are like those of the previous decade.   Others tried, more or less successfully, to build churches of the kind that the Cambridge Camden Society would approve.

After all that has been said, we might expect something very lovely ; but if so we shall be disappointed.   The day-dream was very beautiful ; but when it had to be translated into stone and wood and glass it failed.   In spite of all the good intentions, in spite of the study of the purest examples, in spite of the moral excellence of the clergy, in spite of the advice of the Camdenians to the workmen not to swear ; in spite of every-thing, the new churches were failures.   Genuine Gothic architecture is never prim : the churches of the Gothic Revival always are.   You will see details copied from churches you know ; but all the goodness is gone out of them in the copying, and they now look tame and weak.   You will see angels ; but they are not copied at all.   They are certainly not copied from the homely, flat-nosed angels of the fifteenth century, who bear corbels or spread their magnificent wings in East Anglian roofs, for they dated from days when Gothic architecture, according to the ecclesiologists, had begun to decline.   Nor are they like the graceful angels of the thirteenth and fourteenth centuries.   They are more like the daughters of the Rectory—though surely the most proper of Victorian maidens could hardly have looked so prim.

These churches prove that the ecclesiologists were wrong. The builders had good intentions and holy lives and noble aims ; but they have not succeeded in giving life to these dry bones.

The style of most of the churches is Early English or Decorated—very rarely Perpendicular.   There were fewer Early English churches as the 'forties progressed, for the ecclesiologists maintained their opinion that Decorated was the only permissible style.   And, says Gilbert Scott,[1] " so imperious was their law, that anyone who had dared to deviate

[1] G. G. Scott, *Personal and Professional Recollections*, p. 203.

from or to build in other than the sacred ' Middle Pointed ',
well knew that he must suffer. In my own office, Mr. Street
and others used to view everyone as a heretic who designed in
any but the sacred phase ; and I well recollect, when I was, at
Holbeck, obliged to build in Early English or ' First Pointed ',
the sort of holy and only half-repressed indignation and pity
to which it gave rise. The revived style was one, and its unity
was ' Middle Pointed '. I held this as a theory myself. They
held it as a religious duty. . . . So tyrannical did this law
continue to be, that when I busied myself in forming the
Architectural Museum, it was with fear and trembling that I
introduced some Early English specimens."

There must surely be some exaggeration here,[1] for several
of the architects of whom the ecclesiologists approved designed
Early English churches with comparative impunity. Nevertheless the moral pressure in favour of Middle Pointed was very
great.

Scott's own theory was much the same ; but he considered
that the ecclesiologists' style was too late. He advocated the
earliest expression of Decorated—the late thirteenth- and early
fourteenth-century style which is usually known as Geometrical.
He set forth his argument in his essay on *The Choice of a
Style for Present Adoption.* He takes it for granted, of course,
that Gothic should be revived. It had, he says elsewhere,
like the dove, found no fit resting-place, " and retired *for a time*,
leaving behind its marvellous creations to be taken as models
in some distant but happier age ". Now that the age has come,
what variety of Gothic should be adopted ? We have erred and
strayed from the ways of true Christian architecture : we should
therefore retrace our steps till we find the point in the old path
from which we had deviated—the point of highest development,
after which the path took a descending course. We should
fall in with it, and try to learn by experience and advance
on the ascent. Or rather, we should go a little farther back—

[1] Mr. A. E. Street says, " As a matter of fact my father used, in
his own words, ' to swear by first-pointed ; and we used to call Scott's
work " ogee " because we thought it too late in character ' ". But he
says that he approved of early plate tracery ; so that his position must
have been much the same as Scott's. (*Memoir of George Edmund
Street*, pp. 106 and 107.)

to the point of the path's most vigorous ascent. But where is
that? The Pointed styles are like the celestial bodies : they
are launched into space, but drawn downward by earthly
gravitation. Bearing this in mind, what shall we decide?

Our style must be Pointed. Romanesque is Christian, but
it wants some of the ennobling and glorious sentiments of our
religion.

Then what of early Early English? Is the perfection of the
art to be found in its first appearance? No, for it is confessedly imperfect and not fully developed.

But what of Perpendicular, the latest development? No!
For it wants warmth and religious feeling, and contains an
essential element of corruption and decay. Religious feeling
is giving way to human ingenuity.

Fully developed Early English would successfully claim the
palm had it not excluded mullioned and traceried windows,
and some minor features, which, from habit, have become
almost indispensable.

What of Decorated, when the rigid stone had been rendered
plastic, and taught to bend and entwine itself with all the endless ramifications of vegetable life? But does it give us all that
we want? Are softness and flexibility the great characteristics
of our religion?

But Geometrical unites the essential beauties of First and
Second Pointed ; it is very beautiful, and is also common to *all*
the most favoured nations of Christendom. It retains a
masculine and vigorous character, and Geometrical tracery, in
its best forms, harmonizes better with the grandeur and
majesty which should characterize a Christian church. And it
has no element of enervation or decay. The style had its
phases, and the middle should be taken as the ideal type. But
the whole can be the unquestionable and legitimate field for the
modern architect. Still, he might be allowed to emulate
occasionally the sterner sentiment of earlier and the softer
beauties of later times.

It was always hoped that, having assimilated Decorated, the
architects would be able to progress to a new and even finer kind
of Gothic, not like English Perpendicular or Continental
Flamboyant, but something which would exceed even the

splendours of Early Decorated as much as Early Decorated exceeded Perpendicular.

It is impossible not to admire the wonderful optimism of it all. The 1840's were in many ways a very dark time; but in the ecclesiologists' view of the immediate and more distant future there is very much light. They were good men, and wanted others to be good, and as a consequence to appreciate beautiful things and to build beautiful things. They were sure that they could achieve their ambition if the conditions were right. But the conditions never were. The condition of the souls of the ecclesiologists might be like that of the souls of the mediaeval architects ; but London in the 1840's was not like mediaeval Lincoln or Stamford, nor was Bishop Blomfield like William of Wykeham. The ecclesiologists dreamed of churches which the revived Church of England would build at home, in the Colonies and in the Mission Field :

" Christian architecture, various in form, but one in spirit, like the Faith which it embodies, must take root wherever the foot of Christian bishop has trodden, limited no longer to the narrow peculiarities of European nations, but on the one hand, on the rich and sultry plains of India, amid the wrecks of two false religions, two mighty civilizations, enforced to do them defiance in grandeur and pomp, as well as truthfulness ; and on the other, amid the dreary pine wastes of Newfoundland, commanding ice and snow, frost and cold, to bless THE LORD, praise Him, and magnify Him for ever." [1]

These new Gothic churches were to be the wonder of the world. It was a splendid faith. But some of the churches were built ; and for most people they are now merely objects of ridicule.

It is a pity. But we cannot see things as the Victorians did.

There is a difficulty in describing the churches ; and that is that there is almost nothing to say about them. They are more or less accurate, but very dull copies of some thirteenth- or fourteenth-century church, or of details from various churches which have been assembled into a new one. The exteriors, at any rate in the country, are more successful than the interiors.

[1] Variations of this sentence occur frequently in ecclesiological writings. See p. 173.

The interiors are usually overcrowded and narrow, and the woodwork is very bad.   But not a few of the exteriors, at any rate when seen from a distance, seem to have a considerable amount of quiet charm.

The churches of Benjamin Ferrey are typical.   Ferrey was born in 1810, and became, as we have seen, a pupil of the elder Pugin, with whom he went measuring old buildings in England and Normandy.   Then he entered the office of Wilkins, who was engaged on the building of the National Gallery, and employed Ferrey on the drawings.   In 1834 Ferrey produced, with E. W. Brayley, *Antiquities of the Priory Church of Christchurch, Hants*; and soon after began business as an architect in Bloomsbury.   In the competition for the Houses of Parliament he was honorary secretary to the committee of architects.

In 1841 he became diocesan architect to Bath and Wells, and restored Wells Cathedral in 1842.   In the next year he built St. James's, Morpeth—" a successful adaptation of the grander features of the Norman style "—and St. Stephen's, Rochester Row.   He was one of the consulting architects of the Church Building Society, and one of the original members of the Architectural Society.   He took part in the founding of the Royal Architectural Museum, and was twice vice-president of the R.I.B.A., Fellow of the Society of Antiquaries in 1863, and Royal Gold Medallist in 1870.   The *Recollections of Pugin* were published in 1861.

All the notices of Ferrey seem to relate that he invented an effective and cheap mode of stamping plaster.   This was to " impress common stucco with geometrical and other forms, and applied according to taste, either under string courses, round arches, in spandrels, soffits, or in large masses of diapering ; and texts may be imprinted on the plaster ".   Whippingham Church, in the Isle of Wight, was decorated with coloured devices according to this plan.

It is also said of him that he was well liked by everyone for his winning manners and even temper, and that he was fond of music and had a pleasing baritone voice.   He seems to have been a nice person.

His churches are numerous.   They are all timid, orthodox

and harmless, for Ferrey was " rather a close adherent of precedent than a bold originator ".

They include the following : Elsted ; Penn Street ; All Saints', Blackheath ; St. John's, Eton ; St. Andrew's, Croydon ; Christchurch, Clapham ; Wadesmill ; Shepherdswell ; St. Anne's, Kemp Town ; Coldharbour ; Kingswood ; Brockham Green ; Shalford ; Burton (Hants) ; St. John's, Brixton ; Bengeo ; Buckland St. Mary ; Christchurch, Banbury ; Chetwynde ; Dogmersfield ; St. Mark's, Old Street ; St. Paul's, Dorking ; Esher ; Christchurch, Eastbourne ; Fauls ; Holdenhurst ; Christchurch, Kensington ; East and West Lydford ; Melplash ; Roehampton (Old Church) ; Otterton ; Pett ; Slinfold ; Immanuel, Streatham ; St. Stephen's, Rochester Row (Westminster) ; Vobster ; Whitchurch (Hants).

The Surrey examples are typical : Kingswood and Brockham Green, one standing among trees on the edge of heath, and the other situated attractively in the foreground of the view southwards from Box Hill, are picturesque when seen from a distance, and dull when seen from near by.

In the same county Westcott, near Dorking, by Gilbert Scott, sits satisfactorily on its small hill. And many other country churches, if seen from a quarter of a mile away, are pleasing to the eye, and are almost indistinguishable from old buildings. But the difference is obvious when one approaches them closely.

They are most pleasing when they are least ornamented. Par, Cornwall, by G. E. Street, has a very poor spire. But its interior is attractive in its extreme simplicity. It was built for Mr. G. R. Prynne in 1846–48, and was Street's first church.

For an example of the worst type of village church, grossly over-ornamented and badly designed, we might take Fretherne, Gloucestershire.

Its date is 1847, and it was designed by Francis Niblett. The exterior is prickly and over-ornate ; the interior is a Gothic muddle. Nothing is spared us. In a kind of transept at the south west is a bust of Sir Edward Tierney, Bart., under an elaborate canopy in the Decorated style. Two small angels beneath hold scrolls inscribed " God bless you all ".

Another Gloucestershire church, Highnam (1848–1851), is

a good example of a church arranged in a way that was regarded as completely satisfactory. The *Ecclesiologist* called it " one of the most complete in scale and fitting, and one of the most costly, of the churches built within the last few years ".   Mr. Woodyer was the architect, and it is in the Decorated style, carefully designed and well built.   It was the gift of Mr. Gambier Parry, who himself decorated it with wall paintings— the expulsion from Paradise, the Annunciation and the Entry into Jerusalem in the aisles ; and the Last Judgement over the chancel arch.   The glass is by Wailes, O'Connor, Hardman and Clayton and Bell, and the designs of the windows follow a well-thought-out scheme.   But their colouring is not good, and the wall-paintings have lost their first freshness.   The sun shining through a plain window on to the plainest of whitewashed walls lights up a poor interior and gives it beauty : but the sun shining through one of the archaic windows of Mr. Hardman or Mr. O'Connor, and making red and purple patches on a wall covered with faded fresco, is pitiless in its illumination of poor detail, and destroys the small effect that it had in the semi-darkness.

The town churches of the period are simply larger editions of those in the country.   This was an almost inevitable result of the copy-book method, for the churches which had been most visited and described were naturally those within reach of Oxford and Cambridge.   The churches in those neighbour-hoods are very orthodox specimens of old work ; they are also country churches.   They might be reproduced in the country without incongruity ; but they were also taken as models when town churches were to be built, and spires and gables which were designed to stand above the fields and fens of the Eastern Counties were copied and set up in slum districts of London. Of course they seem out of place.   They do not belong there.

The *Ecclesiologist* itself saw the point.   It published in 1850 a letter from Mr. G. E. Street which contains some sensible remarks on the subject.   He says, " It is a shame and misery indeed that it should ever have been possible, in such a city as London, for architects to attempt to execute copies of country work ".   He points out that some old town churches are much the same as village churches; but that there was also a type particularly appropriate to towns. In Bristol, York and Norwich there are churches of rather late date in which " there does seem to be something which is essentially fitted for the neighbourhood of towns ". He then lays down some points which are of importance in the building of town churches.

First, that the materials and design should avoid rusticity. (That is not very helpful.)

Secondly, that high-pitched roofs are not a necessity.

Thirdly, that a clerestory almost always is.

Fourthly, that regularity of design is essential.

Fifthly, that a spire is often unnecessary. He strongly criticizes some of the new spires. He says of St. Barnabas', Pimlico, which had been recently erected, that it " ought to be in some sequestered spot, far from smoke ". He even compares the new steeples unfavourably with some of those of Sir Christopher Wren.

His last point is that height is all-important.

One of his constructive proposals is that Continental town churches should be imitated. This was almost heresy at the time; but he mitigates it by adding, " if accompanied by a thorough knowledge and respect for those Anglicanisms in art of which we have so much reason to be very proud ". Suggestions of this kind were generally adopted a few years later. But at first they were the utterances of voices crying in the wilderness.

St. Giles's, Camberwell, by Gilbert Scott and Moffatt, is a fair specimen of the overgrown village type of town church— though of course Camberwell a hundred years ago was far more rural than it is now. It was begun in 1842, the year after the destruction by fire of the old church, and consecrated in 1844. The incumbent was determined to have a good church and, according to Scott, so far as his day permitted, he got it. St. Giles's has certainly quite a picturesque exterior, and its tall central spire is not ungraceful. The interior is rather gloomy, and its fittings, like those of most of the churches of the time, are poor. Scott considered the carving (by Mr. Cox) to be fair, except for the human heads, " which are detestable ". It was in the course of building this church that he had his

I

conversion " to the exclusive use of real material ".[1] Details had been designed for execution in plaster ; he then decided that they must be in stone, to the annoyance of those who had to pay for it.

St. Stephen's, Rochester Row, Westminster, by Ferrey, is in a later style of Decorated. The foundress, Miss Burdett Coutts, was not previously known to have " given her adhesion to the principles of ecclesiology ", but the church was praised by the *Ecclesiologist* as being a witness to true principles.

St. Barnabas', Pimlico, designed by Thomas Cundy and consecrated in 1850, was praised for its ritual arrangements, but not for its style, which was Early English. Early English had been selected, it was said, because it was the style most suited for a poor man's church. But, said the *Ecclesiologist*, " why is the poor man's church to be of the plainest style ? We should have taken the opposite tone, and argued that, of all men he, whose own dwelling is mean and poor, has the greatest claim to richness and magnificence in the temple of The LORD. The wealthy and luxurious can better afford to leave their carpets and arm-chairs for a few hours in a plain church, than the inmate of a garret who has such scanty opportunity of drinking in the beauties of external art." It proceeds to admit that St. Barnabas' has rich colours and fittings ; but they are not suitable to First Pointed architecture.

So Decorated, beside its other merits, had that of being suitable for the poor. The Church, of course, at this time, did not think of pulling down the slums.

One of the better architects of this time was R. C. Carpenter. He had been born in 1812, served his articles with John Blyth, and entered practice in London, and was one of the consulting committee of architects of the Incorporated Church Building Society. He was interested in the subsidiary arts of the Church, in the *instrumenta* of worship, and in painted glass. At the age of nineteen he drew up designs for a Gothic church to be erected at Islington, a scheme which fell through owing to the opposition of the vicar.

He made friends with Pugin, and was associated with the Cambridge Camden Society. St. Stephen's and St. Andrew's,

[1] See p. 163.

Birmingham, are specimens of his work.   St. Mary Magdalene's, Munster Square, was pronounced by the *Ecclesiologist*
to be " the most artistically correct new church yet consecrated
in London ".   St. Paul's, Brighton, was built between 1846
and 1848.   Perhaps Lancing College is his best-known work in
England.   He sent out designs for three churches in Tasmania,
and designed cathedrals for Jamaica and Ceylon.   The
Cathedral of Inverness was begun by Carpenter, and finished
after his death by Slater, who had been his first pupil.

The *Ecclesiologist* said in his obituary (June 1855), " He never
seemed to dream of producing a sudden or startling effect,
and yet his works all tell, and are all eminently original and
varied, and peculiarly devoid of mannerism.   His success lay
in the perfect keeping of everything which he did—the harmony
of parts and general unity of proportion running through the
entire building.   The entire mass is broad and manly, and
every detail beautiful, as a single study, and thoroughly
finished, but never frittered into inanity. . . . His eye for
colour was exquisite."

St. Andrew's, Wells Street, designed by Messrs. Dawkes and
Hamilton, and consecrated in 1847, is Perpendicular.   The *Ecclesiologist*, of course, protested vehemently against the style.   Benjamin Webb, the co-founder of the Cambridge Camden Society,
was vicar here for a number of years, and did his best to make
the church ecclesiologically perfect.   It was given a reredos,
screen, font and pulpit designed by Street, and various
other well-known architects designed the other fittings.   The
church was taken down and rebuilt at Kingsbury, Middlesex,
in 1933–1934, and its interior, cleaner and brighter than before,
is now rather attractive.

St. Saviour's, Leeds, the gift of Dr. Pusey,[1] was begun in
1842 and consecrated in 1845.   J. M. Derick was the architect.
Its central tower and spire, long remained unbuilt, but were
completed in 1937.   The whole church was intended to have

---

[1] Pusey at one time thought of buying one of the churches that had
been destroyed in Portugal when convents were suppressed about
1840, and re-erecting it at Leeds.   But the proposal came to nothing.
In the matter of the decorations of St. Saviour's he differed from the
Camden Society.   He desired the introduction of the Ten Commandments, and considered them to be of more value than images or
pictures or tapestry.

" something of the proportions of a foreign cathedral ". It is very tall in proportion to its width, and has transepts and a long chancel : a picturesque but most inconvenient plan.

Two churches stand quite apart from the others that were built at this time : St. Matthias', Stoke Newington, and All Saints', Margaret Street, which were designed by William Butterfield, and are real attempts to build something which would be suitable to a large town.

Butterfield died in 1900, at the age of eighty-six, and much of his work was done later in the nineteenth century. But some account of him seems to be in place here. He was apprenticed to a builder, and, says Professor Lethaby, he remained a builder-architect. Afterwards he was with Inwood (see Appendix). He was associated with the Cambridge Camden Society and was a friend of Benjamin Webb, with whom he prepared a number of illustrations for *Instrumenta Ecclesiastica* (1847). He undertook the management and superintendence of the making of church plate and the binding of office books. Coalpit Heath, his first church, dates from 1844; then he undertook the rebuilding of St. Augustine's Abbey, Canterbury, as a missionary college. This is a simple building, and not particularly Butterfieldian, but quite well planned and attractive. He was, according to Scott, an apostle of the High-Church school. The *Dictionary of National Biography* says [1] that his work " cannot be considered apart from the inner spirit of the Church revival ; [2] his art was entirely inspired by keen churchmanship, and his churchmanship was based on something deeper than ceremonial.[3] Taking the minutest interest in the details of traditional worship, he held in horror anything like fancy ritual. He instilled into the craftsmen associated with him something of his own scruples against working for the Roman Church, and something of his own willingness to labour, if need be without reward, for the Church of England."

The article continues, speaking of his use of colour, that his theory " seems to have been that such combinations were permissible as could be produced by uncoloured natural

[1] *D.N.B. Supplement* 1, p. 362.
[2] But he did design one Nonconformist Chapel—at Bristol.
[3] His manner is said to have been " somewhat clerical ".

materials. This theory will account for the juxtaposition of strongly discordant bricks and marbles, and the bright contrasts thus obtained led on, upon Butterfield's own admission, to his strange choice of garish colours in glass ; but this plea of natural colour cannot be made to cover his views upon the use of similar contrasts in paint. Nor indeed does the consideration that he made a special study of colour in Northern Italy satisfactorily explain the use under the English climate of what may have seemed beautiful beyond the Alps." His first famous church was All Saints', Margaret Street, which was built on the site of Margaret Chapel—a building which had varied fortunes. It was built in the eighteenth century for a congregation of Deists, and was afterwards used by a Mr. David Williams. Then it came into the hands of the Church : the Rev. W. Dodsworth ministered there, then the Rev. Frederick Oakeley, who afterwards joined the Church of Rome, and then the Rev. Upton Richards. The Chapel was noted for some of the first efforts at the revival of ceremonial. Altar lights had been introduced in 1839, and a sung celebration was early established. In 1847 Benjamin Webb wrote, " At Margaret Chapel they have now got up a complete musical Mass. . . . I venture to assert that there has been nothing so solemn since the Reformation."

But the Chapel was not an object of beauty, and it was not capable of much improvement. It was " a combination of everything disgustful, both of bad arrangement and miserable material ". It would clearly have to be rebuilt. The Ecclesiological Society had long wished to build a model church,[1] and it was decided that the new church in Margaret Street would be their attempt at realizing their dream. Sir Stephen Glynne and Mr. Beresford Hope were appointed the executive, and Mr. Butterfield was selected as architect. The result is certainly surprising. For All Saints', Margaret Street, is a

---

[1] In 1841 J. M. Neale had made a proposal to build in Cambridge a large cross church dedicated to St. Alban the Protomartyr. " The style to be Decorated, with lofty cathedral spire. The arrangement to be perfect—open and magnificent wood seats, exquisite font with splendid canopy, painted tiles, magnificent Altar raised on nine steps— in short, in everything except size, to rival Lincoln. The collection to be a national one. . . . We reckon not to build with less than £15,000, or some trifle like that."

decidedly original building. Street said that of all the new churches " this was the most beautiful, vigorous, thoughtful and original ", and Mr. Heathcote Statham says that " it is the one Gothic Revival Church which is still as interesting, externally at least, as when it was built ".[1]

It is of brick, which was against the principles of the early ecclesiologists, and not only of brick, but of many-coloured brick. This was called " polychromatic architecture " or " constructive coloration ", and soon became very common : All Saints' set a fashion. It was, says Mr. Beresford Hope, " the first decided experiment in London of building in polychromatic material ; and the numerous brood of imitations which has followed its path attests the vitality of the attempt ".[2] But not only is there coloured brick : there are also polished red Peterhead granite, Cornish serpentine, Devonshire marble and alabaster ; there are incised patterns filled with coloured mastic ; and the sanctuary and the vault of the chancel have paintings by Mr. Dyce, which make it, according to Mr. Hope, " no whit inferior to the vault of S. Jacques at Liège, or Sta. Anastasia at Verona ".[3]

It was a noble effort, but we cannot but agree with Eastlake that " the frescoes, marbles, geometrical patterns, carving, mosaic, stained glass and gilding dazzle the eye by their close association, and even trench on each other's claim to attention ".

The church had some critics : one was Mr. W. J. Cockburn Muir, who said,[4] " The mind, through the eye, is distracted by a whirling maze of variegated colouring and gilded pictures ; and led wandering from this side to that, and to the other, until fixity of meditation becomes impossible. There is everything to make you look *around*, but very little to direct you heavenward. The Object of worship is forgotten, in the gaudy luxuriousness of the scene of worship." [5] " Strip the walls of their unseemly colouring, and what eloquence of Art do you discern in the naked forms ? This is the test by which to try the pretentions of ostentatious ornamentation. You will not

---

[1] *Short Critical History of Architecture*, p. 531.
[2] *English Cathedral of the Nineteenth Century*, p. 234.
[3] *Ibid.*, p. 250.
[4] W. J. Cockburn Muir, *Pagan or Christian ?*, p. 221.
[5] *Ibid.*, pp. 223–224.

find much beauty certainly in the tracery of the windows; nor in the hard, stiff outline of the niches and their canopies in the choir; nor in the absurd flying-arch at the end of the south aisle. You will not find much rhythm in the arcade at the side of the baptistry, between the slender shafts and the ponderous tracery they make a poor pretence at supporting; not more than a mere inkling of spirituality in the equilateral arches of the nave." Nor does he like the foliated capitals: they are not natural. In another place he says,[1] "Beware of Colour. Let the Pagan Art-harlot paint her bold cheek. But do not you encumber Christian Architecture, and sink her to the dust, with the buffooneries of unmeaning pageantry."

The spire is bold and successful—which is more than can be said of most Victorian spires. The church is small and the site is cramped. The north side is without windows, the nave is only of three bays, and the chancel is not very long—though this is by no means such a misfortune as nineteenth-century Churchmen were apt to imagine.

Mr. Beresford Hope says that his object had been to "work out a higher and more minster-like type of parish church than previously existed in modern English architecture"; but he considers that the parochial and minster-like forms conflict with each other. "The pillars and arches are those of a cathedral, and the clerestory above (whether or not exception may be taken to any of its details) is of a very vigorous character; but the practised eye of 1861 cannot fail to regret that this clerestory should stand sheer upon the arcade, as a triforial story would have doubled the architectural value of all the other members."[2] The roof, he says, is "out of keeping with the rich and massive work below", and the aisle roofs are not satisfactory. We might add that the tracery of the windows is very obvious and dull Gothic Revival. But we can agree that All Saints' is an interesting church. And the most interesting thing about it is that it was the model church of the Ecclesiological Society.

St. Matthias', Stoke Newington, was built in 1850–1852.

---

[1] W. J. Cockburn Muir, *Pagan or Christian?*, p. 276. This is a poor book, with many passages derived from Pugin, and some a long way after Ruskin.

[2] *English Cathedral of the Nineteenth Century*, pp. 234–235.

It is less startling than All Saints'; but it has a decidedly imposing exterior, with a lofty saddle-back tower over the chancel, aisles carried past it, and a sanctuary to the east. The original design, published in the *Ecclesiologist*, had pinnacles to the tower, which were fortunately not executed. The west doorway was passed by the *Ecclesiologist* (which did not like west doorways in parish churches) because all town churches were to be regarded as quasi-collegiate, and their chancels should be adapted for the worship of associated clergy.

The interior is inconveniently planned, but the arcades and the tall clerestory are dignified. As usual, such of the woodwork as is contemporary is poor.

St. Matthias', like All Saints', was a centre of ritualistic worship, and attracted enormous crowds. William Monk, the musical editor of *Hymns Ancient and Modern*, was for a time the organist.

St. Alban's, Holborn, Butterfield's third famous London church, was begun in 1859 and completed in 1863. A picture of the interior at the time of the church's completion shows a riot of constructive coloration. Some of this has been obliterated, and the rest has toned down considerably; so that we can admire the fine proportions of the church without distraction. The treatment of the saddle-back tower is quite masterly. The interior has been considerably altered, and the dominating feature is an enormous reredos by Mr. Garner, of a type which is perfectly in place in a church such as this which has no east window. The window tracery of St. Alban's is extremely feeble.

Butterfield's other churches are mostly of the same type. But in later years he seldom managed to rise to the level of his earlier efforts. His self-confidence helped him to success in the beginning because it enabled him to do his work in the face of opposition and ridicule. But later in his life it caused him to separate himself from others and to become narrow and arbitrary. His early works are his masterpieces; his later efforts tended to become stereotyped and monotonous.

His churches include those of Yealmpton; Helidon; St. John's, Hammersmith; St. Augustine's, Queen's Gate; St. Augustine's, Penarth; Ashford (Middlesex); All Saints',

PLATE XV

ST. JOHN'S, TORQUAY
By G. E. Street

PLATE XVI

WILLIAM BURGES

From a photograph in possession of the R.I.B.A.

GEORGE FREDERICK BODLEY

From a photograph in possession of the R.I.B.A.

Highgate; St. Mary's, Brookfield, Highgate (nave only); St. Michael's, Woolwich; St. Clement's, City Road; St. Mary's, Edmonton (nave only); The Guards' Chapel, Caterham; St. Augustine's, Bournemouth; West Lavington; St. Thomas', Leeds; St. John's, Huddersfield; Emery Down; Beechhill; Braishfield; Cowick; Dropmore; Poulton; St. Mary Magdalene's, Enfield; St. Saviour's, Hitchin, and St. Barnabas', Rotherhithe. The nave of All Saints', Harrow Weald, added to a First Pointed chancel by J. P. Harrison, is a good example of his more restrained style, and has a good deal of character. Rugby Chapel (1875) is not one of his better works. St. John the Baptist's, Barnet, consecrated in 1875, is an enlargement of the old church: Butterfield built a new nave, south aisle, tower, chancel and south chapel to the south of the old nave and north aisle. The new work is rather good; the chancel, with characteristic east window and reredos, is imposing, though the elaborate stalls which were put in later are not suitable.

Keble Chapel was begun in 1873 and completed in 1876. It has been called one of " the last ambitious kicks of the more aggressive Gothic revivalists ".[1] It is of noble proportions, but the interior is very restless. The decoration too often degenerates into tasteless over-elaboration, and the glass is a failure.

His church at Rugby, of which the spire was completed in 1896, is Butterfield's most important provincial work. Ascot Priory Chapel (1885) has some good points and some bad; the fittings have been altered.

There are Butterfield churches outside England: he designed the Scottish cathedrals of Perth and Cumbrae, and there are works in various distant parts of the world—at Madagascar, Port Elizabeth, Capetown, Poona, Bombay, Adelaide and Melbourne. These are not among his best designs. But St. Paul's Cathedral, Melbourne, cannot be taken as an example: only the masonry of the walls is Butterfield's. He resigned during the building of the Cathedral, and a local architect was appointed in his place. And the spires have lately been completed on an entirely new design.

During his life Butterfield was on the whole treated with

[1] R. C. K. Ensor, *England* 1870–1914, pp. 155–156.

respect. The *Ecclesiologist* approved of him, though it felt itself bound to give him a kindly warning. " We are," it said, " no wholesale condemners of mannerism; we have no great prejudice against the recognition of the individual artist by the individual work. But there is a kind of mannerism in idea, arising from the disproportionate importance attached to one true principle, the *telos* of which is to Christian art what heresy is to Christian faith." Butterfield, however, claimed that there was historical precedent for every feature of his work.

Eastlake says,[1] " There is a sober earnestness of purpose in his work widely different from that of some designers, who seem to be tossed about on the sea of popular taste, unable, apparently, to decide what style they will adopt, and trying their hands in turn at French, at Italian, and what not, with no more reason than a love of change or a restless striving after effect. He does not care to produce *showy* buildings at a sacrifice— even a justifiable sacrifice—of constructive strength. To the pretty superficial school of Gothic, busy with pinnacles, chamfers, and fussy carving, he has never condescended. He has his own (somewhat stern) notions of architectural beauty, and he holds to them whether he is planning a cottage or a cathedral. His work gives one the idea of a man who has designed it not so much to please his clients as to please himself. In estimating the value of his skill, posterity may find something to smile at as eccentric, something to deplore as ill-judged, and much that will astonish as daring, but they will find nothing to despise as commonplace or mean."

This judgement may sound rather surprising to us, for Butterfield has come to be regarded as rather a joke. Everyone who has heard of his name knows of his experiments in constructive coloration, and can say smart things about Keble Chapel. It is interesting to find him spoken of as a sober designer of noble buildings. But surely it is the truth.

Butterfield was not a conventional Gothic revivalist, he was a builder who had absorbed Pugin's True Principles. Professor W. R. Lethaby says,[2] " Gothic was to him an essence and a logic rather than a magazine of ' cribs ' for designers, where they might

---

[1] *Gothic Revival*, pp. 262–263.
[2] W. R. Lethaby, *Philip Webb and his Work*, p. 67.

borrow attractive, unexploited features ". " His mind was set on structural results, not on paper schemes." Professor Lethaby divides the nineteenth-century architects into two classes— the Softs and the Hards. The Softs were those who made beautiful paper designs, and produced synthetic churches in a correct mediaeval manner ; the Hards were those with a knowledge of building, who understood their materials and proceeded by experiment. Pugin was by conviction a Hard, but a Soft in practice. Butterfield was a Hard. He did not exhibit designs, and he shunned competitions. His churches are " real ", and, as Eastlake says, he did not sacrifice construction to ornament. He used common materials—brick, slate and cast iron—and " fitted his style to common modes of execution ".

We owe him a debt of gratitude for his bold use of brick, and for making brick once again a respectable material which might be used for the building of churches. It was no doubt Butterfield who converted the ecclesiologists to the use of brick.

All Butterfield's churches have an intense individuality. The details are often crude and harsh. His glass is not attractive, and his woodwork is poor. He failed to appreciate the best English woodwork of the past—no doubt it was considered too late in date to be profitably studied ; and he never grasped the difference between work in wood and work in stone. (This is also true of most nineteenth-century architects.) But the proportions and outlines of his churches are usually good.

He was the first nineteenth-century architect to realize the dignity of a long, unbroken roof-line. Most of the churches of the early revivalists have a fussy outline : there are various levels of roof, and the outline is broken by too many pinnacles and gable crosses. Butterfield avoided this mistake in his churches. The outlines of St. Alban's, Holborn, and of Keble Chapel are very grand. The unbroken roof-line may be generally recognized as a Butterfieldian characteristic. The lead which Butterfield gave was followed by the masters of the later nineteenth century.

His restorations are not satisfactory. He had a great admiration for old churches, but dealt with them most unsympathetically.   He could not keep his individuality in check, and would introduce Butterfieldian features with no regard for appropriateness and no thought of local characteristics.   His obituary in the *R.I.B.A. Journal* (VII, 242–243) states the matter clearly: " We are wrapt in wonder that he could appreciate so much and spare so little. He despised the insipid and empty renovations of Scott, he was altogether blind to the tender and scholarly respect and the delicate abstention of Pearson, and it is perhaps not surprising that the many, whose shallow sense of sentimental respect for ecclesiastical antiquity overrides their grasp of genuine architectural production, appraise the man by the failures which were inherent to his very instincts, and judge his creations by the relentless destruction he wrought upon many cherished monuments. We can regret for our own sake and for his reputation's that he was ever called in to deal with a single ancient fabric."

But it ends, as any remarks on Butterfield are almost certain to do, " But let us not confuse issues. Butterfield was essentially a creator, and when most of the paltry work of the revived Gothic, typified by the churches of West End London squares, has passed out of history as unworthy of aught but scorn, Butterfield's best efforts will remain, full of vigour, strength and virility, types of a strong soul—a master of his craft ".

Towards the end of his life Butterfield lived in the past, and lamented the degeneracy of the age. He led a quiet and retired existence, and wrote no books. But he need not have repined : he had had much more influence than most of his contemporaries. He had broken away from mere copyism, and had dared to be original both in design and material.

The lead which he had given in the 1840's was followed by other architects. From that time onward there were many brick churches, and many which were to some extent unconventional.

We are not concerned with churches of an extremely unconventional type : they were discussed, but did not reach the stage of actually being built.

The Ecclesiological Society published a design for a Gothic Church entirely of iron. According to Scott, it showed that " quite a new version of the beauties of a Gothic interior might be obtained by the use of wrought iron for its entire construction ". The iron, of course, must have made no pretence at being anything else : that would have been an abomination. Nothing came of the scheme of iron Gothic, except in Railway stations. Mr. Beresford Hope was not unfavourable towards iron Gothic; but he ruled out crystal—which presumably meant glass Gothic. The Crystal Palace had evidently struck people's imaginations.

At an earlier date (1845) a book had been published whose title is self-explanatory : *The New System of Architecture, founded on the forms of Nature, and developing the properties of metals ; by which a higher order of beauty, a larger amount of utility, and various advantages in economy, over the pre-existent Architectures, may be practically attained : presenting also, the peculiar and important advantage of being commercial, its productions forming fitting objects for exportation.* The author (William Vose Pickett) hoped that when his system had been adopted, churches, like bridges, would be made in England and exported.

But nothing so original was attempted yet. The unconvention was of a comparatively mild nature. Nevertheless it was a step in advance. Architects began to build churches of brick, and to use materials of various colours. And they began to be interested in styles that had not hitherto been used. To begin with, the architects had been required to imitate exactly English models. Now it began to be fashionable to look abroad and to borrow from other countries.

CHAPTER VII

UNTIL about 1850 the Gothic Revival was on the whole English and insular. To begin with, English Gothic had been regarded as the best simply because very few people knew much about any other kind—just as the English liturgy was regarded as incomparable because it was the only one that was generally known to Englishmen. When the Gothic style became associated with the Church revival it was natural to wish it to be English, for the Tractarians were essentially English in their outlook. It was equally natural for the English Roman Catholics to prefer on the whole Italian fashions. English Gothic prevailed in the Church of England, and the architects' choice of style was limited by the tyranny of the ecclesiologists and the lovers of Second Pointed. Against that tyranny there was a rebellion, and Gilbert Scott was one of the rebels. He wished to take an independent line in the matter of ornament. He had used conventional foliage in his earlier work ; " but subsequently I had come to the conclusion that, though it was lawful to revive bygone forms of a merely mechanical character, it was inconsistent to revive bygone conventionalism in matters originally derived from nature, and that while we might imitate the architecture of another period, we must always go to·nature direct (though perhaps aided by suggestions from art) for objects of which nature was the professed origin, and that if we saw fit to conventionalize, the conventionalism should be our own." He wrote a lecture on the subject of 1853 or 1854, in preparation for which he studied botany. " I remember longing most earnestly to discover a leaf, from which I might suppose our early English foliage to have been derived. The nearest I could find was an almost microscopic wall-fern, and certain varieties of the common parsley. One night I dreamed that I had found the veritable plant. I can see it even now. It was a sear and yellow leaf, but with all the beauty of form which graces the capitals at Lincoln and Lichfield. I was maddened with excitement and pleasure; but while I was exulting, and ready to exclaim, ' Eureka! Eureka! ' I awoke, and behold it was a dream." [1]

After another lecture in which he gave his theory against revived conventionalism, Mr. Clutton whispered in his ear, " You've been preaching heresy ". But Scott did not discover his meaning until 1856, when Messrs. Clutton and Burges won the competition for the new cathedral at Lille.

" This was really the first occasion on which the Ecclesiological Society's law, as regards the ' Middle Pointed ', was set at nought." The ecclesiologists had to praise it, unwillingly. " Clutton and Burges certainly had the credit of overthrowing the old tyranny, and even some of its most rigorous abettors soon found it necessary to outvie each other in setting at nought their former faith, and in trying who could be the *earliest* in the style of their buildings. One thing, however, they never changed: the intolerance shown by them for all freedom of thought on the part of other men. Every one must perforce follow in their wake, no matter how often they changed, or how entirely they reversed their own previous views." [2]

Was the breakdown of the Middle Pointed régime good or bad? Scott agreed, of course, that at the beginning of the Revival it was the duty of its leaders to see that the most complete phase of the style was adopted. He agreed that the Middle was the best, when Gothic had been purged from the leaven of its early rudeness, but had not yet commenced the downward path of enervation and decay. (Enthusiasm for Gothic nearly always led writers to mix their metaphors.) The breakdown of the Middle Pointed theory led to " pious devotion to ' First Pointed ' in its most ultra-

---

[1] Scott, *Recollections*, p. 205.   [2] *Ibid.*, p. 206.

Gallic form ". Scott, who was not always *persona grata* with the ecclesiologists, considered that on the whole this was a good thing. But he lamented the fact that new fetters could be forged to take the place of the old.

That was the first rebellion. The other was the movement towards the introduction of foreign Gothic. The ecclesiologists could not possibly confine architects for ever to England, or prevent them from admiring what they saw if they did venture into foreign countries.

Architects travelled abroad and sketched examples of foreign Gothic: they saw that English Gothic was in some ways inferior, and they refused to be unreasonably limited. From about 1850 onwards the *Ecclesiologist* began to give a cautious blessing to the introduction of foreign detail.

Scott made drawings in France and Germany. Street did not make his first foreign tour until 1850. From that time onwards he went abroad regularly, and studied the architecture of France, Germany, Italy and Spain. His book on *Brick and Marble Architecture of North Italy* was published in 1855. Norman Shaw and W. E. Nesfield made drawings of French buildings. The casts of French detail in the Architectural Museum gave examples to copy; and M. Viollet-le-Duc's *Dictionnaire raisonné de l'Architecture Française du XIe au XVIe Siècle* was a store of useful information.

The *Ecclesiologist* said in April 1858, " We consider ourselves very bold in our eclecticism, and we imagine that the extent to which we advocate the incorporation of ideas borrowed from abroad, and particularly Italy, into the local Gothic of the future, is such as to startle the Rickman–Parker school at home, and that of the 13*me siècle* in France."

It is impossible to draw an exact line between a Middle Pointed English period and a First Pointed and foreign period. Churches of the ecclesiological Middle Pointed type were built throughout the nineteenth century. However, we can say that during the 1850's architects began to use foreign detail in their churches. And how much there was to choose from ! The whole of Europe lay before the Gothic Revivalists: France, with its towering churches; Spain, with its exotic, florid Gothic cathedrals; Italy, with its

PLATE XVII

SKELTON CHURCH
By William Burges

PLATE XVIII

THE TRANSFIGURATION, LEWISHAM

By James Brooks

PLATE XIX

ST. GEORGE'S, CAMPDEN HILL
By Bassett Keeling

PLATE XX

ALL SOULS', HALEY HILL
By Sir Gilbert Scott
" On the whole my best church "

many-coloured buildings glowing in the sunlight; and any other country which could be visited by architects. The old days must have seemed very tame and unexciting. At first, all that had been required was to sit and study Someone's *Architectural Specimens*, and to introduce some of them into your churches. Then it had been necessary only to take a walk to Cherry Hinton or Kidlington, and to copy some of what you saw there. Now, architects began to take foreign tours for granted; they went abroad and returned with a wealth of material from many lands. And some of it went into their churches.

The *Ecclesiologist* began also to be very interested in the subject of constructive coloration. In 1850 it said that it was a question which had not yet received the consideration which it deserved. "We are every day more and more convinced that this is one of the problems which the revived Pointed architecture of the nineteenth century, enterprising and scientific as it is, will have chiefly to work out, if it means to vindicate its position of being a living and growing style."

Two years later, G. E. Street, in a paper read to the Oxford Architectural Society, described the constructive coloration of the churches of Italy and Greece, and mentioned the few specimens of it in England. "It is," he continued, "so far as we can judge, just that element which is required to harmonize and perfect the most elaborate Pointed work, and for the lack of which most modern work, and much old, fails in inspiring that placid and quiet feeling which all great art should inspire; and at the same time it has in it nothing at variance with the real principles of the style, which are, as I have said, entirely constructional, inasmuch as it is in itself most clearly so also. . . . Now, besides these elements of true beauty there are others in foreign buildings which can by no possible reason be said to be in any way properly peculiar to the lands in which we find them." Bricks can be used, tiles, coloured marbles, and the coloured stones of England.

So structural polychrome came into fashion. The coming of the railway had made it possible to convey stone and

K

marble of various kinds without difficulty. Devonshire, Cornish and Derbyshire marbles, and other coloured limestones which had not been generally available a few years previously except in their immediate localities were now carried easily by rail at a moderate cost, and were applicable for building purposes in any part of the country.

The result seems to have pleased the Victorians. They delighted in the rich appearance of the constructive coloration, and loved to write in their guide-books of the various materials in cathedral reredoses and pulpits—lapis lazuli, verde antico, rosso antico, Vecchia marble, Carrara marble, Mexican onyx and the rest. The names are attractive : the things themselves are less so.

The less ambitious churches had to be content with bricks of various colours, voussoirs of various coloured stone, and polished granite columns.

Structural polychrome could, of course, be used in a design in any style : it was best suited to Italian ; but it could be used with French, and Butterfield used it with English. He was not much interested in foreign styles : he " modified English Gothic after his own fashion, but in his hands and perhaps from his attachment to its most characteristic features, its tracery, its mouldings, and its woodwork, it never lost its nationality ".[1]

The adoption of the Early French style by many architects was on the whole a step in advance. It meant that " the small and intricately carved foliage of capitals which had hitherto been in vogue gave place to bolder and simpler forms of leaf ornament. The round abacus was superseded by the square. In place of compound or clustered pillars, plain cylindrical shafts were employed. Arch mouldings grew less complex. Crockets and ball-flower enrichment were reduced to a minimum."[2] The Early French style, at any rate in capable hands, was simpler and stronger and, as Eastlake says, more muscular. In less capable hands it was heavy, and when combined with constructive coloration it was not attractive.

In some cases styles were mixed : such eclecticism was on

[1] Eastlake, *Gothic Revival*, p. 328.   [2] *Ibid.*, p. 319.

the whole approved of. It was customary to scoff at pre-ecclesiological eclecticism, but that was the work of men who did not understand the styles which they were mixing. Those who did were allowed to mix them, and the result was pleasing to the eye of the connoisseur—unless it was carried too far or became too wild.

Scott has some hard things to say about the new architecture.[1] He speaks of " Ruskinism such as would make Ruskin's very hair stand on end : Butterfieldism, gone mad with its endless stripings of red and black bricks ; architecture so French that a Frenchman would not know it, out-Heroding Herod himself ; Byzantine in all its forms but those used by the Byzantians ; mixtures of all or some of these ; ' original ' varieties founded upon knowledge of old styles, or upon ignorance of them, as the case may be ; violent strainings after a something very strange, and great success in producing something very weak ; attempts at beauty resulting in ugliness, and attempts at ugliness attended with unhoped-for success." At the same time, he considered that " much of the best, the most nervous and the most original results of the revival, have been arrived at within the same period ".

Ferrey complained that " many of the strange buildings now erected with the most exaggerated details, utterly wanting in grace and proportion, rendered mainly attractive by the introduction of striped brickwork in imitation of coloured marbles, are the fruits of a fashion which appears to set aside all the sound canons of architecture, and gives reins to every kind of eccentric treatment which the young architect may choose to adopt ". Ferrey remained obstinately English : Scott was tempted to " eclecticism of a chastened kind, and to the union in some degree of the merits of the different styles ". He says that he never used Italian details, but that he gradually fell into a use of French detail in combination with English.

We may say that churches of this type were built approximately between 1855 and 1875. They are of various types and shapes, but they have in common a use of foreign styles

[1] Scott, *Recollections*, p. 210.

or the use of structural polychrome. At the same time, as we have said, many straightforward churches of a correct and more or less dull English type were still being erected.[1]

During these years Symbolism is not so prominent as it was, but, by some at any rate, it was not forgotten. A writer in the *Builder* (June 17, 1871) said, " We architects should infuse a symbolic spirit into the minutest details of all sanctuary work, even in the dimensions of the altar itself. I recommend my brother-architects in no case to carry out an altar less than 7 ft. 5 in. long (both symbolical numerals), and when possible to exceed this length to let the mystic number 5, so closely associated with altar ritual, determine *in the inches* the exact length of the slab."

When Edward White Benson was headmaster of Wellington, he took great interest in the building of the chapel, which was designed by Scott. Scott allowed him to do what he liked with regard to the sculptured foliage, and he worked it out as follows : " In the Antechapel are none but such plants as grow in wild or desert places, out of the Church—thorns, brambles, also the Fig and the Apple which are emblems of our Fall. Over the Archway is a Maple spray with the Joy of Loves therein. Within are rich and glorious plants— and in every window may be seen the significance of the plant in symbol of the subject of the window according to my list. In the Apse every capital has special relation to the window : *i.e.* to the Ascension, Evergreens, Water-lily (Baptism), Pomegranate (Heaven's Treasure), Maple (Power of Keys)." [2] But probably Benson was more interested in this than Scott.

It would hardly be possible in writing of nineteenth-century church architecture to say nothing of John Ruskin. We are not concerned with his political economy or with his

[1] There are at all periods of the nineteenth century a few curious churches which cannot be exactly classified. Gerrards Cross, for instance, which was consecrated in 1859, is of a somewhat non-ecclesiological type. It has a central dome, and was supposed to be " reminiscent of the monuments of Pisa ". Mr. Tite, M.P., was the architect.

[2] A. C. Benson, *The Life of Edward White Benson*, p. 172.

teaching on art in general; but we can hardly ignore what he wrote on the subject of architecture. He wrote with tremendous force and fervour, and he made many disciples.

He is often considered to have been the prophet of the Gothic Revival; but he was certainly nothing of the kind. He loved Gothic architecture, if it was pure and noble; but he first distrusted and finally disliked its revival. He despised Pugin, and scorned most of the other Gothic architects. He wrote in *Modern Painters* (Appendix III), " It is often said that I borrow from Pugin. I glanced at Pugin's Contrasts once, in the Oxford architectural reading room, during an idle afternoon. His ' Remarks on Architects in the *Rambler* ' were brought under my notice by some of the reviews. I never read a word of any other of his works, not feeling, from the style of his architecture, the smallest interest in his opinions."

Ruskin was not an ecclesiologist, and had nothing in common with the Camdenians. They were Anglican High Churchmen : he was a Protestant without sympathy for Catholicism, but with an uncomfortable leaning towards it at times which only led him to attack it more vehemently. The *Ecclesiologist*, reviewing *The Stones of Venice* in August 1851, said, " His speculations concerning questions of art lead him to one conclusion; his religious prejudices drive him to another, wholly irreconcilable. He cannot harmonize the two, nor part with either ; *Hinc illae lacrymae.* Idolizing, as he does, upon conviction, the Campanile of Giotto, or the Frari at Venice, he finds himself loathing the faith of the men who reared them ; while, tortured to the very soul by the architecture of the conventicle, and by that high appreciation of art always shown by the Puritan, he struggles against the conclusion that Protestantism is fairly symbolized by the material exhibition it pleases to make of itself. He cannot understand why Will Dowsing crusaded against art, nor why Wesleyanism, for example, has not enshrined itself in a Cologne, instead of in a Centenary Hall. We can imagine Mr. Ruskin living in constant fear lest, after all, Mr. Pugin should succeed in building a second Westminster Abbey : in constant disgust, that so sound a Protestant as Lord Shaftesbury should prefer a ' Lydian ' worship by the river side,[1] to a stately liturgy in one of those dark old churches of Verona, which no one loves more warmly, nor describes more feelingly, than Mr. Ruskin himself."

That is true : but whatever went on in his own mind, Ruskin succeeded in separating Gothic and Popery in the popular mind. He certainly might have been suspected of Romish leanings, for he spent much time in studying the Gothic of Italy ; but his violent anti-Roman diatribes satisfied even the British public of his soundness.

Eastlake says,[2] " When Mr. Ruskin first entered the lists as a champion of Gothic architecture, it was certainly not as a Ritualist or as an apologist for the Church of Rome. His introduction to *The Seven Lamps of Architecture* partook largely, as indeed much of his writing then did, of a religious tone, but he wrote rather as a moral philosopher than as a Churchman, and though his theological views found here and there decided expression, they could hardly be identified with any particular sect. His book, therefore, found favour with a large class of readers who had turned from Pugin's arguments with impatience, and to whom even the *Ecclesiologist* had preached in vain."

It is surprising that Ruskin should be so generally regarded as a leader of the Gothic Revival.[3] Some ecclesiologists laughed at him and parodied his style. Mr. Freeman spoke of his " unintelligible volumes ". The *Ecclesiologist* regarded him as an unorthodox ally. *The Seven Lamps of Architecture* was welcomed with " feelings of gratitude and admiration ".

The *Ecclesiologist* was delighted to find Mr. Ruskin, in *The Stones of Venice*, to be a " champion for the beauty, as well as the strict architectural propriety, of the Italian method of decoration by horizontal bands of colour ". But there is no suggestion that he suggested any ideas to them for the

[1] Acts xvi. 13.
[2] *Gothic Revival*, p. 266.
[3] The " influence of Ruskin " on nineteenth-century church building seems to be taken for granted. But it is time that it was questioned. John Betjeman's amusing book *Ghastly Good Taste* ends with a panoramic picture of typical buildings, including an obviously Camdenian church labelled " Influence of Ruskin ". But what would the Camdenians have said about that ?

first time. Indeed, the *Ecclesiologist* said the exact opposite. In December 1853 it said, " He has often been anticipated in many of the principles he lays down, and the arguments by which he enforces them ; and we do not think that his work would have been less influential, had its general readers been made to understand that the author did not stand quite alone, nor even foremost in point of time, in his onslaughts on many of the false principles of the day. . . . However, we have always been glad to welcome Mr. Ruskin as a fellow-labourer."

Most of Ruskin's doctrines were not original. We must believe him when he says that he did not borrow his ideas : no doubt they were to a great extent common property. But they must have originated from somewhere, and we cannot think that he was entirely uninfluenced by the ecclesiologists. Probably he encountered ecclesiological ideas, in their less symbolic Oxford form, at the University. In any case, he shared ideas with the ecclesiologists, though he sometimes followed them to conclusions of which no ecclesiologist could approve. Like them, he believed that " certain right states of temper and moral feeling were the magic powers by which all good architecture has been produced ". The difference came when it was asked, What states ? J. M. Neale and Benjamin Webb said, A Catholic state, inspired by a regular life of prayers and daily offices ; Ruskin said, A good life inspired by an undogmatic Protestant faith. Still, Ruskin and the revivalists agreed that some kind of satisfactory state of mind was necessary in the first place.

Ruskin was too sensitive a critic to find fault with everything in Classic architecture : he admired its sculpture and some of the details of Greek work. But he shared the general Victorian horror of the style as a whole, and his denunciation of the Renaissance was more shrill even than Pugin's. It was a Foul Torrent ; it was accursed. It uprooted the love of nature from the hearts of men, and its sign was not the Cross, but the Guillotine. It was base, unnatural, unfruitful, unenjoyable and impious, an architecture invented to make plagiarists of its architects, slaves of its workmen, and sybarites of its inhabitants. The very words connected with it are bad words. Pinnacle, Turret, Belfry, Spire and Tower are pleasant-sounding words, and the things for which they stand are pleasant things. But the words Pediment, Stylobate and Architrave excite no pleasurable feelings, because the things for which they stand are dead, lifeless and useless. So away with Classic architecture! The ecclesiologists of course agreed.

The Gothic revivalists believed in the imitation of Nature. The *Ecclesiologist* described the perfect church, whose capitals were flowers wanting only life to be equal to Nature's. Ruskin agreed, but he carried the principle to almost insane lengths. The pointed arch, he said, should be used because its form is one of those which, as we see from Nature, the Deity has appointed to be an everlasting source of pleasure to the human mind. Leaves are pointed, and they spring from their stalk exactly as a Gothic vault springs from its shaft. All beautiful lines are adaptations of those which are commonest in the external creation. Beyond a certain point, and that a very low one, man cannot advance in the invention of beauty without directly imitating natural form. All the most lovely forms are directly taken from natural objects.

There is beauty in all natural objects. All do not have it in the utmost degree; but absolute ugliness is admitted as rarely as perfect beauty. Ugliness in various degrees is associated with whatever has the nature of death and sin; just as beauty is associated with whatever has the nature of virtue and of life. What Nature does generally is more or less beautiful; what she does rarely is either *very* beautiful, or absolutely ugly. If the rare occurrence is the result of the complete fulfilment of Nature, the thing will be beautiful; if of the violation of Nature it will be ugly. Therefore, since leaves invariably terminate in pointed and not square ends, the pointed arch is one of the forms most fitted for perpetual contemplation by the human mind. (Of course, by Nature he means things that are visible, not those things which Nature keeps hidden—entrails, for instance, and strange minerals in the depth of the earth.) Forms not taken from natural objects must be ugly. The lions' heads in Greek

PLATE XXI

PRIVETT CHURCH
By Sir A. W. Blomfield

PLATE XXII

HOLY TRINITY, SLOANE STREET
By J. D. Sedding

ornament are not like the heads of real lions—which is
seriously harmful to our powers of perceiving truth or beauty
of any kind at any time. Something like the Greek fret is
certainly found in crystals of bismuth ; but that form is
unique among minerals, and is only attainable by an artificial process. Therefore it is not ornament, but monstri-
fication. But a certain ornament found in Lombardic architecture is beautiful because it resembles a crystal of common
salt. No one took this argument seriously. A portcullis
used as a decoration is a monster, absolutely and unmiti-
gatedly frightful ; scrolls are bad, because they are not,
after all, much like seaweed. Of course architectural ornament cannot be an exact imitation of Nature ; it must fall
short in three ways—conventionalism by cause of colour, by
cause of inferiority, and by cause of means. But, accepting
these limitations, we must agree that no work can be beautiful
which is not full of the beauty of Nature.

Colour, without which no building is complete, should
be if possible the colour of the natural stone. Otherwise,
buildings ought to be coloured as Nature would colour one
thing—a shell or a flower or an animal : not as she colours
groups of things. God always arranges colour in simple and
rude forms, and we must not try to refine His arrangements.
Perfect colour and perfect form will never be united : all
arrangements of colour for its own sake in graceful forms are
barbarous. We want simple masses of it—cloudings, flam-
ings, spots or bands, done as Nature does it.

This was the teaching of the ecclesiologists. They agreed
also with his Lamp of Sacrifice—that we should offer valuable
things for building, and build churches rather than expensive
and luxurious private houses.

" Mr. Ruskin," they said, " is acquainted with the true
spirit of a Christian architect, which despises the nicely
calculated less and more, and throws itself freely, generously
and faithfully into its work."

They certainly shared his belief in the Lamp of Truth—
which means that shams should not be used in architecture.
This is pure Pugin. Structural deceit is the suggestion of a
mode of structure or support other than the true one. A

building will be noblest which discloses its structure.[1] Iron must not be used as a support (though it may be used as a cement). Surface deceit means the painting of wood to resemble marble, or anything of that kind. Painting confessedly such is no deception; but if the thing painted may be supposed to be real, it is. " In our cheap modern churches, we suffer the wall decorator to erect about the altar frameworks and pediments daubed with mottled colour, and to dye in the same fashion such skeletons or caricatures of columns as may emerge above the pews." But church furniture should be neither fictitious nor tawdry. " It may not be within our power to make it beautiful, but let it be at least pure." " The smoothly stuccoed walls, the flat roofs with ventilator ornaments, the barred windows with jaundiced borders and dead-ground square panes, the gilded or bronzed wood, the painted iron, the wretched upholstery of curtains and cushions, and pew-heads, and altar railings, and Birmingham metal candlesticks, and, above all, the green-and-yellow sickness of the false marble—disguises all, observe; falsehoods all—who are they who like these things? Who defend them? Who do them? "[2]

Whitewash is not a falsity, nor is gilding, though it ought to be used in moderation. But what of the facing of brick with precious stone? Ruskin is somewhat embarrassed about that; but he defends it by saying that it may be done if we understand that the marble facing does not pretend to be a marble wall. And sometimes the stone is too rare to be used for a complete wall. The facing may be held to be mosaic on a large scale. Operative deceit means the substitu-

---

[1] In this respect there is a difference between Pugin and Ruskin. Pugin believed that a building which showed its construction must be beautiful. But Ruskin would not allow that honest construction and good building constituted architecture: there is, he said, no architecture without ornament. Without ornament there are simply dead walls: they are made to live by the addition of unnecessary features, and by painting and sculpture. A great architect must be a great sculptor or painter, otherwise he will be nothing but a builder. Pugin said that construction was all-important; but his love of Gothic ornament and his skill in producing it seem to show that he really agreed with Ruskin. He would hardly have admitted that a rectangular concrete building without a trace of Gothic detail was true architecture.
[2] *Seven Lamps of Architecture* (1880 edition), p. 87.

tion of cast or machine work for that of the hand. Ornament
has two sources of agreeableness : the abstract beauty of its
forms, and the sense of human labour and care spent on it.
That does not exist in machine-made ornament. It may
look exactly the same as hand work, but it is simply a lie.
" Down with it to the ground, grind it to powder, leave its
rugged place upon the wall, rather; you have not paid for
it, you have no business with it, you do not want it ; nobody
wants ornaments in this world, but everyone wants integrity." [1]
Cast brick may be used because everyone knows that it is
not cut. But cast iron has degraded our national feeling for
beauty.

But there are even more subtle forms of deception—
deceptions of impressions and ideas only—such as the inter-
secting mouldings of late Gothic. Such deception is seen
in the development of tracery. To begin with, the eye of
the architect was on the openings only. But when the
shape of the openings had received the last possible expan-
sion, architects began to think of the stonework, and the
intervening spaces were forgotten. Tracery should never
be considered flexible ; but it was ; and in that it sacrificed
a great principle of truth. It sacrificed the expression of
the qualities of the material. The next step was to consider
tracery as not only ductile, but penetrable. In the early
days mouldings melted into each other. Later, they began
to intersect. And at last Gothic architecture fell. It could
not rise out of the ruins of violated truth.

Ruskin's Lamp of Obedience is altogether Camdenian.
He denies that there is such a thing as Liberty : it does not
exist, in architecture or anywhere else. The architecture of
a nation is great only when it is as universal and as established as its language. " A day never passes without our
hearing our English architects called upon to be original, and
to invent a new style : about as sensible and necessary an
exhortation as to ask of a man who has never had rags enough
on his back to keep out cold, to invent a new mode of cutting
a coat. Give him a whole coat first, and let him concern
himself about the fashion of it afterwards. We want no new

[1] *Seven Lamps of Architecture* (1880), p. 97.

style of architecture. Who wants a new style of painting or sculpture ? But we want some style." [1] A universal system of form and workmanship ought to be everywhere adopted and enforced. " It may be said that this is impossible. It may be so—I fear it is so : I have nothing to do with the possibility or impossibility of it ; I simply know and assert the necessity of it. If it be impossible, English art is impossible. Give it up at once." [2]

The universal style should be one of four : either Pisan Romanesque, or Early Gothic of the Western Italian Republics, or the Venetian Gothic in its purest development, or the English earliest Decorated. Probably the last is the best, but it must be well fenced from the chance of again stiffening into the Perpendicular, and it might be enriched by some mingling of decorative elements from the exquisite decorated Gothic of France. The early ecclesiologists could not approve of the first three suggestions : the rest was their own doctrine.

But in two ways Ruskin differed wholly from the ecclesiologists. In the first place, he was a pessimist. He sometimes showed enthusiasm for a modern building, but it seldom lasted long. He hoped for great things from the Museum at Oxford ; but in the end he hated it. The ecclesiologists were optimists, and very sure of themselves. They were certain that good architecture was possible, and confident on the whole that they were producing it. But Ruskin came to despair of contemporary architecture altogether. In *The Seven Lamps of Architecture* he wrote, " The stirring which has taken place in our architectural aims and interests within these few years, is thought by many to be full of promise : and I trust it is, but it has a sickly look to me." In the 1880 edition he commented on these words in a footnote : " I am glad to see I had so much sense, thus early ;—if only I had had just a little more, and stopped talking, how much life—of the vividest—I might have saved from expending itself in useless sputter, and kept for careful pencil work ! I might have had every bit of St. Mark's and Ravenna drawn by this time. What good this wretched rant of a book can do still, since people ask for it,

[1] *Seven Lamps of Architecture* (1880), p. 368.   [2] *Ibid.*, p. 374.

let them make of it ; and *I* don't see what it's to be. The only living art now left in England is Bill-sticking."

The other matter in which they differed without possibility of agreement was the question of restoration. The ecclesiologists loved restoration : it was a natural result of their principles. The Gothic style had been gloriously revived in their time : now that they understood it, it was inevitable that they should remove what was bad or indifferent and substitute what was good or better. After all, they could build good Gothic : did they not study the purest examples, and were they not men of upright and Catholic life ? To remove post-Reformation work or fifteenth-century work— to remove, if it had been possible, the whole of Peterborough Cathedral [1]—and to substitute work of the best period was their vocation.

But to Ruskin restoration of any kind seemed wicked. A building, he said, does not get into its prime until four or five centuries have passed ; and the entire choice and arrangement of its details should have reference to their appearance after that period. But what was happening to the buildings which had become mature with age ? He said of *The Seven Lamps* in 1880, " I never intended to have republished this book, which has become the most useless I ever wrote ; the buildings which it describes with so much delight being now either knocked down, or scraped and patched up into smugness and smoothness more tragic than uttermost ruin ". Restoration so called is the worst manner of destruction. " It means the most total destruction which a building can suffer : a destruction out of which no remnants can be gathered : a destruction accompanied with false description of the thing destroyed. Do not let us deceive ourselves in this important matter ; it is *impossible*, as impossible as to raise the dead, to restore anything that has ever been great or beautiful in architecture. That which I have above insisted upon as the life of the whole, that spirit which is given only by the hand and eye of the workman, can never be recalled." [2] " Do not let us talk then of restoration. The thing is a lie from beginning to end. You may make a

[1] See p. 235. [2] *Seven Lamps of Architecture* (1880), pp. 353-354.

model of a building as you may of a corpse, and your model may have the shell of the old walls within it as your cast might have the skeleton, with what advantage I neither see nor care : but the old building is destroyed, and that more totally and mercilessly than if it had sunk into a heap of dust, or melted into a mass of clay." [1]

Take care of buildings ; or set up new buildings in the place of the old. But we have no right to restore them. They are not ours to touch. "What we have ourselves built, we are at liberty to throw down ; but what other men gave their strength and wealth and life to accomplish their right over does not pass away with their death."

The *Ecclesiologist* replied, mildly enough, "We are not *artists* only : we have a duty to consult, the comeliness and decency of GOD's house, and this we must harmonize, as well as we can, with a reverent regard for the fabrics considered only as monuments of art".

Ruskin is remembered by many chiefly as the man who first called attention to the Gothic of Italy. *The Stones of Venice* was published in 1851–53 ; and in all his works Italian Gothic is regarded as good Gothic. This was a novelty. Eastlake says,[2] "Up to this time English architects, whether of the Gothic or Classic school, had regarded such buildings as the Doge's Palace at Venice, or the Church of San Michele at Lucca, as curious examples of degenerate design—interesting indeed as links in the history of European art, but utterly unworthy of study or imitation. It was, therefore, with some surprise that they found features from those buildings engraved in *The Seven Lamps* as instances of noble carving and judicious ornamentation." But Ruskin was convincing. "That he made many converts, and found many disciples among the younger architects of the day, is not to be wondered. Students, who but a year or so previously had been content to regard Pugin as their leader, or who had modelled their notions of art on the precepts of the *Ecclesiologist*, found a new field open to them, and hastened to occupy it. They prepared designs in which the elements of

---

[1] *Seven Lamps of Architecture* (1880), pp. 355–356.
[2] *Gothic Revival*, p. 267.

Italian Gothic were largely introduced; churches in which the 'lily capital' of St. Mark's was found side by side with Byzantine bas-reliefs and mural inlay from Murano; town halls wherein the arcuation and baseless columns of the Ducal Palace were reproduced; mansions which borrowed their parapets from the Calle del Bagatin and windows from the Ca' d'Oro. They astonished their masters by talking of the Savageness of Northern Gothic, of the Intemperance of Curves, and the Laws of Foliation; and broke out into open heresy in their abuse of Renaissance detail. They went to Venice or Verona—not to study the works of Sansovino and San Michele—but to sketch the tomb of the Scaligers and to measure the front of the Hotel Danieli. They made drawings in the Zoological Gardens, and conventionalized the forms of birds, beasts, and reptiles into examples of ' noble grotesque ' for decorative sculpture. They read papers before Architectural Societies, embodying Mr. Ruskin's sentiments in language which rivalled the force, if it did not exactly match the refinement, of their model. They made friends of the Pre-Raphaelite painters (then rising into fame), and promised themselves as radical a reform in national architecture as had been inaugurated in the field of pictorial art. Nor was this all. Not a few architects who had already established a practice began to think that there might be something worthy of attention in the new doctrine. Little by little they fell under its influence. Discs of marble, billet-mouldings, and other details of Italian Gothic, crept into many a London street-front. Then bands of coloured brick (chiefly red and yellow) were introduced, and the voussoirs of arches were treated after the same fashion." [1]

But there is no sign in the ecclesiological literature of the time that Ruskin had any particular influence on church-building. His influence on domestic and civil architecture was obvious and regrettable. Most towns have some more or less repulsive specimens of Italian Gothic villas or shops, or libraries or museums. Ruskin wrote in 1872, " I have had indirect influence on nearly every cheap villa-builder between this and Bromley ; and there is scarcely a public-

[1] *Gothic Revival*, pp. 278–279.

house near the Crystal Palace but sells its gin and bitters under pseudo-Venetian capitals copied from the church of the Madonna of Health or of Miracles. And one of my principal notions for leaving my present house is that it is surrounded everywhere by the accursed Frankenstein monsters of, indirectly, my own making."

But as Eastlake himself says, " The general aspect of ecclesiastical architecture was for some time scarcely, if at all, affected by the new doctrines of taste ".[1] Italian influence came, along with French and other foreign influences : but if we had to name any one man who was responsible, we should probably say not Ruskin, but Street.

George Edmund Street was born in 1824. He intended at first to take orders, but changed his mind, and in 1844 entered the office of Scott and Moffatt. His first church was that of Par, Cornwall, his next was that of Sticker, and he was responsible for the restoration of several old Cornish churches. He became a member of the Ecclesiological Society, was connected with Butler of Wantage, and in 1850 settled in Wantage and became diocesan architect of Oxford. He attended church regularly and sang in the choir. He made his first foreign tour (in France) in 1850, and travelled in Germany in 1851. Then he moved to Oxford. In 1853 he began the Theological College at Cuddesdon. This was considered to be a good work : Eastlake says that it is impossible to mistake the genuine *cachet* on the design : it is the production of an artist hand. It is certainly not without picturesqueness ; but no one who has lived in it could call it a convenient building. The *Ecclesiologist* remarked that if there were a death in the College—*absit omen*—it would be difficult to carry out the coffin.

In the same year Street visited Italy, and made the studies that were published in *Brick and Marble Architecture of North Italy* (1855). Then he revisited Germany, and in 1855 moved to London.

He entered for the Lille Cathedral competition and was placed second ; he entered for the Crimea Memorial Church competition and eventually obtained the work ; he entered

[1] *Gothic Revival*, p. 289.

for the Government Offices competition and was awarded a premium. In 1857 he revisited Italy, and then France again. St. James the Less, Westminster, was begun in 1858 and consecrated in 1861. It was built and endowed by the Misses Monk in memory of their father, Dr. J. H. Monk, Canon of Westminster and afterwards Bishop of Gloucester. The style is Italian Gothic, and there is plenty of constructive coloration. Externally it is of red and black brick with bands of Morpeth stone, voussoirs of coloured bricks and marble shafts. The *British Almanac and Companion* for 1864 no doubt had this kind of church in mind when it complained that " irregularity of outline seems now to be the guiding principle in designing a church, symmetry and simplicity the abiding terror of the Church architect. To avoid these, he will snip up the outside of his church into as many odd peaks and projections, and decorate it with as many ' bands ', lines and dubious ornaments, as though he were a Nuremberg toy-maker." Mr. A. E. Street says that in this church we see his father's " strong and masterful imagination not as yet adequately restrained by a sense of purity and beauty of form ".[1] Eastlake says that " there is something to regret in the restless notching of edges, the dazzling distribution of stripes, the multiplicity of pattern forms, and exuberance of sculptured detail. But it is all so clever and so facile, so evidently the invention of a man who enjoys his work . . . that it is impossible but to regard it with pleasure." [2]

St. Paul's, Herne Hill, was rebuilt by Street after a fire in 1858. It was declared by Ruskin to be " one of the loveliest churches of the kind in the country ".

All Saints', Clifton, was begun in 1863. It is chiefly remarkable for its wide nave with passage aisles, into which open the two aisles of the chancel. Mr. Bernard Miller says, " I consider this a very imaginative design, in spite of the fact that there are few to-day who would welcome a return to Street and Butterfield's ' streaky-bacon style '. This is not altogether ' imitation ' Gothic, but shows great powers of adaptation." [3]

[1] A. E. Street, *Memoir of George Edmund Street*, p. 37.
[2] *Gothic Revival*, p. 321.
[3] *Church Quarterly Review*, July–September 1936.

L

St. Mary Magdalene, Paddington, was begun in 1867 and built gradually : it was damaged by fire in 1872, but completed in 1873. The site was constricted and curiously shaped, for " an enemy of the Catholic Faith " bought the land between the site and the Grand Junction Canal, so that a north aisle was impossible. " The lopsided arrangement, which the division of men and women must always demand so long as the churchgoers among the latter predominate so greatly in numbers, is turned to valuable account." [1] The north side has the narrowest of passage aisles ; the arcade has two subsidiary arches beneath each main one. The apsidal chancel is vaulted. The details are partly English, partly Italian.

St. John the Divine, Kennington, begun in 1870 and consecrated in 1874, is of brick, with a wide, unclerestoried nave attached to the chancel by a canted bay—a plan which is also to be seen at SS. Philip and James's, Oxford, and St. Saviour's, Eastbourne. Street's apses are seldom very satisfactory ; at St. John's the small effect that it has is lessened by the enormous reredos designed by Bodley and Garner.

Other churches by Street are St. Peter's, Bournemouth, St. John's, Torquay, Boyne Hill (Maidenhead), Kingstone (Dorset), Wansford and Howsham.

He made three tours in Spain in successive years—1861, 1862 and 1863—and produced a book in 1865 which may fairly claim to rank as the standard work on the Church architecture of Spain. During his whole life he was a keen Churchman ; he was on the Council of the English Church Union, and churchwarden of All Saints', Margaret Street. During his wardenship he insisted on the segregation of the sexes, and kept the ladies of the congregation to their own seats. This resulted in a greater attendance of men. He was always present at the early celebrations on saints' days. He was an adherent of the pre-Raphaelite movement, and made a collection of pictures, modern and early Italian. Appreciation of Fra Angelico was made the test of his own moral state.

He became an associate of the Royal Academy, and entered

[1] *Memoir of George Edmund Street*, p. 110.

the competition for the enlargement of the National Gallery—
which came to nothing. Other important works were the
restoration—which practically amounted to a rebuilding—of
Christchurch, Dublin, and of Kildare Cathedral; and the
rebuilding of the nave of Bristol Cathedral. He entered for
the competition for the Episcopal Cathedral at Edinburgh,
but was beaten by Scott. But he was able to beat Scott in
the matter of the Law Courts, and produced a conscientious
and dignified building. Towards the end of his life he
settled in Surrey, and built the attractive church of Holmbury
St. Mary, which was begun in 1878. He died in 1881.

Street was a religious man, and believed firmly in the
connexion between architecture and religion. In his early
days he even wished to form a college for instruction in
art of which the members should keep a religious rule. He
regarded the phases of Gothic architecture as reflections of
the spiritual life of the Church. It was Christian architecture, and could never be developed properly except by an
essentially Christian intention on the part of the architect as
well as on the part of his employers. He believed in symbolism, and loved truthfulness in architecture; but he was
able to hold these articles of the ecclesiological creed without
developing them to the point of absurdity. Scott is said to
have mistaken one of Street's churches for a fourteenth-
century one, " simply from the presence of that subtle quality
which I have attributed to the spirit which animated him in
his work ".

He regarded Gothic as the most beautiful and useful style,
full of truthfulness, abnegation of self and consistency. But
he was not a fanatic. He " yielded to none in his respect for
the domestic work of the eighteenth century ";[1] and he
loved Rome. " Goth as he delighted to call himself, ancient
Rome held him spellbound; the indefinable attractiveness of
the city, born partly of its associations, and partly of what
it offers to the eye, of humanity as well as of brick and stone,
made itself felt hardly less strongly in him than in the student
whose heart is wrapped up in the Rome of the past."[2]

[1] A. E. Street, *Memoir of George Edmund Street*, p. 115.
[2] *Ibid.*, p. 209.

His earliest work is definitely English ; before long he began to use foreign features, French or Italian.   But he preferred English Gothic to Italian, and tried to adhere to local styles. He always retained a fondness for First Pointed, though he admired it " less for its beauty of form than for its moral attributes and for the rightness of its principles ".   Elaborate line traceries he considered to be wrong in principle.   He thought that the deterioration of Gothic was due to the fact that at first the architect in chief had supreme control and influence which he afterwards lost.   He was deeply attached to this idea of an architect who designed or inspired every detail of a great design : " it was part of his enthusiastic creed that every architect should be, in his degree, as Giotto was or Michael Angelo, and should himself be able to decorate his own building with painting and sculpture."   He could not put it into practice owing to too much work.   But he maintained that " such a way of working could alone give a perfect unity of conception entirely harmonious in all its details ".[1]   This he believed to have been carried out in the early Gothic works.   But he refused to believe the doctrine of the spirituality of the workmen of the Middle Ages. Speaking of Christchurch, Dublin, he said, " The workmen absolved themselves from all responsibility, worked the stones they were ordered to work, and ate their meals between times with the same absolute *sangfroid* that marks their successors at the present day.   They had no more pleasure in their work, no more originality in their way of doing it, than our workmen have at the present time, all the pretty fables to the contrary notwithstanding." [2]

In all his designs he aimed at producing churches that could be used.   Churches were to be made for people, not people for churches.   A church ought to be free and open, efficiently run, and used by everyone, poor as well as rich, and men as well as women.   He believed that a town church should not be like a village church, nor should it be an exact copy of an ancient town church.   The old plan should be modified.   Wide aisles were a hindrance to congregational

[1] A. E. Street, *Memoir of George Edmund Street*, pp. 13–14.
[2] *Ibid.*, p. 117.

worship : the arcade ought to be kept as an architectural feature, but the aisles could be reduced to the width of passages, and the nave made broader. The altar should be raised on steps, so as to be prominent and visible. If there were a chancel it should be divided from the nave only by a light screen ; but he was willing to dispense with the chancel altogether and to place the choir in the nave.

His churches all have some character. The early ones " have an excess of boldness or bluntness, a tinge of eccentricity, a truthfulness in displaying construction, which is too much like that of a candid friend. But if excuse is wanted, it will be found in the intention with which such work was done. It was the strongest form of protest against that dull and meaningless symmetry which had long been the leading character of church architecture before the Revival, and if my father laid himself open to the charge of exaggeration, he did so in good company. The feeling which moved him and others had its exact counterpart in that which then actuated the pre-Raphaelite painters. The same exaggeration is visible in their drawings ; but we forgive it and welcome it because of the purity and loftiness of the conceptions with which it was associated and the great results which it achieved." [1]

Street's taste is not ours ; but we can see that his churches are the product of a strong mind with definite beliefs and whole-hearted convictions.

It has been said that " Street grated upon some people, and was what some of his more sensitive contemporaries called a ' robustious male ', and had besides a flourishing practice ". " So he, duly ballasted with the specifications, bills of quantities, contracts, and the innumerable mundanities of his profession, did not suffer as did poor Ruskin from that Victorian cleavage between a theory of art growing progressively more lyrical and unearthly, and a theory of economics growing more and more utilitarian. Street ran his practice in the old Palladian way. He did not carry his Gothicism so far as to imitate the master-mason methods of the guilds, and so when he died in middle age—a man still full of vigour— it is said that he had about sixty buildings on hand. Here

[1] A. E. Street, *Memoir of George Edmund Street*, p. 104.

was certainly no man of the world, no logician, and—with all his uncanny skill in dating Gothic edifices—at most half a critic, and yet how brave a figure he makes in his epoch. He had the skill to enjoy two worlds. He was, on the one hand, the successful, competent, active professional man, and, on the other, the revered ' ecclesiologist ', the admired of the apostles of ethical architecture, and an archaeologist of European reputation. We find in him again a clinging for the intimate contacts of life to those who presented themselves, rather than to friends of his own choice. His mother and his brother were his first friends. When his first wife died, the circle was disturbed as little as might be, for he married her intimate friend. In later life it was in his son that he confided. The elements of subtlety and adventure which might have been lacking in a circle so wholly domestic he found in his religion." [1]

The churches of William Burges are all of a Continental type. Burges, who was born in 1827 and died in 1881, entered the office of Blore in 1844, and in 1849 that of Digby Wyatt. He visited Normandy, Belgium, Germany and Italy, and acquired a taste for foreign Gothic. His Gothic tastes were most robust, and he expressed a wish to make " that old wretch, Sir Christopher Wren, turn in his grave ". He probably succeeded. He was ready, towards the end of his life, to speak well of Greek architecture ; he said that he could respect it, or even Roman architecture. " But what was usually meant by ' Classic ' was the vilest Renaissance of George III's time. . . . As to working in two styles, a man could never work in two styles equally well. Eclecticism, whether in architecture or language, would only result in a farrago." So Burges " imbued his sensitive and poetical mind in mediaeval lore ", and almost always expressed himself in the style which appealed to him most—French Gothic of the early thirteenth century. He was a thoroughgoing mediaevalist—at least, he loved to play the part. " Architecture to Burges was play-acting—and yet he was earnest and thorough, a real make-believer, although the idea of

[1] C. and A. Williams-Ellis, *The Pleasures of Architecture*, pp. 141–142.

being a mediaeval jester must have occurred to his quick mind." [1] In 1852 Burges designed a Cathedral for Brisbane, which was never built.[2] Working with Henry Clutton, he obtained in 1856 the first award in the competition for Lille Cathedral, with a set of designs so mediaeval in appearance that they were imagined by some to be the work of an architect of the Middle Ages recently discovered. M. Didron, the French ecclesiologist, said, " England has indeed triumphed. . . . The defeat is for us and on our own soil : at Lille the architecture and archaeology of France have met with their Agincourt."

But Burges was not allowed to erect his own work. There were two possible sources of money for the undertaking : the subscriptions of the faithful and a State lottery. But it was thought that the faithful would not subscribe for the erection of a design by non-Romans, nor the general public for a design by Englishmen. And the design itself was unpopular. So the plans were placed in the hands of three Frenchmen, M. Leroy, l'Abbé Godfroy and Père Martin, who altered and enlarged them. The cathedral has not been completed. In 1857 he obtained the first premium in the competition for the Memorial Church at Constantinople, and in the same year he restored with Clutton the chapter house of Salisbury Cathedral, and in 1860 restored Waltham Abbey, for which he provided a new east end. He wished to rebuild the apsidal choir on the old foundations, but money was not forthcoming. This work is incongruous, but surprisingly effective.

In 1862 Burges prepared the designs for the Cathedral of St. Finbar at Cork, in the early French style. The foundation stone was laid in 1865, the cathedral was consecrated in 1870, and the towers and spires were completed in 1876. It was much admired by contemporaries. " In unity of design," it was said, " it excels all modern edifices ; and as the stonework has already been toned down by the smoke, it might easily be taken for a building by one of the best French architects of the thirteenth century transported to its present

[1] W. R. Lethaby, *Philip Webb and his Work*, pp. 72–73.
[2] The fate of rather a large number of his designs.

site." [1]   It is still admired locally; but in spite of its idiomatic French mediaeval detail, it is obviously Victorian. Surely no one could ever really have seen no difference between it and Chartres.

Burges rebuilt Cardiff Castle, and altered Worcester College, Oxford; his designs for the Law Courts and for the decoration of St. Paul's were not accepted. He was a Fellow of the R.I.B.A., and was elected a few months before his death an associate of the Royal Academy. In 1870 he published a volume of his designs. In 1875 he began his house in Melbury Road, which was a kind of architectural shrine, illustrating his artistic ideas, and filled with a large collection of objects, new and old. [2]

His buildings are said to have been characterized by " force and massiveness of general style and composition, combined with great picturesqueness of detail ". It is said of him, as it is said of most of his contemporaries, that he hated shams. Eastlake says [3] that " Mr. Burges has done much to dissipate the frivolous extravagance of detail and wilful irregularities of plan which first found favour with those younger architects who for a while mistook licence for freedom of design ". But Studley Royal Church, begun in 1871, is most extravagant. It has been said that " in its construction no expense has been spared; and so far as general design and richness of ornamentation are considered, it is one of the most perfect churches in the kingdom ".

The chancel walls are internally of alabaster; the shafts are of green, red and black marble. In the floor are depicted the principal buildings of Jerusalem; the pavement of the sanctuary represents the Garden of Eden, and has branches and flowers, an embattled wall with an angel at the gate, and the four rivers, Gihon, Pison, Tigris and Euphrates, flowing from vases held by figures at the angles. The cost of the whole church was about £50,000. The neighbouring church

---

[1] *Architectural Designs of William Burges, A.R.A.*, ed. R. P. Pullan.
[2] Burges remained a bachelor: " but in designing his house he bore in mind the possibility of his entering the ranks of matrimony, and provided Day and Night Nurseries, suitably decorated for the delectation of a family *in posse* ".
[3] *Gothic Revival*, p. 354.

PLATE XXIII

[*Photograph by W. A. Clark.*]

ST. ALBAN'S, BIRMINGHAM

By J. L. Pearson

ST. PETER'S, VAUXHALL

By J. L. Pearson

PLATE XXIV

ST. MICHAEL'S, CROYDON

Pearson's completed design

ST. MICHAEL'S, CROYDON

By J. L. Pearson

of Skelton in the same style is also the work of Burges. St. Faith's, Stoke Newington, which was partly finished by 1873, and completed after the death of Burges by James Brooks, is quite impressive though rather ponderous. It has low passage aisles constructed inside the building with galleries above, a barrel roof and an eastern apse, and is lit by enormously wide lancets.

The enlargement of St. Michael's, Brighton, by Bodley, was designed by Burges in 1868, and carried out in 1893, after his death. It is one of the best of his designs. Other churches by Burges are Fleet and Lowfield Heath.

The churches of James Brooks [1] (1825–1901) are on a higher level than those of Burges. He used French detail, but with common sense; and they are simple and solid, and without the fussiness which makes many of the churches of the period so unattractive. They show to some extent the influence of Butterfield. Brooks was certainly one of the builders, not one of the competition-winners, and his churches have dignity and power. His point of view was not archaeological: he was trying to build nineteenth-century town churches. His style was generally rather early thirteenth century (the handsome Perpendicular church of St. Mary, Hornsey, is an exception); but he interpreted it with freedom and removed unnecessary features. He did not indulge in elaborate foliated capitals, or abuse the gift of coloured marbles. He generally used brick, and his churches are sensible, restrained and usually planned for what was called an advanced ritual.

Robert Brett and Richard Foster were his patrons in his East London churches of St. Saviour's, Hoxton; St. Columba's and St. Chad's, Haggerston. Details of these churches were criticized when they were built; but they were recognized as successful efforts in town church planning.

St. Saviour's (consecrated in 1866) is a parallelogram with an eastern apse, with one line of roof and no chancel arch. The apse has thirteen lancets; the tall clerestory has lancets

---

[1] Some of Brooks's churches were built later in the century; but some account of him seems to belong more naturally to this point than to a later.

alternating with pairs of smaller lancets surmounted by a circle. The aisles are low.

St. Columba's (consecrated in 1869) has an impressive nave with a north-west transept groined in brick, a groined base of central tower forming a choir, quasi transepts and a square-ended sanctuary groined with a brick vault. There are no buttresses and no windows in the aisles. The arches are moulded in brick.

St. Chad's is another imposing brick church, with a western narthex, no aisle windows, quasi transepts, and a chancel of two bays with an apse. I have not been able to get inside; but I understand that the apse and north chapel are groined, and that the nave is ceiled, the roof being carried past the transept arches.

The Annunciation, Chislehurst, has a nave with narrow aisles, thick walls and very large cylindrical piers. Over the arcade is a plain space of wall divided into bays by a stone rib. This is an impressive church.

St. Andrew's, Plaistow, is of somewhat similar type, but with clustered piers and foliated capitals. The sanctuary is apsidal.

St. John the Baptist, Holland Road, Kensington, was built in 1877–1888; the nave and transepts were completed in 1891. It was designed for a tower surmounted by an octagonal stone spire, but this was not carried out. The west end (1911) is by another hand: it has been called " dismal and incoherent ".

The noble church of All Hallows', Gospel Oak (1894–1895), has nave and aisles under separately gabled roofs with a circular window at the west. The ribs of the vault (which is not yet completed) die away into the columns. The chancel (the vault of which is finished) is of three bays, its north aisle is of two stories; the south aisle is carried up without a floor.

Other churches by Brooks are Holy Innocents', Hammersmith; St. Michael's, Shoreditch; The Transfiguration, Lewisham; St. Andrew's, Willesden Green; All Saints', Southend; St. Peter's, St. Leonards; All Saints', Ipswich; Charlton (Dover); St. Michael's, Coppenhall; St. Luke's, Enfield; and All Saints', Perry Street, Northfleet.

Brooks was followed by a number of architects who designed churches more or less of the type that he had introduced : of brick, and " muscular ", with an elimination of pedantic details which were not required. Some of the churches of J. E. K. and J. P. Cutts are fairly successful efforts in this style.

Some of the architects of this time produced extraordinary eclectic buildings. William White (1825–1900) [1] designed All Saints', Notting Hill—a curious church. It is said to have been suggested by the Church of St. Columb Major, but is nothing like it. The western tower, which was intended to be surmounted by a spire, is unlike anything else which the Gothic Revival produced. There is a great deal of constructive coloration : the lower part of the walls internally is lined with black, red and buff tiles, and bricks in courses. There is inlaid work in the heads of the clerestory windows : an arrangement of gold, red and blue circles and triangles, and on the inside flowers with green stems.

The same architect is responsible for Lyndhurst Church, Hants, which was begun in 1858 on the site of an older building. It is large and exceedingly polychromatic, with naturalistic foliage on the capitals. The chancel has a painting by Leighton. The *Ecclesiologist* regretted to see " a thoughtful design spoiled by an affectation of originality ".

St. Stephen's, Hampstead, by Mr. S. S. Teulon, has many details that resemble nothing Gothic. A contemporary description said that the tower surpasses in ugliness even the worst native French examples. But the interior is not unimpressive.

Huntley Church, Glos., was rebuilt with the exception of its tower by Mr. Teulon in 1863. It has striped walls, marble shafts, capitals carved with every possible variety of naturalistic foliage, medallions of the four evangelists in the spandrels of the arches, alabaster pulpit, and many other expensive and unbeautiful things.

[1] Some of White's other churches, such as St. Saviour's, Aberdeen Park, Highbury, and St. Mark's, Battersea Rise, and the other churches which he built at Battersea for Canon Erskine Clarke, are reasonably good, with solid brickwork, and some restraint in the design. A short biography of White, with a list of some of his churches, will be found in the Appendix.

St. Andrew's, Lambeth, was admired by the *Ecclesiologist* (December 1856). " Inside, the changes are made with red and white brick. In the nave each spandril contains, in red brick, a circle bearing the pentalpha ; while the entire chancel wall, east end as well as side, is a chequered diaper of red brick, on the white ground. The effect is rich. . . . The most elaborate brick *instrumentum* in the chancel is the reredos ; which is composed of seven trefoiled arches, borne upon circular shafts of serpentine, with circles of the same in the spandrils, and a bold, projecting cornice above, set with a band of encaustic tiles, bearing monograms and crosses. This combination of brick with a rare species of stone deserves credit for its boldness. Polished as it now is by steam, serpentine can, and we hope will, come into extensive use."

Other works of Mr. Teulon are St. Thomas', Agar Town, and Holy Trinity, Hastings.

Some of the works of the lesser architects are indeed painful.

It is perhaps just worth mentioning the works of Mr. Bassett Keeling—St. Paul's, Upper Penge ; St. Andrew's, Peckham ; St. George's, Campden Hill (Kensington) ; St. Mark's, Notting Dale, etc. Most of them are a caricature of everything that was worst in the foreign Gothic craze. This is St. Mark's, Notting Dale : " The church is built of ordinary yellow stock brick with black bands ; the arches are of bluish-black and white bricks. The ugly angular flying buttresses are of the like magpie polychromy. The walls of the interior are also of many-coloured bricks. The nave arcades and clerestory are borne on cast-iron columns with wrought iron capitals."

The design was presented for the inspection of the Ecclesiological Society, but the style was not such as the committee could sanction. The church has been somewhat improved in recent years.

St. Mark's, Dalston, was designed by Mr. Chester Cheston ; but it is in the true Bassett Keeling style.

A large number of dull churches were built by Ewan Christian (1814–1895). Christian was first articled to Matthew Habershon (see Appendix), and was afterwards with Mr. Brown of Norwich and with Railton. He travelled abroad in 1841–1842, and in 1842 set up business on his own account. His first church was at Hildenborough, near Tonbridge—not a very distinguished effort. In 1847 he competed for the restoration of Scarborough Parish Church, and was appointed architect, and in 1850 he obtained the work of restoring St. Peter's, Wolverhampton. He was architect to the Ecclesiastical Commissioners from 1850, one of the architects of the Church Building Society, consulting architect to the Charity Commissioners from 1887, and P.R.I.B.A. from 1884 to 1886.

" His life was one of quiet domestic happiness, and ceaseless labour—labour, however, which he supremely enjoyed, and which brought him a well-deserved reward of wealth sufficient for his wants and his liberality, of reputation, honourable position, and the esteem of valued friends." [1] He was a Churchman of Evangelical outlook, a regular worshipper at St. John's Episcopal Chapel, Downshire Hill, and superintendent of the Sunday School.

None of his churches rises above mediocrity : they are said to be " distinguished more for quietness and repose than for architectural effect ". " His hatred of shams in architecture was proverbial."

His original efforts include the following : St. Luke's, Nutford Place (Marylebone); All Saints', Bromley by Bow; St. Benet's, Stepney; St. Paul's, Clerkenwell; St. Mary's, Hoxton; Holy Trinity, Dalston; St. Thomas', Finsbury Park; St. Stephen's, Spitalfields; Little Amwell; St. Mark's, Leicester; St. John's, Kenilworth; St. Peter's, Rochester; St. Mary's, Carlisle; Holy Trinity, Scarborough; Christchurch, Winchester; Hamsey; St. James's, Tunbridge Wells; Holy Trinity, Folkestone; Christchurch, Weymouth; St. Matthew's, Cheltenham; St. Antholin's, Nunhead; St. Stephen's, Upper Holloway; St. Barnabas', Kentish Town; St. Dionis', Fulham; St. Peter's, Limehouse; St. Paul's, Longridge; and St. Olave's, Stoke Newington. He was responsible for the restoration of about 350 churches.

---

[1] *Ewan Christian* (Anonymous) (1896), p. 21.

CHAPTER VIII

SIR GILBERT SCOTT, *Vir Probus, Architectus Peritissimus*

No account of church-building in the nineteenth century would be complete without a fairly lengthy account of Gilbert Scott, the man with whom the Gothic Revival is in the minds of most people most closely associated He was, Sir Kenneth Clark says, a popularizer. After his death, Mr. E. M. Barry said in an address to the Royal Academy,[1] " The Tractarian Movement and the Gothic revival went, indeed, hand in hand ; but he was too earnest a champion to wish his cause to be identified with any single party. Like many High Churchmen, he desired to tread the ' *via media* ', very much as did the late Dean of Chichester ; so that Sir Gilbert Scott may almost be termed the Dean Hook of the Gothic revival." That is a very just estimate. He might also be called the Bishop Wilberforce, for " the degree to which the Oxford Movement took hold of the English Church is very largely due to Bishop Wilberforce. The Church has accepted it in the same modified sense as that in which he accepted it himself." [2]

Scott said that " amongst Anglican architects, Carpenter and Butterfield were the apostles of the High-Church school, I, of the multitude. . . . They were chiefly employed by men of advanced views, who placed no difficulties in their ways, but the reverse ; while I, doomed to deal with the promiscuous herd, had to battle over and over again the first prejudices, and had to be content with such success as I could get." [3]

Like Bishop Wilberforce and Dr. Hook, he was a great worker ; and as in the case of the Bishop, " the danger was that he was too successful ".

His *Personal and Professional Recollections* is an extremely interesting book. There is no trace of self-consciousness

---

[1] Quoted in Appendix to Scott's *Recollections*.
[2] S. C. Carpenter, *Church and People*, p. 261.
[3] Scott, *Recollections*, p. 112.

about it, and no disguise of the fact that he considered himself to be a great architect, raised up by Providence for his work, and guided by Providence in it. In the summary of his life which follows, there is no attempt to be ironical: almost everything is simply quoted from the *Recollections*.

Scott was born in 1811. His grandfather was Thomas Scott, the Evangelical commentator on the Bible;[1] his father was incumbent of Gawcott, Bucks. There were other brothers, and Scott considered that he was overlooked. He did not go to school, and made little attempt to study, though he enjoyed the visits of Mr. Jones, the drawing master. " How infinitely important it is for boys to feel the duty and necessity for exertion! Though I have reason to be most thankful for my success in life, the defects of my education have been like a millstone about my neck, and have made me almost dread superior society."

He inspected the churches in the neighbourhood as a boy, and as the result began to develop a love of Gothic architecture. Chetwood Church gave him his first glimpse of Early English, in consequence of which he remained in a state of morbid excitement all day. Then his father decided that he was to be an architect. He was taken in hand by his uncle, and eventually articled to Mr. Edmeston in London. " The first remark of my new master which I recollect was to the effect that the cost of Gothic architecture was so great as to be almost prohibitory; that he had tried it once at a dissenting chapel he had built at Leytonstone, and that the very cementing of the exterior had amounted to a sum which he named with evident dismay." Edmeston was an inferior architect, but kindly. Scott's fellow-pupil, Enoch Hodgkinson Springbett, was not a congenial companion. Scott went to Mr. Maddox (a good draughtsman, but an infidel) for drawing lessons, and in his spare time drew, read and visited more Gothic buildings. Another fellow pupil was Moffatt (intelligent though uneducated), who came later. After Scott left, Moffatt left also.

[1] Thomas Scott seems to have been an alarming old gentleman. He was deaf, and when a joke was made he would beg to be informed what it was. When brought to understand it, he would only deign to utter a single word—" Pshaw! " Family prayers in his household lasted for an hour.

Scott, then, after a visit to Lincolnshire and Yorkshire, returned to London, and procured an introduction to Samuel Morton Peto and Mr. Grissell, builders, to whom he gave his services, and was given in return the run of the workshops and the London works. This gave him an insight into practical work.

In 1832 he entered the office of Henry Roberts, a pupil of Smirke, who was gentlemanly, religious, precise and quiet. During this time he executed a few small works ; but Smirkism and practical work chilled his own tastes.

Then, the new Poor Law having come into operation, Kempthorne, a good, kind fellow, asked Scott to help him in his work of designing workhouses : which he did.

Then his father died, and Scott was left to fend for himself. He wrote a circular to every influential friend of his father's whom he could think of, informing them that he had commenced practice, and begging their patronage. He left Kempthorne and tried with success to be appointed architect to workhouses in the district in which his father was known. " An era of turmoil, of violent activity and exertion. For weeks I almost lived on horseback, canvassing newly formed unions. Then alternated periods of close, hard work in my little office at Carlton Chambers." Moffatt came to help ; and finally became partner. At this time Scott became engaged to his cousin Caroline Oldrid. " This afforded a softening and beneficial relief to the too hard, unsentimental pursuits which at this time almost overwhelmed me." Moffatt worked hard at getting commissions, and the new workhouses were designed and built. But no care was taken over their appearance.

In 1838 Scott married, and his first church was built—at Lincoln, which was better than many then executed. This was the year of the beginning of the Cambridge Camden Society,[1] " to whom the honour of our recovery from the odious bathos is mainly due ". But at that time no idea of ecclesiastical arrangement or ritual propriety had crossed the mind of Scott. Other churches followed—at Birmingham, Shaftesbury, Hanwell, Turnham Green, Bridlington Quay and Norbiton. In none of these was there a chancel ; in all of them, minor transepts

[1] Actually the Society was founded in 1839.

and mouldings of plaster. " As," he says, " I had not then awakened to the viciousness of shams, I was unconscious of the abyss into which I had fallen. These days of abject degradation only lasted for about two years or little more, but, alas ! what a mass of horrors was perpetrated during that short period." This is the familiar language of revivalism. We naturally expect a conversion : and we get it.

The human causes were two : first, acquaintance with the Cambridge Camden Society. Mr. Webb lectured him " on church architecture in general, on the necessity of chancels, etc., etc. I at once saw that he was right, and became a reader of the *Ecclesiologist*."

The second cause was the reading of Pugin's articles in the *Dublin Review*. " Pugin's articles excited me almost to fury, and I suddenly found myself like a person awakened from a long, feverish dream. . . . Being thus morally awakened, my physical dreams followed the subject of my waking thoughts." He wrote to Pugin, was invited to call, and found him tremendously jolly. He did not see him again : " but his image in my imagination was like my guardian angel, and I often dreamed that I knew him ". Scott was now a new man. " Old things (in my practice) had passed away, and, behold, all things had become new, or rather, modernism had passed away from me and every aspiration of my heart had become mediaeval. What had for fifteen years been a labour of love only, now became the one business, the one aim, the one overmastering object of my life. I cared for nothing, as regarded my art, but the revival of Gothic architecture."

In later years he fully thought that his experience, and that of some, perhaps many, others, pointed to a special interposition of Providence for a special purpose. One of the fruits of the conversion was the design for the Martyrs' Memorial at Oxford. He fancied that it was better than anyone but Pugin would then have produced. (But of course Pugin would not have designed a martyrs' memorial. His opinion of reformers was not high.)[1]

[1] They were, according to Pugin, " vile, blasphemous imposters pretending inspiration while setting forth false doctrines ". The subscribers to their memorial were " foul revilers, tyrants, usurpers, extortioners and liars ".

M

Then followed the Infant Orphan Asylum at Wanstead, St. Giles's, Camberwell and Reading Gaol ; the refitting of Chesterfield Church and the restoration of St. Mary's, Stafford. At Stafford too little actual old work was preserved ; but no restoration could, barring this, be more scrupulously conscientious.

All the time Scott was continuing to erect workhouses. These were now Elizabethan, and in many cases of really good design. He was less successful in the matter of lunatic asylums ; but generally speaking his practice was increasing in merit as well as in size.

The restoration of the Bridge Chapel at Wakefield was too drastic, and he consented to an entire renewal of part of it, which he soon regretted. " I never repented but once, and that is ever since." And about this time the Cambridge Camden Society became his enemies.[1] " I suppose that I was not thought a sufficiently High Churchman, and as they fell in at the time with my very excellent friends Carpenter and Butterfield, they naturally enough took them under their wing." But he bore their injustices patiently. " With all its faults, the good which the Society has done cannot possibly be overrated. They have, it is true, often pressed views, in themselves good, too far, and their tendencies have at times been too great towards an imitation of obsolete ritualism ; but in the main their work has been sound and good."

1844 was the year of the beginning of a new era in Scott's professional life—and also of the opposition of the Camdenians. There was a competition for the rebuilding of the Lutheran Church of St. Nicholas, Hamburg, and Scott decided to enter. He paid a visit to the Continent in order to study Belgian and German Gothic. At Frankfort he met Dr. Schopenhauer, an old German philosopher—alas ! a determined infidel. He intended on his return to send the Doctor some religious books ; but he forgot. For he was hard at work on the new design. It turned out to be in the main a good one, and he sent it in. The effect in Germany was perfectly electrical. The Germans considered that Gothic was the German style, " and

[1] Scott exaggerates the *Ecclesiologist's* hostility ; it admired much that he did, and looked for great things from him.

their feelings of patriotism were stirred up in a wonderful manner ". There was some criticism; but the foundations were laid in 1845. The *Ecclesiologist* attacked Scott for designing a church for Lutheran heretics : " how must we characterize the spirit that prostitutes Christian architecture to such a use ? . . . We do earnestly trust that Mr. Scott's example will not be followed. We are sure that the temporal gains of such a contract are a miserable substitute for its unrealness, and— we must say it—its sin." Scott replied with a long letter in which he defended himself and explained the similarity of the Anglican and Lutheran positions. The *Ecclesiologist* reviewed it, but did not publish it. It was not convinced.

At this time he decided to sever his partnership with Moffatt. He made an agreement which turned out less well for Moffatt than for himself; but Moffatt behaved fairly and straight-forwardly throughout. Another circular was written announcing the separation to the world.

Then he was offered the work of restoring Ely Cathedral ; he made a tour of French cathedrals, and at last realized the French origin of Gothic ; he designed a number of new churches ; and in 1849 was appointed architect of Westminster Abbey. In 1851 he went to Italy with Benjamin Ferrey. " The Venetian Gothic, excepting the ducal palace, disappointed me at first, but by degrees it grew upon me greatly. Ferrey was enraged at it, and I could continually hear him muttering the words ' Batty Langley '.[1] . . . I was convinced that Italian Gothic, as such, must not be used in England, but I was equally convinced, and am so still, that the study of it is necessary to the perfecting of our revival."

The Great Exhibition contained among other things a model of the Hamburg church—perhaps the finest of Mr. Salter's models.

He then tried to get the Government to purchase Cotting-ham's collection of mediaeval remains. There was no immediate result ; but this originated the architectural museum.[2] He

[1] Not an appropriate exclamation. See p. 12.

[2] The Museum originated in the sale of Cottingham's collection, and was based on Bruce Allen's idea of a school of applied art for workmen. Some of the architects—Street and Butterfield, for instance—did not encourage it. Waterhouse, Norman Shaw, J. Clarke, E. Christian and J. P. Seddon did. It was begun in Canon Street, Westminster, and then moved to South Kensington.

appealed for help to the Prince Consort, who gave him and Mr. Clutton a lecture on the poor state of contemporary architecture. " I might have replied that . . . there stood before his Royal Highness two architects who, having in three several instances accepted invitations to compete in foreign countries with architects from all Europe, and for buildings of first-rate importance, had in each instance carried off the first prize."

With Doncaster Church, which had to be rebuilt after a fire, he took great pains, and believed it to stand very high amongst the works of the revival. " However, I am not proud of the tower. I missed the old outline, and I never see it without disappointment, though I do not think that this feeling is generally participated in."

The design for the new Rathhaus at Hamburg had its details entirely changed. " I confess that I think it would have been a very noble structure." M. Adolphe Lance wrote, " L'hôtel de ville de Hambourg sera une des plus belles et des plus raisonnables constructions de ce temps-ci. Heureux l'artiste qui y aura attaché son nom, heureuse la ville qui pourra le compter au nombre de ses monuments."

In 1855 Scott was elected associate of the Royal Academy. He gave lectures after Professor Cockerell ceased to do so : they contained much that is original and meritorious. The sketches made in France which accompanied one of the lectures were most noble.

Haley Hill church was built at this time. It was, on the whole, his best church.

Then followed the affair of the Government Offices. There was a competition for the design of the new buildings in 1856, and Scott contributed the best drawings ever sent into a competition, or nearly so. But the judges knew amazingly little about their subject. The first premium for the Foreign Office went to Mr. Coe ; the first for the War Office to Mr. Garling ; Banks and Barry were second for the War Office, and Scott third. But Lord Palmerston set aside the result of the competition and appointed Pennethorne, a non-competitor. Scott therefore considered himself at liberty to stir, and so persistently did he stir that he got himself appointed architect for both the buildings ("L.D."). But he was not allowed to enjoy his triumph in peace. Mr. Tite opposed him in Parliament, and was supported by Palmerston. He wrote to *The Times* next day exposing them, and proving that, whatever they might say, his Gothic windows would certainly admit enough light. But the attacks continued: the " very abjects " now loaded him with their miserable abuse. The *Ecclesiologist*, however, was sporting enough to defend him. It said, " The more we study Mr. Scott's drawings, the better they seem, and the more satisfied we should be to see them carried out in execution ", and, the design " marks another onward epoch in our movement ". The *Saturday Review* was on his side, and so was the Gothic party pretty generally.

Then Parliament was dissolved. Scott says, " I am no politician, though tending to conservatism, but at that time I certainly did take an interest in the election. At length, however, the fatal day arrived, the Government resigned, and my arch opponent became once more autocrat of England." At once he exerted his tyranny. Lord Palmerston " sent for me and told me in a jaunty way that he could have nothing to do with this Gothic style, and that though he did not want to disturb my appointment, he must insist on my making a design in the Italian style, which he felt sure I could do quite as well as the other. That he heard I was so tremendously successful in the Gothic style, that if he let me alone I should Gothicize the whole country, etc., etc., etc." There was another debate, in which Lord Palmerston aired his second-hand knowledge and Mr. Tite talked nonsense. Then a deputation waited on Palmerston to advocate the cause of Gothic architecture. Mr. A—— was a new devil's advocate ; Mr. B—— was a traitor— and the battle continued.

At last Lord Palmerston " sent for me, and, seating himself down before me in the most easy, fatherly way, said, ' I want to talk to you quietly, Mr. Scott, about this business. I have been thinking a great deal about it, and I really think there was much force in what your friends said.' I was delighted at his supposed conversion. ' I really do think that there is a degree of inconsistency in compelling a Gothic architect to erect a classic building, and so I have been thinking of appointing you a coadjutor, who would in fact make the design.'   I was thrown to earth again."

Scott was unable to do justice to the case *vivâ voce*, and so he returned home and immediately wrote a strong and firmly worded letter.   " I dwelt upon my position as an architect, my having won two European competitions, my being an A.R.A., a gold medallist of the Institute, a lecturer on architecture at the Royal Academy, etc., and I ended by firmly declining any such arrangement.   I forget whether he replied.   I also wrote, if I remember rightly, to Mr. Gladstone."

So upset was he that he had to take a holiday at Scarborough. His mental distress was considerable.   To resign would be to give up a sort of property which Providence had placed in the hands of his family.   But there was a way out : might it not be possible to design something that was Italian without being fully Classical ?   He decided on Byzantine " toned to a more modern and usable form ".   He made the design, not without considerable success : the designs were both original and pleasing in effect.   But Professor Cockerell, being a pure classicist, had the greatest difficulty in swallowing the new style.

And unfortunately the idea had to be " toned down, step by step, till no real stuff was left in it.   It was a mere *caput mortuum*."   In any case, it did not please Lord Palmerston.   In 1860 he again sent for Scott.   " He told me that he did not wish to disturb my position, but that he would have nothing to do with Gothic ;   and as to the style of my recent design, it was ' neither one thing nor t'other—a regular mongrel affair— he would have nothing to do with it either ' :   that he must insist on my making a design in the ordinary Italian, and that, though he had no wish to displace me, he nevertheless, if I refused, must cancel my appointment. . . . I came away thunderstruck and in sore perplexity."

What was to be done ?   Mr. Hunt advised him not to resign : so did Mr. Digby Wyatt.   So " I . . . bought some costly books on Italian architecture, and set vigorously to brush up what, though I had once understood pretty intimately, I had allowed to grow rusty by twenty years' neglect.   I devoted the autumn to the new designs, and, as I think, met with great success. . . . My new designs were beautifully got up in outline ;   the figures I put in myself, and even composed the groups, for, though I have no skill in that way, I was so determined to show myself not behind-hand with the classicists, that I seemed to have more power than usual."

The new designs were passed by the House of Commons in 1861, though the Gothic party opposed them, and Scott himself aided the opposition a little. It was a curious position. He determined by God's help to do his very best, just as much so as if the style had been of his own choosing. Even Ruskin said that he had done quite right.

A few other works are described in the *Recollections*. First there is the Albert Memorial. " My idea in designing it was, to erect a kind of ciborium to protect a statue of the Prince ; and its special characteristic was that the ciborium was designed in some degree on the principles of the ancient shrines. These shrines were models of imaginary buildings, such as had never in reality been erected, and my idea was to realize one of these imaginary structures with its precious materials, its inlaying, its enamels, etc., etc. . . . This was an idea so new, as to provoke much opposition. Cost and all kinds of circumstances aid this opposition, and I as yet have no idea how it may end ; I trust to be directed aright."

He says later on that the metal work was by Skidmore, the carving by Brindley, Armstead, Redfern and others, and the sculpture under the special direction of Sir Charles Eastlake ; after his death, of Mr. Layard, and finally of Mr. Newton. The structural work was by Mr. Kelk and Mr. Cross. After describing how the Queen awarded him the honour of knighthood, he goes on to say, " This being my most prominent work, those who wish to traduce me will naturally select it for their attacks. I can only say that if this work is worthy of their contempt, I am myself equally deserving of it, for it is the result of my highest and most enthusiastic efforts." Mr. Layard said, " I am convinced that if so great and splendid a monument had been erected in Italy or in Germany, our countrymen would have gone many thousands of miles to see it, and would have pronounced it an example of the superiority of foreign over English taste. I am equally convinced that such a monument could not have been erected out of England." That is probably true.

Then there is the Midland Railway Terminus at St. Pancras.

" My own belief is that it is possibly *too good* for its purpose, but having been disappointed, through Lord Palmerston, of my ardent hope of carrying out my style in the Government Offices . . . I was glad to be able to erect one building of that style in London." Other buildings in the same style are Kelham Hall, Preston Town Hall and Old Bank, Leeds.

Another great building was to have been the Law Courts. There was a competition early in 1866, and Scott of course sent in designs. " I do not know that my general architectural design was of much merit, though I think that it was fully as good as any recent work I know of by any other architect. Of its parts, I am bold to say, that many exceeded in merit anything that I know of among modern designs."

But his design was not accepted—though Mr. Layard considered it one of the finest things that he had ever seen. The reason was that enemies whom he had innocently supposed not to exist were brought out of their lurking-places.

Nor was his design for the Albert Hall accepted. There were, in fact, two designs : one based on the Byzantine churches of the South of France, the other Gothic. Both were worthy of more consideration than they received.

The *Recollections* are rather scrappy towards the end ; but there is some account of the cathedrals which Scott restored— Ely, Winchester, Hereford, Lichfield, Peterborough, Salisbury, Chichester, St. David's, Bangor, St. Asaph, St. Albans, Chester, Gloucester, Ripon, Worcester (where " I fear I am jointly responsible for the removal of the Jacobean and Elizabethan canopies, and of the choir screen, but I forget now how this was "), Exeter and Rochester. The Appendix also mentions Durham and Canterbury, where very little work was done.

He died in 1878, and was buried in the Abbey. The coffin bore the words

" *Georgii Gilberti Scott equitis*
viri probi architecti peritissimi
parentis optimi reliquiae hic
. . . *resurrectionem*
expectant. . . ." [1]

---

[1] The beginning of the inscription, in the nominative case, is on his brass in the Abbey.

PLATE XXV

St. Michael's, Brighton

By G. F. Bodley

" A boyish, antagonistic effort "

PLATE XXVI

St. Augustine's, Pendlebury

By G. F. Bodley

Dean Stanley preached the funeral sermon. In the course of it he said, " Others may have soared to loftier flights or produced special works of more commanding power ; but no name within the last thirty years has been so widely impressed on the edifices of Great Britain, past and present, as that of Sir Gilbert Scott ".

That is true. The *Recollections* give no idea of the number of buildings with which he was concerned. The number is said to have been over seven hundred and thirty after the year 1847 [1] —and he had been working for years before that. He seems to have been quite untroubled by the unmanageableness of it all. A correspondent in the *Builder's Journal* about twenty years after his death spoke of the " insensate greed " with which he grasped all the opportunities which came his way. Someone else has said more temperately that he " was not strong enough to resist the pressure and temptations which his lucrative professional engagements brought upon him, or he was of an irresolute and vacillating disposition ". He would have been deeply hurt by such language. He considered himself a great architect, and was sure that all the work that came to him was only his due.

But was he a great architect ? His obituary in the *Builder* compared him to Palladio. " It will be recognized that what the name of Palladio in common parlance is to the Classic Renaissance in Italy in the sixteenth century, the name of Scott is to the similar and equally remarkable movement which may be called the Gothic Renaissance in England." But, it continues, his influence was healthier than Palladio's, for he was always an advocate of honest construction, and Palladio was not. But it admits later on that Ruskin's " wolfish " element had no place in Scott's designs, and quotes someone who said that he " wanted a little more *devil* in them ". Mr. T. F. Bumpus, who was an enthusiastic admirer of the Gothic Revival, extravagantly eulogizes in his book on London churches the works of most of the architects. But this is all that he can say of Scott :

" When a man of real ability, diligence, knowledge and technical skill finds that the public holds him to be the best in his calling and confides to him the most important works it

[1] See the *Builder*, XXXVI, p. 360.

desires to have executed, he is not to blame for accepting its estimate as the true one; for diffidence, in any department of activity, except pure literature, is not the road to fortunate achievement. Perhaps to some Sir Gilbert's claims do not seem high. He may not have been endowed with the divine gift of genius. . . . But he had all the other qualities named above. But, just as these same qualities in the literary field, or in that of pure art, are not enough to make a poet or a painter, so they do not suffice for an architect of the first class." [1]

The *Architect* gave Scott quite a friendly obituary, but it had to admit that there was nothing exciting about his works. " The great mannerism of Sir Gilbert Scott was a certain simple, moderate, permanent graciousness."

We may be now too near to the Victorian age to be able to judge its heroes impartially; but will anyone ever admire the works of Scott? It is hard to believe that they will, for there is nothing in particular in them to admire. The works of some of the other Gothic Revivalists have some character. When I visited Denstone Church, Staffordshire, I said " Street"; and so it was. But is it possible to visit one of Scott's churches for the first time and to say " Scott "? At the best it must be a guess. It may be the work of Scott; but it may equally well be the work of any one of a hundred less well known men. Any one of Scott's churches might be the work of someone else. If we discover, after all, that Scott was the architect, we shall not be surprised: when we see a commonplace church we are prepared for the information. But we shall not in consequence inspect the church with any greater interest. If we know beforehand, we know what to expect. And in every single instance we find it.

[1] T. F. Bumpus, *London Churches Ancient and Modern*, Vol. 2, p. 238.

CHAPTER IX

ABOUT 1850, Scott was looking forward to the future, and speculating as to the probable development of the Gothic Revival in England. There must, he said, be no mere variation from the acknowledged styles *for the sake of* gaining individuality ; still less must there be mere eccentricity. There will be no development from the architects who affect contempt for those who look to what *has been* as a stepping-stone to what *shall be*. There will be no development save through the perfect knowledge and appreciation of pointed architecture as it has already existed, but servile copying must be avoided. In its future development we may hope for its perfect adaptation to the requirements of the present day. How suitable Gothic architecture is ! It has an innate principle of universal adaptability. But we must strike off the features which do not belong to it intrinsically, but which were the result of its adaptation to customs that have now for ever passed away ; and we must add such other and new features as are necessary to render it a genuine and living art, suited to the habits and requirements of the present day. It must also be adapted to different climates. Our architecture should everywhere be *English* and *Christian* ; but it should have in it that intrinsic principle of life which would admit of its ready adaptation to the climate of the torrid or the frozen zone, to the scorched plantations of Jamaica or the icy rocks of Labrador.

All that is really beautiful and intrinsically valuable in the hitherto attained developments of the pointed arch should be amalgamated. We can engraft on our chosen period the essential beauties of the earlier and late periods. He looks forward to the infusion into the reanimated art of a life and reality which

173

does not belong to ages long gone by, but which is the distinct and genuine inspiration of our own.[1]

In 1857 he wrote,[2] " Let it not be imagined that the ecclesiastical branch of our work is anything like complete. On the contrary, I think that one great effort is still before us ; we have still to make our style thoroughly *our own*, and, divesting ourselves of the *shackles*, though not of the *aid* of precedent, to strike out boldly and fearlessly for ourselves." " I am no mediaevalist : I do not advocate the styles of the Middle Ages as such. If we had a distinctive style of our age, I should be content to follow it ; but we have not ; and the middle ages having been the latest period which possessed a style of its own, and that style having been in part the property of our own country, I strongly hold that it has greater *primâ facie* claims to be used as the nucleus of our developments than those of ancient Greece or Rome."[3] " Classical buildings have not been " so pre-eminently successful as to lead us, so religiously as is the fashion, to adhere to their worn-out style, as if it were as much part and parcel of us as Magna Charta or the Thirty-nine Articles."[4] Anything might be possible in the future : there would be Gothic warehouses and statues : why not Gothicize the Orders ? The Corinthian columns with naturalistic foliage would look very beautiful, though the Ionic would present difficulties.

In the *Recollections* he seems at times to be rather disillusioned. The Revivalists, he says, began without premeditation ; reproduction ripened into revival, first for ecclesiastical, then for general use. Then they began to flatter themselves that they would supplant Classicism ; then they began to entertain a religious horror of Classic. He traces the course of the revival : first, free choice of style was seen to be inconsistent with an organized revival, and Middle Pointed was fixed on and Norman and Perpendicular shunned. Then there was a shift to Early Pointed ; then foreign features were introduced ; then there was an English reaction ; and now, he says, we are at sea again. A liberal spirit has been produced which renders restorations

[1] *Faithful Restoration of our Ancient Churches*, pp. 110–118.
[2] *Gothic Architecture Secular and Domestic*, p. 12 (footnote).
[3] *Ibid.*, p. 191–192.   [4] *Ibid.*, p. 200.

more conservative ; and a study of foreign architecture cannot fail to supply us with much valuable matter.   Still, the position is anomalous.

The revivalists had been disturbed by the " Queen Anne " style which was then coming into fashion, and which seems to have meant anything from the style of the reign of Elizabeth to that of the mid-eighteenth century.   He says, " The movement in favour of this style, or family of styles, has been no doubt a vexatious disturber of the Gothic movement.   The ardent promoters and sharers in the Gothic movement had fondly flattered themselves that theirs was a preternatural heaven-born impulse ; that they had been born, and by force of circumstances trained, and led on, by a concurrence of events wholly apart from their own choice and will, to be instruments under Providence in effecting a great revival.   They viewed that revival as in part religious, and in part patriotic." [1]   He would hardly have said " fondly flattered themselves " thirty years earlier.

But Gothic was not yet dead : the best Gothic work was to be done from this time onward.

There are many churches of the last quarter of the nineteenth century which are entirely nondescript : red-brick suburban churches dedicated to All Saints, St. Philip or St. Andrew, which have no merit and need no description.   Prebendary Mackay's description of St. Uriel's, Clump End, applies satisfactorily to most of them :   " a church built of bright red brick with free-stone dressings, seated with pitch pine and possessing a morning chapel." [2]   They are rather less attractive than the Camdenian churches of forty years earlier, and there is nothing to be said about them.   But the better churches are better than anything that had been done before.

The question of Style was coming to be regarded as being of small importance : at any rate, there was no polemic fervour aroused by it.   The " Queen Anne " style was used chiefly for domestic work, and the churches of this character are not very important.

There were a few Renaissance or Romanesque churches.

[1] *Recollections*, p. 372.
[2] *Pilgrims' Progress in the World To-day*, p. 92.

St. Agatha's, Landport, which was opened in 1895, and was designed by Mr. J. H. Ball, is of the Basilican type, " not the Renaissance Basilican of Palladio . . . but the Romanesque variety of North Italy, and suggested to Mr. Ball by studies of the churches of Lombardy, though not a copy of any one of those churches ". Fr. Dolling, for whom the church was built, considered that this type of church was best for mission work among the people. Sedding's church of the Holy Redeemer, Clerkenwell, is Renaissance. But, on the whole, Gothic was used, for most of the laity and clergy were used to it, and con-sidered—as many still do—that a non-Gothic building is unecclesiastical.

The foreign Gothic craze (which was connected with the adoption of an early style : the borrowers from abroad had not imitated Flamboyant) had come to an end. Mr. Goodhart-Rendell speaks [1] of " that return of English designers to Eng-lish models which took place in the last quarter of the nineteenth century ". He says that " those who had been the first to stray in foreign pastures—Pearson, Bodley, Street—were first to return and crop their native fare. In their student days even Philip Webb, Norman Shaw and Sir Ernest George had fallen in with the taste for Gothic exotics, and patriotic stalwarts such as Micklethwaite and G. G. Scott, junior, were few. Generally the wanderers returned richer for their experience."

Street's Church of Holmbury St. Mary, Surrey, is of an Eng-lish type ; but Street died soon after it was built.

There was now no limitation of style. Pearson (of whom we shall speak later) had his own characteristic version of thirteenth-century Gothic, and a considerable number of the " St. Uriel's, Clump End " churches have lancet windows. But, on the whole, the tendency was towards a later style. Bodley's late fourteenth-century details were widely imitated, and many architects designed churches in fully developed Perpendicular—All Saints', Hertford, and a number of other churches by Paley and Austin are typical examples.

Camdenian doctrines had been forgotten (except by some of the clergy, who have not yet forgotten them). It was no longer believed that Gothic architecture and Christianity were in-

[1] *Architectural Review*, Vol. XLIV.

separably connected, nor that it was wrong to love Gothic for its beauty rather than for its moral qualities. Gothic was admired and used when it was wanted. But it was not defended on theological grounds. In fact, by the end of the century the situation was much the same as it had been at the beginning of it. Gothic had once more become a matter of taste : the Church had followed Mr. Petit, and not J. M. Neale.

But the ecclesiologists had not worked in vain. Their architectural theory had been more or less without value ; but they had done invaluable work in their studying of old buildings, their liturgical researches and their determination to raise standards in the worship of God. Much that they defended was not worth fighting for ; but that was inevitable. We are not interested in Symbolism ; and we regret, among other things, the choir-stalls and the surpliced choir which have been introduced into almost every church. But we admit that the general reverence and decency of our church services are due to the pioneer work of the ecclesiologists. We can hardly exaggerate our debt to them in this matter.

But long before the last of the old brigade had died, the question of style had ceased to be of supreme importance. The architects were more interested in the question of how to build churches that should be suitable to present-day needs.

In earlier years that had been done naturally. Style, plan and internal arrangements developed with the religious needs and social conditions of the time. The belief and manners of the people, as Pugin said, were embodied in their buildings. Styles changed ; and the plan of the mediaeval churches developed in new ways to suit new conditions. An increase of ceremonial meant an enlargement of chancels ; the preaching activities of the friars resulted in large open naves ; the multiplication of guilds and of masses for the dead produced many side chapels and altars.

The churches built after the Reformation are exactly suited to the type of service that was held in them, from the churches of Wren to the large, rectangular, galleried churches of the early nineteenth century. It was not merely habit or lack of imagination which made the early nineteenth-century architects design churches in the way that they did. They agreed with Barry's contention that deep chancels, rood-screens and other features of mediaeval arrangement were not suited to the carrying out of a service that was truly Common Prayer.   And some are now beginning to feel that they were right.

But the ecclesiologists did not agree.   If modern needs [1] did not require a mediaeval arrangement, so much the worse for modern needs.   They were inadequate ; they were unimaginative, and were independent of the rubrics and of the true teaching of the Prayer Book.   That was true.   The ritual and ceremonial of most Anglican churches a hundred years ago were slovenly, jejune and uninspiring.[2]   It was necessary to instruct Church-people and to inspire their imaginations, so that they should desire the services to be carried out properly. And the parish churches would have to be adequate to the new standards—which, as the ecclesiologists were never tired of pointing out, were not new, but old.   The Camdenians, and even Pugin, maintained that the present-day needs of the Anglican Church were almost exactly the same as those of the Church of the Middle Ages ;   therefore churches must be built and arranged in the mediaeval manner.   The Reformers had made no alteration in this respect.   Obedience to the Anglican rubrics made the old arrangements necessary.   If it had not been found to do so in the past, that was because the rubrics had never been properly obeyed.   The ecclesiologists imagined indeed a short golden age in the seventeenth century ;   but their reconstruction of the state of affairs at that time was based upon too few examples to be really convincing.   And many Churchmen were not convinced.   But the ecclesiologists, as we have seen, succeeded on the whole in carrying their point.   They allowed no intermediate or " semi-Catholic " position.   The demands of the Prayer-Book ritual were evident.   They could be satisfied by nothing less than a thorough-going reproduction of the old churches.   Adaptation had been tried but it had failed.

[1] It is worth remembering that to the ecclesiologists " modern " was almost always a term of reproach.

[2] Here are some liturgical curiosities from the 1840's.   The font of St. George's, Hanover Square, ran on castors, and was wheeled out from under the altar.   At All Hallows' and St. Petrock's, Exeter, the altar had a drawer in which papers were kept.   At Spofforth the legs of the stone altar were polished with blacking every Sunday. In several churches the pulpit ran on castors.

We have dealt with the question of Style, and with the Third Pointed dogma. The question of Plan is not unconnected with that of Style. For if it was not legitimate to use a style later than that of the fourteenth century, and if the churches of that period had to be reproduced literally, it was not legitimate to use any type of plan that had been developed since then.

The ecclesiologists were dissatisfied with the usual plans of the churches of their time. Small churches were usually wide and aisleless, with no structural chancel; large churches were rectangular and aisled, with only a small projecting sanctuary. But there was ancient precedent for both types. Wide, aisleless churches were built all through the Middle Ages. Many of the churches of the fifteenth century had no structural chancel : the aisles were continued from west to east, and the whole formed one large rectangle. In some cases the chancel projected one bay beyond the side chapels—which is, after all, not unlike the single-bay chancel of the early nineteenth-century church. Some of the churches of the 1820's and 1830's combined Gothic detail with a most un-Gothic plan : but many others were planned in almost exactly the same way as a large late fifteenth-century town church. It would have been possible to have argued that this was the latest and best development of the mediaeval plan. It was noble and practical, it combined dignity with usefulness, and it was well lit. But this was answered by saying, " Yes : it was the latest development ; but it was not the best. It was a falling off : it was the product of debasement and decay. The earlier styles represented Gothic at its best, and they are the styles that we must adopt." If that were the case, the late plan was ruled out, and a structural chancel was almost a necessity. Decorated churches of the late thirteenth and of the fourteenth centuries usually had well developed chancels.

There is no lack of evidence as to the type of church which the ecclesiologists favoured. Their ideal church was in the Decorated style—not too early and not too late. It had a nave with aisles and porch and, if possible, a tower and spire. In England alone among the countries of Europe the normal place for a tower was at the west end ; the central tower, usually combined with transepts, tended to die out ; when there is a

N

tower of the fourteenth or fifteenth century it is usually a
rebuilding of an earlier tower. Flanking towers were comparatively uncommon.

The ecclesiologists did not favour a central tower. At the
beginning of the Gothic revival the tower was almost always
placed at the west end ; then there was a reaction, and towers
were placed in various other positions. A flanking tower can
be made to appear dignified more easily than a tower at the
west, for it has not to rise to so great a height. But a west
tower gives greater dignity to the church as a whole.

The nave should contain the font, which ought to be at the
south-west rather than at the west end of the central passage of
the nave. Benches should be low and not closed by doors ;
at the east end would be the pulpit and the lectern.

With regard to transepts there is a curious inconsistency in
ecclesiological writings. In theory the transept was a necessity,
for Symbolism required a cruciform church, and without the
transept a great deal of symbolical theory was meaningless.
And yet if a church were built with well-developed transepts,
the architects were taken to task. Old churches with deep
transepts did not afford appropriate models for imitation.
Lip service might be paid to the cruciform plan by building
transepts of very slight projection ; but large transepts were
inconvenient for congregational purposes ; those who sat in
them could neither hear nor see the service. In this respect,
at least, ecclesiological theory was tempered by common sense.
In the Middle Ages transepts had not been built to hold a
number of worshippers, but to contain altars. The ecclesiologists did not think of restoring side-altars in parish churches,
and their objection to long transepts was sensible.

The chancel was raised on one step, and in the chancel arch
was the screen, of open work, with a solid base closed by doors.
A reading-pew outside the screen and facing west was on no
account to be tolerated : the clergy must sit inside the chancel
facing north and south ; or, better still, their seats might be
returned and face east. The ecclesiologists did not succeed in
introducing returned stalls, which have post-Reformation as
well as pre-Reformation authority. Reading-pews were at
first often adopted against the wishes of the architects. But

they became rare later in the century, except in definitely
Evangelical churches; and the arrangement of clergy-stalls
facing north and south became general. Beside the clergy-
stalls, there should be stalls for a choir of " laicks ". Except
at Holy Communion, the choir should be the only laymen
admitted to the chancel. The organ might stand in a choir
aisle or chapel.

The altar was raised on two steps. Altar rails were not
approved of, but custom demanded them, and their use in the
nineteenth century was universal. The sacrarium [1] contained
the altar, credence, sedilia (not altar chairs) and piscina. The
sacristy in a small church would be on the north side of the
chancel towards the east, with a lean-to roof and no external
door : in a large church it might be anywhere, so long as it
was near the altar. It should not be detached, or look like a
chapter house. The chancel might have a priest's door.

This was the correct plan; and if combined with correct
details would form a model church. Mere utilitarianism in
planning was condemned; but the plan, it was claimed, was
useful as well as correct and beautiful, and had " a moral effect
in promoting community of worship ".

There is no doubt that the model churches of the ecclesiologists were well attended, and that the congregations were
strong and united. But this cannot have been due entirely to
the revival of the Decorated style and fourteenth-century
planning and arrangement. The revived sense of Churchmanship, combined with the consciousness of being in opposition
to most of the Church, the novelty of surpliced choirs and stoles
and altar flowers, and, without doubt, the appeal of deep
spirituality, were enough to fill the churches of Camdenian
clergymen whether the churches were " correct " or not. There
was a keen congregation at Margaret Chapel before the building
of All Saints', Margaret Street. It is hard not to feel that the
needs of the congregation were an afterthought : modern
requirements had to be fitted to Gothic churches rather than

---

[1] Anglican ecclesiologists used the word sacrarium to mean sanctuary; Romans used it to mean piscina. Hence the Romans were
amused when in an account of a function in an Anglican church the
officiant was said to have sat in the sacrarium.

Gothic churches to modern requirements. Still, the congregations, when they had accepted Camdenian ideals, demanded
Gothic as loudly as their priests, and were willing at first to
undergo discomfort in the good cause. For the more ardent
mediaevalists were ruthlessly ascetic. They would not allow
their windows to admit much light, and they maintained that a
church window should never be made to open. That was a
piece of modern luxury. Stoves and heating apparatus were
looked upon with suspicion : it was enough to bring a brazier
into the church and remove it before the service began. The
extreme mediaevalism of the earlier revivalists passed away.
There are limits to unpracticalness ; it was realized soon that
Gothic would have to be adapted. Nevertheless, for some
years style was the first consideration, and planning and
arrangement came afterwards.

When foreign Gothic was recognized and borrowed,
developments in plan were certain to follow. With the whole
of Europe to choose from, it was not difficult to find precedents
for all kinds of variety of plan.[1] But precedent began to count
for less, and practical considerations for more.

In the latter part of the nineteenth century very much less
was written on ecclesiological subjects than during the first
part, and in what was written there was a different emphasis.
There is no longer the continual stress upon precedent, and not
much stress upon style. But there is an attempt to work out
types of building which would be suited to the needs of congregations of worshippers of the nineteenth century.

The *Ecclesiologist* published in 1862 a remarkable article
advocating a Basilican arrangement of churches, of which some
of the paragraphs have a very modern sound. " The presi-
dents of our churches *do* not administer the Holy Communion
to us. The Holy Communion, as the common act of the organized Body of Christ instinct with a common life by the HOLY
SPIRIT, can hardly be said to exist among us." Mediaeval
churches were built for the mass—which was considered to be
offered by the priest as a mediator between God and

[1] William Burges said, " We want churches in this city something
like Angevin churches, with great thick walls, domed or vaulted,
filled with mosaic inside, and perhaps majolica or mosaic or marble
outside ".

the people; and a congregation was not necessary. At the Reformation belief in Transubstantiation was abandoned; but the Church did not revert to the primitive way of celebrating Holy Communion. " As in cathedrals so in parish churches, the parson, *as such*, has no place in the assembly of the faithful. He is not one of a certain order of men extrinsic to the congregation, without the presence of one of whom to consecrate the elements, and also to preside with Christ's authority in His organized Body and Communion, the Sacrament may not be had. Yet at a family dinner the head of the household presides, not because he is a qualified carver, but by right of his relationship."

A return to the primitive method of celebrating Communion, and the old Basilican arrangement of churches, is the cure for and solution of all the *isms* which have so fatally beclouded the highest act of Christian worship. The suggestion was not carried out : but it called attention to an important principle.

Street was one of the first architects to remember the needs of the congregation, and to insist that churches were made for people and not people for churches. The congregation should be able to see and to hear, and to this end he introduced into some of his churches wide naves with, in some cases, aisles merely of passage width. And he was willing to dispense with a chancel.

J. T. Micklethwaite quoted on the title-page of his book on *Modern Parish Churches* the lines of Pope :

" Something there is more needful than expense
And something previous even to Taste—'tis sense."

And the book applies this important principle to church-building. He says,[1] " As for *symbolism* which some people would have us believe was the ruling influence in the old plans, I do not think it had anything in the world to do with them. Ceremonial was sometimes symbolical, as also were some of the decorations of the churches, but the churches themselves were arranged to suit the practical requirements of those who were to use them." Considerations which would have seemed to J. M. Neale to be worldly and unworthy of the considerations

[1] J. T. Micklethwaite, *Modern Parish Churches*, p. 56.

of a truly Catholic architect were given first place : they determined the plan. Style was certainly not to be an afterthought
in the sense that the Rev. J. L. Petit had wished it to be : an
architect would not plan a church first, and afterwards add
ornamental details to taste and as funds allowed. But the
Gothic styles had become so far learned that they were becoming accepted and instinctive, and were less obviously in the
forefront of the architect's mind.

J. T. Micklethwaite says that style is comparatively unimportant. " Judging from the amount of quarrelling which has
been going on for many years about this, one might imagine
it to be the most vital subject connected with architecture.
But really it is one of comparatively little importance." [1] The
laws of style are good for beginners, but no real artist is bound
by them. Everyone is bound by the laws imposed by the
necessities of construction, the properties of materials, and the
like ; but the conventional laws are arbitrary and subject to
change. Modern Gothic work has suffered both from pedantry
and from vulgarity. Pedantry was inevitable at the beginning
of the revival, but it must not now be repeated. Old churches
must be studied but not copied. The mediaeval styles developed in some respects more than in others. In the thirteenth century masonry was good, but woodwork poor ; and
joiner's work hardly existed until the early fifteenth century.
If one particular period is chosen for imitation, it should be
Perpendicular. Perpendicular contains a larger number of
good qualities than any other style, and is most suitable for
modern requirements. But there need be no direct imitation,
and new materials and the advance in mechanical science must
be taken into consideration.

Vulgarity is produced largely by the quality called " go ".
It is manifested chiefly in the efforts of the early French Gothic
school. " The common symptoms of it in our churches are
harshness, even to brutality, of general design, with studied
ugliness and systematic exaggeration and distortion of details,
stumpy banded pillars, stilted arches, a profusion of coarse
carving, notches, zigzags, curves, whose

'Wily turns and desperate bounds'

---

[1] J. T. Micklethwaite, *Modern Parish Churches*, p. 250.

baffle all description, and long, wiry crockets, bursting out of unexpected places." [1] " Go " is the perpetual forcing into notice of the personality of the architect. One cause of vulgarity is the ease with which coloured building materials can now be obtained.

A style must be chosen, preferably a severe style (which is not the same as early), because we must work within our power. Then we must learn to apply the style : find out what is wanted, and then do it simply, naturally and straightforwardly. " If ever again we are to have a real living architecture, we must, before all things, BE NATURAL."

But Taste is more important than style. Aesthetic beauty is not a matter of ornament : it is the taste of the designer which elevates construction to the rank of architecture. The ecclesiologists had been deeply suspicious of Taste. But a reminder of its existence and importance was badly needed in the 1860's and 1870's. There was much lamentable vulgarity in design and fittings. The early ecclesiological efforts at glass-painting and wood- and stone-carving are poor and crude ; but they are obviously the result of a genuine desire to do well, and they are sincere. But the mid-nineteenth-century architects and church furnishers let loose a flood of bad work, unrestrained by any taste, with only the merit of correctness according to the ideas of the moment, and without the note of sincerity which is there in the earlier, more naïve work. Mr. Micklethwaite gives a long description of an imaginary church. This kind of thing is quite easy to do ; but as he does it quite well and amusingly his description may be worth quoting. He pictures

" St. Simeon's, which cost perhaps £25,000, and will hold, without accommodating, 700 worshippers, and which is on all sides acknowledged to be Mr. Flick's masterpiece. We have spoken of the harmony in the old church, what is the music like at St. Simeon's ? I fear very much like that traditional Dutch chorus in which every man played his favourite tune on the instrument most to his liking. Mr. Flick leads off with, it may be, an original composition, or it may be a more or less judicious selection from his library and note-books. Then

---

[1] J. T. Micklethwaite, *Modern Parish Churches*, p. 264.

start many carvers, ' foliage hands ', and ' figure hands ', who
follow each his own devices, on caps, corbels, and other things
' left for carving ', and fill up the niches and other vacant spaces
with figures and ' subjects ' of their own choosing. Messrs.
Stencil & Daub, ' ecclesiastical decorators ', perform astound-
ing feats on the walls and roofs, whilst Mr. Twister, the eminent
' mediaeval metal-worker ', executes marvellous flourishes on
gas lamps and altar-rails. Nor are the glass painters behind-
hand ; here one bellows ' God save the Queen ' on a ' Prince
Consort memorial ', mostly pink and blue ; there one of a
newer school chants a *Te Deum*, all in green and yellow. On
one side a worthy churchwarden feebly sounds the Jews' harp
in a medley of subjects from the Old Testament, whilst on the
other the squire of the parish blows his own trumpet with a lot
of crudely-coloured heraldry, most likely from the Apocrypha.
And so on, all through the windows, each trying to outroar the
rest. This is surely bad enough, but the chorus is yet far from
complete, for even the very pavement is made a vehicle for
loudness, and the smallest and most insignificant objects assert
their right to add to the din, whilst, regardless of every one's
feelings, the ' warming engineer ' drives his horrible organ-
grind of pipes and gratings throughout the whole. Then the
squire's wife executes a (very) brilliant *fantasia* on the altar
frontal, arranged by the famous Mrs. Berlin Babylinen of Regent
Street, whose taste in such matters is so well known, whilst,
simultaneously, the ' ladies of the parish ' perform a number of
others equally brilliant, but each in a different key, on the
kneeling mats, and hangings for the pulpit, and sedilia, and the
like. And last, but by no means least, Messrs. Snip & Co.,
ecclesiastical tailors, supply diluted thunder, in the shape of
carpets and curtains." [1]

What is wrong with St. Simeon's ? Even if the details were
good, it wants system and unity.[2] It is the business of the
architect both to compose the piece and to conduct the performance. And he must continue to look after his church :
his work is never finished as long as any work has to be done

[1] J. T. Micklethwaite, *Modern Parish Churches*, pp. 246–247.
[2] See also the last two chapters of T. G. Jackson, *Modern Gothic
Architecture*.

PLATE XXVII

ECCLESTON CHURCH

By G. F. Bodley

PLATE XXVIII

[Photograph by J. S. Simnett.

HOAR CROSS CHURCH
By G. F. Bodley

there. " If the work outlast the architect, let it be put into the hands of another at least as good, and after him another, and so on.   So it was that our ancient churches grew to be what they are, and so it must be again, if ever we are to rival them." [1]

Micklethwaite takes the different parts of a church one by one, and makes suggestions about their design.   The altar ought to be the principal object in a church ; but it need not be visible from every corner.   He believes in aisles, and considers that some modern architects have reduced them too much. Without them the chancel appears to be too wide.

The chancel should be little narrower than the nave, and a little more than half its length.   Every chancel ought to have an aisle or chapel on one side or on both.   A central tower is only desirable when placed over a chancel.   If it is not there, the best position for a tower is at the west end.   If there is a tower at the side of the chancel, it may serve as an organ chamber.

Vestries ought to be much larger than they usually are ; a sacristy ought to be on the north or south of the chancel.   A side chapel ought to be a real chapel, complete in itself.

The entrance to the church had better be at the west end, not half-way up the nave, so that the congregation will not be divided by a passage running through the middle of the pews. Windows should be adequate.

West galleries may sometimes be used ; the pulpit of every large church ought to have a sounding-board ; a pulpit ought to be of wood, and not of stone or marble, which do not furnish a church well.   The Georgian three-decker was " much more worthy of our respect than three-fourths of the ' correct arrange-ments ', of the present day ".   " What is most convenient is most correct "—in the arrangement of choir seats and desks, and in everything else.   A wall of stone or marble between the nave and chancel is enough for practical purposes ; but for architectural effect a high screen is necessary.   The rood should show the glorified Christ, a figure expressing majesty, power and beneficence, not suffering and death.   Every town church ought to have a loft, which may be used for the reading of the Gospel, and is useful for the accommodation of an

1 J. T. Micklethwaite, *Modern Parish Churches*, p. 249.

orchestra. Lecterns for the reading of the lessons at Mattins
and Evensong are not necessary ; the eagle form had better be
confined to the Gospel lectern, which may stand in the sanctuary
of a large church, and be used for the reading of the Gospel.

The altar steps ought to be as far east as possible, and in
small churches there ought not to be too many. At the entrance
of the sanctuary there should be only one. A few feet of altar
rail at the end of the step is all that is necessary. A turned
wood rail often looks very well; " and it is scarcely credible
that ' correctness ' should have caused so many really good
altar-rails of this sort to be turned out of our old churches, to
make room for vile tailors' trash, in the shape of what are called
' iron standards ' ".

The altar and reredos are dealt with at considerable length.
The altar ought to be well proportioned and simple ; there
should be a shelf for candlesticks a few inches above the altar.
The reredos consists of two parts : the base, containing an
arrangement of shelves ; and the upper part. There should
be no pictures over the altar ; they usurp the interest which
should belong to the altar itself. A single figure is worse than
a picture. Small subjects are a different matter ; but sculpture
and painting must be severely disciplined. The lower part of
the reredos he calls the retable. The upper part, the reredos
proper, extends beyond the altar shelf and retable in height or
length. It should be treated as a single composition, and
such figures as Christ in Majesty or the Adoration of the Lamb,
which are out of place in the retable, are appropriate here.
Painting is preferable to sculpture.

There are sections dealing with credence, piscina, sedilia,
minor altars, confessionals, sacristy, vestry, bells, clock, sand-
glasses and sundials, artificial lighting, warming and ventilation,
almsboxes, notice-boards, and monuments and inscriptions.

Here is a picture of the better type of later nineteenth-century
town church. It is certainly Gothic, and it has continuity
with the past. But, for all that, it is a new thing. New needs
are provided for ; room is found for the organ either in a
chamber or in a gallery ; it does not seem to be an intruder.
The clergy and choir are accommodated in vestries which are
more than mere lean-to's. Both the convenience and the

edification of the people are considered, and their new demands are met. Micklethwaite's book reminds us that there were by this time large and united Catholic-minded congregations. He mentions side-chapels with altars, vestries with room for the keeping of vestments, sacring bells, and many other things which were neither demanded nor supplied twenty years before. He speaks of rood-screens and rood-lofts and crucifixes and stations of the Cross.

Churches of this type have their faults. The altar is often raised on a flight of steps, which is theatrical in effect and dangerous in use. A long flight of steps to the altar was regarded as essential by High Churchmen. The *Church Times* in its obituary of Scott (March 29, 1878), after remarking that " his churches, though they rarely have striking merit, are almost always creditable ", goes on to say, " His worst failing was rather in the arrangement of the buildings than in the buildings themselves ; and thus it was a failing which can be remedied ; for to raise an altar two or three steps higher is a task that does not present insuperable difficulties ". If Scott did not raise his altars (but he did sometimes), that would now be regarded as one of his good points. However, advanced Churchmen did not think so : they liked plenty of steps— seven, if possible.

Churches of this type usually have too many shelves behind the altar. Micklethwaite was one of the last architects of any importance to defend the " gradine ". He realized that it had no ancient precedent, and only a certain amount of precedent after the Reformation, and in any case he would limit its height to a very few inches. " The altar shelf," he wrote,[1] " like many other things, is sometimes made offensive by vulgar exaggeration, as when it is raised excessively high or developed into something like a flight of stairs." Gradines like flights of stairs are all too common in later nineteenth-century churches. They support (or used to) an enormous quantity of flower vases and candlesticks (single, triple or even seven-branched) ;[2]

[1] *Ornaments of the Rubric*, p. 24.
[2] I do not know why the nineteenth-century Churchmen and architects, who hated shams, should have allowed their candles to be raised on wooden stocks painted to look like wax. Was not this a serious piece of deceit ? But it was not only allowed : it became orthodox.

in the middle is the cross, raised very high on a kind of sham tabernacle. The reredos generally looms too large.

But these faults can be rectified, and in many churches have been. On the whole the better of these churches are noble, satisfying and sensible.

Micklethwaite in his churches carried out what he advised in his book. He had been a pupil of Scott from 1862, and began independent practice in 1869. In 1876 he entered into partnership with Somers Clarke, and the partnership lasted until 1892. Micklethwaite was appointed surveyor to the Dean and Chapter of Westminster in 1898, on the death of Pearson; in 1900 he was appointed architect to St. George's, Windsor. He was an enthusiastic Churchman, with a keen interest in ceremonial. He was one of the founders of the Alcuin Club, and his tract on the Ornaments of the Rubric was the first publication of the society. Micklethwaite's antiquarian knowledge was very extensive. His churches are good, sound designs, if not particularly original, and they are planned with liturgical requirements in view. His association with Somers Clarke was so close that is not always possible to say which of them was responsible for what. It is said that St. John's, Gainsborough; All Saints', Brixham; St. Paul's, Wimbledon, and the chancel of St. Peter's, Brighton, were designed and begun by Somers Clarke and completed by Micklethwaite. At All Saints', Wimbledon, Micklethwaite completed Somers Clarke's plans and designed the screens and furniture. Stretton was Somers Clarke carried out by Micklethwaite. Churches exclusively or distinctively Micklethwaite's are St. Hilda's, Leeds; St. Bartholomew's, East Ham; St. Peter's, Bocking; Widford (rebuilt but for tower); and St. Saviour's, Luton. Other churches not mentioned in this list are St. Martin's, Brighton (by Somers Clarke alone) and St. Saviour's, Folkestone.

Arthur William Blomfield (1829–99) was an architect who designed some noble churches, and a considerable number of St. Uriel's, Clump End's. He was the fourth son of Bishop Blomfield of London, who was a keen Church builder. After coming down from Cambridge he was articled to P. C. Hardwick; in 1855 he made a Continental tour with F. P. Cockerell, and in 1856 opened his first office. His clerical associations assured him of work. He was president of the Architectural Association in 1861, Fellow of the R.I.B.A. in 1867 and vice-president in 1886 ; in 1888 he became an associate of the Royal Academy, in 1889 he was knighted, and in 1891 received the gold medal of the R.I.B.A. He is said to have been a charming companion and a true English gentleman—happy, prosperous and modest.

He was essentially an ecclesiastical architect, though some of his works were not ecclesiastical. In 1883 he became architect to the Bank of England, for which he built the Law Courts branch. After the death of Street he was associated with his son in the Law Courts ; other unecclesiastical works were Whitgift School, Croydon, King's School, Chester, Sion College Library, Queen's School, Eton, and the Church House, Westminster.

He was a careful restorer ; the new nave of Southwark Cathedral, though not an exact restoration, has the spirit of old work.

In his church work he admitted the possibility of individuality in ecclesiastical art, and held that " where convenience is at stake we ought not to be too much confined by the precedent of mediaeval architecture. Neither our ritual nor our congregations are the same as those for whom our ancient churches were built, and it is scarcely to be expected that if they were exactly suited to the one they would be equally so to the other." In the matter of materials he did not consider that architects need be afraid of the use of iron. He advocated the use of iron columns, because they could be much lighter than stone and did not obstruct the view. He saw no reason for thinking that iron was an unecclesiastical material. St. Paul's, Haggerston (his first church), and St. Mark's, Marylebone, are examples of Blomfield churches with iron columns.

In the matter of planning he believed that churches should not impose mortification upon a congregation—a wise opinion.

He said that " our churches should be so designed as to meet perfectly all the requirements of an auditorium, and at the same time be equally well adapted for the due observance of all the rites and ceremonies of our Church, whether carried out in the highest development of ritual, or in a simpler manner ".

Importance should be given to the altar : it ought to be raised
and conspicuous.   He recommended the use of a stone reredos.
There should be some architectural indication of the presence
of the font.   The reading-desk ought to be an architectural
feature ;   and he believed in placing sounding-boards over
pulpits.

He was " inspired by the tradition of the Gothic Revival, and
his hold on that method never slackened, while he was thoroughly
conversant with its difficulties and limitations ".[1]   But he had
no strong opinions on the subject of style : he produced
churches in almost any style.   He was influenced at first by
Street's *Brick and Marble Architecture*, and by his own studies
in Italy.   St. Barnabas', Oxford, is of Italian Romanesque
type, with a campanile.

He recast St. Mark's, North Audley Street, and St. Peter's,
Eaton Square, in a style which has been called both Auvergnat
Romanesque and also Byzantine Romanesque.   Anyhow, it is
Romanesque.   St. Luke's, Stepney, is Italian Romanesque.

But the Italian influence disappeared.   St. John's, Wilton
Road, has some, but not much.   He became fond of Perpendicular, and the large and important church of St. Mary,
Portsea, is in that style.   The exterior is not particularly
successful ; but the interior is broad and dignified, and suitable
for its purpose.   It was begun in 1884.

Many of his churches are Early English, often built of brick,
and of the type which one expects to see in suburbs which were
developed during the 1880's.

Blomfield " excelled in the charitable but unremunerative
art of keeping down the cost ".   St. John's, Wilton Road, was
a cheap church.   In the case of St. Barnabas', Oxford, Blomfield
wrote as follows :

" The idea usually conveyed by this term (cheap church) is
that of a showy exterior, flimsy construction, and a mean and
disappointing interior.   Now, as the exact opposites of these
are found in St. Barnabas', I object to its being classed with
cheap churches ; it is true that no money was wasted on it,
and it was in that sense economically designed and economically
carried out ; but, as I have before said, no expense was spared

---

[1] W. A. Pite in the *Builder's Journal* (November 8, 1899).

to secure strength and solidity of construction; the work was put without any competition into the hands of a thoroughly good contractor, and not one single item of the design from first to last was altered or cut down in the slightest to reduce the cost; everything was carried out as originally designed, and this is more than can be said for many churches that have cost three times as much." [1]

Blomfield's many churches include All Saints', Caldecote; St. Mary's, Strood; Privett; St. Mary's, Portsea; St. Matthew's, Croydon; St. John's, Wilton Road (Westminster); St. Barnabas', Edgware Road; St. James's, West Hampstead; Christchurch and St. John's, St. Leonards; St. Luke's, Brighton; St. Andrew's, Worthing; St. John's, Bognor; St. Jude's, Peckham; St. Andrew's, Surbiton; St. Mary's, Bourdon Street (Westminster); Holy Trinity, Stevenage; St. Paul's, Haggerston; St. Saviour's, Raynes Park; Christchurch, Epsom; St. Mary's, Walmer; St. Mark's, Marylebone; St. Werburgh's, Derby; St. Mary's, Aberdare; St. Peter's, Upton Cross; All Saints', Highgate; East Sheen; St. Matthew's, Fulham; Leamington Parish Church (new nave and tower); St. John's, Great Marlborough Street (Westminster).

Other than parish churches: St. Alban's, Copenhagen; Lower Chapel, Eton College; Chapel of Haileybury College (Classic); Chapels of Malvern College and of Queen Anne's School, Caversham; St. George's, Cannes; Cathedral of St. George, George Town, Demerara; Cathedral of the Falkland Islands.

There is nothing in particular which is characteristic of the works of Blomfield. The same could be said of the churches of many nineteenth-century architects: of those of Gilbert Scott, above all, and those of others, such as Ewan Christian. The churches of Butterfield have obvious features. Street had a recognizable style of his own, and when he used it, he built a church which can safely be ascribed to him. Some of the inferior architects designed churches that are so bad that there can be little doubt about their origin: most of the churches of Mr. E. B. Lamb or of Mr. Bassett Keeling are recognizable; they are too bad to be the work of anyone else. But, on the

[1] A. T. Bassett, *St. Barnabas', Oxford*, pp. 20–21.

whole, there were few architects who developed a style so characteristic as to leave no doubt as to the authorship of their churches. Gothic had not been sufficiently assimilated; or the architects were men with no particular personality, or they were too busy to do more than turn out designs according to the accepted pattern. Most nineteenth-century churches bear no particular signs of the mind which conceived them.

But three men at any rate in the latter part of the century developed a recognizable and characteristic style of their own; Sedding, Pearson and Bodley.

John Dando Sedding was born in 1839, and in 1858 became a pupil of Street. His brother Edmund was already a member of the group under Street's influence; William Morris had been in the office for a year, Philip Webb was a pupil, and was succeeded by Norman Shaw, who came back here from his foreign studentship. Norman Shaw said that Street's pupils were loyal, and believed in their master entirely; but Norman Shaw did not follow him in the matter of style, nor did Sedding. Sedding reacted from Street's teaching, and began to study the later types of church, which appealed to him very strongly. He left Street in 1865, and joined his brother at Penzance. Edmund was considered to be the more gifted of the two, but his life was short. He had lived in Bristol, then in London, and lived at Penzance from 1862. He built or restored a number of churches in the west country, and died in 1868.

After his death John began work at Bristol, where he had little to do. He designed embroidery, altar-cloths, frontals, etc., adorned with sacred symbols, angels, birds, squirrels, foliage and flowers. Many of these designs were made at St. Raphael's Home, Bristol, where Sedding was precentor. He made a prolonged study of the mediaeval work of Somerset, and knew the churches as they were built. He was much interested in local types, and had a feeling for the churches as part of the landscapes in which they stood. Gothic art, he considered, was not a product of England as a whole, but of Yorkshire, Norfolk, Somerset or Cornwall. This is an obvious fact which has only recently begun to be dealt with as a general rule in books on mediaeval architecture. The variations are

obvious, though they have hardly yet been satisfactorily ac-
counted for. Sometimes they are clearly due to varieties in
building material; always there is a wonderful, instinctive
fitting of the kind of church to the kind of countryside. But
there are many curious instances of local varieties which it
would be difficult to explain. Sometimes the last church on
this side of a county boundary is of one type, and the first
church over the boundary has a new set of characteristics. The
earlier nineteenth-century ecclesiologists were aware of this;
but they did not attach much importance to it, and in designing
their new Gothic churches took it very little into consideration.
But Sedding was interested in it and studied it.

In 1872 he married Miss Rose Tinling, who was a kindred
spirit, and helped him with his work. In 1875 he went to
London. Here again he had little to do at first, and made
designs for furniture, embroidery and gold and silver ornaments. In 1876 he made the acquaintance of Ruskin, and came
under his influence. Ruskin told him that he " must always
have pencil or chisel in hand if he were to be more than an
employer of labour on commission ". Sedding tried to form
a school of masons and carvers and modellers from Nature, and
succeeded in influencing greatly his workmen.

He was diocesan architect to Bath and Wells, and restored
many churches in the west. He died in 1891.

Sedding's churches are all original and interesting. He did
not confine himself to one style, and did not work for long in
any one. He used in his own way the Gothic of the late fourteenth and fifteenth centuries; but he expressed himself in
many different ways, using all of them with sympathy and
ability. He had a great dislike of trade art, and wanted the
best in everything. He was not content to design a church and
leave it to the ecclesiastical furnishers to fit it out. He designed
screens, reredoses, crosses, plate and decorations. The con-
ventions of ecclesiastical ornament made no appeal to him,
and he never descended to the mechanical use of symbolical
devices. He did not pepper his work with conventional sacred
monograms, As and Ωs and evangelistic symbols. He
wanted " fresh life and reality ". A church ought to be " a
design *by* living men *for* living men "; and he pictured a church

o

" wrought and painted over with everything that has life and beauty—in frank and fearless naturalism covered with men and beasts and flowers ".

His churches include the Holy Redeemer, Clerkenwell; St. Dyfrig's, Cardiff; All Saints', Falmouth; Holy Trinity, Sloane Street (Chelsea), and St. Clement's, Bournemouth.

St. Clement's was planned in 1872. It consists of nave, chancel, north aisle and porch, lady-chapel, vestries and west tower, which was finished after the architect's death. The style is rather advanced fourteenth century, freely treated. There are elaborate open stone screens both to the chancel and to the side-chapel. The life of St. Clement appears on the font, and his emblem is to be found in the floor, the lamps and the pulpit rail; his monogram is in the windows, alternating with roses and crowns. St. Clement, holding his own church, also appears as a bench end.

Holy Trinity, Sloane Street, which was consecrated in 1890, is a noble church, very eclectic, and showing its architect in his " rôle of wilful improvisatore ". It is an attempt to carry out Sedding's ideas on a large scale, and includes the work of a large number of artists—Sir Edward Burne Jones, William Morris, Messrs. Powell, C. W. Whall, H. Starkie Gardiner, F. W. Pomeroy, Harry Bates, F. Boucher, Onslow Ford, Hamo Thornycroft, etc. But the several artists have hardly worked as a team, and the church as a whole hardly " hangs together ". The fittings are mostly very good, though in some cases rather " arty ", but they are not very congruous with one another. The church as a whole is a brilliant attempt : but it can hardly be called a success. Perhaps, under the circumstances, it could hardly be that.

Holy Redeemer, Clerkenwell, consecrated in 1888, is of Renaissance design.

The later churches of John Loughborough Pearson are almost all instantly recognizable. If you know one, you know them all. That is not to say that they are all alike. Each one has something peculiar to itself. But similar features are to be seen in all of them—features which are undoubtedly thirteenth century, but which in their use and disposition are simply Pearsonic. Pearson was not particularly interested in style as such : his domestic work is in various styles, and he is said to have had ideas of producing a Renaissance work on a large scale. But in his churches he came to adhere to one style in which his architectural ideas could be adequately expressed.

And his planning and construction are characteristic. His churches are unmistakably late nineteenth century, in spite of their mediaevalisms. They may remind travelled ecclesiologists of churches in France ; but in fact they are not like any others. They are English, in spite of certain features borrowed from abroad. They are churches designed for the carrying out of the services of the English Prayer Book in the manner that became customary in a large number of parishes during the second period of the Catholic revival, and for the accommodation of large Anglican congregations. And they are planned according to the good taste, common sense and deep ecclesiological knowledge of one man.

Pearson was born in 1817. He was the son of William Pearson, a water-colour painter and etcher of Durham. At the age of fourteen he entered the office of Ignatius Bonomi.[1] He spent much time in Durham Cathedral, especially in the Chapel of the Nine Altars, and studied the thirteenth-century abbeys of Yorkshire. His interest was not confined to the buildings : he also studied all kinds of church furniture and fittings. After leaving the office of Bonomi he went to London, and worked for A. Salvin and Philip Hardwick. He began independent practice in 1843. He was made a Fellow of the Society of Antiquaries in 1853, F.R.I.B.A. in 1860, A.R.A. in 1874 and R.A. in 1880. He received a gold medal at the Paris Exhibition in 1878, and was made Knight of the Legion of Honour, and received the Royal Gold Medal of the R.I.B.A. in 1880. He was for many years consulting architect of the Church Building Society.

Pearson was not connected with the Camdenians, and the *Ecclesiologist* confessed that it knew little of him. His understanding and appreciation of mediaeval work developed independently, and he did not involve himself in ecclesiological controversies. " At the height of the . . . ' battle of the

[1] Architect of St. Cuthbert's Roman Catholic Church, Durham, etc.

styles ', he well-nigh alone of his school kept a balanced mind."

His earlier churches are not particularly interesting, though some of them contain hints of his future developments. The earliest is Ellerker (1843); Elloughton dates from 1844. Laverstock also dates from 1844 ; it is of flint, with a central tower and shingled spire. Ellerton and North Ferrilby date from 1846. St. James's, Weybridge, was rebuilt in 1847–1848 : it is a commonplace but not unattractive effort in early Middle Pointed, with a spire. It has been since enlarged.

Holy Trinity, Vauxhall Bridge Road, the gift of the Archdeacon of Westminster, was built in 1849–1852, and was enthusiastically praised by Barry, Pugin, Gilbert Scott and the *Ecclesiologist*. The *Ecclesiologist* said, " When in this church we behold the ideas for which we have fought and suffered obloquy so prominently exhibited, we can indeed thankfully and sincerely offer our *Deo gratias* as the only suitable expression of our feelings at such a result ". Holy Trinity is a most orthodox specimen of early Middle Pointed, consisting of nave with aisles and clerestory and north and south porches, central tower and spire, transepts, and chancel with aisles of one bay and sacristy on the north. The only unusual feature is that the chancel, owing to the nature of the site, is wider than the nave. The church is fitted according to the best taste of its time.

Dalton Holme Church (1858) has a nave with south porch and western tower with spire ; transepts, and a chancel with aisles. The north aisle serves as vestry and organ chamber, and the south as a mortuary chapel of the Hotham family. The sanctuary is without aisles. The tower has an elaborate belfry-stage with three tall windows on each face, and octagonal turrets with slender pinnacles : the spire is very lofty.

By this time Pearson's churches were beginning to show the influence of the study of French Gothic.

Daylesford (1859) is not a great success : it is somewhat over-elaborate. But the central tower is picturesque.

Titsey (1861) is a small village church, rather above the average.

The first really fine church is St. Peter's, Vauxhall, built between 1862 and 1864. This church shows a strong French

influence.   It consists of nave and apsidal chancel of equal
height.   There are baptistery, narthex, aisles, double aisles on
the north of the chancel, with vestries beyond, and organ chamber on the south.   The light is mainly admitted through the
clerestory and the west windows.   The west end has double
windows with a buttress between, and a circular window above.
The triforium stage of the nave is plain : in the chancel it has
openings, and is lit by lancets.   The entire church is vaulted,
with stone ribs and brick filling.   St. Peter's is said by more
than one writer to be the first example of this treatment in the
nineteenth century ; but Street's St. James the Less, Westminster, which has brick vaulting to the chancel and sanctuary,
is just previous to St. Peter's.

Appleton le Moors, Yorkshire (1863), is a church of the same
type as St. Peter's, on a smaller scale.   The west end has a
circular window and a shallow porch built between two buttresses.   The tower, on the south side, has double windows in
the belfry stage, and a gable above on the faces of the spire.
The chancel is apsidal.   The piers are of a more elaborate
type than those at St. Peter's, with clustered and banded
shafts.

St. Peter's was the first of a long series of noble churches in
which Pearson developed his best manner, and which have
much the same characteristics.

Their style is thirteenth century.   St. Peter's, Vauxhall, is
very French ; but the French elements tended to disappear
from the later churches, or at any rate to combine with English
features, especially with details suggested by the Early English
abbeys of the North and the churches of Lincolnshire.   The
proportions are Pearson's own.

The plan was in every case suggested by the site, and any
difficulties of the site were turned to the best advantage.   St.
John's, Red Lion Square, is a notable example of this.   In
Truro Cathedral the whole conception was governed by the
existence and position of the old church of St. Mary, of which
an aisle was kept as part of the new building.

The exterior outlines are simple and dignified, and the roof-
line is usually unbroken.   Pearson in his later days dispensed
with central towers in his parish churches.   His transepts do not

project far beyond the outer walls of the aisles. Many of his chancels have apsidal ends.

The apse is not a natural English growth. There are some Norman apses, but only a very few later mediaeval examples. England preferred the square east end. But on the Continent the apse was almost universal. It was therefore inevitable that the ecclesiological English Gothic churches should as a rule have square east ends, but that the apse should be used as soon as Continental architecture was imitated. The square east end filled with a large window is obviously easier to deal with successfully. An apse may look dark or mean or " pokey ". There are very few Gothic Revival apses that do not. It has been said that Pearson naturalized the apse : " Gilbert Scott could not do it—his looks pinchbecked and Frenchy; Street could not—his looks mean and stupid. All the other masters avoided it; the minor men rushed at it with excruciating results. Pearson succeeded. His are the only truly English apses in existence. But he grew to love them less and less, and reverted to the square end with fine compositions of grouped lancets." [1]

Pearson's towers were not the least imposing part of his designs. He exhibited at Paris in 1862 a large sheet of tower designs in his earlier manner, about half of which had been erected. His later manner was far finer ; but all too many of his later towers have never been built at all—as at St. Michael's, Croydon, St. John's, Red Lion Square and St. Alban's, Birmingham. St. Stephen's, Bournemouth, lacks its spire : the tower now has a pyramidal cap. Pearson's towers and spires were strongly influenced by northern French examples. The buttresses, if there are any, are slight, and there is an absence of unnecessary set-offs. Vertical lines are emphasized. The stories are " graded with an admirable intuition "; the belfry stages are tall, with long windows. Spires are comparatively short : the junction of the spires with the towers is well managed.

Most of the large churches are vaulted. Very few Gothic Revival churches had vaults ; perhaps this was partly due to reaction by the architects from the efforts of their predecessors

[1] E. Milner White, " Architecture and Art of the Oxford Movement ", *Theology*, July 1933.

at the beginning of the nineteenth century, who vaulted their churches with iron and plaster. It was also a result of the exclusive copying of English examples; for almost all English churches of the Middle Ages have timber roofs. But when French examples began to be copied there was a beginning of vaulting in the new churches, for most French churches are covered with a vault—as, indeed, Gothic churches ought to be.

Pearson delighted in the construction of vaults, and understood them perfectly. He vaulted any space, regular or irregular in plan, with apparent ease. A vault needs support; and the buttresses and flying-buttresses which support it can be disposed in various ways. An outer wall can be built beyond the buttresses, and a way pierced through them to make an outer aisle. Flying-buttresses may be displayed or concealed; Pearson sometimes hid the straining arches which take the thrust of the main vault under the roof of the aisles. This was done, *e.g.*, at Truro and St. John's, Upper Norwood.

A feature of the large Pearson churches is the side-chapel, which is a real chapel, distinct from the rest of the church, and giving scale to the rest of the building. It is very often elaborately treated, with complex vaulting. A processional path in some cases is carried round the whole building.

Internally there is an effect of great height. Pugin sometimes aimed at this effect by designing a high arcade and a small clerestory: in a Pearson church the arcades are kept comparatively low, and the clerestory is high. The vault is high pitched and without a ridge rib. If the chancel is less wide than the nave, its vault rises to the same height as that of the nave, but springs from a higher level. The chancel arch is eliminated, but in some churches a thickening of a rib of the vault marks the division.

The triforium stage is variously treated. St. John's, Red Lion Square, has a developed triforium. St. Michael's, Croydon, like St. Peter's, Vauxhall, has a blank stage marked by string courses. St. Augustine's, Kilburn; St. John's, Upper Norwood; St. Agnes', Sefton Park; St. Stephen's, Bournemouth, and other churches have a gallery carried round the church beneath the clerestory; the front of the gallery forms a low triforium stage. At Kilburn and Norwood this is plain,

at St. Agnes' and St. Stephen's it is pierced.   The open quatre-
foils at St. Stephen's are hardly the most successful part of the
design.   This arrangement entails the setting back of the walls
and windows of the clerestory stage, and a charming effect of
light and shade.

There are usually picturesque vistas through the arcades
to the transepts and side-chapels.

Pearson's own furniture is to be seen in most of his churches.
He designed no particularly striking fonts or pulpits; his stone
screens, as at Upper Norwood and Kilburn, are perhaps less
successful than his light-metal screens at St. John's, Red Lion
Square, and Headingly.   His reredoses are on a larger scale
than is now customary; but whether they are painted triptychs
or carved stonework, they are exactly suited to the churches.

He used various materials, brick or stone.   His stonework is
not rubbed smooth and set with fine joints, but dressed on the
face with the chisel, set with wide joints and pointed with dark
mortar.   He often used red bricks, and did not disdain sometimes to use in his interiors common London stock bricks, which
the ecclesiologists had despised as being mean.   But they
undoubtedly have a good effect.

St. Augustine's, Kilburn, was begun in 1871; chancel 1872,
nave 1877.   The chancel was consecrated in 1880, and the spire
built in 1897–1898.   The tower stands at the north-west.   The
lofty nave and chancel are under one roof; there is a processional path all round the church, and above the arcade a gallery
and lofty clerestory with lancets.   The arcades and gallery
are continued past the transepts.   An apsidal chapel opens
from the south transept; the vestries and organ-chamber are
on the north.   There is an open stone screen of five arches with
elaborate sculptures on its west face; these are continued at the
same level on the walls of the chancel.   The chancel suffers
from an excess of ornamentation, and is less successful than
many of Pearson's: he did better work when he had less money
to spend.   The east wall has two tiers of triplets.   The west
end, with its wheel window and five small lancets, contained
under an imposing arch externally, is good.   On the whole this
is a remarkable and noteworthy church.

Wentworth, Yorkshire, was built between 1872 and 1876

PLATE XXIX

ST. AGNES', KENNINGTON
By G. G. Scott, junior

PLATE XXX

[From a sketch made in 1829 by courtesy of R. S. Morrish.

STOKE D'ABERNON CHURCH BEFORE RESTORATION

for Earl Fitzwilliam. It has a lofty aisled nave, transepts, chancel, and central tower and spire, and is groined throughout. The interesting old church with Wentworth monuments was abandoned; the chancel was repaired in 1925, but the nave is in a ruined condition, and the north wall has disappeared. I found it impossible to visit the new church without considerable prejudice against its existence and great anger at the fate of the old. The new church appears to be a suburban intruder, rather vulgarly showing off. But even a visitor who rejoiced in the humiliation of the old church, or who was not aware of its existence, and who approached the new building with the intention of being pleased, could hardly say that it is one of Pearson's more inspired works.

St. John's, Red Lion Square (1874–1878), was built on a piece of ground of curious shape, and is ingeniously planned to make the most of the site. There is almost an excess of pretty corners and picturesque peeps; but we cannot fail to wonder at Pearson's virtuosity in the construction of vaults. The church has a broad and rather short nave with aisles and additional outer aisles; there is a west gallery and a semi-circular baptistery. The chancel and its aisles open into the nave. There is an elaborate chapel at the south-east. The triforium stage is fully developed; the vaulting of the nave and of the chancel is of the same height, the vault of the narrower chancel springing from a higher level. The east wall has a successful double row of five lancets. The gilt metal screen and the painted triptych are characteristic and good.

Horsforth Church, near Leeds, was begun in the same year as St. John's. It is a good, solid-looking building, with a tower and spire. The roof is of timber, not stone.

It would be impossible to write of Pearson without saying something about Truro Cathedral, though this book is concerned not with cathedrals, but with parish churches.

The Act constituting the new diocese of Truro was passed in 1876, and in 1878 Pearson was asked to prepare plans for a cathedral. He had sent in nothing but photographs of work that he had already done: Bodley, an unsuccessful competitor, had sent a complete design, and alternative designs as well. The building was begun in 1879, and the foundation stone laid in 1880. Choir and transepts were consecrated in 1887; the foundations of the nave were laid in 1898; the nave (carried out by Mr. Frank L. Pearson after the death of his father) was dedicated in 1903; and in 1910 the western spires were completed. One bay only of the Cloisters has been built: and the Chapter House, Song School and Library have not yet been begun.

The Cathedral consists of nave and aisles of nine bays, with two western towers and south and west porches; central tower; transepts with east and west aisles, and a circular baptistery to the west of the south transept; and choir, with one bay behind the high altar, eastern transepts and aisles. There is a single aisle on the north of the choir, and there are three on the south, the outermost being St. Mary's aisle, the remains of the old parish church. The transverse arches of the second aisle have solid walls above them to receive the buttresses which cross the first aisle and support the vault of the choir. At the west of St. Mary's aisle, and abutting the south transept, is a small tower and spire. The vestries are in a vaulted crypt beneath the choir.

The spirit in which Pearson designed the Cathedral is revealed in the now rather hackneyed story told in the *Life of G. H. Wilkinson* by A. J. Mason: [1] " Before he would put pen to paper, or even begin to imagine what sort of building he should design, he made his Communion in the little old church of St. Mary, which had been assigned to the Bishop as his Cathedral by the Act which founded the see. Mr. Wilkinson had the opportunity of praying with Mr. Pearson then and there. No doubt it was under such influences as his that Mr. Pearson gave a memorable answer to someone who offered a criticism upon his design before he had fully worked it out. ' My business,' he said, ' is to think what will bring people soonest to their knees '."

Probably few other architects of the time could have done as well as Pearson; but the design is less inspired than those of many of his parish churches. The picturesqueness, however, of the exterior is undeniable, and Pearson has grouped his towers and spires with great effect. The view from the south-

[1] *Life of G. H. Wilkinson*, vol. II, p. 120.

east is charming. The west front, with its twin towers and spires is pleasing. There is some variety in the designs of the towers: there might well have been more. The central tower and spire are said to have been Pearson's favourite among his works. Neither the south nor the west porch can be considered to be very successful.

The interior is rather monotonous. In many of Pearson's churches there is an excess of thirteenth-century detail; in Truro there is so much of it that we become almost bored. The east end recalls Whitby Abbey; parts of the choir were suggested by the thirteenth-century work in the Chapel of the Nine Altars at Durham; other features are derived from Lincoln and Westminster. They are welded together by the genius of Pearson, and the whole Cathedral is obviously far more than an enormous collection of choice " bits ". As in the other buildings, the nobility of the whole conception atones for the monotony of some of the detail; but at Truro it only just does so.

The baptistery is a memorial of Henry Martyn the missionary. It has eight slender piers and is vaulted, with eight principal ribs and intermediate and ridge ribs, with carved bosses at each intersection. There is a wall arcade with shafts of various marbles. The baptistery as a whole is over-elaborate. Pearson seldom designed a really pleasing font: this one, of red porphyry (" as recalling the fire of the Holy Ghost ") is commonplace.

The reredos is very ambitious, but it does not greatly appeal to our taste. Nor do the elaborate canopied sedilia: there is far too much of them.

Truro Cathedral is not by any means a failure; but it would hardly be possible to call it a complete success. It was recognized at the time that it would be the last great building of its kind. It expressed a great deal, and was a wonderful result of faith and devotion; but future cathedrals would have to use a different idiom in which to express what they had to say.

During the time that Truro was being built Pearson was busy with many other churches, of which we can mention only some.

St. Alban's, Birmingham, was built in 1879–1881. It has

nave and aisles, western narthex, transepts, apsidal chancel and ambulatory and a chapel on the south of the chancel. The church is built of red brick. The inside walls are faced partly with stone and partly with the same red brick. The more prominent parts and the vaults are all of stone. The whole church is vaulted. The west end is characteristic: there are octagonal turrets, and an arch enclosing the west windows—five lancets and a circular window. A gallery over the windows connects the two turrets at the level of the springing of the gable; in the gable is a triplet. The lower portion of the tower is south of the west bay of the south aisle. The clerestory is lofty, with two light windows, deeply recessed to allow a passage in front of them over the arcades of the nave and chancel. The passage has a perforated parapet. The chapel is entered from the transept by a double arch: it has elaborate vaulting at its east end.

St. Michael's, Croydon, is a very fine example of Pearson's work: it was begun in 1880, dedicated in 1881 and consecrated in 1885. It is built of red brick externally and of London stock brick internally. It consists of an aisled nave with lofty clerestory, base of tower at the south-west, transepts, apsidal chancel with aisles and ambulatory, and south apsidal chapel south of the chancel and opening from the south transept. The chapel of St. George is under the organ-loft to the east of the north transept. There is an internal narthex in the west bay of the nave under the gallery—a common feature in Pearson's churches. There are two flanking turrets to the chancel, and an attractive copper flèche at the crossing. The organ case, pulpit and font are the work of Mr. G. F. Bodley; the choir stalls are by Temple Moore; the tester and hangings of the lady-chapel altar were designed by J. N. Comper. Pearson is recorded to have remarked on visiting this church, " This is a place of real worship ".

Speke church dates from 1881; and in the same year a beginning was made of St. Stephen's, Bournemouth. The nave and aisles of this church were consecrated in 1885, the chancel and lady chapel were begun in 1896, and the tower was built in 1907–1908. The spire has not yet been completed. The nave is of six bays with double aisles; there are transepts, an apsidal chancel with ambulatory, and two chapels, of Our Lady and of All Souls. The east bay of the nave is slightly canted. Here is another iron screen, and an elaborate triptych.

St. John's, Upper Norwood, was also begun in 1881 ; the chancel was dedicated in 1882, and the whole church consecrated in 1887. It consists of a nave of four bays with double aisles ; there is a shorter western bay without aisles with baptistery under the gallery and western narthex beyond. There are transepts : the south transept forms the base of the tower which is not yet completed. The choir is aisled, with an ambulatory behind the altar, which is continued down the choir, inside the arches and behind the choir-stalls. The apsidal lady chapel is to the east of the tower ; the vestries are to the east of the north transept. The stone screen resembles that at St. Augustine's, Kilburn : it is of five arches, of which the outer two lead into the ambulatory. The ten lancets in the east wall are less successful than the six at Kilburn or the ten at Red Lion Square : they are somewhat squat in effect, and the additional vaulting ribs which are carried on shafts within the outer lancets have not a particularly good effect. The lady chapel has seven two-light windows in its apse, divided by seven vaulting ribs. This is not the only chapel in which Pearson seems to have attempted rather too much in a small space. The walls of this church were to have been covered with painting, but this has not materialized.

St. Barnabas', Hove, was designed in 1882 : this is another characteristically Pearsonic church. Headingley was begun in 1883 : it has a tower and spire at the west. The nave is spanned by a series of transverse arches which support the timber roof.

St. Agnes', Sefton Park, Liverpool, was built in 1883–1885, a memorial to Robert, father of Howard Douglas Horsfall. This is another grand, apsidal cruciform church, with the features that we have learned to recognize.

St. George's, Cullercoats, is an example of Pearson's simpler and less ambitious style. It was built by the sixth Duke of Northumberland, in memory of the third Duke, and was consecrated in 1884. According to Bishop Lightfoot, it " set an ideal of something better in the way of church-building than that to which we are commonly accustomed ". It has a nave with aisles of five bays; the western bay of the nave is flanked by porches. The tower is on the south of the choir balancing the transept on the north; it has a plain, graceful spire. The chancel is apsidal with a lofty arcade of blind arches. All the church is vaulted. The triforium stage is rudimentary, indicated by string courses. The aisle windows are single lancets, the clerestory is double, and the west end has two three-light windows and a circular window in the gable.

Hersham (1887) has a nave of four bays, aisles, low tower and spire at the north-west, shallow transepts and a long chancel. It must be pronounced an indifferent specimen of Pearson's work.

St. John's, Redhill, is an ingenious enlargement of an earlier church (1843). It was reconstructed in 1889, and the tower and spire built in 1895. The church was extended, a new chancel built, and a lofty clerestory raised on the old arcades.

Highcliffe, near Winchester, was built in 1889–1896. All Saints', Hove, was begun in 1890, and completed by Mr. F. L. Pearson. It is early Geometrical in style, and has a timber roof supported on transverse arches.

Other noteworthy churches are the Catholic Apostolic Church, Maida Vale (one of his latest works); St. Matthew's, Northampton; St. Patrick's, Birmingham; Port Talbot, and St. Bartholomew's, Nottingham.

Pearson died in 1897.

We are hardly concerned with his restoration work: it will be sufficient to mention a few of his more important works. At Lincoln he partly rebuilt the south-west tower, restored the vaulting of the north transept, and did work in the Chapter House and cloisters. At Peterborough he rebuilt the tower and refitted the choir. At Bristol he completed the towers which Street had designed and begun, restored the Elder Lady Chapel and fitted the choir. At Rochester he restored the west end and completed the turrets; this work did not give general satisfaction. At Exeter he rebuilt part of the cloister, and at Canterbury restored the Chapel of St. Anselm. Scott had designed the porches of the north transept at Westminster Abbey; Pearson completed the transept front. He also restored many parish churches. But this work, though mostly well done, is of less interest than his original parish churches. They showed what Gothic forms could become in the hands of a master, gave a new ideal and set a new standard. Pearson did not live to see a new century: but he had brought to a very high level the art of the old.

George Frederick Bodley gained his first interest in ecclesiology by reading Bloxham's *Gothic Architecture*. Then he met Scott at Brighton, where Scott's brother married his sister. He became Scott's first pupil, went to live with him, and stayed there for five years.

His first work was at Bussage:[1] other early works were France Lynch (1857), St. Michael's, Brighton, consecrated in 1862, and St. Martin's, Scarborough, consecrated in 1863. In his early days he expressed himself in French Gothic. St. Martin's shows a certain amount of thirteenth-century French Gothic influence. In St. Michael's,[2] which he called " a boyish antagonistic effort ", he broke away from the manner of his master : he was " tired of mouldings ", and tried in this church to eliminate them, and use flat bands and un-chamfered arches. His French Gothic was original, and good in its way, but he soon came back to an English style. St. Salvador's, Dundee, built between 1865 and 1870, is purely English Middle Pointed; and All Saints', Cambridge, is characteristically English also, of an early fourteenth-century type. The *Ecclesiologist* greeted this church with pleasure. " We note, with some satisfaction, that Mr. Bodley has restricted himself to pure English forms. The time for reaction from exclusively French or Italian types has at length arrived." This seemly and restrained church must certainly have provided a relief from many of the buildings of the time, though Cambridge suffered less than Oxford from foreign Gothic structures.

In about 1870 Bodley entered into partnership with Thomas Garner, who had also been a pupil of Scott. St. John's, Tue Brook (1868–1870), was the last church of Bodley's before the partnership began, though Garner co-operated in it. It is

[1] An enlargement of a church by J. P. Harrison. It was largely built from the subscriptions of Oxford undergraduates.
[2] Since enlarged, see p. 155.

English mid-fourteenth century in style, and plentifully adorned with painting.

During the first half of their partnership Bodley and Garner were so much in harmony that it is not easy to say which was responsible for any particular piece of work. Generally speaking, Bodley had the greater influence in glass and in colour work, while Garner had more say in matters of carved ornament in stone or wood. Latterly, Bodley did most of the church work and Garner the domestic. The partnership was broken in 1898: Garner became a Roman Catholic, and Bodley remained faithful to the English Church.

In 1878 Bodley failed in the competition for Truro Cathedral. He had been certain of winning, and sent a complete design and alternative designs as well as illustrations of completed works. In the design which he preferred the Cathedral had two towers, over the transepts, and two bays of the old parish church were kept as a lady chapel.

In the Liverpool competition he was one of the assessors with Norman Shaw in 1903: Giles Gilbert Scott was selected architect, but in view of his youth Bodley was asked to collaborate with him. The collaboration was not a great success.

In 1906 he was invited to prepare, with H. Vaughan of Boston, plans for the Episcopal Cathedral of SS. Peter and Paul at Washington. The scheme was well advanced at the time of his death in 1907.

Bodley was associate of the Royal Academy in 1882 and R.A. in 1902. He received the gold medal of the R.I.B.A. in 1889, was elected Fellow, and served on the Council. He had advisory appointments to several Cathedral Chapters—York, Peterborough, Exeter and Manchester.

He was a poet and a musician, with a strong dislike for the business side of his work. His brother, the Rev. William Bodley, made out his accounts for him: he is said to have used his pass-book for making sketches. He travelled in his younger days, but never did very much sketching. He would gaze for a long time at an old building from various points of view, and make up his mind about it on the spot. But he kept a large and carefully ordered quantity of material for reference.

In spite of his gentleness, he always insisted on his designs being carried out as he wished. When in 1879 a narthex and a new bay were to be added to St. Martin's, Scarborough, Lord Grimthorpe, the chancellor, returned the plans with marginal notes. Bodley had the notes rubbed out and the specifications returned. He became in later years very sure of himself, and unwilling to rely on the judgement and the help of other people. Towards the end of his life he came to be regarded as somewhat of a survival from the past. Certainly there were then few equally ardent Gothicists.

A Bodley church is generally recognizable. The style is almost always English Decorated. In some of his churches he used the style that prevailed a little later than the time of the Black Death, with a mixture of Perpendicular and flowing tracery in the windows. This was a later style than it had been considered proper to imitate : it was thirty or forty years later than the early middle Middle-Pointed period when architecture was considered to have reached its height. There is not much old work of this type. In some parts of England the Decorated style lingered on unaltered during the later part of the fourteenth century; in others, the new Perpendicular style appeared ready-made almost at once.[1] Obvious transitional work, of a type which would serve as an illustration to an architectural text-book, is rare. But Bodley was not anxiously seeking a satisfactory number of precedents for what he did : he was trying to continue in his own way the development which was just beginning at that time.

St. Augustine's, Pendlebury (consecrated in 1874), is an example of this kind of style : so are the Church of the Holy Angels, Hoar Cross, and St. Michael's, Folkestone, begun in 1873 and finished ten years later. And many other churches are of this type. The window tracery is usually flowing, but combined with a square head, or with the two mullions of the centre light carried straight up to the head of the window, and made slightly thicker than the others—a type of window which became very fashionable with certain architects.

In St. Michael's, Camden Town, which was begun in 1876,

---

[1] I have never seen an adequate explanation of the fact that the windows in the belfry stage of many indubitably fifteenth-century towers have flowing tracery of a much earlier type.

P

and in many other later works, Bodley turned to an earlier style of English Decorated which was less original but wonderfully refined and tasteful.   But it is not possible to divide his later work into periods : sometimes he inclined to earlier detail and sometimes to later, and he did not despise Perpendicular.   His work is always charming : perhaps it may be found rather too much so.   Mr. T. H. Lyon considers that Bodley confused religion with refinement : he says that Queens' College Chapel, Cambridge, reminded him of an Anglican sisterhood, and made him picture the nuns primly curtseying to the altar.   That is a justifiable criticism.   But it is quite pleasant to visit churches like that after visiting a number of others which remind one of very fierce-looking bearded clergymen, or of wealthy manufacturers of Protestant views.

Bodley brought Gothic to a state of refinement which it had probably never reached before.   Whether Gothic ought to be refined is a different question.   The lack of refinement of certain details of old churches was always a source of embarrassment to the revivalists : a good deal of mediaeval carving is coarse in execution and in subject.   Sometimes the subjects are positively indelicate—a reminder that the ancient artists were not always the pure-souled idealists that Pugin had imagined.   It was out of the question for the revivalists to reproduce anything of that kind, which even Symbolism could not explain away : all details must be edifying.   But quite apart from that, it was felt from the beginning that the vigour of the old workmen had not been recaptured : the best of the new Gothic churches were Gothic very much toned down. Bodley was not able to restore the old vigour and toughness ; but he was able to put into Gothic a new quality which had not been there before.   Its presence altered its nature very considerably, however orthodox the fourteenth-century details may have been.   But if Gothic and religion went together (and Bodley would not have denied that they did), it was right that late nineteenth-century Gothic should be different from mediaeval Gothic—as different as the better type of late nineteenth-century Anglican Catholicism, with its scholarship and refinement, was from the popular religion of the Church of the Middle Ages.

The plans of Bodley's churches are varied. The general plan is a straightforward one of nave and aisles. His chancels are always lofty, and generally of the same height as the nave : at Hoar Cross the chancel is longer and loftier. A chancel arch is usually dispensed with, and a screen marks the division. The aisles are generally high, though at St. Augustine's, Pendlebury, there are passage aisles four feet wide pierced through the internal buttresses. All Saints', Cambridge, has nave and south aisle of equal width. St. Luke's, Warrington, has a central arcade and a north aisle. At the little church of Hom Green the central arcade is rather clumsy, and hides the altar unnecessarily. Clumber is cruciform, with a central tower and spire. St. Matthew's, Chapel Allerton, has a detached tower.

Bodley was the first architect of the nineteenth century who knew how to colour a church. Others were apt to leave the colouring to other people, and many otherwise fairly respectable churches are spoiled by haphazard decoration and by a rather mixed assortment of windows by different artists. Bodley superintended all this part of the work, and regarded the decoration as an integral part of the church. He and his partner, and Gilbert Scott, junior, began the firm of Watts and Co., Baker Street, and obtained for Burne Jones one of his first commissions—a triptych at Brighton. The work of C. E. Kempe appears in many of his churches, and is exactly suitable to them. Bodley's artistic ideals were those of the pre-Raphaelites. Though he did not belong to the brotherhood, he was a friend of William Morris, Burne Jones, Ford Madox Brown, and Rossetti. He gave Morris his first chance of executing ecclesiastical stained glass (at King's Stanley) ; and he designed some of Morris's early wall-papers, and helped with his glass, tiles and church fittings.

The west windows of St. Michael's, Brighton, have some of the earliest glass of William Morris : the cartoons were the work of Ford Madox Brown, Rossetti and Morris. All Saints', Cambridge and St. John's, Tue Brook, were decorated by Kempe.

At St. Martin's, Scarborough, the central panel of the east wall is the work of Burne Jones, and the side panels are the work of Morris. The painting on the organ case is by R.

Spencer Stanhope, and the chancel roof was decorated by Morris with the assistance of Philip Webb. Bodley himself was responsible for the painting over the chancel arch. Morris drew the cartoons for the lower panels of the pulpit; a side panel is by Rossetti. The earlier windows are by Morris from the designs of Burne Jones, F. M. Brown, Rossetti and Philip Webb.

Unfortunately, much of Bodley's painted decoration has already a faded look. Structural polychrome—alas !—does not fade, and nor does most painted glass, however much we may wish that it would. The polished marble and coloured mastic of many nineteenth-century churches will be glaring as long as the churches last: it is sad that a great deal of Bodley's refined colouring has lost its first freshness, and will lose still more. Those of us who were born in the twentieth century have missed the privilege of seeing these churches when they were first built. They will need restoration from time to time. But it is to be hoped that the decoration will not be obliterated : much as we appreciate whitewash, we can still appreciate the work of Bodley and his fellows, and find it beautiful.

Churches of a somewhat Bodleian type were built by other architects. Gilbert Scott, junior, built St. Agnes', Kennington, and All Hallows', Southwark. St. Agnes', which was attacked in the architectural press and defended by Sedding, was consecrated in 1877. Its style is late fourteenth century, of the type that Bodley loved, refined and restrained, with unnecessary features eliminated. There are, for instance, no capitals to the arcades. Nave and chancel are under one roof, and there is a carved, open wooden screen. The tower which was originally designed has not been executed. There is a west gallery— an early instance of the return of this particular feature. The church is fortunate in having a complete set of windows by Kempe. .

St. Agnes' could not possibly be mistaken for a fourteenth-century church : no fourteenth-century architect ever built a church like this. But to say that is not to find fault with it. Scott had succeeded in doing what his father, in all his enormous practice, had never been able to do: he had built a church which had continuity with the best work of the past, but which was at the same time a new thing—inspired by nineteenth-century churchmanship, and able to be used by nineteenth-century—and by twentieth-century—churchmen.

All Hallows', Southwark, is a church of similar type, with a beautiful and spacious interior.   There is no screen here : the church is open from end to end, and terminates in a high altar raised on a flight of rather too many steps.   One noteworthy feature is the prominent position of the font.   It is rather uncommon even in well-planned later nineteenth-century churches to find a font whose position suggests that it is a thing of importance.   There is very often a small apsidal baptistery at the west, combined with porches, in which the font is hidden—not as insignificant as the average Roman baptistery, but nevertheless unnecessarily obscure.

St. Mark's, New Milverton, Leamington, by the same architect is more commonplace.   It has rather more elaboration but rather less charm.[1]

Temple Lushington Moore (1856–1920) was a pupil of Gilbert Scott, junior.   His churches are of a similar type, though he tried to carry the development of Gothic beyond that of the Bodley school.   Many of his churches were built in this century, and therefore fall outside the scope of this book. St. Wilfrid's, Harrogate, and All Saints', Tooting Graveney, can only be mentioned.   A list of his works will be found in the Appendix.   Temple Moore's large churches are exceptionally beautiful; but his many smaller designs are attractive and distinguished.

---

[1] Scott occasionally did non-Gothic work.   His addition of a sanctuary to the Chapel of Pembroke College, Cambridge, improved a good work of Christopher Wren.

CHAPTER X

WE may become reconciled to some of the more absurd buildings by remembering the vigorous parish life of which they
were the centre. Not that every Victorian parish was vigorous :
there were too many of them for that. Until the early part of
the nineteenth century it was possible to form a new parish
only by Act of Parliament, as a civil as well as an ecclesiastical
area was thus formed. The Building Act of 1818 and the Act
of 1824 provided not only for the building of churches, but also
for the formation of parishes. But clearly little advance was
possible until this state of affairs was changed.

The formation of a parish without an Act of Parliament was
first made possible by Sir Robert Peel's Act in 1843. It was
now easy, by means of an Order in Council, on the recommenda-
tion of the Ecclesiastical Commissioners, to establish new
ecclesiastical parishes. The first parish to be formed was
St. Andrew's, Wells Street; and this was followed by a multitude of others.

This was not always satisfactory. Mr. Beresford Hope
said that the Act was in many ways a blessing. " Greater
facilities were unquestionably needed for the subdivision of
parishes than already existed, and these the Act provided upon
the broad and intelligible principle, then for the first time
admitted into our Parliamentary legislation for ecclesiastical
matters, that the creation of the cure of souls was of more
importance than the completion of the material fabric, and that
the new autonomy ought therefore to date from the endowment
of the incumbent and not from the building of the church.
That Sir Robert Peel's Act has, however, proved an unmixed
blessing, no man unconnected with the Ecclesiastical Commission would, I should think, be bold enough to asseverate."
In many cases " the church is either unbuilt . . . or else it

has been built with a debt which is breaking the backs of all who have taken part in that good work ". The Church Rate " has either been refused for years past, as the new church stands in a populous place, or else it is levied for the benefit of the mother-church, and the new institution gets nothing at all, or much less than its right proportion ". The character of the incumbent tends to deteriorate under these circumstances —and altogether the situation of these parishes is most serious. " Where three puny churches, each with a single ill-endowed clergyman, and a proportionately feeble tariff of services, have been erected in a locality where one large church with a staff of four or five clergy, and constant opportunities of worship at all hours, would have been infinitely more beneficial, and not have cost one farthing more at the outset, then these churches must, I suppose, be still maintained as a vested interest. But at least we can be more wise for the future in the institutions which we raise up to meet the growing wants of an increasing population, and to palliate, if not remove, the inconveniences of the existing organization." [1]

The idea that all churches were full in the nineteenth century must be dismissed as a mistake. In London more and more churches were built. In 1854 the London Diocesan Church-Building Society took the place of the former Metropolitan Churches Fund. Bishop Tait, who succeeded Bishop Blomfield in 1856, was in full agreement with his predecessor. In 1857 he held a meeting of property-owners, and proposed the raising of a million pounds for church-building in the next ten years. But after ten years only £467,910 had been received. The *Ecclesiologist* considered that the scheme was spoiled from the beginning by the proposal to demolish some of the City churches. Londoners were not willing to destroy. " They will not only keep their churches, but will make them sumptuous. They decline to be iconoclastic ; they will rather take to ecclesiology."

In 1874 it was decided to continue the Bishop's fund as a permanent diocesan institution. But many of the new churches were failures from the beginning. Bishop Walsham

[1] J. Beresford Hope, *The English Cathedral of the Nineteenth Century*, pp. 15–19.

How, as Suffragan Bishop of Bedford (from 1879), did good work in the East End, and aimed at increasing the number of the clergy.   But in 1885 it was said that " in many districts in East London, taking the average attendance on Sunday, one church would suffice where there are now six ".[1]   A great deal of money and labour had been spent in trying to perform impossibilities.

Unnecessary churches were also built in country districts. New parishes were formed and expensive churches built for small populations.   In many places an old, small church was abandoned or pulled down, and a new and large one built, in which the small congregation felt itself out of place and ill at ease.

On the other hand, there were parishes run as Mr. Beresford Hope desired, which were extraordinarily successful.   They had large churches and a large staff of clergy, and ran the organizations which are now generally accepted, but were then attractive novelties.   In some the services were of a ritualistic type which attracted large numbers from outside the parish.

St. Mary Magdalene's, Paddington, began with a temporary church which was opened in 1865, under the charge of the Rev. R. T. West.   A daily celebration was introduced in the next year.   One paper spoke of it as a church with " a high ritual, but where the poor attend in large numbers, and where the offertory in the course of three months has been close upon £1000 ".   The permanent church, of which we have spoken, was begun in 1867.   When it was decided that it must be larger than was first intended, two ladies sold their house and furniture.   The sale of their plate and jewels procured the alms-dish and lectern.   The Holy Communion was first celebrated there in 1868.   On the Sunday after the fire in 1872, five celebrations were held in the temporary church.   In that year there were 1122 Easter communicants, and the collections amounted to £1189.   The parish soon had a choir school, sisters' home, penitentiary home, working-men's club, nurses' institute, schools and a dependent church of St. Martha.   Mr. Street seemed to imply that women composed the majority of the

[1] *Church Quarterly Review*, Jan. 1885.

PLATE XXXI

[Photo by courtesy of R. S. Morrish.

STOKE D'ABERNON CHURCH TO-DAY

The result of a restoration by Messrs. Ford and Hesketh in 1866. The pulpit was moved and dismembered at the restoration, and reinstated later

PLATE XXXII

ST. MICHAEL'S, CORNHILL

A Wren Church restored by Scott. "An attempt to give tone to the existing classic architecture"

congregation ; but the Bishop of Nassau said that " St. Mary Magdalene's was largely attended by men, many of whom were seniors, and to retain these men in their allegiance, and deepen their love for the church by every lawful means, was (the Vicar's) great and earnest desire. . . . We sometimes had as many as a hundred male communicants, not on great festivals only, but on ordinary first Sundays of a month." [1] It was said of Mr. West that " he would go any distance, and take any trouble to help and minister to his spiritual children, and those who looked to him for help ".[2]

In 1856 Charles Lowder took charge of a mission in the parish of St. George in the East. In the same year an iron church of the Good Shepherd was built, in which there were celebrations of Holy Communion at 7 on weekdays and at 8 and 11 on Sundays. In 1857 a sisterhood was begun in the parish. The neighbourhood was very rough and degraded, and there was much opposition ; nevertheless, large numbers were attracted to the church. Then Lowder secured the old Danish Church in Wellclose Square, and decided that all the clergy should live there. A very strict rule of life was observed in the Clergy House. The riots which continued for a long period in the parish church " tended to consolidate and establish " Lowder's work. In 1860 a Working-men's Institute was formed, at which classes were held in various subjects.

The permanent church of St. Peter (by J. F. Pownall) was consecrated in 1866. It is " in the style of the later First Pointed Gothic, being faced externally with yellow stock bricks, relieved with stone dressings, and internally with red bricks, having bands and patterns of black bricks. The columns of the main arches are of blue Pennant stone. The plan consists of a lofty nave, 68 feet by 27 feet, with clerestory lights. . . . The chancel is 35 feet long by 22 feet wide, with two trefoiled windows in the east end, surmounted by a shafted wheel window about 17 feet in diameter."

The last resistance to the Church was broken down by the heroic service of the clergy and workers in the cholera epidemic.

---

[1] Appendix to *Richard Temple West*, by T. T. Carter.
[2] *Ibid.*, p. 79.

Attempts by the Church Association to stir up trouble came to nothing. Open-air preaching was begun, and an open-air Good Friday procession—the first in 1869.

There were 180 Easter communicants in 1868, 206 in 1869, and 400 in 1880. Schools were built (in 1871), and St. Agatha's Mission was opened. At St. Peter's on Sunday there were celebrations of Holy Communion at 7, 8 and 9; Mattins at 10.15, and High Celebration at 11; classes in the afternoon, Catechism at 2.30, with guild meetings afterwards; Mission service at St. Agatha's at 6.30; Evensong at St. Peter's at 7, followed by a Bible class and boys' class.

On weekdays the services were, Holy Communion at 6.45 and 8; Mattins at 7.30, and Evensong at 8.

Father Lowder died in 1880, and enormous crowds mourned at his funeral.

Other important London churches were St. Matthias', Stoke Newington, from which at great festivals about 500 people had sometimes to be turned away; and St. Alban's, Holborn. St. Alban's was opened in 1863, and quickly achieved fame under A. H. Mackonochie. It was said that the congregation was " made up . . . after allowing for a few rich and a good many poor, of shopmen, warehousemen, tradesmen, professional men, students of medicine, etc.; the very men whom the Church generally finds it so hard to hold together ". The church attracted notice as the result of the ritual prosecutions which continued through a number of years, but the prosecutions did little to disturb the building up of the life of the parish. There were schools, various classes, district visitors, an association of laymen, sisters, choir school, orphanage, infant nursery, youths' institute, soup kitchen, working-men's club, recreation society, cricket and swimming clubs, night schools, perseverance association, C.E.M.S., E.C.U.; and from 1877 Father Stanton's St. Martin's League for Postmen.

Christchurch, Hampstead, was a flourishing centre of Evangelical life under E. H. Bickersteth, vicar from 1855 to 1885.

The parish life of Leeds Parish Church was wonderfully transformed by W. F. Hook, who was afterwards Dean of

Chichester. It has been called " the most stirring centre of parochial life at that period ". Hook found when he arrived little more than fifty communicants in his enormous parish, hardly any of whom were men. After two or three years there were 400 or 500 communicants at Easter, and before he left Leeds the number was often doubled. In 1844 he at last succeeded in obtaining an Act of Parliament for the division of the parish. About 20 chapels of ease became parish churches. He took a great interest in education and in everything that concerned the welfare of working people : he advocated the Factory Ten Hours Bill, and supported the early closing movement.

Particulars of one or two unnamed parishes are given in the appendix to *The Parish Priest of the Town* by John Gott : " Parish A.—A town of this generation ; wholly mechanic, a pure creation of the railway, with no legacy of the past . . . 14,000 population ; clergy, 6 ; communicants last Easter, 610 ; weekly average, 111 ; church workers, 396 ; Sunday scholars, 1,883 ; confirmed in last three years, 360 ; lay preachers, 7, conducting children's services in lecture hall."

" Parish B.—A new district of a great town. . . . Population, 6,000, mixed poor and lower middle ; clergy, 5 ; church workers, 235 ; communicants last Easter, 1,180, *i.e.* one-fifth ; weekly average, 177 ; 973 (573 adults) are in Holy Communion classes ; confirmed in last three years, 373, *i.e.* 2 per cent. a year ; Sunday-school children (on books), 1,400."

Several new parishes had been formed in Derby in the nineteenth century. At the beginning of the 1890's the services at St. Andrew's combined " evangelical simplicity with comeliness of church order ". There were 50 wardens and sidesmen, 40 choristers and ringers, and a men's Bible class of 200 ; the Sunday collections brought in £535 in the year. St. Anne's had seven services on Sundays and three a day during the week ; there were eight guilds, and various meetings, classes and clubs. St. Barnabas' had 1000 Sunday-school scholars : the Langley Street schools were built entirely by the working men of the parish. St. Chad's had 1200 children in the Sunday schools. The iron church of St. Augustine had a musical and hearty service ; the collections for one year covered the expense of the services, and left £20 over for the maintenance of the clergy.   Christchurch had flourishing schools, Total Abstinence Society, Band of Hope, Bible classes, Y.M. Mutual Improvement Society, parish library, sewing classes and mothers' meetings.   Holy Trinity had schools, library, classes, cottage lectures and communicants' and teachers' meetings.   At St. James the Greater there were two daily services and four on Sundays ; the training of the young was given a prominent place in parochial arrangements.   St. Dunstan's had Bible classes, meetings, P.S.A., brass and drum-and-fife bands, and a men's institute ; it was considered to be a proof that the Church of England is truly the Church of the poor.   The services at St. John's were highly musical, hearty and congregational.   St. Luke's enjoyed the purest English ritual in the town ; it had been visited by many famous preachers.   St. George's had 400 children in its Sunday schools.   At St. Paul's the services were musical ; the Vicar intoned.   Processional and recessional hymns were *de rigueur*. The parochialia included C.E.T.S., G.F.S., communicants' union, mothers' meetings, clothing club and Bible classes. At Easter 1891 there was a credit balance of 13s. 11d. in the accounts of the previous year.   St. Thomas's had many organizations, 700 in the Sunday school, and choral services.[1]

Important work was done in many country parishes.

W. J. Butler, afterwards known as Butler of Wantage, was appointed incumbent of Wareside in 1844.   A chapel of the Holy Trinity had been built by a former vicar.   He visited the whole parish with regularity, and found no real knowledge of religion.   He said that the men attended church in large numbers, but that the women, who had to prepare dinners, would not come in the morning.   Butler's famous work was done at Wantage ; but at Wareside he was able to accomplish not a little.

In 1861 James Skinner was appointed to the very small parish of Newland, near Malvern.   He found that the Holy Communion had been celebrated three times a year ; then once in every second month.   He increased the number of celebrations, until after seven years there was a daily Eucharist.

[1] From C. J. Payne, *Derby Churches Old and New*.

On Christmas Day 1863 the church was so full that there was scarcely standing room. There were two celebrations and an increase of fifty communicants. The church was an interesting one of wood, said to date from the fourteenth century. But it was " in a rickety state ". It was therefore unfortunately pulled down, and a new church built in 1862–64. This was filled every Sunday, though not entirely by parishioners ; and in 1867 there were 136 Easter communicants. Vestments were introduced in 1868.

And in a great number of other parishes there were large congregations and many good works.

The number of new parishes and new churches was enormous. 106 new churches were built in the Diocese of Oxford during the Episcopate of Bishop Wilberforce.

Bishop Sumner was appointed to Winchester in 1827 ; in 1837 the Diocesan Church Building Society was formed. By 1864 the Bishop had consecrated 82 new churches in Hampshire, and 65 which had been rebuilt ; in Surrey 87 new ones and 33 rebuilt ; and in the Channel Islands seven and two. Between that time and his resignation, the Bishop had consecrated about 40 new churches, and 400 restored or enlarged. In 1864 the expenditure on Church building had been £1,704,914.

In the Diocese of Manchester, Bishop Lee (1848–69) consecrated 110 new churches, the cost of erection, exclusive of endowments and cost of sites, being £451,344. Twenty new churches were built in place of old ones. 163 new district parishes and ecclesiastical districts were formed. In the time of Bishop Fraser (1869–85) 105 new churches were built at a cost of £730,079. Twenty new ones were built in place of old. The number of new parishes was 117.

In Wales also there was plenty of church-building. In the Diocese of St. Asaph a Diocesan Church Building Society was formed in 1834 ; by the year 1888 it had assisted in the building of 58 new churches, the rebuilding of 26, and the restoration and improvement of 93 others.

In the Diocese of St. David's eight churches were built between 1831 and 1851, and about 30 between 1851 and 1881.

In the Diocese of Llandaff, 47 new churches were built or rebuilt and 69 restored or enlarged between 1890 and 1899.

And, even if we regret the way in which money was spent, we admire the generosity which church-building inspired.

Almost all the money for all this was raised voluntarily. Church Rates had been a grievance for many years, and in many places were not paid at all. Nonconformists were naturally unwilling to pay for buildings which they would never enter. The English Church Union vigorously defended the existing law, and resolutions on the subject occur frequently in the records of the meetings. The Society considered that all that was necessary was the improvement of the machinery, and resisted attempts at abolition. However, in 1868 Gladstone's Compulsory Church-Rate Abolition Bill removed the power of enforcing any claim for the rate, and it disappeared. The Ecclesiastical Commissioners gave grants, and the Church Building Society.[1]   The latter would not give a grant if it was intended to charge for seats. But pew-rents were sometimes used as a means of raising money. The *Ecclesiologist* complained in 1853 that of the sum of £10,000 required for the building of St. Mary's Church, Stoke Newington, half was expected from subscriptions, £1000 from sermons by popular preachers, something from the Church building societies, something from the mortgage of estates, and the remainder from pew-rents. The pew-rent part of the scheme was in this case given up : but it was used in others.

Sometimes money came in but slowly. Mr. J. T. Micklethwaite says [2] that in many cases the clergyman " tries to get some other people interested in the matter, but they do not see it as he does ; one gives a small subscription, and another a small subscription, and at last, after a great deal of begging and scraping, the anxiety and labour of which ought not to have been thrown upon the parson at all, two or three thousand pounds are got together. Mr. Flick is called upon to furnish

[1] In 1936 the amount contributed by the Society from its foundation was £1,025,477 in 9762 grants from its general fund ; and 1094 grants amounting to £35,750 from the Mission Buildings Fund.
[2] J. T. Micklethwaite, *Modern Parish Churches*, pp. 331–332.

a design, and in due time there rises what the newspapers are pleased to call a ' neat Gothic edifice '."

But in many cases the nobility and gentry and clergy, if they could afford it, were very liberal. After the Rev. W. J. E. Bennett had been for a short time vicar of St. Paul's, Knightsbridge, he made an appeal to his congregation : " The existence of this poor population now immediately around you depends entirely upon *yourselves*. You are the indirect creators of it. It is you that have brought them here, from the magnificent dwellings in which you live, and the houses and carriages which you keep, and the many servants whom you require to minister to your wants. . . . Come with me into the lanes and streets of this great city. Come with me and visit the dens of infamy, and the haunts of vice, ignorance, filth and atheism, with which it abounds. Come with me and read the story of Dives and Lazarus. Come with me and turn over the pages of the Holy Book, by whose precepts your lives are, at least, in theory, guided. Then look at your noble houses, and the trappings of your equipages, the gold that glitters on your sideboards, and the jewels that gleam on your bosoms ; then say within your secret conscience, as standing before the great and terrible God at the day of judgement, what shall I do if I give not of the one, to relieve the other ? " Large sums were given as the result of the appeal, and the school and church of St. Barnabas', Pimlico, begun.

There were several London laymen who did noble work in the cause of the church-building. William Cotton of Leytonstone, known as the lay archdeacon, was the first lay promoter of Bishop Blomfield's Building Scheme. He built and endowed, among many other works, the church of St. Paul, Bow Common. Robert Brett of Stoke Newington was one of the founders of St. Matthias'. Richard Foster helped the building of the group of new churches in Haggerston, and was responsible for St. Barnabas', Walthamstow, St. Bartholomew's, Bermondsey, and other London churches.

Sir Tatton Sykes built or rebuilt many churches in the Yorkshire wolds—including East Heslerton, Hilston, Kirby Grindalythe, Luttons Ambo, Sledmere, Thixendale, Fimber, Helperthorpe, and Weaverthorpe. St. Alban's, Holborn, was the gift of the Right Hon. J. G. Hubbard and Lord Leigh. Mr. Douglas Horsfall was a most generous benefactor of the Church in Liverpool.

Of the clergy, Dr. Pusey sent anonymously a gift of £5000 towards the building of churches in London; Holy Trinity, Vauxhall, was built and endowed at the sole cost of Archdeacon Bentinck; St. Stephen's, Lewisham, by the Rev. S. Russell Davies; All Saints', Hawkhurst, by the Rev. H. A. Jeffreys and his family. The Rev. A. D. Wagner of Brighton gave liberally of his means to build the Church of the Resurrection (no longer in use), St. Mary Magdalene, Bread Street, the Church of the Annunciation, St. Bartholomew's, and St. Mary's, Buxted. A great church-builder was John Erskine Clarke, Vicar of St. Michael's, Derby, who rebuilt his church after it had partly fallen down in 1856, and then raised money for (and himself subscribed to) the building of St. Andrew's, of which he afterwards became the first incumbent. In 1872 he became Vicar of Battersea, and during his time there was responsible for the building and maintaining of five new churches.

Mrs. Norma Hunt of Godstone helped the Church in South London, and built the church of All Hallows, Southwark.

Clearwell, Gloucestershire, was the gift of the Dowager Duchess of Dunraven; Bicton, Devon, was erected by Louisa Lady Rolle; Edvin Loach and Tedstone Wafer, Herefordshire, were built by E. Higginson; Welsh Bicknor, Herefordshire, by the Rector and Stephen Allaway. These are a few taken at random from hundreds of examples.

But the poor also sometimes contributed. When St. Mary Magdalene's, Paddington, was being built, a working-man was heard to say as he dropped his offering into the bag, " That, at any rate, will pay for one brick ".

CHAPTER XI

ENORMOUS sums of money were spent not only on the building of new churches, but also on the restoration of the old. And in this matter neither the generosity of the subscribers, nor the vigorous church life which led to the restoration of churches, and which increased in vigour as the result of it, can induce us to regard with favour the work that was done.

The old parish churches of England are still of extraordinary interest and beauty to-day ; but their value was far greater one hundred years ago.

There has never been a time in which some work has not been done to the old churches. All through the Middle Ages most churches underwent alterations and repairs and enlargements : only very small chapels in very small hamlets escaped altogether. Of course all repairs were done in the manner of the time. In a few cases in which building was spread over a large number of years—as at Westminster and Beverley —there was a deliberate assimilation of style to that of the earlier work. But such cases are very rare. When cathedrals and parish churches were enlarged or altered, the work was done in the manner that was then natural. And there is no incongruity at all with the older work.

After the Reformation, in the latter part of the sixteenth and the seventeenth centuries, there was very little enlargement : the churches were simply kept more or less in repair. Probably far more work was done than is commonly imagined. Though at the time Renaissance modes were being introduced, the ordinary mason probably continued to work on the old lines, and what he did was hardly distinguishable from similar work of a century or two before. What looks like fifteenth-century work may really belong to the seventeenth. The old traditions died hard.

Q

227

By the eighteenth century Classical fashions had become almost universal, and additions and repairs were made in a more or less Classical style. Sometimes windows were slightly pointed and had wooden mullions; but they were obviously not Gothic. And still there was very little incongruity. A red brick Classical mausoleum might be expected to look out of place by the side of a thirteenth-century chancel; but it seldom does. A white wooden cupola rather improves a fifteenth-century tower. And Classical altar-pieces and pulpits often enhance the beauties of a Gothic interior.

It is often forgotten how much was done to churches in the seventeenth and eighteenth centuries, because so much of the work has disappeared. But it is hardly fair to destroy it, and then to speak as though it was never there.

Nevertheless, by the beginning of the nineteenth century many churches were in bad repair, and restoration was necessary.

The early numbers of the *Ecclesiologist* give many examples of churches that were desecrated, mutilated, or ruinous. In the south chapel of Rippingale " the scene of desolation on entering the interior is a disgrace to all parties who knowingly tolerate such an atrocious perversion of its use. The floor is torn up, uneven, and literally falling to pieces. . . . The east wall is falling outwards, and a most magnificent Early Decorated window of four lights has its tracery intercepted by the low roof, and filled up with mortar. The floor is of course strewed with filth, rubbish, deal forms, and unsightly and indescribable piles of deal woodwork."

At Cliffe-at-Hoo " the north aisle is used as a day-school, with all the accompanying juvenile nastiness; the west end of the same aisle is a rubbish hole, and is now filled with a store of brambles, coals, and cinders: the transepts are falling, and the tower is shored up with a gigantic buttress of brick ". A north chapel at Hingham was used as a gaol and as a dog-kennel.

This is the kind of thing which writers of the Oxford-Move-ment-Shown-to-the-Children school love to rake up. They like to give the impression that all the old churches were on the brink of ruin. Of course they were not; nevertheless there were many which urgently needed restoration. But what does restoration mean ? It may mean simply preservation, or it may mean preservation with a certain amount of unnecessary reconstruction; it may even mean complete rebuilding on a new design. Of the first there are very few instances before the late nineteenth century; [1] almost every Victorian restoration was of the second or third kind.

Destructive restoration was sometimes done in the eighteenth century in accordance with a particular theory—the theory that a Gothic church should present an uninterrupted vista from end to end.

Wyatt's restorations of Salisbury and Lichfield were of this type : he opened the cathedrals from end to end to procure an uninterrupted view. This was no doubt ill-advised; but at any rate he knew what he wanted to do. The same process was carried out at Durham later, though there the altar screen was left.

But often in the early nineteenth century unnecessary alteration was carried out without any theory at all.

The pre-Conquest top of the tower of Whittingham Church, Northumberland, was rebuilt in 1840 in the Gothic style; and most of the north arcade was removed to make room for a copy of the one on the south. In Daglingworth Church, Gloucestershire, some very interesting work was destroyed in 1845, and a window was given away to Barnsley Church. This kind of restoration continued at intervals throughout the nineteenth century. In 1866 the whole appearance of Stoke d'Abernon, Surrey, was altered, and much interesting work destroyed. In 1878 Sir Gilbert Scott removed a pre-Conquest arch at Godalming to make room for an imitation thirteenth-century one.

Probably the most destructive of nineteenth-century architects was Lord Grimthorpe, who restored St. Albans Cathedral and the churches of St. Michael and St. Peter, St. Albans. He " claimed the right to alter old buildings exactly as we

[1] The small church of Llandegveth, Mon., was rebuilt in 1875–1876 with a minimum of alteration. The chancel arch is new, otherwise the church is exactly as it was. The windows on the south side are " debased " ; ninety-nine out of a hundred Victorian architects would not have been able to resist the temptation to alter them. Llandegveth is exceptional enough to deserve mention.

feel like ", and was perfectly self-confident and impenitent. His little book on St. Albans Cathedral and its Restoration describes his own doings, and includes a great deal of abuse of Scott for his timidity, conservatism and incompetence. Lord Grimthorpe was vigorously attacked, and he says that he would have been overwhelmed " if I did not, like Nehemiah, hold the trowel in one hand and the (feathered) sword in the other, and use it every now and then. I never threw the first stone, but only laid them ; which in this case seems to be thought worse." [1] The book is amusing ; but, of course, his work was quite unjustifiable.

But the most dangerous type of nineteenth-century restoration was that which was animated by a theory : the ecclesiological theory of pure style and correct arrangement. The ecclesiologists had an ideal of what a church should look like. But of course most churches did not look like that. They did not do so because much work had been done to them since the thirteenth and fourteenth centuries ; and even then they probably did not look as the ecclesiologists imagined. That was unfortunate ; but it was easily to be remedied. They could be made to look like it. And they were.

There was much talk of the " original style ". As a matter of fact the original style of many churches was Saxon ; in the case of many others—probably the majority—it was Norman. But it was out of the question to restore them to a primitive, undeveloped and unsymbolic style. The original style meant the style that the ecclesiologists liked, which, as we have seen, was late thirteenth-century Geometrical and fourteenth-century Decorated. Most churches had some remains of these styles which could be worked into the reconstruction ; or, if there was not enough to suggest a pattern, a model could be found in some local church which gave some idea as to how the church might have looked if it had ever been like what the restorers wished it to be.

It is interesting to read Gilbert Scott's *Plea for the Faithful Restoration of our Ancient Churches*, published in 1850, for it sets out clearly the folly of much that was going on at the time, and gives some wise advice on the subject. Scott did not take his own

---

[1] *St. Albans Cathedral and its Restoration*, p. x.

advice, either then or later.   But the essay is worth reading.   It
begins with a conventional description of the rise of Christian
architecture, its retirement like the dove which found no fit
resting-place on the still-deluged earth, and its revival in the
nineteenth century.   The revival has, of course, been a good
thing ; but unhappily we are so ready from *learners* to become
judges, and to conduct restorations without humility.   " Nearly
every restorer has his favourite style, or some fancy notion,
to which he wishes to make everything subservient ; and it is a
most lamentable fact, that there has been far more done to
obliterate genuine examples of pointed architecture, by the
tampering caprices of well-meant restorations, than had been
effected by centuries of mutilation and neglect.   A restored
church appears to lose all its truthfulness, and to become as
little authentic, as an example of ancient art, as if it had been
rebuilt on a new design.   The restorer too often preserves
only just what he fancies, and alters even that if it does not
quite suit his taste.   He adds what features his caprice dictates
and removes such as do not happen to please him, without
the smallest consideration that the building should be treated
with more veneration than if it had been erected yesterday.
It is against this system of so-called restoration, a system
which threatens to deprive us of all authentic examples of
the humbler forms of this sacred art, that I wish to take this
opportunity of PROTESTING." [1]

Three modes of Restoration had been mentioned : the
Conservative, Destructive and Eclectic.   A conservative
restorer would reproduce the exact details of every piece of
ancient work which presented itself at the time of the restoration.   A destructive restorer would do what the mediaeval
architects did—disregard the work of the past, destroy what
was there already, and rebuild it in the best style of art.   An
eclectic would take a middle course : in some cases restoring
and in others remodelling.

The Destructive architects " plead the example of the
mediaeval architects, who, *disdainful* of past, and *discontented*
with present attainments, were ever earnestly pressing after
new developments of their art, and sometimes destroyed, to

[1] *Plea for the Faithful Restoration of our Ancient Churches*, pp. 20-21.

make room for them, the beautiful works of their predecessors ".[1]
But our position is *totally distinct* from that of the ancient
architects. They were led by Providence to originate a new
style of art : we are called to reawaken one that has for centuries
lain dormant.   We have to learn from the works of our masters ;
and therefore we must not destroy the works from which we
learn.   " We should view the remains of the whole range of
pointed architecture, whether in its earlier or later forms, in
its humbler or more glorious examples, as the one vast treasury
of Christian art, wonderfully produced, and as wonderfully
preserved for our use ; as a chain *every link* of which is necessary
to its future uses ; as a wreath, now faded and disarranged,
but every flower of which, we may hope, is destined to revive,
and to be woven anew, by hands more skilful than our own."[2]

The restorer should be a Conservative, however hard it may
be consistently to carry out his own principles.   " As a general
rule, it is highly desirable to preserve those vestiges of the
growth and history of the building which are indicated by the
various styles and irregularities of its parts ; they often add
interest to a church in other respects poor ; they frequently
add materially to its picturesque character ; and nearly always
render it more valuable as a study.   This rule is, however,
open to many exceptions ; and it is here, perhaps, more than
on any other question, that a sound judgement and freedom
from caprice is needed.   In some cases the *later* are the more
valuable and beautiful features ; but in these the architect
of true feeling will be very unwilling to obliterate earlier
features, however simple or even rude, to bring them into
uniformity with more ornamental additions.   Indeed, it may
be laid down as a rule that some vestige *at the least* of the oldest
portions should always be preserved, as a proof of the early
origin of the building.   In other cases, some one of the *earlier*
styles claims the finest and most beautiful features ; but it
by no means follows that later parts should be removed, even
though they may infringe upon finer forms : in some instances,
however, this may seem to be desirable, particularly when, as
is often the case, the later portions are themselves decayed,

[1] *Plea for the Faithful Restoration of our Ancient Churches*, pp. 22–23.
[2] *Ibid.*, p. 26.

and the earlier may be restored with absolute certainty. It may, however, be assumed as a rule that an authentic feature, though late and poor, is more worthy than an earlier though finer part *conjecturally restored*. . . . Above all, I would urge that *individual caprice* should be *wholly excluded* from restorations. Let not the restorer give undue preference to the remains of any one age, to the prejudice of another, merely because the one *is*, and the other *is not, his own favourite style*." [1] Lost details should not be restored from conjecture; there may be indications of the nature of the original, or neighbouring churches may supply it. Fragments of mural painting, tiles, glass, ironwork, seating and screenwork should be carefully preserved, and the general character of the church should not be lost. " It is often preferable to retain reminiscences of the age of Elizabeth, or James, or the martyred Charles, rather than to sweep away, as is now the fashion, everything which dates later than the Reformation."

The essay ends with a quotation of some " appropriate lines " by Mr. Petit. They end :

> " It were a pious work, I hear you say,
> To prop the fallen ruin, and to stay
> The work of desolation. It may be
> That ye say right ; but, O ! *work tenderly ;*
> Beware lest one worn feature ye efface—
> Seek not to add one touch of modern grace ;
> Handle with reverence each crumbling stone,
> Respect the very lichens o'er it grown ;
> And bid each ancient monument to stand,
> Supported e'en as with a filial hand.
> Mid all the light a happier day has brought,
> We work not yet as our forefathers wrought ! "

This is all very well, and we agree with nearly all of it. But it would hardly be possible to find among the enormous number of Sir Gilbert Scott's restorations one which was conducted exactly according to these principles. He said in an address in 1875 to the Institute of British Architects, " One may say that a certain proportion of our churches have been carefully dealt with ; another proportion treated with fair intention but less success ; but that, as I fear, the majority are almost utterly despoiled, and nine-tenths, if not all, of

[1] *Plea for the Faithful Restoration of our Ancient Churches*, pp. 29–31.

their interest swept away ". As the result, " a church-tour is one of the most distressing and sickening of adventures ".

But, with a great display of injured innocence, he always defended himself. This description fitted the work of others : it did not suit his own. His own work had always been most conscientious, and he had only once had reason to repent.[1] He always considered himself to be a conservative ; and others agreed. The writer of his obituary in the *Builder* (April 6, 1878) says that Scott was "incapable of putting on to an old building any feature which was a pure invention of his own". And the claim is supported by Dean Burgon in his preface to Scott's *Recollections*. He compares the work of the average restorer, as the result of whose work hardly a single point of interest remains in the greater number of the lesser country churches, with that of Scott, and tells of his restoration of Houghton Conquest church, in which everything (very nearly) was preserved. Scott also, he says, preserved the Laudian porch of St. Mary's, Oxford. But against that must be set his work at St. Mary's, Cambridge, where he altered the top of the tower, which had been finished in the early seventeenth century, and replaced the Renaissance west door with a new one. And against Houghton Conquest must be set many hundreds of parish churches with faked Geometrical work and gutted interiors.

Scott complained that the anti-restoration party tried to make him out to be the " ring leader of destructiveness ". But, he says, if there has been any destruction, it has been the fault of his employers. That is probably to some extent true ; but the excuse was not allowed to Wyatt. In any case, he admits that " the best of us have been blameable, and even our conservatism has been more or less destructive ".[2] He says that it is not possible in all cases to be consistent in conservatism ; but need the cases have been quite so frequent ? Neither he nor the many other architects who restored churches through the nineteenth century could confine themselves to conservatism : they were eclectic or destructive.

---

[1] In the matter of the restoration of the Bridge Chapel at Wakefield. But he seems also to have repented at St. Asaph.

[2] Sir G. G. Scott, *Personal and Professional Recollections*, p. 359.

Mr. E. A. Freeman was certainly exaggerating when he said, " There are persons calling themselves admirers of ancient art, lovers of ancient churches, who have sent forth, in a style which would not have disgraced King Harry himself, a solemn mandate for the entire destruction of Peterborough Cathedral and King's College Chapel, with the single proviso that buildings supposed to approach more nearly to some fancied ideal may be erected in their place ".   But it was an exaggeration of something that had really been said.   At a meeting of the Ecclesiological Society on May 18, 1847, J. M. Neale announced his willingness to see Peterborough Cathedral pulled down, " if it could have been replaced by a Middle Pointed Cathedral as good of its sort ".   The members of the Society having expressed their opinions, Mr. Neale said that mediaeval architects only destroyed the works of their predecessors in the belief that their own were better.   He himself, could he know that a better style than Middle Pointed was discovered, would destroy all Middle Pointed building.   The *Ecclesiologist* agreed that Destructive restoration was the safest.   " There is no use in believing or asserting one style of Christian art to be superior to others, if nevertheless we are not to employ it because it happens to have been removed to make way for another."   But it advised waiting for a time " until architects have complete mastery of their art.   But every year will diminish the force of this objection."

But the architects did not wait.   They light-heartedly reconstructed and rebuilt, in many cases obliterating all traces of the history of the church, and in many cases falsifying it. " The south transept, let us say, has a particularly fine five-light late Perpendicular window, with fragments of coeval glass in the upper tracery beneath its obtusely pointed Tudor head.   There are some stately large Early English windows in the chancel.   The architect, enamoured of these designs, sets out a clever triplet of lancets and—if funds are abundant— suggests that ' the painfully debased transept window ' should be removed in favour of his pretty sketch, and the roof-pitch raised.   The rector and his committee, overawed by the big man's name and impressed by the prettiness of the sketch, consent.   One parishioner, of more knowledge than his fellows, offers a vain protest.   The church-breakers are set vigorously to work. In pulling down the end of the transept, several hidden fragments of undoubted mouldings of thirteenth-century Early-English window-jambs come to light. The architect produces these in triumph, and the least intelligent of the committee regard the great man in hushed awe, as akin to a magician. Had the objector known a little more, he would have gone to the heap of dislodged masonry, turned up a stone or two closely marked with Norman axeing and another perchance bearing Saxon tooling, and told the architect that there was just as much justification in giving transept windows of the days of Athelstan or Stephen as those of Henry III. And this is exactly the kind of thing that went on in a score or two of highly interesting parish churches in the mid-Victorian epidemic of rash restoration, when many a period was obliterated to satisfy the ideal fancies of some would-be purist." [1]

We agree with Scott's advice to retain work of the reigns of Elizabeth, James and Charles ; but in how many cases did he do it ? He says that he always saved Jacobean pulpits and altars and tried to keep sounding-boards. But did he ? It would perhaps be too much to expect him to have kept work of the period of the Georges, for, as we said, " Georgian " and " hideous " have been until the present day almost synonymous. But work of the seventeenth century would seem to have had a special claim to be preserved.

The theologians of the Oxford Movement were interested in the work of the Caroline Divines, and regarded them as supplying the basis and authority for the Anglicanism which they were attempting to revive and preserve. They appealed to Laud and Ken and Andrewes, Bancroft, Wren, Montague and Thorndike—and rightly : their works are of the greatest importance, and provide the necessary link between the Reformation and the Anglicanism of the present day.

The Ecclesiological Society published a valuable book of extracts illustrative of the ritual of the Church of England after the Reformation under the title of *Hierugia Anglicana.* The compilers say in the preface,[2] " We take our stand on the ground held by Andrews, Bancroft, Laud, Wren, Montague,

---

[1] J. C. Cox, *English Parish Church*, pp. 209–210.
[2] *Hierugia Anglicana*, p. 9.

and their fellow confessors, and we claim, with them, for the English Church, the revival of all the vestments and ornaments to which, it can be proved, she is justly entitled ".

It might have been expected that all the work of their period would have been carefully preserved as an outward sign of the continuity which the theologians stressed.

But the architects—and the clergy, who were even more to blame—seemed to take a pleasure in removing from their churches all that was post-Reformation, and doing their best to make them look as though the seventeenth century had never existed.

The Oxford Architectural Society suggested that a church ought to be restored to the state in which it was in the year 1550. G. E. Street considered that this was a good working rule. It was certainly put into practice.

Islip, Oxfordshire, is a particularly egregious example. " The old chancel falling into disrepair was rebuilt in 1680 by Robert South, then rector, and his chancel was a valuable specimen of church architecture and ritual at this date, fitted with a wooden lectern, altar, and credence-table complete. A so-called restoration in 1861 swept all this away, modernized and ' beautified ' the nave, and built the present chancel of vapid Dec. in the place of South's work." [1] Even the *Ecclesiologist* called the seventeenth-century work "an interesting testimony to the Catholic practice of the reformed Anglican Church ". A screen dating from 1610 was removed from Wimborne Minster.

Altar rails mostly dated from the seventeenth century ; some were probably introduced in the sixteenth, but there were none before that. And yet in innumerable churches they were thrown away, and superseded by altar rails in the style of the Middle Ages—when there were none. Seventeenth-century pulpits were removed in favour of new pulpits in the style of the thirteenth century—when there were no pulpits. It is hard to see how this kind of thing could ever have been called restoration.

The destruction of screens had begun in the eighteenth century. Pugin had opposed it, and put the case for screens very strongly. The ecclesiologists liked them because they

[1] Murray's *Handbook to Oxfordshire*, p. 97.

could be given a symbolical meaning.   But in the restoration
of churches screens were often light-heartedly destroyed.
There can be no excuse whatever for this.   Mr. Aymer Vallance
gives many flagrant examples.   Eighty-two screens were mentioned in 1896 as having disappeared from Devonshire churches
" during comparatively recent times ".   Iffley, Asthall, Bodicote,
Long Combe and Swinbrook in Oxfordshire, Worth in Sussex
and Ashwell in Herts, are typical of many other such cases.

It was often customary in the fifteenth century, unless the rood
was higher than the chancel arch, to fill the arch with painted
boarding, which served as a background to the rood.   Many
of these tympana remained until the nineteenth century ;
but now they are rare.   The Rev. J. L. Fulford read a paper to
the Exeter Diocesan Architectural Society in 1848 in which he
said, " We must commence with necessary repairs, unless there
should be . . . a plaster division reaching from the screen to
the point of the chancel arch, which may be at once altered ".[1]

The boardings had in many cases been plastered over or
painted with the Royal Arms, and the restorers, in their
ignorance, probably imagined them to be post-Reformation.
So they were removed.   A few remain in their place (as at
Llangwm Uchaf and Bettws Newydd, Monmouthshire) ; a few
remain in some other position—as at Wenhaston, Suffolk ;
but most of them have gone.

Many seventeenth-century fonts, of course, were removed ;
and even fonts of the twelfth and thirteenth centuries were
displaced in favour of new and more symbolical modern ones.
I have even seen a church in which the old font stands unused
beside an exact but very uninteresting copy of itself.

It is a very sad story indeed.   Some of the mischief has been
repaired in this century ; but most of it is quite irreparable.

In 1877 the Society for the Protection of Ancient Buildings
was formed, with William Morris as secretary ; the first annual
meeting was held in 1878.   The Society did useful work ;
and it certainly succeeded in annoying the architects.   The
building journals contain many gibes at the " Anti-Restora-
tionists ".   Scott found three faults in them ; first, they had
been silent while destruction had been going on, and not

[1] Quoted in Aymer Vallance, *English Church Screens*, p. 25.

encouraged those who for years had raised their voices against it—(*sc.* himself). Secondly, they attacked those whose protests they had all along refused to support—(himself again). Thirdly, they took an impracticable line, advocating abstaining from doing anything but the barest sustenance. Certainly they were unreasonable at times ; but their unreasonableness was justified many times over. They did their best to stem the tide of senseless destruction. But no one can replace the things that have been destroyed.

We can look tolerantly on the removal of galleries. Many churches had unnecessary and ugly galleries, and as the accommodation on the floor was increased by the substitution of benches for the old square pews,[1] it was quite reasonable to remove them. We do not like to see galleries in the aisles of a Gothic church. But in most cases the west gallery should not have been destroyed. It was the direct descendant of the old rood-loft. It was probable that rood-lofts were some-times used for choirs ; and when they were demolished their place was taken by the gallery at the west. In some instances the gallery was simply the rood-loft transferred bodily to the west end of the church. It was the tradition for the musicians to be in a gallery ; and the custom of the seventeenth and eighteenth centuries perpetuated the mediaeval one. A mixed choir of men and women singers and a selection of instruments were customary in the eighteenth century if there was not an organ. When the Rev. T. Castley entered the living of Cavendish, Suffolk, in 1806, " there was a small gallery in . . . which the clerk and a few neighbours with flutes and a bass viol performed their respective shares with good effect ". He says that " the singers and performers were John Brockwell, clerk—who sang—John Blakelock—sang—Brockwell—a lame man—played on the Bazoon—Charles Motton—the claronet— another played on the violin—Thomas Woods played on the violincello ". The gallery was enlarged to make room also for the children of the Sunday School and the free boys of Cavendish School. In 1838 an organ was erected. It was

[1] The word " pew " (or pue) in ecclesiological literature usually means a square or high pew. What we call pews were referred to as open seats or benches.

purchased from the Marquis of Bute's mansion at Luton, " and it may be presumed that it is the Marquis's coronet, is on the top of the organ, with the representation of a trumpet to render the summit, or top, of the organ more ornamental ". All of this was destroyed later in the nineteenth century.

A west gallery was anathema to the restorers. Sir Gilbert Scott called it the " beastly loft ", and everyone agreed with him. The beastly loft had to come down. The organ, if there was one, was rebuilt in a side-chapel, or a new organ was provided, the minstrels were disbanded (and probably departed to the Methodist Chapel), and the choir was put into surplices and crowded into the chancel, which was too small for them.

Smaller things, such as tiles and scraps of old glazing, were removed wholesale. Mr. J. D. Le Couteur mentions the removal of old glass from Newington-by-Sittingbourne (in 1862) and Milton (in 1873) ; " while in Exeter Cathedral a complete Decorated window which had been found in the Minstrels' Gallery was actually cut to pieces by the Chapter glazier to make coloured borders for his plain glazing. Much glass has been lost by the insertion of new memorial windows. As late as 1882 it was seriously proposed to clear the great west window of Winchester Cathedral of its vast collection of ancient glass, itself a jumble of many dates, in order to insert a memorial to Bishop Wilberforce." [1] A valuable coat of arms of the Bohun family, together with fragments of figures and canopies, scroll work and inscriptions, were in the east window of Rochford Church when its restoration was taken in hand in 1862. During the restoration it was removed, and has never been replaced.[2]

Many monumental brasses also disappeared. Mr. J. S. M. Ward mentions an exceptionally bad case in which a partner in a firm of art-metal workers found that one of the workmen who were engaged in restoring a country church was using a brass from the church as a frying-pan. " He rescued it, and many others which had been cast out into the churchyard. Then he brought the matter to the notice of the incumbent, who absolutely refused to have anything to do with them, and

[1] J. D. Le Couteur, *English Mediaeval Painted Glass*, p. 166.
[2] F. S. Eden, *English Stained and Painted Glass*, p. 147.

declared that he would not have them in the church.   Further,
he told the partner that he could take them away.   The
latter hesitated to do so, and left them behind.   A few days
later he received a box containing them.   Not knowing what
to do with them, he stored them away and forgot all about
them.   Some twenty years later they were rediscovered by
his son, who showed them to some friends, and in the end he
returned them to the church, suggesting that they should be
restored to their proper places.   He never even received an
acknowledgment, but learned later they were still lying neglected in the box." [1]

Renaissance monuments were in many cases spoiled, or removed to some more or less inaccessible part of the church.
In Kentchurch, Herefordshire (rebuilt by Pritchard and Seddon
in 1859), the figures from the monument of John Scudamore
(1616), Amy his wife, and family are lying forlornly in the
church.   When Hagley Church was rebuilt by Street, the
Lyttleton monuments were " relieved of urns and other pagan
emblems ", and the inscriptions collected at the west end of the
church.   At Pangbourne the monument of Sir John Davis
(1625) has been concealed by the organ.

Wall paintings were sometimes obliterated for religious
reasons, but more often they disappeared because the plaster
was removed from the walls.   Sometimes the removal was
necessary for the repair of the walls, often it was quite unnecessary.   In any case, if it had to be removed, it could have
been replaced.   Most mediaeval walls were meant to be
covered with plaster, and in their unplastered state are extremely
ugly and unattractive.   But the restorers, for some reason,
did not like plastered walls—and so the plaster, and the paintings
on it, were removed.

Mr. Gambier Parry wrote in 1858, " It is the friends of the
Church who are now doing us an injury—injury which is
irremediable.   Walls are to be cleaned—churches to be restored—away goes everything down to the bare stone—whitewash and yellow dab would often be luxury in comparison
to what is left ; where walls never intended to be bare were
built rough, to be coated with plaster and then fresco-painted—

[1] J. S. M. Ward, *Brasses*, p. 103.

but away it has all gone, frescoes, powderings, diapers, scrollage, symbols, inscriptions—everything !—and this happens more often than people suppose. . . . If church restoration and repairs go on as they have done, in a few years all record of old polychromatic art will be lost."

We have become used to restored churches, and do not realize how much they have lost until we see one that has escaped restoration. It has a quiet homeliness and charm which are very largely lacking in the others. Fortunately there are some such churches left. Compare Icklingham All Saints', Suffolk, which is unrestored, with Icklingham St. James, which was restored in 1864. No one would wish to stay for more than a few minutes in St. James : in All Saints' one could stay happily for hours. We agree with J. C. J., who wrote in 1863, " It is scarcely to be doubted that the present race of restorers will be a hissing and an astonishment to those who come after ".[1]

Let us, after the manner of J. M. Neale and Benjamin Webb, pay a visit to a restored church.

We notice that most of the windows have been restored in the Decorated style, in an unpleasant yellow stone. A clerestory of small circular windows has been added and the roof raised ; [2] the roof has slates of an unpleasant hue and a metal cresting. There are crosses on every gable. The porch has been entirely rebuilt.

We enter, and observe the font, which is in the Decorated style, by Farmer and Brindley of Westminster Bridge Road. It has marble shafts with foliated capitals. In a corner we see the broken bowl of a Norman font. Raising our eyes, we observe that the walls of the church have been stripped of their plaster and aggressively repointed. The roof is supported

---

[1] The following are the names of some of the more active Victorian restorers : G. G. Scott, B. Ferrey, S. S. Teulon, E. Christian, A. Salvin, G. E. Street, H. Woodyer, R. J. Withers, R. C. Carpenter, W. Butterfield, J. Clarke, W. White, J. E. Giles, P. C. Hardwick, J. P. Seddon and J. Pritchard (mostly in Wales and the West), J. Hayward (mostly in Devonshire), W. Slater, J. P. St. Aubyn (mostly in the West), J. Norton, E. G. Paley (mostly in the North), G. M. Hills.

[2] The *Ecclesiologist* advised the removal of Perpendicular clerestories and roofs. Circular windows ought to be inserted in place of large clerestory windows.

on corbels representing angels ; from it depend gas brackets with clusters of rather tarnished gilt ivy-leaves. A north aisle has been added, separated from the nave by a heavy arcade with polished granite columns and foliated capitals. The aisle, like the nave, is full of pews. Each pew in the nave is adorned with a brass stand for umbrellas. Most of the glass is tinted Cathedral glass ; but there are two windows by Clayton and Bell : one, representing the Good Samaritan, is to the memory of a local J.P. ; the other, depicting the story of Martha and Mary, is to the memory of his wife.

The pulpit is of stone. On its faces are circular openings from which protrude the heads of the four Evangelists. The lectern is a well-developed brass eagle.

The screen has been removed and the chancel arch rebuilt. There is, however, a low screen of brass. Over the arch is the legend O WORSHIP THE LORD IN THE BEAUTY OF HOLINESS.

The chancel is filled with stalls which leave but a narrow central alley, and scarcely allow kneeling at the altar steps. Under a low arch on the north is the organ, its pipes liberally painted and gilded. The chancel floor is paved with shiny tiles by Minton. The sanctuary within its brass rails is small, and space is further reduced by a pile of steps. The altar has a frontal of elaborate workmanship, brass candlesticks supporting two feet of painted wood and two inches of candle, and brass flower-vases. The reredos is mainly of alabaster, and consists of three compartments, each surmounted by a pediment with crockets. The central one contains a cross in low relief surrounded by a vesica ; in the left-hand one is A ; in the right, Ω. The east window (of three lights) is modern, in the Geometrical style. It has glass by Hardman representing the Crucifixion, Resurrection and Ascension. The subjects are archaically treated.

On the walls throughout the church we observe a large number of monuments and brasses to the members of county families.

If we go into the vestry, we may see an old sketch of the church before restoration. We are glad of the legend beneath which identifies it : without it we should not have known that it represented the same church.

R

What does all this symbolize ?

Spiritual pride, self-sufficiency, clericalism, complacency, Philistinism and patronage of the poor ?

Verily as we contemplate it we may say " *Comederunt Jacob et locum ejus desolaverunt* ".

Towards the end of the century there were some excellent restorations, such as that conducted by Mr. W. S. Weatherley at Shere, Surrey, in 1895. But by that time there were few churches left to restore. Most of them had been through the process, and a great deal of their charm had been sacrificed to an arbitrary theory.

The process of restoration was even applied to Classical churches of the seventeenth and eighteenth centuries. Sometimes they were simply transformed into Gothic ; sometimes a curious style was invented which was partly Gothic and partly not ; sometimes Romanesque details were borrowed from various foreign countries. Some of Wren's City churches were pointlessly maltreated. St. Michael's, Cornhill, was spoiled by Scott : " He fuses the vaulting," said the *Ecclesiologist*, " into something transitional between Pointed and Italian. And he inserts tracery in all the round-headed windows, and the great ugly stable-like circles of the clerestory become roses under his plastic hand." [1]

St. Mary, Aldermanbury, and St. Swithun's, London Stone, were altered and had tracery inserted in the windows by Mr. Woodthorpe.[2]

Wolverton, Hants (1717), " was originally a complete masterpiece of good Classic treatment on a small scale, both in fabric and fittings . . . but in 1872 . . . the round-headed windows were actually divided up after a vulgar fashion with brick mullions to provide a quasi-tracery effect ". The gallery and chancel gates were removed " and a remarkably well-executed vase-font of right proportions was cast out into the churchyard to give place to a feeble Gothic successor absolutely unsuited to the building ".[3]

Hinton Admiral Church (1786) has been given Gothic

[1] He called the work " an attempt to give tone to the existing classic architecture ". It has been partly undone.
[2] In these churches the mischief has been to some extent remedied.
[3] J. C. Cox, *Little Guide to Hampshire*, pp. 250–251.

windows. The windows of Tyberton, Herefordshire (1720), have been altered to singularly mean lancets.

St. Mary's, Monmouth, was rebuilt in 1736 by Mr. Smith of Warwick,[1] one of the provincial architects who stood out above the status of tradesman builders, and " dominated a locality, and yet were not confined to it ".[2] It was considered to be an elegant building : Archdeacon Coxe in his *Historical Tour of Monmouthshire* (1801) said that " the body of the church is extremely light and well proportioned ; the range of columns which separate the nave and the aisle and support a strait entablature have a pleasing effect ". But the later nineteenth century had not a good word to say for it. The Bishop of Llandaff spoke of the church as one on which " the bad taste of past ages had laid its ruthless hands " ; and Mr. G. E. Street said that " it might almost be said to have no style at all ; at any rate, it was extremely unattractive and uninteresting ". Street's first design for the entire rebuilding of the church was too expensive ; finally it was enlarged towards the east, and given Gothic arcades and lancet windows. But the proportions are still those of the eighteenth-century church, and the lancet windows designed to fit the tall side walls of the nave recall those of the Gothic Commissioners' churches. At the reopening in 1882 the Bishop of Llandaff preached on St. Mark xiv. 4 : " Why is this waste of the ointment made ? " Comparing the work of Mr. Street with the vanished work of Mr. Smith, we may consider that his lordship did not satisfactorily answer the question.

In such cases there was no question of restoring the original style. The restorers might have taken down Mr. Smith's church at Monmouth and made an imaginary reconstruction of the former Priory Church of which a few partial descriptions and one print survive. But to supply an eighteenth-century church with Gothic detail cannot be called a restoration in any

---

[1] Smith built the Court House at Warwick after the fire of 1694, and helped in the rebuilding of the nave of St. Mary's Church. Also Four Oaks Hall, Warwickshire, Stoneleigh Abbey and Ditchley Park, Oxfordshire. James Gibbs, in *Biblioteca Radcliviana* (1730), says that among the tradesmen employed on the Radcliffe Library was Smith of Warwick.

[2] A. Dale, *James Wyatt*, p. 2.

sense.   The truth is, as Sir Kenneth Clark says, that the average man of the nineteenth century felt an inexplicable need for pointed arches ;[1] and if a church was not fortunate enough to have them already they had to be supplied.

St. Mary's, Ealing, is an example of the nondescript style which was considered to be an improvement on the eighteenth-century one.   The history of the church is not unlike that of St. Mary's, Monmouth.   The old building fell into disrepair and began to collapse in 1729 ; a new one was built with the assistance of a brief, and was completed about ten years afterwards.   Between 1866 and 1872 it was remodelled by S. S. Teulon in a most unattractive style.   Bishop Tait spoke of the alteration as " the conversion of a Georgian monstrosity into the semblance of a Constantinopolitan basilica ".   Semblance is perhaps the right word.   Sunbury, Middlesex, is another unfortunate Byzantinized eighteenth-century church. This was also the work of Teulon.

Some of the Grecian churches of the early part of the century were restored.   St. Mark's, North Audley Street, and St. Peter's, Eaton Square, as we have seen, had their interiors altered into Byzantine or Auvergnat Romanesque by the late Sir Arthur Blomfield.

Early Gothic Revival churches were also " ameliorated ". As the years of the nineteenth century passed, Gothic enthusiasts learned more of the style, and looked back on their earlier efforts with a kind of amused tolerance.   The *Ecclesiologist* once referred to " those *very early* restorers " (meaning those of a few years ago), and added " for every year is now an age ". In December 1846 it said, " There is no modern church so unsatisfactory that it cannot, in the hands of a Catholic-minded incumbent, be very considerably ameliorated, and rendered not altogether unsuitable for the performance of Catholic worship.   Such a task will, we doubt not, be often a very difficult one, and still more often a very distasteful employment of time and thought. . . .   Still, however, this

---

[1] Probably not the poor.   An old woman told me that Monmouth Church never should have been altered.   " It was a beautiful old church.   I don't know what they were thinking of."   The Gothic Revival and ecclesiology were apt to be the hobby of the clergy and the well-to-do.

undertaking may be in reality more truly meritorious than the very attractive one of rendering beauty still more beautiful. It may be a more real and unadulterated act of love, a more entire offering DEO et Ecclesiae, than the former, where aesthetical feeling, the desire of the gratification of one's own sense of beauty may have mixed itself up (who can tell how far ?) with our wish of doing our duty to The Giver of all good things, and may therefore bring down greater blessings on those by whom it has been undertaken."

Eight years after it could be said (or at any rate, it was said) that " Church architecture is no longer tentative. It approaches to something of the completeness of an exact science. It is admitted to be a subject not so much of taste as of facts. It has its rules, principles, laws."

Mr. Beresford Hope, as we have seen, looked back at the building of All Saints', Margaret Street, with " the practised eye of 1861 ", and saw faults which the less practised eye of the 1840's had overlooked. As early as 1840, however, Mr. Hope had undertaken to rectify the faults of Kilndown Church, Kent, which had been begun in 1839. Messrs. Carpenter, Butterfield and Willement co-operated in the amelioration.

St. Mary's, Haggerston, and St. Margaret's, Lee, Kent, were satisfactorily altered by Mr. Brooks, and hundreds of other churches underwent the same kind of process. In many cases they were certainly improved, in others the new work is hardly an improvement on the older. The later chancel of Christchurch, Harrogate, is little better than the nave and tower designed by Mr. Oates, and consecrated in 1831.

EPILOGUE

WHEN the nineteenth century ended, church-building was still continuing at a rapid rate. Bentley's Roman Catholic Cathedral at Westminster had been begun. Bentley had been a Gothic man to begin with : a rather unhappy man, pessimistic about the possibility of art in modern life, and contemptuous of a great deal that was done. He does not come into our view, as he joined the Church of Rome at an early date, and most of his work was done for that Church. He was bold and decided in his stand against clerical interference : much as he respected the clergy, he had no faith in their artistic abilities, and withstood them firmly. He would have preferred a Gothic Cathedral ; but in this case he gave way, and admitted that the Cardinal (Vaughan) was right. The Byzantine style was best suited for seeing and for hearing : it was economical, and it would not challenge comparison with the neighbouring Westminster Abbey. When he went to visit Italy in preparation for making the design, he fell in love with the style, and considered this visit to be the turning-point in his career. But the merit of the Cathedral is in its masterly construction rather than in its Byzantine details.

At about the same time that Westminster Cathedral was being begun, a move was being made towards the erection of the Cathedral at Liverpool, and Giles Gilbert Scott was soon to win the competition with his noble design. Both Westminster and Liverpool had great influence on the design of smaller churches.

Truro Cathedral was being completed ; but Truro was already being looked upon as something belonging to the past, and it was agreed that there would be no more cathedrals quite like that.

*   *   *   *   *

Most of the architects whom we have mentioned were either dead or approaching death. The survivors should have been satisfied. They had seen an immense development, the acceptance of most of their own ideals, and a considerable harvest from the seed that they had sown.

It is important to remember that the seed had borne fruit. The undistinguishing scorn which was poured on the nineteenth century and all its works during the 1920's is now becoming out of date. There are distinct signs of a growing appreciation of the church-building achievements of the Victorian age. It is surely the duty of English Churchmen to take an interest in them and to try to understand them.

There is a certain amount that is comic in the history that we have tried to sketch, and a little that is irritating, and a great deal that is regrettable. But there is also much that is noble and good. If this book has seemed to emphasize what is comic or contemptible, that has not been my purpose. The story of nineteenth-century church-building is an interesting and—it would be safe to say—a wonderful chapter in the history of our beloved Church of England.

We can laugh at some of it; but for most of it we should be grateful, and for much of it we should do well to thank God.

APPENDIX I

(In most cases only specimens are given, not the complete works of the architect. In this list no distinction is usually made between an entirely new church, and a rebuilding of an old church on a new design.)

ASHPITEL, ARTHUR (1807–1869). St. Barnabas', Homerton; St. John's, Blackheath; Ripple; Vernham Dean; Aldborough Hatch.

ASHWORTH, EDWARD (1815–1896). Articled to Robert Cornish, Cathedral architect of Exeter, then to Charles Fowler. Went to the colonies, and then returned to Devonshire. Withycombe Raleigh; Topsham; St. Mary Major, Exeter; Whipton.

BAKER, ARTHUR (1841–1896). A pupil of Scott. St. Paul's Kensington; St. Lawrence's, Northampton; Llanberis.

BARRY, SIR CHARLES (1795–1860). Chiefly remembered as architect of the Houses of Parliament. Barry was self-educated; he travelled abroad and studied Classic architecture. The design for the Houses of Parliament was accepted in 1836; he was knighted in 1852. Churches at Prestwich, Campfield (Manchester), Oldham, Brighton, Holloway, Cloudesley Square and Balls Pond (Islington) and Hurstpierpoint.

BARRY, CHARLES and EDWARD MIDDLETON (1830–1880). Sons of Sir Charles; both practised architecture. The former was at work independently; the latter acted as his father's coadjutor, after having been in the office of T. H. Wyatt. He became partner of R. R. Banks. Works mostly secular. Was R.A. Professor of Architecture. St. Saviour's, Haverstock Hill; Clifton (near Manchester).

BARRY, T. DENVILLE (d. 1905). St. Peter's, Birkdale; Holy Trinity, Tulse Hill.

BARTLEET, W. GIBBS (1829–1906). Had an extensive practice in the neighbourhood of London. St. George's, Beckenham.

BENTLEY, JOHN FRANCIS (1839–1902). A pupil of Clutton; he was influenced by Ruskin and the Continental Gothic school. Joined the Church of Rome in 1861, and began work independently in 1868. His work was mostly done for the Roman Catholic Church; he received the commission for Westminster Cathedral in 1894. The Immaculate Conception and St. Francis', Bocking; Holy Rood, Watford; Our Lady of the Holy Souls, Kensal New Town; Corpus Christi, Brixton; additions to St. Francis', Notting Hill and to Our Lady of Victories', Clapham, etc. Some Anglican work: St. Luke's, Chiddingstone Causeway (1898).

BIDLAKE, W. H. (1862–1938). Churches in Birmingham: St. Agatha's, St. Oswald's, Bishop Latimer, St. Stephen's (additions).

BILLING, ARTHUR (1824–1895). In the offices of Ferrey and Hardwick. From 1860 to 1873 was partner of A. S. Newman; from 1890

of A. E. Billing; and from 1893 of J. W. Rowley. All Saints',
Hatcham; Holy Trinity, Anerley; St. Peter's, Lee; St. John's,
Chelsea; St. Peter's, Fulham; Hammerwich.

BLACKBURNE, E. L. (1803–1888). A pupil of Mr. Taylor, F.S.A.
Author of *History of the Decorative Painting of the Middle Ages*
(1847), etc. Martyrs' Memorial Church, Clerkenwell; St. Paul's,
Paddington, etc. Some restorations.

BLOMFIELD, SIR ARTHUR WILLIAM (1829–1899). See pp. 190–193.

BLORE, EDWARD·(1787–1879). More of a draughtsman than an
architect. He made sketches for various books of antiquities, and
produced in 1824 *The Monumental Remains of Noble and Eminent
Persons*. At his death he left behind forty-eight books of drawings.
Blore corresponded with Rickman on the subject of Gothic architecture. He was special architect to William IV and to Queen Victoria
in the early part of her reign; he did work at Windsor, Hampton Court
and Buckingham Palace, and was architect to Westminster Abbey. He
was one of the founders of the Royal Archaeological Institute, and
Fellow of the Royal Society. Domestic work included the Palace of
Prince Woronzow at Aloupka in the Crimea: restorations included
Glasgow Cathedral, Merton College Chapel, and the rebuilding of most
of Lambeth Palace.

Christchurch, Hoxton; St. James's, Shoreditch; St. George's,
Battersea; Chapel of St. Mark's, College, Chelsea; Holy Trinity,
Windsor.

BODLEY, GEORGE FREDERICK (1827–1907). See pp. 209–214. An
almost complete list of his works may be found in the *Builder*
(XCIII, p. 447). This is a selection: France Lynch; St. Michael's,
Brighton; All Saints', Cambridge; St. Martin's, Scarborough;
St. Salvador's, Dundee; St. Wilfrid's, Haywards Heath; St.
Michael's, Folkestone; St. Saviour's and St. German's, Roath,
Cardiff; St. John's, Cowley; St. Luke's, Warrington; Holy Inno-
cents', South Norwood; St. George's, Nottingham; All Saints',
Weston-super-Mare; Clumber; St. Mary of Eton, Hackney Wick;
St. Mary's, Eccleston; St. Matthew's, Chapel Allerton; Holy
Trinity, Kensington Gore; Horninglow; St. Raphael's, Bedminster,
Bristol; St. Bride's, Glasgow; St. Aidan's, Bristol; Chandler's
Ford; All Souls', Leicester; Hom Green; St. John the Baptist's,
Epping; St. Faith's, Brentford. With Garner: St. John's, Tue
Brook; Hobart Cathedral, Tasmania; St. Michael's, Camden Town;
Hoar Cross; St. Augustine's, Pendlebury, etc.

Other works: restorations at Magdalen Chapel, Oxford; Little
Bowdon; Whitkirk; Hartshorne; All Saints', Gainsborough;
Hickleton; Elvaston; Headcorn; Grimston. New tower at Long
Melford; sacristies at St. Andrew's, Wells Street; alterations at
Christchurch, Ealing; chancel at Ham, Surrey; enlargement at
Christchurch, Mold Green; new tower at Soulderne; alterations
at St. Paul's, Burton-on-Trent; restoration of Winchester Cathedral
reredos. Reredoses at St. Margaret's, King's Lynn; St. Peter's
Sudbury (Suffolk); St. Mary's, Leicester, etc. With Garner:
decoration of St. John the Divine, Kennington; enlargement of
chancel of St. Paul's, Knightsbridge; reredos at St. Paul's Cathedral;
work at St. Peter's, Harrogate, etc. At the time of his death Bodley
was engaged on plans for the Cathedral at San Francisco and the
enlargement of two cathedrals in India.

BRANDON, JOHN RAPHAEL (1817–1877). With his brother, JOSHUA

ARTHUR, wrote several books on Gothic architecture (see p. 77).
St. Peter's, Great Windmill Street; Catholic Apostolic Church,
Gordon Square; Leverstock Green; Datchett.

BROCK, EDGAR PHILIP LOFTUS (1833–1895). A pupil of W. G.
and E. Habershon: stayed with the latter. Numerous church buildings and restorations. St. Augustine's, Highbury; Hammerwood;
Wallington; Hethersgill. After the retirement of Habershon, Brock
continued work alone.

BROOKS, JAMES (1825–1901). See pp. 155–156. Pupil of Lewis Stride,
and attended the classes of Professor Donaldson at University College.
Entered as pupil at the R.A. Schools. F.R.I.B.A. 1866 and Vice-
President 1892–1896. Architect to Canterbury Diocese from 1888.
He took his son Martin into partnership.

BURGES, WILLIAM (1827–1881). See pp. 152–155.

BURTON, DECIMUS (1800–1881). Made his reputation early;
designed few churches, and had " no comprehension of Gothic ".
St. Peter's, Southborough; Riverhead; Goring (near Worthing);
Holy Trinity, Eastbourne; Fleetwood; Flimwell.

BURY, THOMAS TALBOT (1811–1877). A pupil of Augustus Pugin,
and began practice in 1830. In 1847 he published his *Remains of
Ecclesiastical Woodwork*, and in 1849 *History and Description of the
Styles of Architecture of Various Countries, from the Earliest to the
Present Period*. He prepared, with Pugin, the designs of the Houses
of Parliament, under Barry. The number of his churches and chapels
is said to have been thirty-five. All Saints', Clapham Park; Christchurch, Battersea; St. Anne's, Stamford Hill; St. John's, Weymouth;
St. James's, Dover; St. John's, Burgess Hill.

BUTTERFIELD, WILLIAM (1814–1900). See pp. 118–126.

CARPENTER, RICHARD CROMWELL (1812–1855). See pp. 116–117.

CHAMPNEYS, BASIL (1842–1935). Son of a Dean of Lichfield.
Articled to Pritchard of Llandaff. Designed school and college
buildings, and some churches. St. Luke's, Kentish Town; St.
George's, Glascote.

CHATWIN, JULIUS ALFRED (1829–1907). Articled in 1851 to Sir
Charles Barry, and helped in preparation of the drawings of the
House of Lords. Practised at Birmingham.

Churches in Birmingham: St. Martin's; chancel of the Cathedral;
Christchurch, Summerfield; St. Augustine's; St. Clement's; Holy
Trinity, Birchfield; All Souls', Witton; Aston Parish Church;
St. George's (additions); St. Mary's, Acock's Green, etc. Many
restorations.

CHRISTIAN, EWAN (1814–1895). See pp. 158–159.

CLARKE, JOSEPH (1819–1888). St. Luke's, Heywood; Dane Bridge;
St. Bartholomew's, Whitworth; St. Mary's, Farnham (Essex); St.
Alban's, Rochdale; St. Stephen's, Congleton. About fifty new
churches altogether.

CLARKE, SOMERS (1841–1926). With Micklethwaite in Scott's
office. A learned antiquary and great ecclesiologist. Collaborated
with Micklethwaite. St. Martin's, Brighton; St. Mary's, Stretton,
Burton-on-Trent. Surveyor of St. Paul's from 1897. Resigned,
retired to Egypt for his health and practised there.

CLUTTON, HENRY (1819–1893). A pupil of Blore, and friend of
Burges. With Burges, won first place in the competition for Lille
Cathedral. Subsequently they worked apart. He built schools,
houses and churches. In 1875 he was selected architect for the

proposed Roman Catholic Cathedral of Westminster. Churches at Tavistock, Woburn, Woburn Sands, Ewell, Stanmore, Dunstall; St. John's, Limehouse.

COCKERELL, CHARLES ROBERT (1788–1863). Did important antiquarian work, and " in his exquisite refinement of taste was like an ancient Greek come to life again ". His work was mostly secular, but he designed Hanover Chapel, Regent Street, now demolished, and St. Bartholomew's, Moor Lane, also demolished. (See p. 107.)

COLSON, JOHN (d. 1894). Built or restored over 120 churches, including new churches at Awbridge, Herriard, Fair Oak, Ovington, Portsdown, Ramsdell, Sholing, Stockbridge, Lockerley, Wyke.

COTTINGHAM, LEWIS NOCKALLS (1787–1847). Apprenticed to a builder at Ipswich. He " did a great deal to promote the revival of Mediaeval Gothic Architecture, but as an architect is now esteemed more for his draughtsmanship than the works that he carried out " (D.N.B.). Author of Henry VII's Chapel (two volumes). Restored Rochester Cathedral; Magdalen Chapel, Oxford; St. Albans; Hereford; Louth.

His son NOCKALLS JOHNSON COTTINGHAM (1823–1854) helped his father. He designed the reredos at Hereford, and designed stained glass.

CROWTHER,' JOSEPH STRETCH (d. 1893). Author, with Bowman, of Churches of the Middle Ages. For a time partnered by Bowman. St. Mary's, Moss Lane, Manchester; St. Philip's, Alderley Edge; St. Alban's, Cheetwood, Manchester; St. Mary's, Crumpsall; St. Andrew's, Eccles; Scunthorpe. Restored Manchester Cathedral.

CUNDY, THOMAS (1790–1867). Was the son of another Thomas Cundy (1765–1825), a domestic architect. He succeeded his father as surveyor to Earl Grosvenor's London estates. In later years he designed some churches: Holy Trinity, Paddington; St. Paul's, Knightsbridge; St. Barnabas', St. Michael's, St. Gabriel's and St. Saviour's, Pimlico; St. Mark's, Hamilton Terrace (St. John's Wood). He was father of a third Thomas Cundy, who was born in 1820 and also practised architecture.

CURREY, HENRY (1820–1900). Was articled to Decimus Burton. Churches at Burbage (Derbyshire), Buxton, Chiswick, and Notting Hill; St. Peter's, Eastbourne.

CUTTS, J. E. K. and J. P. St. Luke's, Camberwell; St. Matthew's, Sydenham; The Ascension, Victoria Docks; St. George's, Enfield; St. Mark's, Southampton.

DAWKES, SAMUEL WHITFIELD (1811–1880). Articled to Pritchard of York, and later entered practice at Gloucester and Cheltenham simultaneously. Designed Colney Hatch and several railway stations. Churches at Hampstead and New Brompton; St. Andrew's, Wells Street (see p. 117); St. Peter's, Cheltenham; St. Stephen's, Portland Town; Holy Trinity, Malvern.

DERICK, JOHN MACDUFF (d. 1861). Irish, and did work in Ireland. Resigned, but as the result of various misfortunes had to resume his profession. Went to America and practised there. St. Saviour's, Leeds (see pp. 117–118) and a church at Manchester.

DOBSON, JOHN (1787–1865). A pupil of David Stephenson of Newcastle, and a friend of Sydney Smirke. Much domestic work: designed Newcastle Central Station, and was concerned with prison-building and town-planning. His churches are mostly non-ecclesiological in type. St. John Lee; Humshaugh; Greenhead; Walker-on-Tyne; St. Cuthbert's, Bensham; All Saints', Monkwear-mouth; Shotley Bridge; St. Paul's, Hendon, Sunderland; Cowpen; St. Thomas', and St. Peter's (now demolished), Newcastle; Otterburn; St. Mary's, Tyne Dock, etc. Some Roman Catholic Chapels. Restored St. Nicholas', Newcastle, Hexham Abbey, etc.

DOLLMAN, FRANCIS THOMAS (1812–1900). A pupil of the elder Pugin. "The last of a good old school." Author of *Examples of Ancient Pulpits* and *Examples of Ancient Domestic Architecture*. Eye, Northamptonshire; St. Matthew's, Upper Clapton; St. Saviour's, Walthamstow; All Saints', Lower Clapton; All Souls', Clapton Park; St. Stephen's, Haggerston; All Saints', Stoke Newington (with Allen).

EMERSON, WILLIAM (1843–1925). A pupil of Habershon and Pite and of Burges, whose French Gothic he followed at first. Went to India and built several churches there. Was first in Liverpool Cathedral competition. Knighted in 1902. St. Mary's, Brighton.

FERREY, BENJAMIN (1810–1880). See pp. 112–113.

FLOCKTON, T. J. (1825–1900). Designed a number of churches in and around Sheffield.

FOWLER, CHARLES (1791–1867). Apprenticed to John Powning: in 1814 in the office of David Laing. Charmouth; St. Paul's, Honiton; St. John's, Paddington.

FOWLER, CHARLES HODGSON (1840–1910). A pupil of Scott. Architect to Rochester Cathedral, 1898; Lincoln, 1900: and to Durham. Restored Chapter House at Durham, Selby Abbey tower, and tower and spire of Rochester. St. Columb's, Notting Hill; St. Ambrose, Bournemouth; Marsden; Cudworth; St. Hilda's, Halifax; Crosland Moor; St. Aidan's, Cleethorpes, Grimsby; St. Aidan's, Sunderland; St. Saviour's, Ravensthorpe; Great Habtoh; Romanby; Burton Leonard; St. Nicholas', Hedworth; Cheltenham Training College Chapel (with H. W. Chatters) and many others. Many restorations, and designed many reredoses, stalls, etc.

FOWLER, JAMES (1828–1892). A pupil of Potter of Lichfield: began practice 1851. Lived at Louth, but did work all over the country. St. Mary's, Newington ("one of the finest modern churches in London": Scott); St. Swithin's, Lincoln; Holy Trinity, Wanstead; St. Matthew's, Skegness; St. Michael's, Louth; St. Mary's, Lichfield.

FRANCIS, HORACE (1821–1894). Ringwood; Christchurch, Lancaster Gate, four churches at Hampstead, etc.

GIBSON, JOHN (1819–1892). A pupil of Hansom and of Barry. Charlecote; Shenstone; Bodelwyddan; Bix.

GODWIN, EDWARD WILLIAM (1833–1886). Practised in Bristol, first alone and then with Henry Crisp. Moved to London and was friendly with Scott, Street and Burges. He failed to fulfill his early promise, and turned to literature, the designing of furniture and theatrical costumes and scenery. There are churches of his in and around Bristol.

GOLDIE, GEORGE (1828–1887). Inspired by Pugin: a pupil of Hadfield and Weightman. Roman Catholic churches of St. Wilfrid's, York; Our Lady of Victories', Kensington; St. Peter's, Bradford; Middlesbrough Cathedral.

St. James's, Spanish Place, was designed by the son Edward, with the elder Goldie and Child.

GOUGH, ALEXANDER DICK (1804–1871). Entered the office of Benjamin Wyatt: was entrusted with the superintendence of the Duke of York's column. Began practice with R. L. Roumieu in 1836. St. Peter's (enlargement) and St. Matthew's, Islington; St. Pancras' (Old Church). Independent from 1848. St. Paul's, Chatham; St. Mark's, Tollington Park (Holloway); St. Philip's, Arlington Square and St. Jude's, Mildmay Park (Islington); St. John's, Tunbridge Wells; St. John's, Marchington; St. John the Evangelist's, Hull; St. Saviour's, Camberwell.

GOUGH, HUGH ROUMIEU (1843–1904). Son of the preceding: began practice by himself in 1870. St. Cuthbert's, Kensington; Hammersmith Parish Church with Seddon; Killamarsh; Kippax, etc. Several restorations.

GWILT, JOSEPH (1784–1863). Architectural writer. Lee, near Lewisham.

HABERSHON, MATTHEW (1789–1852). Articled to William Atkinson. Was deeply interested in missions to Jews, designed an Anglican Cathedral for Jerusalem, and wrote books on Biblical prophecy. Churches at Belper, Kimberworth, etc. Two sons, Edward and W. G. Habershon, were also architects. Toft (Cheshire); Risca; Coedkernew; Machen. The brothers were partners: then W. G. Habershon became associated with A. R. Pite.

HADFIELD, MATTHEW ELLISON (1812–1885). Articled to Woodhead and Hurst: in practice from 1836. In 1838 he took John Gray Weightman into partnership, and in 1850 George Goldie. In 1858 Weightman retired, and in 1864 Charles Hadfield joined his father. Roman Catholic churches at Worksop, New Mills, Matlock, Bath, Birkenhead. In 1844 began the Cathedral of St. John, Salford. St. Marie's, Sheffield; Church of Sisters of Notre Dame, Liverpool; St. Chad's, Manchester; St. Marie's, Burnley, etc.

HAKEWILL. There were several architects of this name. HENRY (1771–1830) designed Rugby School, Wolverton Church (Gothic) and St. Peter's, Eaton Square (Grecian): but the first design was Gothic. St. Peter's was burned in 1836 and rebuilt by one of his sons. Both of his sons, John Henry and Edward Charles, practised architecture.

JAMES brother of Henry, was an architect and artist; his son Arthur William (1808–1856) was a pupil of Decimus Burton; he was best known as a writer and lecturer.

HANSOM, JOSEPH ALOYSIUS (1803–1882). Articled to Mr. Philips at York. Settled at Halifax, and became assistant to Mr. Oates. Then went into partnership with Edward Welch. Churches at Toxteth Park, Acomb and Hull, and three in the Isle of Man. From 1854–1859 he was partner with his brother Charles Francis, 1859–1861 with his eldest son, and 1862–1863 with Edward Welby Pugin. All Roman Catholic churches. St. Ignatius', Preston (enlarged); Roman Catholic Cathedral, Plymouth; Jesuit Church, Manchester; St. Philip Neri, Arundel; the Priory Church, St. Marychurch; Our Lady and The English Martyrs', Cambridge, St. Aloysius', Oxford, and many others.

Hansom's name is known to everyone as the inventor of the Hansom cab.

HARDWICK, THOMAS (1752–1829). Was a pupil of Chambers. St. Mary's, Wanstead; St. Paul's, Covent Garden (rebuilt after fire);

St. James's, Pentonville; St. James, Hampstead Road; St. John's Chapel, St. John's Wood; Marylebone Church.

His son Philip (1792–1870) was a pupil of his father: his buildings are secular. Euston Station.

HARDWICK, PHILIP CHARLES (1822–1892). Was the son of Philip. He designed a number of churches: Shotton; Camp Church, Aldershot; St. John's, Deptford; St. Mary's, Lambeth; Newland, Great Malvern.

HAWKINS, RHODE. St. Paul's, Bow Common; St. Michael's, Paddington; St. Michael's, Exeter.

HAYLEY, WILLIAM HENRY (1827–1871). Bowdon; Christchurch, Bradford; Sale Moor.

HAYWARD, CHARLES FORSTER (1830–1905). Assistant of P. and P. C. Hardwick. St. Andrew's, Haverstock Hill.

HAYWARD, J. Many restorations and new churches in Devonshire and the West. SS. Philip and James's, Ilfracombe; Bicton.

HEALEY. Churches in Bradford: St. Augustine's, Undercliffe; St. John the Evangelist's, St. Luke's, Manningham; St. Luke's, Harrogate; St. Giles's, Cambridge. Mallinson and Healey: St. Mary's, Wyke; Baildon; Shelf; Mytholmroyd; Heptonstall; All Saints', Horton; All Saints', Leeds.

HICKS, WILLIAM SEARLE (1849–1902). Articled to Austin and Johnson, and in 1875 became partner of the firm of Austin, Johnson and Hicks. In 1882 he began independent work with the rebuilding of Shilbottle. New churches: Lambley and St. Cuthbert's, Blyth. In 1888 he was joined by H. C. Charlewood, with whom he designed St. Aidan's, Newcastle; St. Margaret's, Brotton in Cleveland; St. John's, Crewe; Eston Grange; St. Oswald's, West Hartlepool; St. Chad's, Bensham; St. Luke's, Thornaby; St. Barnabas', Jesmond. Many restorations.

HILLS, GORDON MACDONALD (1826–1894). Under Butler of Chichester and R. C. Carpenter. Diocesan architect of London, Rochester and St. Albans. St. Saviour's, Everton; All Saints', Princes Park, Liverpool, etc. Many restorations.

HOLME, ARTHUR (1814–1857). A pupil of Rickman. Churches in Liverpool: St. Paul's, Prince's Park; St. Matthias', Great Howard Street; All Souls'; St. Aidan's; St. Alban's; All Saints', Great Nelson Street; St. Mary's, Grassendale.

INWOOD, WILLIAM (1771 ?–1843). St. Pancras' (together with his son H. W. Inwood): also (with his son) Camden Town Church; St. Peter's, Regent Square; St. Mary's, Somers Town (see pp. 41–42). Published *The Erechtheion at Athens.*

INWOOD, HENRY WILLIAM (1794–1843). Studied under his father, travelled in Greece and helped his father in St. Pancras' and other London churches. All Saints', Great Marlow.

JACKSON; THOMAS GRAHAM (1835–1924). Author of *Modern Gothic Architecture*—a protest against mere archaeological revival. Much secular work. St. Luke's and St. John's, Wimbledon: churches at Annesley, Hornblotton, Curdridge, Narberth, Northington, Stratton. Enlargement of Old Malden.

JOHNSON, JOHN (1808–1879). Travelled in Italy. Author of *Johnson's Churches of Northampton.* St. Paul's, Camden Town; Christchurch, Stratford; St. Matthew's, Oakley Square (S. Pancras); St. Mary's, Greenhithe; St. Edmund's, Romford;

Holy Trinity, Wimbledon; St. Saviour's, Walmer; Woolhampton; Midgham; Brimpton; Bramcote.

JOHNSON, ROBERT JAMES (d. 1892). Author of *Specimens of Early French Architecture*. Had a large practice in church-building in the North. St. Matthew's and St. Stephen's, Newcastle; St. Hilda's, Whitby; St. Aidan's, Leeds; Skelton-in-Cleveland.

KEELING, BASSETT (1836–1886) (see p. 158). Specialized in cemetery chapels. " Cultivated the Victorian style." Not approved of by the *Ecclesiologist*.

KELLY, JOHN (1840–1904). Head of the firm of John Kelly and Sons. With G. E. Street for three years: partner with Adams. Work in Leeds: Emmanuel, All Hallows', etc. St. Patrick's, Soho (Roman Catholic); All Saints', Petersham; All Saints', Acton; St. Luke's, Kingston.

KEMPTHORNE, SAMPSON. St. James's, Gloucester; Holy Trinity and All Saints', Rotherhithe. He left England for New Zealand in 1841, and is supposed to have died soon afterwards.

KENDALL, HENRY EDWARD (1776–1875). St. George's, Ramsgate; St. John's, Kensal Green; Trent Park, Middlesex.

LAMB, EDWARD BUCKTON (1806–1869). Articled to Cottingham; had a large practice and designed a number of churches. He was a *bête noir* of the *Ecclesiologist*. St. Philip's, Clerkenwell; St. Mary Magdalene, Addiscombe; Christchurch, West Hartlepool; All Saints', Thirkleby; Healey (Yorkshire); St. Martin's, Gospel Oak. Wrote several books.

LEE, EDWARD CLAUDE (1846–1890). Influenced by Burges. Parish Church, Whitechapel; churches at Brentwood and elsewhere.

MICKLETHWAITE, JOHN THOMAS (1843–1906). A pupil of Scott, and an earnest Churchman. He was in constant collaboration with Somers Clarke, with whom he designed St. John's, Gainsborough; All Saints', Brixham; St. Paul's and All Saints', Wimbledon. Alone he designed St. Hilda's, Leeds; St. Bartholomew's, East Ham; St. Peter's, Bocking; Widford; St. Saviour's, Luton; St. Matthew's, Southsea.

MIDDLETON, JOHN (d. 1885). Churches in Cheltenham: St. Luke's, St. Mark's, All Saints', St. Stephen's, SS. Philip and James's, Leckhampton.

MITCHELL-WITHERS, JOHN BRIGHTMORE (1837–1894). A pupil of Samuel Worth of Sheffield: partner with William Blackmore. St. Andrew's, Sharrow, etc.

MOORE, TEMPLE LUSHINGTON (1856–1920). A pupil of G. G. Scott, jun., and associated with him in his work. After Scott gave up practising about 1890, Temple Moore gradually developed individuality. " His buildings, although purely Gothic, appear to have been designed with no constraint save that of his vigilant good taste " (*D.N.B.*). All Saints', Peterborough; St. Peter's, Barnsley; St. Augustine's, Newland, Hull; St. John's, West Hendon; St. Mark's, Mansfield; St. Cuthbert's, Middlesbrough; St. Wilfrid's, Lidget Green, Bradford; St. Columba's, Middlesbrough; St. Wilfrid's, Harrogate; St. Luke's, Eltham; St. Margaret's, Leeds; Uplands (Stroud); All Saints', Tooting Graveney; All Saints', Basingstoke; St. Augustine's, Gillingham; Sledmere; Walesby; St. Anne's, Royton; Bessingby; Carlton; East Moors; St. Cuthbert's, Preston; St. Mary's, Sculcoats; St. Luke's, Walsall. Many restorations of churches in Yorkshire.

MOUNTFORD, F. W. (1855–1908). Articled to Habershon and Pite. Chiefly secular works. Enlargement of All Saints' and St. Anne's, Wandsworth; St. Mary's, Wandsworth; St. Andrew's, Earlsfield.

NASH, EDWIN (1814–1884). A pupil of Mr. Field and worked with Scott. St. John's, Penge; Crocken Hill; North Cray; St. Nicholas', Sutton; St. Philip's, Sydenham.

NASH, JOHN (1752–1835). Famous as the designer of Buckingham Palace and Regent Street, and the laying out of large areas in London. A few churches: All Souls', Langham Place; St. Mary's, Haggerston; East Cowes.

NICHOLL, S. J. (1826–1905). Apprenticed to J. J. Scoles. Assisted T. J. Willson in his churches. After the end of the partnership he designed churches at Oldcotes and Wellingborough. St. Walburge's, Preston.

NICHOLSON, THOMAS (1823–1895). Began independent work at Hereford; diocesan surveyor and architect of Hereford. One new church and three enlargements at Hereford; St. Michael's, St. James's and St. Thomas's, Swansea; churches at Aberystwyth, Penrhiwceiber and Pembroke Dock.

NORTON, JOHN (1823–1904). In the office of Benjamin Ferrey. Designed many churches: Stapleton; Stoke Bishop; Frampton Cotterell; Highbridge; Congresbury; St. Luke and St. Matthias', Bristol; Emmanuel, Clifton; Bedminster; Pontypridd; Neath; Ebbw Vale; Blaina; Abertillery; Ystrad Mynach; Penmaen; Dyffryn; St. Matthew's, Brighton; St. John's, Middlesbrough; Christchurch, Finchley; Croxley Green (enlarged later).

PALEY, EDWARD GRAHAM (1823–1895). A grandson of Paley of " Evidences " fame. Was a pupil of Edmund Sharpe of Lancaster, and joined him as his partner in 1845. Parish Church of Wigan, and churches at Knowsley, Lever Bridge and Rusholme. Independent from 1851 to 1868. St. George's and St. James's, Barrow-in-Furness; St. Peter's (Roman Catholic), Lancaster; Ringley; Allithwaite; Aughton; St. Thomas's, Blackburn; Holy Trinity, Bradford; Bradshaw; Higher Walton; Penwortham; Ince; Wrightington; Lowton; Walney Island; Blawith; Great Singleton; Quernmore; Over Darwen; Thwaites; Livesey; St. Mark's, Preston, etc. From 1868 he was a partner of H. J. Austin, and the pair built over forty new churches. Altogether he was responsible for building or restoring about 150 churches, mostly in the North. Mossley Hill; The Saviour, Bolton; St. Mary's, Beswick; Higher Broughton; St. John's, Cheetham; St. Clement's, Salford; Leigh Parish Church; St. George's, Stockport; St. Lawrence's, Morecambe; Winmarleigh; Howe Bridge; Crosscrake; St. Cuthbert's, Darwen; Daisy Hill; Holy Cross, Knutsford; Hutton Roof; Mansergh; Langho; Scorton; Pilling; St. Barnabas', Crewe; Dalton-in-Furness Parish Church; Lower Ince; Grimsargh; Burnage; Finsthwaite; Torver; Burton-in-Lonsdale; Cloughfold.

PEACOCK, JOSEPH (1821–1893). St. Jude's, Gray's Inn Road (now demolished); St. Stephen's, Kensington; St. Simon's, Chelsea; Holy Cross, St. Pancras; St. James's, Derby.

PEARSON, JOHN LOUGHBOROUGH (1817–1898). See pp. 196–209.

PENNETHORNE, JAMES (1801–1871). In the office of Nash. Studied abroad and helped Nash. A town-planner: knighted in 1870. Christchurch, Albany Street; Holy Trinity, Gray's Inn Road (now demolished). His brother John was also an architect.

PENSON, RICHARD KYRKE (1816–1886). Restored and built churches in Salop, Cheshire, Hereford and Wales.

PHIPSON, RICHARD MAKILWAINE (1827–1885). In 1849 took an office at Ipswich : much work in Suffolk and Norfolk. Restored about 100 churches. Rebuilt St. Mary le Tower, Ipswich.

PORDEN, WILLIAM (1755–1822). Studied under Wyatt and S. P. Cockerell. Ecclestone and South Kelsey.

PORDEN, CHARLES FERDINAND (1790–1863). Was his nephew and pupil. St. Matthew's, Brixton.

POYNTER, AMBROSE (1796–1886). A pupil of Nash. St. Andrew the Great, St. Paul's and Christchurch, Cambridge ; St. Katherine's Hospital and Chapel, Regent's Park. He retired in 1858, owing to bad eyesight.

PRITCHARD, JOHN (1818–1886). A pupil of Walker. Lived at Llandaff, and restored the Cathedral. Was in partnership with J. P. Seddon for ten years.

PRYNNE, GEORGE HALFORD FELLOWES (1853–1927). Son of the Rev. G. R. Prynne ; a pupil of Windyer of Toronto and of Street. He was almost exclusively a church architect. He was fond of a traceried stone chancel screen, such as may be seen in the old churches of Great Bardfield and Stebbing, Essex. St. Peter's, Plymouth ; All Saints', West Dulwich ; St. Peter's, Staines ; Budleigh Salterton ; Roehampton ; St. Saviour's, Ealing ; All Saints', Elland ; St. John's, Sidcup ; St. Peter's, Ilfracombe ; St. Peter's, Whitstable ; St. Wilfrid's, Bognor ; St. Alban's, Bournemouth ; St. Mark's, Purley ; St. Peter's, Bushey Heath ; St. Nicholas', Taplow ; St. Michael's, Beaconsfield.

PUGIN, AUGUSTUS WELBY NORTHMORE (1812–1852). See pp. 46–71. Some of Pugin's churches have been demolished, and some greatly altered. The appendix to *Pugin* by Mr. Trappes-Lomax gives a more or less complete list. Here are some specimens of his work : St.Peter's, Marlow ; St. Alban's, Macclesfield ; Warwick Bridge ; St. Mary's, Derby ; St. Mary's, Stockton ; St. Oswald's, Old Swan (Liverpool) ; St. Wilfrid's, Hulme ; St. Thomas', Fulham ; St. Mary's Cathedral, Newcastle ; St. Barnabas' Cathedral, Nottingham ; St. Mary's, Brewood ; St. Giles's, Cheadle ; St. Chad's Cathedral, Birmingham ; St. Augustine's, Kenilworth ; St. Osmund's, Salisbury ; Our Blessed Lady and St. Thomas of Canterbury, Dudley ; St. George's Cathedral, Lambeth ; St. Anne's, Keighley, etc. His Anglican work includes several restorations, and the church at Tubney.

PUGIN, EDWARD WELBY (1834–1875). Eldest son of A. W. N. Pugin. On his father's death he undertook the entire management of the business. Like his father, was a hard worker, and was lively and depressed by turns. His works were almost all Roman Catholic : they are very numerous. Our Lady of Seven Dolours, Peckham ; St. Monica's, Hoxton ; The English Martyrs', Tower Hill ; St. Joseph's, Highgate ; St. Goderic's, Durham ; Ushaw College Chapel ; Queenstown Cathedral ; Churches at Workington, Hastings, Northampton, Great Harwood, Dover, Liverpool, Much Woolton, Westby, Rugby, Euxton, Cleator, Belmont (Hereford), etc.

PUGIN, PETER PAUL (1851–1904). Third son of A. W. N. Pugin : of the firm of Pugin and Pugin. Franciscan Church, Glasgow ; Abbey of Fort Augustus and other work in Scotland. Our Lady of Lourdes and St. Bernard, Liverpool ; Aigburth ; St. Bonaven-

S

t'ra's, Bishopton; St. Joseph's, Lancaster; Coatbridge, etc. Reredoses, altars, etc.

RICKMAN, THOMAS (1776–1841). Practised medicine, 1801–1803; in business, 1803–1808; clerk in an insurance broker's, 1808–1818. In 1809 began to study churches, and is said to have examined 3000. In 1812 he began to write on Gothic architecture, and in 1817 set up as an architect in Liverpool. Helped with Parker's *Glossary*. The ecclesiologists admired him as a pioneer, but could not treat him very seriously as a church architect because he was a Quaker. St. George's, Birmingham; St. Peter's and St. Paul's, Preston; Hampton Lucy (altered by Scott); Albury (Oxford).

ROGERS, WILLIAM (d. 1857). A pupil of C. Beazley. All Saints', Lambeth Lower Marsh (now demolished); St. Michael's, Stockwell.

ROPER, DAVID RIDDAL (d. *circa* 1852). St. Mark's, Kennington.

ST. AUBYN, JAMES PIERS (1815–1895). Educated chiefly at Gloucester, and pupil of Mr. Fulljames. Surveyor of Middle Temple. "In his work," so it was said, "will always be found strength, good detail, suitable material and . . . a good interpretation and translation, without servility, for modern purposes and usages of our own unequalled and indigenous architecture." All Saints' and St. Luke's, Reading; St. Mary's, St. James's, St. Stephen's, St. Paul's and St. Barnabas', Devonport; St. James-the-Less, Plymouth; Christchurch, Erith; St. Mark's, New Brompton; St. John's, Penzance; All Saints', Marazion; Halsetown; St. Mary's, Clifton; St. Clement's, Notting Dale; Blackfordby; St. John the Baptist's, Enfield. An unsuccessful competitor for Truro Cathedral.

SALTER, STEPHEN (1825–1896). Articled to T. H. Wyatt. St. Paul's, Kent Town; Christchurch, Hendon.

SALVIN, ANTHONY (1799–1881). A pupil of Nash. An authority on mediaeval military architecture, restored many castles and manor houses, and built some new mansions. Failed in competition for the Houses of Parliament and Fitzwilliam Museum. He was fellow of the R.I.B.A. in 1836, in 1839 vice-president, and Fellow of the Society of Antiquaries from 1824 until his death. St. Paul's, Alnwick; St. Anne's, Bishop Auckland; Aberford; Runcorn; St. Mark's and St. Mary Magdalene's, Torquay.

SAVAGE, JAMES (1779–1852). St. Luke's, Chelsea; Holy Trinity, Sloane Street (now removed to make room for a new church); St. James's, Bermondsey; Holy Trinity, Tottenham Green; St. Mary's, Ilford; St. Michael's, Burleigh Street (now demolished); St. Thomas', Brentwood (now removed to make room for a new church); Speenhamland (also rebuilt); Addlestone.

SCOLES, JOSEPH JOHN (1798–1864). Articled in 1812 to Ireland, a leading Roman Catholic architect of the day. The influence of Dr. Milner drew the attention of both master and pupil to Gothic. About 1818 Ireland built a Roman Catholic Chapel in Leicester. Scoles began practice in 1819, and travelled from 1822 to 1826. In 1831 he began St. Peter's, Great Yarmouth; he also designed a church at Edgbaston, and at Southtown, Yarmouth. Roman Catholic churches at Stonyhurst, St. John's Wood, Holywell, Preston, Colchester, Newport, Cardiff, Bangor, Merthyr Tydfil, Lydiate, Chelmsford, Great Yarmouth. Immaculate Conception, Farm Street. Began a church at Prior Park, not completed. Temporary church of Brompton Oratory. His pupil S. J. Nickoll completed some of his later works.

SCOTT, SIR GEORGE GILBERT (1811–1878). See pp. 160–172. The following are thirty examples selected at random from the immense total number of his works. St. Andrew's, Westminster; St. Matthew's, Westminster; St. Mary's, Stoke Newington; St. Mary Abbots, Kensington; St. Stephen's, Lewisham; St. Clement's, Barnsbury; St. Peter's, Croydon; St. Barnabas', Ranmore; West Meon; St. Giles', Camberwell; St. Matthew's, City Road; Westcott; Holy Trinity, Halstead; Christchurch, Turnham Green; St. Matthias', Richmond; Holy Trinity, Manchester; Haley Hill; Normacot; St. Gregory's, Canterbury; Ambleside; Holy Trinity, Rugby; St. Paul's, Dundee; Shirley; Hartshill; Holy Trinity, Hulme; Ridgmont; St. George's, Doncaster; Christchurch, Ealing; St. John's, Taunton.

SCOTT, GEORGE GILBERT, jun. (1839–1897). Eldest son of Sir G. G. Scott. Had a distinguished career at Cambridge. Helped his father and J. O. Scott. Became a Roman Catholic after his father's death: edited *Personal and Professional Recollections*. Gradually withdrew from practice, and left J. O. Scott to finish his works. All Hallows', Southwark; St. Agnes', Kennington; St. Mark's, Milverton; Roman Catholic Church, Norwich (finished by J. O. Scott).

SCOTT, JOHN OLDRID (1842–1913). Second son of Sir Gilbert, and his pupil. He " accepted his father's architectural faith implicitly ". Associated with Sir Gilbert in many works, including the Foreign Office and St. Mary's, Edinburgh. Lahore and Grahamstown Cathedrals, Hereford west front. Design for Liverpool was honourably mentioned. Restored Selby. Greek Church, Bayswater; St. Paul's, New Cross (Manchester); St. Mary's, Slough (rebuilding): Holy Trinity, Burton-on-Trent; St. Augustine's, Croydon; Sunningdale; St. Andrew's, Boscombe (with his son and C. T. Miles); St. John's, Boscombe; All Saints', Stourwood (Bournemouth); St. John's, Palmer's Green; St. Mark's, Harrogate; St. Michael's, Bournemouth (tower); new designs for choir, transepts and tower of Roman Catholic Church, Norwich; completion of tower and spire of St. Mary's, Stoke Newington, etc.

SEDDING, JOHN DANDO (1839–1891). See pp. 194-196.

SEDDON, JOHN POLLARD (1827–1906). Articled to Professor Donaldson in 1847 and had a Classic upbringing. A diligent student of Mediaeval architecture, and developed a style of his own, which owed something to his love and study of Venetian Gothic. Author of *Progress in Architecture* (1852). From 1852 to 1862 partner with J. Pritchard, restored and built many churches, mostly in Wales and Monmouthshire. Canton; St. John's, Maindee; Llandogo, etc. Was a consulting architect of the Incorporated Church Building Society, and surveyor for the Archdeaconry of Monmouth. In 1885 took John Coates Carter as partner: partnership was dissolved in 1904. Among his works (including those carried out in co-operation with his partners) are: St. James's, Great Yarmouth; St. Barnabas', Swindon; Hoarwithy; St. Paul's, Hammersmith (with H. Roumieu Gough); Chigwell Row; Ayott St. Peter; Ullenhall; Redbrook; Wyesham; St. John's, Lacey Green; Grangetown; All Souls', Adamstown, etc.

SHARPE, EDMUND (1809–1877). A pupil of Rickman. Practised at Lancaster for fifteen years. Took up engineering in 1851. He designed about forty churches, many in the Romanesque style. Author of

Architectural Parallels. Lever Bridge (with E; G; Paley), Platt, Holy Trinity, Blackburn, etc.

SHAW, JOHN (1776–1832). Articled to George Gwilt the elder. St. Dunstan's, Fleet Street.

His son, JOHN SHAW (1803–1870), was a pupil of his father. Christchurch, Watney Street.

SHAW, RICHARD NORMAN (1831–1912). Studied under Burn and Street. Began practice with W. E. Nesfield in 1862. He built houses for artists in South Kensington and Hampstead: " Queen Anne " style. His later style is shown in Great Scotland Yard: his churchbuilding was mostly, though not entirely, done in earlier years. Harrow Mission Church, Notting Hill; All Saints', Leek; St. Michael's, Chiswick; St. Margaret's, Ilkley.

SHELLARD, E. H. Churches mostly in the North: Biggin; St. Stephen's, Chorlton-on-Medlock; St. Mark's, City Road, Manchester.

SLATER, WILLIAM (1819–1872). Was a pupil of Carpenter, and completed some of his work after his death. He worked with Carpenter in some churches; and built or restored many others. St. Peter's, Devizes; Harpenden; Oborne; Burwash Weald.

SMIRKE, SIR ROBERT (1781–1867). Articled to Soane. Travelled in Italy and Greece between 1801 and 1805. His works are mostly Classical, and rather heavy: St. Mary's, Bryanston Square; St. Anne's, Wandsworth; St. John's, Chatham; St. Nicholas', Strood; St. George's, Brandon Hill, Bristol; St. Philip's, Salford; St. Andrew's, Netherton; West Hackney; St. George's, Tyldesley; Markham Clinton; West Markham.

SMIRKE, SYDNEY (1798–1877). Was a brother and pupil of Robert. Loughton, Theydon Bois, etc.

SMITH, WILLIAM BASSETT (1830–1901). Of the firm of William and Charles Aubrey Bassett Smith. Christchurch, Penge; St. John's, Highbury Vale; St. Mary's, Caterham (additions); St. Barnabas', Clapham Common; St. Paul's, Plumstead. (With R. P. Day) St. Gabriel's, Willesden.

SOANE, SIR JOHN (his real name was Swan) (1753–1837). Was an errand-boy to Dance the younger, and was then taken into Dance's office. He entered the office of Henry Holland, and then spent three years in Italy. He made a wealthy marriage, and collected works of art (Soane Museum). Architect of the Bank of England and of many country houses. St. Peter's, Walworth; Holy Trinity, Marylebone; St. John's, Bethnal Green.

STREET, GEORGE EDMUND (1824–1881). See pp. 146–152. A short selection of his church works: Ashley Green; Bettisfield; All Saints', Bolton-le-Moors; St. Peter's, Bournemouth; Boyne Hill; Bracknell; Bristol Cathedral nave; Carlton (Yorkshire); All Saints', Clifton; St. Saviour's, Eastbourne; Denstone; East Grinstead Convent; Holy Trinity, Eltham; Farlington; Filkins; Fimber; Fylingdales; Helperthorpe; East Heslerton; Holmbury St. Mary; Howsham; All Saints', Hull; Kingstone; St. Peter's, Leicester; St. Margaret's, Liverpool; London: All Saints', Putney; St. James's, Paddington; St. James-the-Less, Westminster; St. John the Divine, Kennington; St. Mary Magdalene, Paddington; Long Ditton; All Saints', Middlesbrough; Milnrow; Monmouth; SS. Philip and James's, Oxford; Par; St. James's, Pokesdown; St. Mary's, Southampton; Swinton; SS. Peter and Paul's, Teddington;

Thixendale; Tinsley; St. John's, Torquay; Wansford (Yorkshire);
Wheatley; St. Michael's, Wigan.

TEULON, SAMUEL SAUNDERS (1812–1873). Of French descent.
A pupil of George Legg and George Potter. St. Stephen's and St.
Paul's, Hampstead; St. Paul's, Bermondsey; Riseholm; Fosbury;
Huntley; Uley; Oare; Burringham; St. John's, Ladywood;
St. James's, Edgbaston; St. Thomas's, Agar Town; Holy Trinity,
Hastings; Christchurch, Croydon; St. Andrew's, Watford.

TRUEFITT, GEORGE (1824–1902). Pupil of the elder Cottingham.
Erected sixteen churches and chapels. St. George's, Tufnell Park;
St. George's, Worthing; St. John's, Bromley; Davyhulme; St.
John's, Hulme.

VULLIAMY, LEWIS (1791–1871). Articled to Smirke. Travelled in
Italy and Greece. St. Barnabas', Addison Road; Highgate; Christchurch, Woburn Square (Bloomsbury); St. James the Great, Bethnal
Green; All Saints', Ennismore Gardens (Westminster); Christchurch, Rotherhithe; St. John's, Richmond; St. Bartholomew's,
Sydenham; St. James's, Clapham; St. James's, Norlands (Kensington).

WADMORE, J. F. (1822–1903). St. Mary's, Mistley.

WALTERS, FREDERICK ARTHUR (1850–1932). A pupil of Goldie:
designed over forty churches (Roman Catholic). St. Anselm, Kingsway; The Sacred Heart, Wimbledon; St. Peter's, Winchester;
St. Anne's, Vauxhall; Buckfast Abbey.

WARDELL, WILLIAM WILKINS (1823–1900). An acquaintance of
Pugin, and caught his enthusiasm. Many Roman Catholic churches:
first in 1846. From this time to 1858 he designed about fifty churches.
Went to Australia. Designed St. Mary's Cathedral, Sydney, and
St. Patrick's Cathedral, Melbourne.

WATERHOUSE, ALFRED (1830–1905). Articled to Richard Lane, and
completed his studies in France, Germany and Italy. Began work in
Manchester and then moved to London. Fond of terra cotta, and was
one of the first architects to make free use of constructional ironwork.
Few churches. St. Elizabeth's, Reddish; St. Mary's, Twyford;
St. Bartholomew's, Reading (chancel by Bodley); St. John's, Brooklands.

WEBB, SIR ASTON (1849–1930). A pupil of Banks and Barry.
Was P.R.I.B.A. and P.R.A. Mostly secular works. Restored St.
Bartholomew's, Smithfield.

WHICHCORD, JOHN (1790–1860). Holy Trinity and St. Philip's,
Maidstone.

WHITE, WILLIAM (1825–1900). A great-nephew of White of
Selborne. Placed with Mr. Squirrell of Leamington. Came to
London and worked with Scott: was also a friend of Street and Bodley.
In practice at Truro, and built or restored many churches in Cornwall.
He identified himself with the revival of Gothic architecture, and tried
to set a proper standard of church arrangement. His works have been
called "simple, reserved and eminently sincere". He was interested
in the Ecclesiological Society. Had certain theories of proportion in
design, which were explained in the *Ecclesiologist* (1853). All Saints',
Notting Hill; St. Mark's, Battersea Rise; St. Peter's and St.
Matthew's, Clapham; St. Mark's, Hanwell; Lyndhurst; Masborough; Parkgate (Sheffield); North Ormesby; Sharow; Freemantle; Holy Trinity, Barnstaple; Felbridge; Fenny Stratford;
Smannell; St. Hilary; Axford; Elvington; St. Saviour's, Highbury.

WILD, JAMES WILLIAM (1814–1892). Articled to Basevi. Travelled in the Mediterranean, 1842–1848. Discovered the construction of the Great Pyramid. Studied the mosques and domestic architecture of the Arabs, and was an authority on the subject. Curator of Soane Museum from 1878. Coates; St. Lawrence's, Southampton; Barton; Christchurch, Streatham.

WILLIAMS, S. W. (1837–1900). Restored or erected numerous churches in mid-Wales. Newbridge-on-Wye.

WILLSON, T. J. (1823–1903). A friend of Pugin. Roman Catholic Churches of St. Charles Borromeo, Ogle Street; Sacred Heart, Accrington; St. Catherine's, West Drayton.

WITHERS, ROBERT JEWELL (1823–1894). A pupil of T. Hellyer. Built or restored nearly 100 churches. He built a " good, cheap type of brick churches, erected with regard to style and public worship ". St. Mary's, Graham Street; St. Anselm's, Streatham; Little Cawthorpe; Church of the Resurrection, Brussels; Llanychllwydoc and many other churches in Wales. He " imparted to many a barn-like structure some semblance of artistic life and feeling ".

WOODYER, HENRY. A pupil of Butterfield. St. Paul's, Wokingham; Christchurch, Reading; St. Augustine's, Northam, Southampton; Langleybury; Waterford; Hascombe; St. Augustine's, Haggerston; Smeaton; St. Michael's, York Town; Highnam; Bayford; St. Martin's, Dorking; St. Stephen's, Redditch; St. Michaels, Tenbury, etc.

WYATT, JOHN DRAYTON (1820–1891). Articled to H. W. Inwood, and in 1841 became assistant draughtsman to Scott and Moffatt. After the dissolution of the partnership stayed on with Scott and was known as " Scott's Wyatt ". Helped to form the British Association of Architectural Draughtsmen, which became the Architectural Association. Left Scott in 1867. Diocesan architect for Bath and Wells. Many restorations. Christchurch, Gretton.

WYATT, THOMAS HENRY (1807–1880). In office of P. Hardwick. Partner with David Brandon in 1838. From 1850 he was helped by his son Matthew. As a designer or restorer was connected with more than 150 churches. Wilton, and many other churches in Wiltshire, including Crockerton; Fonthill-Gifford; Cholderton; Semley; Hindon; Woodborough; Christchurch, Savernake; St. Katherine's, Savernake; Holy Trinity, Haverstock Hill; St. Matthias', Bethnal Green; St. Peter's, Wimblington; Bredenbury; Weston Patrick, etc. Many in Wales. Many restorations.

WYATT, SIR MATTHEW DIGBY (1820–1877). Younger brother and pupil of Thomas Henry.

APPENDIX II

SOME TOWNS AND THEIR CHURCHES

(This is only a small selection of towns and a small selection of churches. The churches mentioned are typical, not necessarily particularly good.)

LONDON:
St. Dunstan in the East.—Tite and Laing.
St. Dunstan in the West.—James Shaw.

LONDON SUBURBS:

BATTERSEA:
St. Mark.—William White.

BERMONDSEY:
St. James.—J. Savage.

BETHNAL GREEN:
St. John.—Sir J. Soane.

BRIXTON:
St. Matthew.—C. F. Porden.
Corpus Christi (R.C.).—J. F. Bentley.

CAMBERWELL:
St. Giles.—G. G. Scott.
St. George.—F. Bedford.

CAMDEN TOWN:
Parish Church.—W. and H. W. Inwood.
St. Michael.—G. F. Bodley.

CHELSEA:
Holy Trinity, Sloane Street.—J. D. Sedding.
St. Luke.—J. Savage.

CLAPTON:
All Saints'.—T. F. Dollman.
St. Matthew.—T. F. Dollman.

CLERKENWELL:
Holy Redeemer.—J. D. Sedding.

DULWICH:
All Saints'.—G. H. Fellowes Prynne.

265

EALING :
  Christchurch.—G. G. Scott.

FULHAM :
  St. Etheldreda.—A. H. Skipworth.

HACKNEY :
  West Hackney Parish Church.—Sir R. Smirke.
  St. John, South Hackney.—E. C. Hakewill.
  St. Mary of Eton, Hackney Wick.—G. F. Bodley.

HAGGERSTON :
  St. Augustine.—H. Woodyer.
  St. Chad.—J. Brooks.
  St. Columba.—J. Brooks.
  St. Mary.—J. Nash.   Altered by Brooks.

HAMMERSMITH :
  Holy Innocents.—J. Brooks.
  St. John.—W. Butterfield.

HAMPSTEAD :
  St. Mary, Primrose Hill.—W. P. Manning.
  St. Stephen.—S. S. Teulon.

HERNE HILL :
  St. Paul.—Alexander and Stevens.   Burned 1850, and rebuilt by
    G. E. Street.

HIGHGATE :
  St. Michael.—L. Vulliamy.   Chancel by Mileham 1881.

HOLBORN :
  St. Alban.—W. Butterfield.
  St. John, Red Lion Square.—J. L. Pearson.

HOXTON :
  St. Saviour.—J. Brooks.

KENNINGTON :
  St. Agnes.—G. Scott, junior.
  St. John the Divine.—G. E. Street.
  St. Mark.—D. R. Roper.

KENSINGTON :
  All Saints', Notting Hill.—W. White.
  St. Augustine.—W. Butterfield.
  St. Cuthbert.—H. R. Gough.
  Holy Trinity.—G. F. Bodley.
  St. John the Baptist, Holland Road.—J. Brooks.
  St. Mary Abbots.—G. G. Scott.
  Our Lady of Victories (R.C.).—G. Goldie.

KILBURN :
  St. Augustine.—J. L. Pearson.

LAMBETH :
St. John, Waterloo Road.—F. Bedford.
St. George (R.C. Cathedral).—A. W. N. Pugin.

LAVENDER HILL :
The Ascension.—J. Brooks.

LEWISHAM :
St. Stephen.—G. G. Scott.
The Transfiguration.—J. Brooks.

NORWOOD :
Holy Innocents.—G. F. Bodley.
St. John.—J. L. Pearson.

PADDINGTON :
St. Mary Magdalene.—G. E. Street.

ST. MARYLEBONE :
Parish Church.—T. Hardwick.   Chancel 1883–1884, T. Harris.
All Saints', Margaret Street.—W. Butterfield.
All Souls', Langham Place.—J. Nash.
The Annunciation, Bryanston Street.—W. Tapper.
St. Cyprian.—J. N. Comper.

ST. PANCRAS :
All Hallows', Gospel Oak.—J. Brooks : completed by Scott, jun.
St. Luke, Kentish Town.—B. Champneys.
St. Mary Magdalene, Munster Square.—R. C. Carpenter.
St. Pancras New Church.—W. and H. W. Inwood.
Catholic Apostolic Church, Gordon Square—R. Brandon.

SHOREDITCH :
St. Michael.—J. Brooks.

SOUTHWARK :
All Hallows.—G. Scott, jun.

STEPNEY :
St. Philip.—A. Cawston.

STOKE NEWINGTON :
St. Faith.—Begun by W. Burges, finished by J. Brooks.
St. Mary.—G. G. Scott.   Tower and spire completed by J. O. Scott.
St. Matthias.—W. Butterfield.

STREATHAM :
Christchurch.—J. W. Wild.

TOOTING :
All Saints'.—Temple Moore.

VAUXHALL :
St. Peter.—J. L. Pearson.

WALWORTH :
St. Peter.—Sir J. Soane.

WANDSWORTH :
St. Anne.—Sir R. Smirke.

WESTMINSTER :
St. Andrew.—G. G. Scott.
St. Barnabas, Pimlico.—T. Cundy.
Holy Trinity.—J. L. Pearson.
St. James-the-Less.—G. E. Street.
St. John, Wilton Road.—A. Blomfield.
St. Matthew.—G. G. Scott.
St. Peter, Great Windmill Street.—R. Brandon.
St. Stephen.—B. Ferrey.
Roman Catholic Cathedral.—J. F. Bentley.

WHITECHAPEL :
St. Mary Matfelon.—E. C. Lee.

BIRMINGHAM :
St. Agnes.—W. H. Bidlake.
St. Alban, Bordesley.—J. L. Pearson.
St. Andrew, Bordesley.—R. C. Carpenter.
St. Augustine, Hagley Road.—J. A. Chatwin.
Christchurch, Summerfield.—J. A. Chatwin.
St. Clement.—J. A. Chatwin.
St. George.—T. Rickman.
St. George, Edgbaston.—Enlarged 1884.   J. A. Chatwin.
Holy Trinity, Birchfield.—J. A. Chatwin.·
St. James, Edgbaston.—S. S. Teulon.
Bishop Latimer Church, Handsworth.—W. H. Bidlake.
St. Oswald, Bordesley.—W. H. Bidlake.
St. Patrick, Bordesley.—J. L. Pearson.
St. Chad's Roman Catholic Cathedral.—A. W. N. Pugin.
Convent and Church of Sisters of Mercy, Handsworth.—A. W. N.
    Pugin.

BOURNEMOUTH :
All Saints', Stourwood.—J. O. Scott.
St. Clement's.—J. D. Sedding.
Holy Trinity.—Charles J. Fergusson.
St. James, Pokesdown.—G. E. Street.
St. John the Evangelist, Boscombe.—J. O. Scott and C. T. Miles.
St. John the Baptist, Moordown.—G. E. Street.   Enlarged, A.
    Blomfield.
St. Peter.—A rebuilding of an earlier church extending over a
    number of years, G. E. Street.
St. Stephen.—J. L. Pearson.
St. Swithun.—Norman Shaw.

BRIGHTON :
All Saints', Compton Avenue.—R. C. Carpenter.
St. Anne's, Kemp Town.—B. Ferrey.
All Saints', Hove.—J. L. Pearson.
St. Barnabas, Hove.—J. L. Pearson.

BRIGHTON :

St. Bartholomew.—E. Scott.
St. Martin.—Somers Clarke.
St. Mary.—W. Emerson.
St. Mary and St. Mary Magdalene.—G. F. Bodley.
St. Michael.—G. F. Bodley. Enlarged from designs of W. Burges.
St. Paul.—R. C. Carpenter. Lantern of tower by Carpenter, jun.
St. Peter.—C. Barry. Chancel by Somers Clarke.

LEEDS :

St. Aidan.—R. J. Johnson and A. C. Hick.
All Saints.—Mallinson and Healey.
All Souls.—G. G. Scott.
St. Andrew.—G. G. Scott.
St. Bartholomew, Armley.—Walker and Athron.
St. Chad, Headingley.—Gibbons.
St. Edward, Holbeck.—G. F. Bodley.
Emmanuel.—Adams and Kelly.
St. Hilda.—J. T. Micklethwaite.
St. John the Evangelist, Holbeck.—G. G. Scott.
St. Margaret.—Temple Moore.
St. Mary, Quarry Hill.—Taylor (typical of many of its kind.
    Decidedly grim Gothic).
St. Matthew, Chapel Allerton.—G. F. Bodley.
St. Michael, Headingley.—J. L. Pearson.
St. Saviours.—J. M. Derick.
St. Thomas, Leylands.—W. Butterfield.

LEICESTER :

All Souls.—G. F. Bodley.
St. Andrew.—G. G. Scott.
St. John.—G. G. Scott.
The Martyrs.—E. Christian.

NOTTINGHAM :

St. Bartholomew.—J. L. Pearson.
St. George, Sutton Chancel.—G. F. Bodley.
St. John the Baptist.—G. G. Scott.
St. Barnabas Roman Catholic Cathedral.—Pugin.

OXFORD :

St. Barnabas.—A. W. Blomfield.
St. Frideswide.—S. S. Teulon.
St. John the Evangelist (Cowley Fathers' Church).—G. F. Bodley.
St. Margaret.—H. C. W. Drinkwater. Tower and porch, G. F.
    Bodley.
St. Peter le Bailey (now the Chapel of St. Peter's Hall).—B.
    Champneys.
SS. Philip and James.—G. E. Street.
St. John the Evangelist, New Hinksey.—Bucknall and Comper.

INDEX

ABERDARE, St. Mary, 193
Aberford, 260
Abertillery, 258
Aberystwyth, 258
Abram, 23
Accommodation, church, 3, 21–28
Accrington, Sacred Heart (R.C.), 264
Acock's Green, St. Mary, *see* Birmingham.
Acomb, R.C. Church, 255
Acton, All Saints', 257
Adams, Mr., architect, 257
Adamstown (Cardiff), All Souls', 261
Addiscombe, St. Mary Magdalene, 257
Addlestone, 260
Adelaide, Butterfield's work at, 123
Aigburth, R.C. Church at, 259
Albert, Prince Consort, 166
   Hall, 170
   Memorial, 169
Albury (Oxon), 260
Alcuin Club, 190
Aldborough Hatch, 250
Alderley Edge, St. Philip, 253
Aldershot, Camp Church, 255
Alexander, Mr., architect, 266
Allaway, Stephen, 226
Allen, Bruce, 165 n.
Allithwaite, 258
Allom, Mr., architect, 107
Alnwick, St. Paul, 260
Aloupka, Palace at, 251
Altars, 49, 99, 134, 188, 189–190, 243
Ambleside, 261
Ambonoclasts, 59, 66
Amwell, Little, 159
Analysis of Gothic Architecture, by J. R. and J. A. Brandon, 77
Ancient Architecture of England, by J. Carter, 17
Anerley, Holy Trinity, 251
Anglican Church Architecture, by J. Barr, 42 n., 43 n.
Annesley, 256

Antiquities of Athens, by Stuart and Revett, 33
Antiquities of England and Wales, by Grose, 17
Antiquities of Ionia, by R. Chandler, 33
Antiquities of the Priory Church of Christchurch, Hampshire, by B. Ferrey, 112
Apology for the Revival of Christian Architecture in England, by Pugin, 49 n., 55–58, 61
Apology for the Separated Church of England, by Pugin, 66
Apostolic Succession, 29
Appleton le Moors, 199
Apses, 200
Architect, The, 172
Architectural Antiquities of Great Britain, by J. Britton, 17
Architectural Association, 191, 264
Architectural Designs of William Burges, A.R.A., 154 n.
Architectural Museum, 109, 112, 130, 165–166
Architectural Parallels, by E. Sharpe, 262
Architectural Review, 176 n.
Architectural Society, 112
Architecture of Humanism, by Geoffrey Scott, 68 n.
Armstead, Mr., sculptor, 169
Arnold, Rev. T. K., 99
Arundel, St. Philip Neri (R.C.), 255
Asceticism of ecclesiologists, 182
Ascot Priory Chapel, 123
Ashford (Middlesex), 122
Ashley Green, 262
Ashpitel, A., architect, 250
Ashwell, 238
Ashworth, E., architect, 250
Asthall, 238
Aston (Birmingham), 252
Atkinson, W., architect, 255
Attempt to discriminate, etc., by Rickman, 18
Attercliffe, 31
Aughton, 258

Aunt Elinor's Lectures on Architecture, 77
Austen, Jane, 11
Austin, H. J., architect, 176, 258
Avington, 9
Awful sentiments inspired by Gothic, 10, 12
Axford, 263
Ayott St. Lawrence, 33
  St. Peter, 261

Baildon, 256
Baker, A., architect, 250
Ball, J. H., architect, 176
Banbury, Christchurch, 113
Bangor, R.C. Church at, 260
Bank of England, 191, 262
Banks, R. R., architect, 166, 250, 263
Barcombe, North, 23
Bardfield, Great, 259
Barley, 100
Barnet, St. John the Baptist, 123
Barnsbury, St. Clement, 261
Barnsley (Glos), 229
  (Yorks), St. Peter, 257
Barnstaple, Holy Trinity, 263
Barrington, 23
Barrow-in-Furness, St. George, 258
  St. James, 258
Barry, Rev. A., 39 n., 64 n.
Barry, Sir C., architect, 28, 38–39, 40–41, 53, 75, 177, 198, 250, 252, 254, 269
Barry, C., junior, architect, 250
Barry, E. M., architect, 160, 250, 263
Barry, T. D., architect, 250
Bartleet, W. G., architect, 250
Barton, 264
Basevi, G., architect, 264
Basilican arrangement of churches, 182–183
Basingstoke, All Saints', 257
Bassett, A. T., 193 n.
Bates, H., 196
Bath, R.C. Church at, 255
Battersea, Christchurch, 252
  St. George, 251
  St. Mark, 263, 265
  St. Mary, 4
  Canon Erskine Clarke's church-building at, 157 n., 226
Bayford, 264
Bayswater, Greek Church, 261
Beaconsfield, St. Michael, 259
Beasley, C., architect, 260
Beauties of England and Wales, by J. Britton, 17

Beauties of Wiltshire, by J. Britton, 17
Beckenham, St. George, 250
Beckford, Wm., 12
Bedford, F., architect, 36, 265, 267
Bedminster, 258
Beechhill, 123
Belmont (Hereford), R.C. Church, 259
Bengeo, 113
Bennett, H. G., M.P., 36
Bennett, Rev. W. J. E., 225
Bensham, St. Chad, 256
  St. Cuthbert, 254
Benson, A. C., 134 n.
Benson, Most Rev. E. W., 134
Bentham, Rev. J., 16, 17
Bentinck, Archdeacon, 198, 226
Bentley, J. F., architect, 248, 250, 265, 268
Bermondsey, St. Bartholomew, 225
  St. James, 39, 260
  St. Paul, 263
Bessingby, 257
Beswick, St. Mary, 258
Bethnal Green, church-building in, 26–27
  St. James the Great, 263
  St. John, 262, 265
  St. Matthias, 264
Betjeman, J., 136 n.
Bettisfield, 262
Bettws Newydd, 238
Beverley Minster, 227
Bezaleel, type of Christian architect, 31, 107
Bickersteth, Rev. E. H., 220
Bicton, 226, 256
Bidlake, W. H., architect, 250, 268
Biggin, 262
Billing, A., architect, 250–251
Billing, A. E., architect, 251
Birchfield (Birmingham), Holy Trinity, 252
Birkdale, St. Peter, 250
Birkenhead, R.C. Church at, 255
Birmingham, Church accommodation at, 27
  Cathedral, St. Philip, 3, 252
  St. Agatha (Sparkbrook), 250
  St. Agnes (Moseley), 268
  St. Alban, 200, 205–206, 268
  St. Andrew, 117, 268
  St. Augustine, 252, 268
  Bishop Latimer, 250, 268
  Christchurch (Summerfield, 252, 268
  St. Clement (Nechells), 252, 268
  St. George, 40, 260, 268

Birmingham (*contd.*)
St. George (Edgbaston), 252, 268
St. James (Edgbaston), 263, 268
St. John (Ladywood), 263
St. Mark, 162
St. Martin, 252
St. Mary, Acock's Green, 252
St. Oswald (Bordesley), 250, 268
St. Patrick, 208, 268
St. Stephen, 116, 250
St. Chad (R.C. Cathedral), 62, 259, 268
Convent of Sisters of Mercy, Handsworth, 268
Bishop, Rev. H. H., 69n.
Bishop Auckland, St. Anne, 260
Bishopton, St. Bonaventura (R.C.), 260
Bix, 254
Blackburn, Holy Trinity, 262
St. Thomas, 258
Blackburne, E. L., architect, 251
Blackfordby, 260
Blackheath, All Saints', 113
St. John, 250
Blackmore, W., architect, 257
Blaina, 258
Blandford, 9
Blawith, 258
Blomfield, Rt. Rev. C. J., Bishop of London, 26, 42, 43, 111, 190, 217, 225
Blomfield, Sir A. W., architect, 190–193, 251, 268, 269
Bloomsbury, Christchurch (Woburn Square), 263
St. George, 9
Blore, E., architect, 152, 251, 252
Bloxham, M. H., architectural writer, 76, 209
Blyth, St. Cuthbert, 256
Blyth, J., architect, 116
Bocking, St. Peter, 190, 257
R.C. Church, 250
Bodelwyddan, 254
Bodicote, 238
Bodley, G. F., architect, 148, 154, 176, 203, 206
his early work, 209
his later work, 209–210
character, 210–211
characteristics of churches, 211–212
some of his churches, 211–212
plans of churches, 213
colouring of churches, 213–214, 251, 263, 265, 266, 267, 269
Bodley, Rev. W., 210
Bognor, St. John, 193
St. Wilfred, 259

Bolton, All Saints', 262
The Saviour, 258
Bombay, Butterfield's work at, 123
Bonomi, I., architect, 197
Booton, 105
Boscombe, St. Andrew, 261
St. John, 261, 268
Boucher, F., 196
Bourton, 23
Bournemouth, St. Alban, 259
All Saints' (Stourwood), 261, 268
St. Ambrose, 254
St. Augustine, 123
St. Clement, 196, 268
Holy Trinity, 268
St. James (Pokesdown), 262, 268
St. John the Baptist (Moordown), 268
St. Michael, 261, 262, 268
St. Peter, 262, 268
St. Stephen, 201, 202, 206–207, 268
St. Swithin, 268
Bowdler, J., 22, 30
Bowdon, 256
Bowdon, Little, 251
Bracknell, 262
Bradford, All Saints' (Horton), 256
St. Augustine (Undercliffe), 256
Christchurch, 256
Holy Trinity, 258
St. John the Evangelist, 256
St. Luke (Manningham), 256
St. Wilfred (Lidget Green), 257
St. Peter (R.C.), 254
Bradshaw, 258
Braishfield, 123
Bramcote, 257
Brandon, D., architect, 264
Brandon, J. A., architect, 77, 251
Brandon, J. R., architect, 77, 251, 267, 268
Brasses, by J. S. M. Ward, 241 n.
Brayley, E. W., 112
Bredenbury, 264
Brentford, St. Faith, 251
Brentwood, 257, 260
Brett, R., 155, 225
Brewood, St. Mary (R.C.), 259
Brick, use of for church-building, 87, 125, 131, 155, 202, 206
Brick and Marble Architecture, by G. E. Street, 130, 146, 192
Bridlington Quay, 162
Briefs for church-building, 3, 4, 24
Brighton, All Saints', 269
St. Anne (Kemp Town), 113, 269
The Annunciation, 226
St. Bartholomew, 226, 269

Brighton (contd.)
Chapel Royal, 51
St. Luke, 193
St. Martin, 190, 252, 269
St. Mary, 254, 269
SS. Mary and Mary Magdalene, 269
St. Matthew, 258
St. Michael, 155, 209, 251, 269
St. Paul, 117, 269
St. Peter, 40, 190, 250, 269
The Resurrection, 226
Pavilion, 46
Brimpton, 257
Brindley, sculptor, 169
Brisbane, Burges' design for Cathedral, 152
Bristol, Cathedral, 149, 208, 262
St. Aidan, 251
St. George, 262
St. Luke, 258
St. Mary Redcliffe, by J. Britton, 17
St. Mary Redcliffe, 51, 70
St. Matthias, 258
St. Raphael, Bedminster, 251
St. Raphael College, 194
Architectural Society, 103
British Almanac and Companion, 147
British Critic, 21, 22, 25, 32, 41, 59, 75
British Magazine, 27
" British Museum " ceremonial, 67
Britton, J., 17
Brixham, All Saints', 190, 257
Brixton, St. John, 113
St. Matthew, 35, 259, 265
Corpus Christi (R.C.), 250, 265
Brock, E. P. L., architect, 252
Brockham Green, 113
Bromley, St. John, 263
Bromley-by-Bow, All Saints', 159
Brompton, New, Dawkes's Church at, 253
St. Mark, 260
Brookfield (Kentish Town), 83
Brooklands, St. John, 263
Brooks, J., architect, 155–157, 247, 252, 266, 267
Brooks, M., architect, 252
Brotton-in-Cleveland, 256
Broughton, St. John, 101
Broughton, Higher, 258
Brown, Ford Madox, 213, 214
Brown, of Norwich, architect, 158
Brussells, Church of the Resurrection, 264
Buckfast Abbey, 263
Buckingham Palace, 251, 258

Buckland, St. Mary, 113
Bucknall, architect, 269
Budleigh Salterton, 259
Builder, 101n., 134, 171, 234
Builder's Journal, 171, 192 n,. 251
Bumpus, T. F., 171, 172 n., 246 n.
Burbage, (Derbys), 253
Burdett Coutts, Miss, 116
Burges, William, architect, 129, 152–155, 182, 252, 254, 257, 267, 269
Burgess Hill, St. John, 252
Burgon, Dean, 234
Burn, architect, 262
Burnage, 258
Burne Jones, Sir E., 196, 213, 214
Burnley, St. Mary (R.C.), 255
Burringham, 263
Burton, 113
Burton, Decimus, architect, 252, 253, 255
Burton, Leonard, 254
Burton-in-Lonsdale, 258
Burton-on-Trent, Holy Trinity, 261
St. Paul, 251
Burwash Weald, 262
Bury, T. T., architect, 252
Bushey Heath, St. Peter, 259
Bussage, 209
Butler, Rev. W. J., 146, 222
Butler, architect, of Chichester, 256
Butterfield, W., architect:
his churchmanship, 118
his use of colour, 118–119
All Saints', Margaret Street, 119–121
other churches, 121–123
character of his buildings, 124–125
his restorations, 125–126
Also 132, 147, 160, 164, 165 n., 193, 242 n., 247, 252, 264, 266, 267, 269
Buxted, St. Mary, 226
Buxton, 253

Caldecote (Beds.), 193
Cam, 84
Camberwell, St. Giles, 115–116, 164, 261, 265
St. George, 265
St. Luke, 253
St. Saviour, 255
Cambridge, St. Alban, proposed model church, 119 n.
All Saints, 209, 213, 251
St. Andrew the Great, 84, 259
Christchurch, 259
St. Giles, 256

Cambridge (*contd.*)
St. Mary the Great, 234
St. Paul, 81–83, 259
St. Sepulchre, 100
Our Lady and the English Martyrs (R.C.), 255
College Chapels: King's, 18, 86, 235
Queens', 212
Pembroke, 215 n.
Cambridge, Archdeacon, 24
Cambridge Architectural Society, 102
Cambridge Camden Society, 75, 77, 78, 79, 81, 89, 98, 99, 100, 101, 102–103, 106, 108, 116, 117, 118, 135, 162, 163, 164, 177, 178, 180
Campfield, 250
Cannes, St. George, 193
Canterbury, Cathedral, 170, 208
St. Gregory, 193
St. Augustine's College, 118
Canton (Cardiff), 261
Capetown, Butterfield's work at, 123
Cardiff, St. Dyfrig, 196
St. Mary, 42
Castle, 154
Carlisle, St. Mary, 159
Carlton (Yorks.), 257, 262
Caroline Divines, 236
Carpenter, R. C., architect, 116–117, 160, 164, 242 n., 247, 252, 256, 262, 267, 268, 269
Carpenter, R. H., architect, 269
Carpenter, Rev. S. C., 160 n.
Carter, J., architectural writer, 13, 17, 65
Carter, J. Coates, architect, 261
Carter, Rev. T. T., 219 n.
Castle of Otranto, A Gothic Story, by Horace Walpole, 12
Caterham, St. Mary, 262
Guards' Chapel, 123
Cathedral Antiquities of Great Britain, by J. Britton, 17
Catholic Encyclopedia, 47 n.
Catshill, 24
Cavendish, 239–240
Caversham, Queen Anne's School Chapel, 193
Cawston, A., architect, 267
Cawthorpe, Little, 264
Cemetery Chapels, 257
Century Dictionary, 76
Ceylon, Carpenter's Cathedral for, 117
Chalmers, Dr., 21
Champneys, B., architect, 252, 267, 269

T (Church Builders)

Chancels, 39, 73, 82, 84, 93, 121, 151, 162, 163, 177–178, 179, 187
Chambers, Sir W., architect, 101, 255
Chandler, R., 33
Chandlers Ford, 251
Chantrell, R. D., architect, 40, 100
Chantrey, F., sculptor, 51
Chapel, A. Trimen's definition of, 31 n.
Chapel Allerton, 213, 251, 269
Chapel and School Architecture, by F. J. Jobson, 104
Charity Commissioners, 159
Charlecote, 254
Charlewood, H. C., architect, 256
Charlton (Dover), 156
Charminster, 23
Charmouth, 254
Chatham, St. John, 262
St. Paul, 255
Chatters, H. W., architect, 254
Chatwin, J. A., architect, 252, 268
Cheadle, 24
R.C. Church, 259
Cheap Churches, 27–28, 48, 83, 192
Cheetham, St. John, 258
Chelmsford, R.C. Church, 260
Chelsea, Holy Trinity, Sloane Street, 196, 260, 265
St. John, 251
St. Luke, 39, 260, 265
St. Mark's and St. John's College Chapel, 251
Cheltenham, All Saints', 257
Christchurch, 42, 99
St. Luke, 257
St. Mark, 257
St. Mary, 99
St. Matthew, 159
St. Peter, 253
(Leckhampton) SS. Philip and James, 257
St. Stephen, 257
Training College Chapel, 254
Cherry Hinton, 131
Chester, Cathedral, 170
King's School, 191
Chester, Bishop of, 25
Chesterfield, 164
Cheston, C., architect, 158
Chetwood, 161
Chetwynde, 113
Chiddingstone Causeway, 250
Chigwell Row, 261
Child, Mr., architect, 254
Chinese Style, confused with Gothic, 14

Chislehampton, 9
Chislehurst, The Annunciation, 156
Chiswick, Christchurch, Turnham
   Green, 261
   St. Michael, 262
Choice of a Style for Present Adoption,
   by G. G. Scott, 109–110
Cholderton, 264
Chorlton-on-Medlock, St. Stephen,
   262
Christian, E., architect, 158–159,
   165n., 193, 242, 252, 269
Christian Observer, 20
Christian Remembrancer, 85 n.
Church and People, by S. C. Car-
   penter, 160 n.
Church Achitecture, by Rev. J. L.
   Petit, 84–85
Church Architecture of Protestantism,
   by A. L. Drummond, 72,
   104 n.
Church Architecture Scripturally Con-
   sidered, by Dr. Close, 98
Church and Chapel Architecture, by
   A. Trimen, 31
Church Association, 220
Church Building Acts, 24, 216
Church Building and Endowment
   Fund, 26
Church Building Society, Incor-
   porated, 23–24, 30, 112, 116,
   159, 197, 224, 261
Church Enlargement and Church
   Arrangement, 75
Church in Danger, by Rev. R. Yates,
   20 n., 22
Churches in the Middle Ages, by
   Crowther and Bowman, 253
Church Quarterly Review, 27 n., 64 n.,
   147 n., 218 n.
Church Times, 188
Clapham, All Saints', 252
   St. Barnabas, 262
   Christchurch, 113
   St. James, 263
   St. Matthew, 263
   St. Peter, 263
   Our Lady of Victories' (R.C.), 250
Clapham, Lower, All Saints', 254,
   265
   Park, All Souls', 254
   Upper, St. Matthew, 254, 265
Clark, Kenneth, 12 n., 62, 69, 104,
   160, 245
Clarke, J., architect, 165 n., 242 n.,
   252
Clarke, Rev. J. Erskine, 157, 226
Clarke, Somers, architect, 36, 190,
   252, 257, 269

Clayton and Bell, glass-painters, 114
Clearwell, 226
Cleator, R.C. Church at, 259
Cleethorpes, St. Aidan, 254
Clerical Architects, 105
Clerkenwell, Holy Redeemer, 176
   196
   St. Paul, 159
   St. Peter (Martyrs' Memorial), 251
   St. Philip, 257
Cliffe-at-Hoo, 228
Clifton, All Saints', 147, 262
   Emmanuel, 258
   St. Mary, 260
Clifton (Manchester), 250
Close, Rev. F., of Cheltenham, 98, 99,
   100
Cloughfold, 258
Clumber, 213, 251
Clutton, H., architect, 129, 153, 166,
   250, 252
Coalpit Heath, 118
Coatbridge, 260
Coates, 264
Cockerell, C. R., architect, 36, 107,
   166, 168, 253
Cockerell, F. P., architect, 190
Cockerell, S. P., architect, 259
Coddington, Mr., of Ware, 89, 97
Coe, Mr., architect, 166
Coedkernew, 255
Colchester, St. Martin, 23
   R.C. Church, 260
Coldharbour, 113
Colney Hatch, 253
Colonies, Gothic in, 104, 111, 123,
   173
Colour, constructional, 119, 120–121,
   122, 123, 124, 125, 131–133,
   136, 139, 147, 154, 157, 158,
   214, 219
   painting, 213–214, 241–242
Colson, J., architect, 253
Colwyn, 24
Commissioners for church-building
   and their churches, 24–25,
   245
Companion to the Glossary, by J. H.
   Parker, 76
Comper, J. N., architect, 206, 267,
   268
Congleton, St. Stephen, 252
Congresbury, 258
Coningsby, by B. Disraeli, 98 n.
Constantinople, Crimea Memorial
   Church, 146, 153
Contrasts, by Pugin, 49–53
Copenhagen, St. Alban, 193
Coppenhall, St. Michael, 156

Cork, St. Finbar's Cathedral, 153–154
Cornish, R., architect, 250
Cornwall, chapel-building in, 4
Cost of new churches, 25, 27, 33 n., 40, 154, 192–193
Cottingham, L. N., architect, 165, 253, 257, 263
Cottingham, N. J., architect, 253
Cotton, W., 27, 225
Coulton, Dr. G. C., 52
Countess of Huntingdon's Connexion, Hymn-book of, 11
Cowes, East, 258
Cowick, 123
Cowley, St. John the Evangelist, 251, 269
Cowpen, 254
Cox, Dr. J. C., 1, 9 n., 236 n., 244 n.
Cox, Mr., carver, 115
Coxe, Archdeacon, 245
Cray, North, 258
Crewe, St. Barnabas, 258
St. John, 256
Criticisms of new churches, 25–26
Crocken Hill, 258
Crosland Moor, 254
Cross, Mr., and Albert Memorial, 169
Crosscrake, 258
Crowther, J. S., architect, 253
Croxley Green, 258
Croydon, St. Andrew, 113
St. Augustine, 261
St. Matthew, 193
St. Michael, 200, 201, 206
St. Peter, 261
Whitgift School, 191
Crumpsall, St. Mary, 253
Crystal Palace, 127, 146
Cuddesdon College, 146
Cudworth, 254
Cullercoats, 207
Cumbrae Cathedral, 123
Cundy, T., architect, (1) 253
Cundy, T., architect (2), 253, 268
Cundy, T. C., architect, 253
Curdridge, 256
Currey, H., architect, 253
Cutts, J. E. K. and J. P., architects, 157, 253

Daglingworth, 229
Daisy Hill, 258
Dale, Dr., of Birmingham, 28
Dale, A., 66 n., 245 n.
Dalston, Holy Trinity, 159
St. Mark, 158
Dalton Holme, 198

Dalton-in-Furness, 258
Dance, G., architect, 51, 262
Dane Bridge, 252
Darwen, Over, 258
St. Cuthbert, 258
Datchett, 252
Daubeny, C., 22
Daveyhulme, 263
Davies, Rev. S. Russell, 226
Dawkes, S. W., architect, 117, 253
Day, R. P., architect, 262
Daylesford, 198
Dedications, 84, 104
Deering, J. P., architect, 36
Denstone, 172, 262
Deptford, St. John, 256
Derby, Church Life in, 221–222
All Saints' Cathedral, 9, 62
St. Alkmund, 62
St. Andrew, 221, 226
St. Anne, 221
St. Augustine, 221–222
St. Barnabas, 221
St. Chad, 221
St. Dunstan, 222
St. George, 222
Holy Trinity, 222
St. James, 222
St. John, 222
St. Luke, 222
St. Michael, 226
St. Paul, 222
St. Thomas, 222
St. Werburgh, 193
St. Marie (R.C.), 62, 259
Derby Churches Old and New, by C. J. Payne, 222 n.
Derick, J. M., architect, 117, 253, 269
Devizes, St. Peter, 262
Devonport, St. Barnabas, 260
St. James, 260
St. Mary, 260
St. Paul, 260
St. Stephen, 260
Dewsbury Moor, 31
Dictionnaire Raisonné, by V. le Duc, 130
Dictionary of National Biography, 118, 253, 257
Discourses on the Scope and Nature of University Education, by J. H. Newman, 45
Disraeli, Benjamin, 98n.
Dissent, growth of, 4, 20, 22, 32
and Gothic, 104, 118 n., 161
Dobson, J., architect, 253–254
Dodsworth, Rev. W., 119
Dogmersfield, 113

Dolgelly, 105
Dolling, Father, 176
Dollman, F. T., architect, 254, 265
Donaldson, Professor, 252, 261
Doncaster, St. George, 166, 261
Dorking, St. Martin, 264
    St. Paul, 113
Dover, St. James (New), 252
    R.C. Church, 259
Downshire Hill, St. John's Chapel,
    159
Downside Priory, 63
Drayton, West, St. Catherine (R.C.),
    264
Drinkwater, H. C. W., architect, 269
Dropmore, 123
Drummond, A. L., author, 72, 104 n.
Dublin, Christchurch, 149, 150
Dublin Review, Remarks by Pugin in,
    49 n., 63, 163
Dudley, R.C. Church, 259
Dudley, Rev. J., 87 n.
Dundee, St. Paul, 261
    St. Salvador, 209, 251
Dulwich, West, All Saints', 259, 265
Dunraven, Dowager Duchess of, 226
Dunstall, 253
Durandus, W., Bishop of Mende,
    87, 92-94, 96, 105
Durham, Cathedral, 13n., 14, 15,
    51, 170, 197, 205, 229, 254
    St. Cuthbert (R.C.), 197 n.
    St. Goderic (R.C.), 259
Dyce, Mr., artist, 120
Dyffryn, 258

Ealing, Christchurch, 251, 261, 266
    St. Mary, 246
    St. Saviour, 259
Earlsfield, St. Andrew, 258
Earnest Address, by Pugin, 67
Eastbourne, Christchurch, 113
    Holy Trinity, 252
    St. Peter, 253
    St. Saviour, 148, 262
    Grant for new church, 24
East Grinstead, convent, 262
Eastlake, C., 12, 37, 40, 62, 72, 120,
    124, 125, 132, 136, 144, 146,
    147, 154, 169
East Moors, 257
Ecclectic Review, 100
Eccles, St. Andrew, 253
Ecclesiastical Commissioners, 159,
    216, 224
Ecclesiological (late Cambridge Cam-
    den) Society, 101, 119, 121,
    126, 129, 146, 158, 235, 236,
    263

Ecclesiologist, 60, 63, 79-87, 94, 97,
    99, 100, 101, 102, 103, 104,
    107, 114, 116, 117, 122, 124,
    130, 131, 135, 136, 137, 138,
    144, 146, 157, 158, 163, 164,
    165, 167, 182, 197, 198, 209,
    217, 224, 228, 235, 237, 242,
    244, 246, 257, 263,
Ecclesiology, meaning of word, 75-
    79
Eccleston (Chesh.), St. Mary, 251
    (Lancs.), Porden's church at, 259
Eden, F. S., 240 n.
Edgbaston, see Birmingham.
Edifices of London, by A. Pugin, 46
Edinburgh, St. Mary's Cathedral,
    149, 261
Edmeston, Mr., architect, 161
Edmonton, St. Mary, 123
Edvin Loach, 226
Eeles, F. C., 9
Egham, 57
Eighteenth century, church-
    building in, 3-4
    styles of architecture in, 9-14
Elland, All Saints', 259
Ellerker, 198
Ellerton, 198
Ellingham, 105
Elloughton, 198
Elsted, 113
Eltham, Holy Trinity, 262
    St. Luke, 257
Elvaston, 251
Elvington, 263
Elwin, Rev. Whitwell, 105
Ely Cathedral, 165, 170
Embroidery, 194, 195
Emerson, W., architect, 254, 269
Emery Down, 123
Enfield, St. George, 253
    St. John the Baptist, 260
    St. Luke, 156
    St. Mary Magdalene, 123
England, 1870-1914, by R. C. K.
    Ensor, 123 n.
English Cathedral of the Nineteenth
    Century, by A. J. B. Hope,
    18 n., 41 n., 120 n., 121 n.,
    217 n.
English Church in the Nineteenth
    Century, by J. H. Overton,
    25 n.
English Church Screens, by A.
    Vallance, 238 n.
English Church Union, 148, 220,
    224
English Mediaeval Painted Glass, by
    J. D. le Couteur, 240 n.

English Monumental Sculpture since the Renaissance, by K. A. Esdaile, 37 n.
English Parish Church, by J. C. Cox, 1 n., 236 n.
English Parish Church, by A. R. Powys, 2 n.
English Stained and Painted Glass, by F. S. Eden, 240 n.
Enquiry into the Principles of Taste, by Payne Knight, 16
Ensor, R. C. K., 123 n.
Epping, St. John the Baptist, 251
Epsom, Christchurch, 193
Erectheion at Athens, by Inwood, 256
Erectheum, 35, 37
Erith, Christchurch, 260
Esdaile, K. A., 37
Esher, Christchurch, 113
Essay on the Origin of Gothic Architecture, by Sir J. Hall, 15–16
Essays on Gothic Architecture, by Milner, Bentham and Grose, 7, 17, 18
Eston Grange, 256
Eton, St. John, 113
  College : Lower Chapel, 193
  Queen's Schools, 191
Eusebius, 90
Euston Station, 256
Euxton, R.C. Church at, 259
Evangelical fear of Gothic, 28, 72
Evelyn, J., opinion of Gothic, 7
Everton, St. Saviour, 256
Evidences, by Paley, 258
Ewan Christian, Anonymous, 159 n.
Ewell, 253
Examples of Ancient Domestic Architecture, by F. T. Dollman, 254
Examples of Ancient Pulpits, by F. T. Dollman, 254
Examples of Gothic Architecture, by A. Pugin, 46
Exeter, Cathedral, 170, 208, 210
  St. Mary Major, 250
  St. Michael, 256
  strange practices at, 178 n.
  Architectural Society, 103, 238
Eye (Northants), 254
Faber, Rev. F. W., 48
Fair Oak, 253
Falkland Islands, Cathedral, 193
Fallacies : Ethical, 69
  Mechanical, 68 n.
Falmouth, All Saints', 196
Farleigh, East, 24
Farlington, 262
Farnham (Essex), 252

Fauls, 113
Felbridge, 263
Fenny Stratford, 263
Fergusson, C. J., architect, 268
Fergusson, J., architectural writer, 35
Ferrey, B., architect, 46, 47, 51, 52, 68, 112–113, 116, 133, 165, 242 n., 250, 254, 258, 268, 269
Ferrilby, North, 198
Few Words to Church-Builders, 75
Few Words to Churchwardens, 75
Field, Mr., architect, 258
Filkins, 262
Fimber, 225
Finchley, Christchurch, 258
Finsbury Park, St. Thomas, 159
Finsthwaite, 258
Fitzwilliam, Earl, 203
Fitzwilliam Museum, 260
Flaunden, 23
Fleet, 155
Fleetwood, 252
Flimwell, 252
Flockton, T. J., architect, 254
Floriated Ornament, by Pugin, 58
Folkestone, Holy Trinity, 159
  St. Michael, 211, 251
  St. Saviour, 190
Fonthill Abbey, 12–13, 38
Fonthill-Gifford, 264
Fonts, 28, 83–84, 192, 215, 238
Foord, E., 13 n.
Ford, C. B., 9 n.
Ford, Onslow, 196
Foreign Gothic, approved of, 128–159
  not approved of, 43–44, 85, 165
Fort Augustus Abbey, 259
Fosbury, 263
Foster, Mr., architect, 40
Foster, R., 155, 225
Fowler, C., architect, 250, 254
Fowler, C. Hodgson, architect, 254
Fowler, J., architect, 254
Frampton Cotterell, 258
France Lynch, 209, 251
Francis, H., architect, 254
Fraser, Bishop of Manchester, 223
Freeman, E. A., 235
Freemantle, 263
Fretherne, 113
Froude, Hurrell, 46
Fulford, Rev. J. L., 238
Fulham, St. Dionis, 159
  St. Etheldreda, 266
  St. Matthew, 193
  St. Peter, 251
  St. Thomas (R.C.), 259

Fulljames, Mr., architect, 260
Furniture, Gothic, Pugin's designs
    for, 47
Fylingdales, 262

Gainsborough, All Saints', 251
    St. John, 190, 257
Galleries, 5, 34, 43, 187, 214, 239–
    240
Gandy, Mr., architect, see Deering,
    J. P.
Gardiner, H. Starkie, 196
Garling, Mr., architect, 166
Garner, T., architect, 122, 148, 209,
    210, 251
Gawcott, 161
Gentleman's Magazine, 17, 39, 41
George IV, 36, 69
George, Sir E., architect, 176
Georgetown, Demerara, 193
Gerrards Cross, 134 n.
Ghastly Good Taste, by J. Betjeman,
    136 n.
Gibbs, J., architect, 6, 35, 62, 245 n.
Gibson, J., architect, 254
Giles, J. E., architect, 242
Gillingham, St. Augustine, 257
Gladstone, W. E., 168, 224
Glascote, St. George, 252
Glasgow, Cathedral, 251
    St. Bride, 251
    Franciscan Church, 259
Glass, not suitable material for
    Gothic, 127
Glass, painted, 210, 213, 214, 240,
    243, 253
Glastonbury Abbey, 15
Glossary of Architecture, by J. H.
    Parker, 76, 260
Glossary of Ecclesiastical Ornament
    and Costume, by Pugin, 58
Gloucester, Cathedral, 18, 170
    St. James, 257
Glynne, Sir S., 119
Godalming, 229
Godfroy, l'Abbé, 153
Godwin, E. W., architect, 254
Goldie, E., architect, 254
Goldie, G., architect, 254, 255, 263,
    266
Goodchild, T., 101 n.
Goodhart-Rendell, H. S., architect,
    9, 176
Goring (Sussex). 252
Gothic, Evelyn's opinion of, 7
    origin of name, 6–8
    churches in eighteenth century, 10
    domestic in eighteenth century,
        12–14

Gothic (contd.)
    references in literature, 10–12
    attempts to find dates of, 14–17
    theories of origin of, 14–17
    names of styles of, 16–19, 87
    use of, in Commissioners' churches,
        38–41
    is Christian architecture, 45 ff.,
        104, 149
    and construction, 53–54, 64–65,
        124, 125, 140 n.
    foreign, 128–159, 198, 199, 209
    prospects for development, 173–174
    return to English, 209, 211
Gothic Architecture Improved, by B.
    Langley, 12
Gothic Architecture Secular and
    Domestic, by Scott, 174 n.
Gothic Revival, by K. Clark, 12 n.,
    69 n., 104 n.
Gothic Revival in England, by C.
    Eastlake, 12, 37 n., 62 n.,
    72 n., 124 n., 132 n., 136 n.,
    144 n., 145 n., 146 n., 147 n.,
    154 n.
Gott, Rt. Rev. J., 221
Gough, A. D., architect, 255
Gough, H. R., architect, 255, 261,
    266
Government Offices, 147, 166–169,
    261
Grahamstown Cathedral, 261
Grangetown (Cardiff), 261
Grassendale, St. Mary, 256
Gray, Rev. S., 105
Gray, T., poet and antiquary, 12, 16
Great Exhibition, 60, 165
Greek style adapted to churches, 33–
    48
Greenhead, 254
Greenhithe, St. Mary, 256
Greenwich, St. Alphege, 9
    (West), Holy Trinity, 43
Grenville, Lord, 30
Gretton, Christchurch, 264
Grimsargh, 258
Grimston, 251
Grimthorpe, Lord, 54, 211 n., 229–
    230
Grissell, Mr., builder, 162
Grose, Captain, Writer on Architec-
    ture, 7, 17
Gwilt, G., architect, 262
Gwilt, J., architect, 255

Habershon, E., architect, 252, 255
Habershon, M., architect, 158, 255
Habershon, W. G., architect, 252,
    254, 255, 257

Habton, Great, 254
Hackney, South, St. John, 266
Hackney, West, 262, 266
Hackney Wick, St. Mary of Eton, 251, 266
Hadfield, C., architect, 255
Hadfield, M. E., architect, 41, 254, 255
Haggerston, St. Augustine, 264, 266
    St. Chad, 155, 156, 266
    St. Columba, 155, 156, 266
    St. Mary, 41, 247, 258, 266
    St. Paul, 191, 193
    St. Stephen, 254
Hagley, 241
Haileybury College Chapel, 193
Hakewill, A. W., architect, 255
Hakewill, E. C., architect, 255, 266
Hakewill, J., architect, 36, 255
Hakewill, J., architect, 255
Hakewill, J. H., architect, 255
Haley Hill, 166, 261
Halifax, St. Hilda, 254
Hall, Sir J., 15
Halstead, Holy Trinity, 260
Halsetown, 260
Ham (Surrey), 251
Ham, East, St. Bartholomew, 190, 257
Hamburg, St. Nicholas, 164–165
    Rathhaus, 166
Hamilton, Mr., architect, 117
Hammersmith, Holy Innocents, 156 266
    St. John, 122, 266
    St. Paul, 255, 261
Hammerwich, 251
Hammerwood, 252
Hampstead, Christchurch, 220
    St. James, 193
    St. Mary, Primrose Hill, 266
    St. Paul, 263
    St. Stephen, 157, 263, 266
Hampton Court, 251
Hampton Lucy, 260
Hamsey, 159
Handbook to Oxfordshire, 237 n.
Handsworth, 24
Hanging Heaton, 31
Hanover Chapel, Regent Street, 36, 253
Hansom, C. F., architect, 255
Hansom, J. A., architect, 254, 255
Hanwell, St. Mark, 263
    St. Mary, 162
Hardman, glass-painter, 114
Hardwick, Philip, architect, 197, 250, 264

Hardwick, P. C., architect, 190, 242 n, 256
Hardwick, T., architect, 36, 255–256, 267
Harpenden, 262
Harrison, J. P., architect, 123, 209 n.
Harrogate, Christchurch, 247
    St. Luke, 256
    St. Mark, 261
    St. Peter, 251
    St. Wilfrid, 215, 257
Harrow Weald, 123
Hartshill, 261
Hartshorne, 251
Hartlepool, West, Christchurch, 257
    St. Oswald, 256
Hartwell, 10
Harwood, Great, 259
Hascombe, 264
Hastings, Holy Trinity, 158, 263
    R.C. Church, 259
Hatcham, All Saints', 251
Haverstock Hill, St. Andrew, 256
    Holy Trinity, 264
    St. Saviour, 250
Hawkesmoor, N., architect, 6, 9
Hawkhurst, All Saints', 226
Hawkins, R., architect, 256
Hawton, 79
Haydn, 89
Hayley, W. H., architect, 256
Haynford, 23
Hayward, J., architect, 242 n., 256
Haywards Heath, 251
Headcorn, 251
Headingley, St. Chad, 269
    St. Michael, 207, 269
Healey, Mr., architect, 256, 269
Healey (Yorks), 257
Heckington, 79
Hedworth, St. Nicholas, 254
Helidon, 122
Hellyer, T., architect, 264
Helperthorpe, 225, 262
Helps to the Building of Churches, by Rev. W. Carus Wilson, 27
Hendon, Christchurch, 260
    St. John, 257
Henry VII's Chapel, by L. N. Cottingham, 253
Heptonstall, 256
Herbert, Sidney, 107
Hereford, Cathedral, 13 n., 51, 66, 170, 252, 261
    T. Nicholson's work at, 258
Herne Hill, St. Paul, 147, 266
Herriard, 253
Hersham, 208
Hertford, All Saints', 176

Hervey, Rev. J., 10
Heslerton, East, 225, 262
Hethersgill, 252
Hetton, South, 23
Hexham, Abbey, 254
Heywood, St. Luke, 252
Hick, A. C., architect, 269
Hickleton, 251
Hicks, W. S., architect, 256
Hierologus, or *The Church Tourists*,
    by J. M. Neale, 77–78
Hierugia Anglicana, 236
Higginson, E., 226
Highbridge, 258
Highbury, St. Augustine, 252
    St. John, 262
    St. Saviour, 157, 263
Highcliffe, 208
Highgate, All Saints', 122
    St. Barnabas, 263
    St. Mary, 123, 266
    St. Michael, 41
    St. Joseph (R.C.), 259
Highnam, 113–114, 264
Hildenborough, 159
Hills, G. M., architect, 242 n., 256
Hilston, 225
Hindon, 264
Hingeston-Randolph, Prebendary,
    105
Hingham, 228
*Hints for the Practical Study of
    Ecclesiastical Antiquities*, 75
Hints to Workmen, 75
Hinksey, New, 269
Historical Tour of Monmouthshire,
    by Archdeacon Coxe, 245
History and Antiquities of Ely, by
    J. Bentham, 16, 17
*History and Description of the Styles
    of Architecture*, by T. T.
    Bury, 252
*History of the Decorative painting of
    the Middle Ages*, by E. L.
    Blackburne, 251
*History of Gothic and Saxon Archi-
    tecture in England*, by Bent-
    ham and Brown Willis, 17
History of Modern Architecture, by
    Fergusson, 35
Hitchin, St. Saviour, 123
Hoar Cross, 211, 213, 251
Hoarwithy, 261
Hobart Cathedral, 251
Holbeck, St. Edward, 269
    St. John the Evangelist, 109,
    269
Holborn, St. Alban, 122, 125, 220,
    225, 266

Holborn (*contd.*)
    St. John, Red Lion Square, 199,
    200, 203, 207, 266
    St. Peter, Saffron Hill, 41
Holdenhurst, 113
Holland, H., architect, 262
Holland, Rev. H. Scott, 96
Holloway, Upper, St. John, 41,
    250
    St. Mark (Tollington Park), 255
    St. Stephen, 159
Holmbury, St. Mary, 149, 176,
    262
Holme, A., architect, 256
Holywell, R.C. Church, 260
Homerton, St. Barnabas, 250
Hom Green, 213, 251
Honiton, St. Paul, 254
Hook (Surrey), 84
Hook, Rev. W. F., 40, 160, 220–221
Hope, A. J. Beresford, 18, 41, 76,
    119, 120, 121, 127, 126, 217 n.,
    218, 247
Horninglow, 251
Hornblotton, 256
Hornsey, St. Mary, 155
Horrid Novels, 11, 12
Horsfall, H. D., 207, 226
Horsfall, R., 207
Horsforth, 203
Houghton Conquest, 234
Hove, All Saints' 208
    St. Barnabas, 207
How, Rt. Rev. W. Walsham, 217
Howe Bridge, 258
Howley, Most Rev. W., 22
Howsham, 148, 262
Hoxton, Christchurch, 251
    St. Mary, 159
    St. Saviour, 155–156, 266
    St. Monica (R.C.), 259
Hubbard, Hon. J. G., 226
Huddersfield, St. John, 123
Hugo de Sancto Victore, 94
Hull, All Saints', 262
    St. Augustine, Newland, 257
    St. John the Evangelist, 225
Hulme, Holy Trinity, 261
    St. John, 263
    St. Wilfrid (R.C.), 259
Humshaugh, 254
Hunt, Mrs., 226
Huntley, 157, 263
Hursley, 45
Hurstpierpoint, 250
Hunt, Mr., 168
Hutton Roof, 258
Hymns Ancient and Modern, 80 n.,
    122

Icklingham, All Saints', 242
St. James, 242
Iffley, 238
Ilford, St. Mary, 260
Ilfracombe, SS. Philip and James, 256
St. Peter, 259
Ilkley, St. Margaret, 262
Ince, 258
Lower, 258
Instrumenta Ecclesiastica, 118
Introduction to the Study of Gothic Architecture, by J. H. Parker, 76
Introductory Discourse on the Principles of Gothic Architecture, by Mr. Murphy, 15
Inverness Cathedral, 117
Inwood, W. and H. W., architects, 35, 36, 51, 118, 256, 264, 267
Ipswich, All Saints', 156
St. Mary le Tower, 259
Ireland, Ecclesiology in, 103
Ireland, Mr., architect, 260
Iron, use of in Architecture, 126–127, 140, 191
Irving, Rev. E., 47
Islington, church-building in, 26
Carpenter's design for Church at, 116
St. Jude, Mildmay Park, 255
St. Matthew, 255
St. Paul, Balls Pond, 40, 250
St. Peter, 255
St. Philip, 255
Islip (Oxon), 237
Italian fashions in Roman Catholic Churches in England, 48–49, 67

Jackson, T. G., architect, 186 n., 256
Jamaica, Carpenter's Cathedral for, 117
James Wyatt, by A. Dale, 66 n., 245 n.
Jearred, R. W. C., architect, 42
Jeffreys, Rev. H. A., 226
Jerusalem, M. Habershon's designs for Cathedral for, 255
Jesmond, St. Barnabas, 256
Jobson, F. J., architect, 104
John Nash, by J. Summerson, 36 n.
Johnson, J., architect, 256–257
Johnson, R. J., architect, 257
Johnson's Churches of Northampton, 256
Jones, Inigo, architect, 6
Jones, Rev. W., of Nayland, 21 n.
Jones, R. J., architect, 105

Jones, drawing-master of Scott, 161
Judkin, Mr., divine and poet, 41
Mr. Judkin's Chapel, *see* St. Pancras, St. Mary's, Somers Town.

Keble, Rev. J., 29, 45
Keble College Chapel, *see* Oxford.
Keeling, Bassett, architect, 158, 193, 257
Keighley, St. Anne (R.C.), 259
Kelham Hall, 170
Kelk, Mr., and Albert Memorial, 169
Kelly, J., architect, 257, 269
Kelsey, South, 259
Kempe, C. E., glass-painter, 213, 214
Kempthorne, S., architect, 162, 257
Kendall, H. E., architect, 257
Kenilworth, St. John, 159
St. Augustine (R.C.), 259
Kennington, St. Agnes, 214–215, 261
St. John the Divine, 148, 251, 262
St. Mark, 260
Kensal Green, St. John, 257
New Town, R.C. Church, 250
Kensington, St. Augustine, Queen's Gate, 122
Christchurch, 113
St. Cuthbert, 255
St. George, Campden Hill, 158
Holy Trinity, 251
St. James, Norlands, 263
St. John the Baptist, 156
St. Mary Abbots, 261
St. Paul, 250
Brompton Oratory, 260
Our Lady of Victories' (R.C.), 254
Kentchurch, 241
Kent Town, St. Paul, 260
Kidlington, 131
Kilburn, St. Augustine, 201, 202, 207
Kildare Cathedral, 149
Killamarsh, 255
Kilndown, 247
Kimberworth, 255
Kingsbury, 117
King's Lynn, St. Margaret, 251
Kingston, St. Luke, 257
Kingstone, 148, 262
Kingswood, 113
Kippax, 255
Kirby Grindalythe, 225
Knight, Payne, 16
Knowsley, 258
Knox, Rev. Ronald, 96
Knutsford, 258

Lacey Green, 261
Lahore Cathedral, 261
Laing, D., architect, 254, 265
Lamb, E. B., architect, 193, 257
Lambley, 256
Lambeth, All Saints', Lower Marsh, 260
    St. Andrew, 158
    St. John, Waterloo Road, 267
    St. Mary, 256
    St. Mary-the-Less, 42
    St. George's R.C. Cathedral, 59, 61-62, 259, 267
    Palace, Blore's work at, 251
Lamps of Architecture according to, Ruskin : Obedience, 141-142
    Sacrifice, 139
    Truth, 139-141
Lancaster, St. Joseph (R.C.), 260
    St. Peter (R.C.), 258
Lance, M. Adolphe, 166
Lancing College, 117
Landport, St. Agatha, 176
Lane, R., architect, 263
Langho, 258
Langley, Batty, architect, 12, 165
Langleybury, 264
Laud, Archbishop, 1
Lavender Hill, The Ascension, 267
Laverstock, 197
Lavington, West, 123
Law Courts, 149, 170, 191
Layard, Mr., 169, 170
Leamington, 193
Le Couteur, J. D., 240
Lee, Professor, Rector of Barley, 100
Lee, E. C., architect, 257
Lee, Rt. Rev. Prince, Bishop of Manchester, 101, 223
Lee (Kent), St. Margaret, 247, 255
    St. Peter, 251
Leeds, St. Aidan, 257, 269
    All Hallows', 257
    All Saints', 256, 269
    All Souls', 269
    St. Bartholomew, Armley, 269
    Emmanuel, 257, 269
    St. Hilda, 190, 257, 269
    Holy Trinity, 3
    St. Margaret, 257, 269
    St. Mary, Quarry Hill, 31, 269
    St. Peter, 40, 220-221
    St. Saviour, 117-118, 253, 269
    St. Thomas, 123, 269
    Old Bank, 170
Leek, All Saints', 262
Legg, G., architect, 263
Leicester, All Souls, 251, 269
    St. Andrew, 269

Leicester (contd.)
    St. John, 269
    St. Mark, 159
    St. Mary, 251
    St. Peter, 262
    The Martyrs, 269
Leigh (Lancs.), 258
Leigh, Lord, 226
Leighton, Lord, artist, 157
Leroy, M., 153
Lethaby, Prof. W. R., architect, 118, 124-125, 153 n.
Lever Bridge, 258, 262
Leverstock Green, 252
Lewis, Mr., on Symbolism, 88
Lewisham, St. Stephen, 226, 261, 267
    The Transfiguration, 156, 267
Leytonstone, Chapel at, 161
Lichfield, Cathedral, 13 n., 66, 170, 229
    St. Mary's, 254
    Architectural Society, 103
Life of E. W. Benson, by A. C. Benson, 134 n.
Life of G. H. Wilkinson, by A. J. Mason, 204
Lightfoot, Bishop, 207
Lille Cathedral, 129, 146, 153, 252
Limehouse, St. Anne, 9
    St. John, 253
    St. Peter, 159
Lincoln, Cathedral, 83, 119 n., 205, 208, 254
    St. Swithin, 254
Little Guide to Hampshire, by J. C. Cox, 244 n.
Littlemore, 105
Liverpool, Cathedral, 210, 248, 254, 261
    St. Agnes, Sefton Park, 201, 202, 207
    St. Aidan, 256
    St. Alban, 256
    All Saints', 256
    All Saints', Princes Park, 256
    All Souls', 256
    St. Margaret, 262
    St. Matthias, 256
    St. Paul, Princes Park, 256
    St. Oswald, Old Swan (R.C.), 259
    Our Lady of Lourdes and St. Bernard (R.C.), 259
    Church of the Sisters of Notre Dame (R.C.), 255
Liverpool, Lord, 20, 22
Livesey, 258
Llanberis, 250
Llandaff, Cathedral, 259
    Church-building in diocese of, 224

Llandaff, Bishop of, 245
Llandegveth, 229
Llandogo, 261
Llangorwen, 84
Llangwm Uchaf, 238
Llanychllwydoc, 264
Lockerly, 253
Lombardic Architecture, 42–43
London, St. Paul's Cathedral, 7, 69, 70 n., 96, 251, 252
    St. Bartholomew, Moor Lane, 107, 253
    St. Bartholomew the Great, Smithfield, 263
    St. Dunstan in the West, Fleet Street, 262
    St. Mary Aldermanbury, 244
    St. Mary Woolnoth, 9
    St. Michael, Cornhill, 244
    St. Stephen, Walbrook, 101
    St. Swithin, London Stone, 244
    Growth of, in eighteenth century, 5, 19
    Diocesan Church Building Society, 217
    Guildhall, 51
London Churches Ancient and Modern, by T. F. Bumpus, 172 n., 246 n.
Long Combe, 238
Long Ditton, 4, 262
Long Melford, 251
Longridge, St. Paul, 159
Loughton, 262
Louth, St. James, 252
    St. Michael, 254
Lowder, Rev. C., 219, 220
Lowfield Heath, 155
Lowton, 258
Luther, Martin, 29
Luton, St. Saviour, 190, 257
Luttons Ambo, 225
Lydford, East and West, 113
Lydiate, R.C. Church at, 260
Lyndhurst, 157, 263
Lyon, T. H., architect, 212

Macaronic Style, 41–42
Macclesfield, St. Alban (R.C.), 259
Machen, 255
Mackay, Rev. J. F. B., 175
Mackonochie, Rev. A. H., 220
Madagascar, Butterfield's work at, 123
Maddox, Mr., 161
Maidenhead, All Saints', Boyne Hill, 148, 262
Maidstone, Holy Trinity, 263
    St. Philip, 263

Maindee, St. John, 261
Malden, Old, 256
Mallinson, Mr., architect, 256, 269
Malvern, Holy Trinity, 253
    College Chapel, 193
Man, Isle of, Hansom's churches in, 255
Manchester, Cathedral, 210
    St. Alban, Cheetwood, 253
    Holy Trinity, 261
    St. Mark, 262
    St. Mary, Moss Lane, 253
    St. Paul, New Cross, 261
    St. Chad (R.C.), 253
    Jesuit Church, 255
    Gothic Chapel at, 104
    church-building in diocese of, 223
Manning, W. P., architect, 266
Mansergh, 258
Mansfield, St. Mark, 257
Mant, Richard, 24
Marazion, All Saints', 260
Marchington, St. John, 255
Marlow, Great, 256
    St. Peter (R.C.), 259
Markham Clinton, 262
    West, 262
Marsden, 254
Martin, Père, 153
Martineau, Harriet, 21
Martyn, Henry, Missionary, 205
Masborough, 263
Mason, A. J., 204
Materials for building, 43, 125, 126–127, 202
Matlock, R.C. Church, 255
Meditations among the Tombs, by Hervey, 10
Melbourne, Australia, St. Paul's Cathedral, 123
    St. Patrick's Cathedral (R.C.), 263
Melbury Road, Burges's house in, 154
Melplash, 113
Memoir of Sir Charles Barry, by Rev. A. Barry, 39 n., 40 n., 64 n.
Memoir of George Street, by A. E. Street, 109, 147 n., 148 n., 149 n., 150 n., 151 n.
Meon, West, 261
Merthyr Tydfil, R.C. Church, 260
Methodism in Cornwall, 4
Metropolitan Churches Fund, 217
Micklethwaite, J. T., architect, 176, 183, 184, 185, 186, 187, 189, 190, 224, 252, 257
Middlesbrough, All Saints', 262

Middlesbrough (*contd.*)
  St. Columba, 257
  St. Cuthbert, 257
  St. John, 258
  R.C. Cathedral, 254
Middleton (Derbys), 24
Midgham, 257
Mileham, Mr., architect, 266
Miles, C. J., architect, 261, 268
Miller, B., architect, 64, 147
Milner, Rev. J., 7, 15, 16, 17, 260
Milnrow, 263
Milton (Kent), 240
Mistley, 263
Mitchell-Withers, J. B., architect, 257
Milverton, New, St. Mark, 215, 261
Modern Gothic Architecture, by T. G. Jackson, 186 n., 256
Modern Painters, by Ruskin, 135
Modern Parish Churches, by J. T. Micklethwaite, 183–189, 224 n.
Moffatt, architect, partner with Scott, 115, 146, 161, 165, 264
Mold Green, 251
Molesworth, Mr., 2
Money, raising of, for church-building, 3, 4, 23, 24, 26, 217, 223, 224–226
Monk, Rev. Dr. J. H., 147
Monk, W., musician, 122
Monk Bretton, 23
Monkwearmouth, All Saints', 254
Monmouth, St. Mary, 5, 245, 246, 262
Monumental Remains of Noble and Eminent Persons, by E. Blore, 251
Monuments, Christian style of, 57
Moore, T. L., architect, 206, 215, 257
Morals and architecture connected, 52, 68–69, 137, 150, 176–177
Morecambe, St. Lawrence, 258
Morpeth, St. James, 112
Morris, W., 194, 196, 213, 214, 238
Mossley Hill, Liverpool, 258
Mountford, F. W., architect, 258
Mozley, T., 21 n., 35, 45 n.
Muir, W. J. Cockburn, 69 n., 120, 121 n.
Murphy, Mr., 15
Myers, Pugin's builder, 60
Mystical Mirror of the Church, by Richard de Sancto Victore, 94
Mytholmroyd, 256

Naology, by Rev. J. Dudley, 87 n.
Narberth, 256
Nash, E., architect, 258

Nash, J., architect, 36, 41, 46, 51, 71, 258, 259, 260, 266, 267
National Gallery, 149
National Society, 22
Nature, Imitation of, 138–139
Neale, Rev. J. M., 75, 77, 87, 95, 97, 119, 137, 177, 183, 235, 242
Neath, 258
Nesfield, W. E., architect, 130, 262
Netherton, St. Andrew, 262
Newbridge-on-Wye, 264
Newcastle, St. Nicholas Cathedral, 254
  St. Aidan, 256
  All Saints', 4
  St. Matthew, 257
  St. Peter, 254
  St. Stephen, 257
  St. Thomas, 254
  St. Mary's R.C. Cathedral, 259
  Central Station, 253
Newington (South London), St. Mary, 254
Newington, Sittingbourne, Kent, 240
Newland, Malvern, 222–223, 256
Newman, A. S., architect, 250
Newman, Rev. J. H., 21 n., 46, 48, 105
New Mills, R.C. Church, 255
New Monthly Magazine, 13
Newport (Mon.), R.C. Church, 260
New System of Architecture, by W. V. Pickett, 127
Newton, Mr., and Albert Memorial, 169
New York Ecclesiologist, 104
New Zealand, churches in, 80–81, 84
Niblett, F., architect, 113
Nicholl, S. J., architect, 258, 260
Nicholson, T., architect, 258
Norbiton, Kingston, St. Peter, 162
Normacot, 261
Norman style for modern use, 42, 81, 84, 102, 112
Northampton, St. Lawrence, 250
  St. Matthew, 208
  R.C. Church, 259
  Architectural Society, 103
Northanger Abbey, by Jane Austen, 11
Northington, 256
Norton, J., architect, 242 n., 258
Northumberland, Duke of, 207
Norwich, St. Martin-at-Oak, 24
  St. John (R.C.), 261
Norwood, South, Holy Innocents, 251, 267
  Upper, All Saints', 39
    St. John, 201, 202, 207, 267
  West, St. Luke, 36

Notting Dale, St. Clement, 260
St. Mark, 158
Nottingham, St. Bartholomew, 208
St. George, 251
St. Barnabas Cathedral (R.C.), 64, 259
Notting Hill, All Saints', 157, 263
Holy Trinity (Harrow Mission), 262
St. Columb, 254
St. Francis (R.C.), 250
Nunhead, St. Antholin, 159

Oakeley, Rev. F., 119
Oare (Wilts), 263
Oates, Mr., architect, 247, 255
O'Connor, glass-painter, 114
Oldham, 250
Oldrid, Caroline, afterwards wife of Scott, 162
Open Roofs of the Middle Ages, by Brandon, 77
Ormesby, North, 263
Ornamental Timber Gables, by A. Pugin, 46
Ornaments of the Rubric, by J. T. Micklethwaite, 189 n., 190
Orsett, 24
Oscott, St. Mary's College, 48, 53
Otterburn, 113
Overton, J. H., 25
Ovington (Hants), 253
Oxford, St. Barnabas, 192–193, 269
S. Frideswide, 269
St. John the Evangelist (Cowley Fathers' Church), 269
St. Margaret, 269
St. Peter-le-Bailey, 269
SS. Philip and James, 148, 262
St. Aloysius (R.C.), 255
College Chapels : Keble, 123, 124, 125
Magdalen, 251, 252
Merton, 251
Worcester, 154
Martyrs' Memorial, 163
Museum, 142
Architectural Society, 89, 103, 131, 237
church-building in diocese of, 223
Oxford Movement, 29, 128, 160, 228, 236
Oxford Dictionary, 76

Paddington, Christchurch, Lancaster Gate, 254
Holy Trinity, 253
St. James, 262

Paddington (*contd.*)
St. John, 254
St. Mary Magdalene, 148, 218–219, 226, 262, 267
St. Michael, 256
St. Paul, 251
church-building in, 26
Paganism in church architecture, 50, 56, 70–71, 74
Pagan or Christian?, by W. J. C. Muir, 69 n., 120 n., 121 n.
Paley, E. G., architect, 176, 242 n., 258
Paley, Archdeacon W., 258
Palladio, architect, 6, 171, 176
Palmer's Green, St. John, 261
Palmerston, Lord, 166, 167, 168
Pangbourne, 241
Par, 113, 146, 262
Parentalia, by Wren, 7–8
Parish Churches, by Brandon, 77
Parish Churches of England, by Cox and Ford, 9 n.
Parishes, new, 216–218
Church life in, 218–223
Parish Priest of the Town, by J. Gott, 221
Parker, J. H., architectural writer, 76, 260
Parkgate, 263
Parliament, Acts of, for church-building, 3, 24
grants for church-building, 24
Parliament, Houses of, 38, 53, 112, 250, 252, 260
Parry, Gambier, 114, 241
Payne, C. J., 222 n.
Peacock, J., architect, 258
Pearson, F. L., architect, 204, 208
Pearson, J. L., architect, 126, 176, 190
his life, etc., 196–197
earlier churches, 198–199
characteristics of his churches, 199–202
later churches, 202–208
restorations, 208–209, 258, 266 267, 268, 269
Pearson, W., 197
Peckham, St. Andrew, 158
St. Chrysostom, 42
St. Jude, 193
Our Lady of Seven Dolours (R.C.), 259
Peel, Sir Robert, 216
Pembroke Dock, 258
Penarth, St. Augustine, 122
Pendlebury, St. Augustine, 211, 213, 251

Penge, Christchurch, 262
St. John, 258
Upper, St. Paul, 158
Penmaen, 258
Pennethorne, James, architect, 166, 258
Pennethorne, John, architect, 258
Penn Street, 113
Penny Sunday Reader, 2
Penrhiwceiber, 258
Penson, R. K., architect, 259
Penwortham, 258
Penzance, St. John, 260
Perry Street, Northfleet, 156
Personal and Professional Recollections, by Scott, 108 n., 129 n., 133 n., 160, 161, 169, 170, 171, 175 n., 234, 261
Perth Cathedral, 123
Peterborough, Cathedral, 170, 208, 210, 235
All Saints', 257
Petersham, All Saints', 257
Petit, Rev. J. L., 84–85, 177, 184, 233
Peto, S. M., 162
Pett, 113
Pews, 102, 239
Philip Webb and his Work, by W. R. Lethaby, 124 n., 153 n.
Philips, Mr., architect, 255
Phipson, R. M., architect, 259
Pickett, W. V., 127
Pictorial Architecture of the British Isles, by Rev. H. H. Bishop, 69 n.
Pilgrim's Progress in the World To-day, by J. F. B. Mackay, 175
Pilling, 258
Pimlico, St. Barnabas, 115, 225, 253
St. Gabriel, 253
St. Saviour, 253
Pite, A. R., architect, 254, 255, 258
Pite, W. A., architect, 192 n.
Plaistow, St. Andrew, 156
Plans of churches, 90, 148, 150–151, 155, 177–183, 187–188, 191, 192, 199–200, 213
Platt (Lancs.), 262
Plea for the Faithful Restoration of our Ancient Churches, by Scott, 174 n., 230–233
Pleasures of Architecture, by C. and A. Williams-Ellis, 152 n.
Plumstead, St. Paul, 262
Plymouth, St. James-the-Less, 260
St. Peter, 259
R.C. Cathedral, 255
Pomeroy, F. W., 196

Pontypridd, 258
Poona, Butterfield's work at, 123
Poore, Bishop of Salisbury, 87
Popery, 13, 29, 39, 52, 72, 98, 99
Population, growth of, 3, 4, 19, 20–27, 81
Porden, C. F., architect, 35, 259, 265
Porden, W., architect, 259
Port Elizabeth, Butterfield's work at, 123
Portsdown, 253
Portsea, St. Mary, 192, 193
Portugal, destruction of monasteries in, 117 n.
Potter, of Lichfield, architect, 254
Powell, Messrs., 196
Pownall, J. F., architect, 219
Powning, J., architect, 254
Powys, A. R., architect, 2
Poynter, A., architect, 259
Pre-Raphaelites, 145, 148, 151, 213
Present State of Ecclesiastical Architecture in England, by Pugin, 58
Preston, St. Cuthbert, 257
St. Mark, 258
St. Paul, 260
St. Peter, 260
St. Ignatius (R.C.), 258
St. Walburge (R.C.), 258
Town Hall, 170
Preston-on-Stour, 10
Prestwich, 250
Prince Regent, 22, 23, 46, *see also* George IV.
Principles of Gothic Architecture, by M. H. Bloxham, 76, 209
Prior Park, R.C. Church, 260
Pritchard, J., architect, 241, 242 n., 252, 261
Pritchard, of York, architect, 253
Progress in Architecture, by J. P. Seddon, 261
Proprietary Chapels, 20
Propriety in architecture, according to Pugin, 54–55
Prynne, G. H. F., architect, 259, 265
Prynne, Rev. G. R., 113, 259
Pudsey, 51
Pugin, A., architect, 38, 46–47, 112, 252, 254
Pugin, A. W. N., architect:
his boyhood, 46–47
love of the sea, 47
marriage, 47
joins Roman Church, 47–48
dreams of, 49, 52, 55, 61, 62, 65, 70
produces *Contrasts*, 49–51
help in Houses of Parliament, 53

Pugin, A. W. N. (*contd.*)
  produces *True Principles*, 53–55
  produces *Apology*, 55–58
  produces *Treatise on Screens*, 58–59
  insanity and death, 60
  character of churches, 60–64
  romance of, 64–65
  attitude to Wyatt, 65–66
  attitude to Church of England, 66–68
  attitude to shams, 68–69
  prophetic character of, 70
  Also 72, 73, 87, 97 n., 104, 116, 121 n., 124, 125, 135, 136, 137, 139, 140 n., 163, 177, 178, 198, 212, 237, 252, 254, 259, 263, 264, 267, 268
Pugin, E. W., architect, 255, 259
Pugin, P. P., architect, 259–260
Pugin, by M. Trappes-Lomax, 62, 70 n., 259
Pullan, R. P., 154 n.
Purcell, E. S., 48, 67
Purley, St. Mark, 259
Pusey, Dr. E. B., 29, 226
  opinions on ecclesiology, 117 n.
Putney, All Saints', 262
Pyramid, Great, 96, 264

Queenstown Cathedral (R.C.), 259
Quernmore, 258

Radipole, 84
Railton, D., architect, 158
Rambler, 59 n., 135
Ramsdell, 253
Ramsgate, St. George, 257
  St. Augustine (R.C.), 62–63
Ranmore, 261
Rates for church-building, 3, 217, 224
Rationale Divinorum Officiorum, by Durandus, 87–94
Ravensthorpe (Yorks), 254
Raynes Park, St. Saviour, 193
Reading, All Saints', 260
  St. Bartholomew, 263
  Christchurch, 264
  St. Luke, 260
  Gaol, 164
Recollections of Pugin, by Ferrey, 46 n., 47, 48 n., 53 n., 60 n., 67 n., 68 n., 112
Redbrook, 261
Reddish, St. Elizabeth, 263
Redditch, St. Stephen, 264
Redhill (Surrey), St. John, 208
Refinement of Bodley's Gothic, 212

Reformation, 1–2, 73, 177, 236
Regents Park, St. Katherine's Hospital, 259
Regent Street, 36, 258
  Hanover Chapel, 36, 253
  St. Philip, 36
Remains of Ecclesiastical Woodwork, by T. T. Bury, 252
Remains of Hurrell Froude, 46
Reminiscences, by T. Mozley, 35, 45 n.
Renaissance, 5–6, 45
Repton, G., architect, 36
Restorations, 13, 125–126, 143–144, 170, 208, 227–247
Restoration of Churches is the Restoration of Popery, a sermon by Dr. Close, 99–100
Revett, N., architect, 33
Richard Temple West, by T. T. Carter, 219 n.
Richards, Rev. Upton, 119
Richmond (Surrey), St. John, 263
  St. Matthias, 261
Rickman, T., architect, 18, 19, 40, 89, 251, 256, 260, 261, 268
Ridgmont, 261
Ringley, 258
Ringwood, 254
Rious, Mr., author, 15
Ripon Cathedral, 170
  Mr. Taylor's work at, 31
Rippingale, 228
Ripple, 250
Risca, 255
Riseholm, 263
Riverhead, 252
Roath (Cardiff), St. German, 251
  St. Saviour, 251
Roberts, H., architect, 162
Rochdale, St. Alban, 252
Rochester, Cathedral, 170, 208, 252, 254
  St. Peter, 159
Rochford, 240
Rock, Dr., 48
Roehampton, Holy Trinity (Old Church), 113
  (New Church), 259
Rogers, W., architect, 260
Rolle, Louisa, Lady, 226
Romanby, 254
Roman Church and Gothic Architecture, 48–49, 57, 66–68, 72–74, 128, 135–136
Rome, city of, 149
  St. Peter's, proposal to rebuild in Gothic, 70
Romford, St. Edmund, 256

Roper, D. R., architect, 260, 266
Rossetti, D. G., 213, 214
Rotherhithe, All Saints', 257
  St. Barnabas, 123
  Christchurch, 263
  Holy Trinity, 257
Roumieu, R. L., architect, 255
Rowley, J. W., architect, 251
Royal Academy, 148, 154, 160, 166,
  191, 197, 210, 250, 252, 263
Royal Archaeological Institute, 251
Royal Institute of British Architects,
  112, 154, 159, 191, 197, 210,
  233, 252, 260, 263
R.I.B.A. Journal, 126
Royal Society, 251
Royton, St. Anne, 257
Rubrics, 73, 74, 75, 78, 82, 178
Rugby, St. Andrew, 123
  Holy Trinity, 261
  R.C. Church, 259
  School, 255
  Chapel, 123
Runcorn, 260
Runcton, North, 9
  South, 23, 24
Rusholme, 258
Ruskin, J., 61, 69, 121 n., 133–146,
  147, 151, 169, 171, 195, 250

Sacred Gems from the British Poets,
  10–11
St. Albans, Cathedral, 170, 252
  St. Michael, 229
  St. Peter, 229
St. Albans Cathedral and its Res-
  toration, by Lord Grimthorpe,
  54 n., 230 n.
St. Asaph, Cathedral, 170, 234 n.
  church-building in diocese, 223
St. Aubyn, J. P., architect, 242 n.,
  260
St. Barnabas', Oxford, by A. T.
  Bassett, 193 n.
St. Columb Major, 157
St. Columb Minor, 105
St. David's, Cathedral, 170
  church-building in diocese, 223
St. George in the East, 9
  Christchurch, Watney Street, 43,
  262
  St. Peter, London Docks, 219
  Fr. Lowder's work in, 219
St. Hilary, 263
St. John Lee, 254
St. John's Wood, St. John, 256
  St. Mark, Hamilton Terrace, 253
  St. Stephen, Portland Town, 253
  Our Lady (R.C.), 260

St. Leonards-on-Sea, Christchurch,
  193
  St. John, 193
  St. Peter, 156
St. Luke's, St. Clement, City Road,
  123
  St. Matthew, City Road, 261
St. Marychurch, Priory Church
  (R.C.), 255
St. Marylebone, Parish Church, 255,
  267
  All Saints', Margaret Street, 118,
  119–121, 122, 148, 181, 247,
  267
  All Souls', Langham Place, 36, 51,
  258, 267
  St. Andrew, Wells Street, 117,
  216, 251, 253
  The Annunciation, Bryanston
  Street, 267
  St. Barnabas, 193
  Christchurch, Lisson Grove, 36
  St. Cyprian, 267
  Holy Trinity, 35–36, 262
  St. Luke, Nutford Place, 159
  St. Mark, 191, 193
  St. Mary, Bryanston Square, 262
  St. Charles, Ogle Street (R.C.),
  264
  Immaculate Conception, Farm
  Street (R.C.), 260
  St. James, Spanish Place (R.C.),
  254
  Catholic Apostolic Church, Maida
  Vale, 208
St. Pancras, All Hallows, Gospel
  Oak, 156, 267
  St. Barnabas, Kentish Town, 159
  Camden Town Church, 56, 256
  Christchurch, Albany Street, 258
  Holy Trinity, Grays Inn Road,
  258
  St. James, Hampstead Road, 256
  St. Jude, Grays Inn Road, 258
  St. Luke, Kentish Town, 252, 267
  St. Martin, Gospel Oak, 257
  St. Mary, Somers Town, 41, 51,
  256
  St. Mary Magdalene, Munster
  Square, 117, 267
  St. Matthew, Oakley Square, 256
  St. Michael, Camden Town, 211–
  212, 251
  St. Pancras (Old Church), 255
  St. Pancras (New Church), 25, 33,
  35, 90, 256, 267
  St. Paul, Camden Town, 256
  St. Peter, Regent Square, 256
  St. Thomas, Agar Town, 158, 263

St. Pancras (*contd.*)
  Catholic Apostolic Church, Gor-
    don Square, 252, 267
  church-building in, 26
  Railway Hotel, 169–170
St. Patrick's Society, 103
Sale Moor, 256
Salford, St. Clement, 258
  St. Philip, 262
  Cathedral of St. John (R.C.), 255
Salisbury, Cathedral, 13 n., 14, 51,
    70, 153, 170, 229
  St. Oswald (R.C.), 259
Salter, S., architect, 260
Salvin, A., architect, 197, 242 n., 260
San Fransisco, Bodley's cathedral at,
    251
Saturday Review, 60, 167
Savage, J., architect, 59, 72, 260, 265
Savernake, Christchurch, 264
  St. Katherine, 264
Scarborough, Holy Trinity, 159
  St. Martin, 209, 211, 213–214, 251
  St. Mary, 159
Schopenhauer, Dr., philosopher, 164
Scoles, J. J., architect, 258, 260–261
Scorton, 258
Scott, E., architect, 269
Scott, Geoffrey, 68 n.
Scott, Sir George Gilbert, architect,
    29, 41 n., 73, 84 n., 108, 109,
    113, 115–116, 118, 126, 128–
    130, 133, 134, 146, 149
  populariser of Gothic, 160
  his education, 161–162
  workhouses, etc., 162
  conversion, 163
  relations with Camden Society, 164
  builds church at Hamburg, 164–
    165
  some of his activities, 165–166
  Government offices, 166–169
  Albert Memorial, 169
  failures, 170
  restorations, 170
  death, 170
  estimates of, 171–172
    Also 190, 193, 198, 200, 208, 209,
    214, 229, 230, 231, 233–234,
    236, 238–239, 240, 242 n., 244,
    250, 252, 254, 257, 258, 260,
    261, 263, 264, 265, 266, 267,
    268, 269
Scott, G. C., Junior, architect, 176,
    213, 214–215, 266, 267
Scott, Sir Giles G., architect, 210,
    248
Scott, J. O., architect, 261, 267, 268
Scott, Rev. T., 161

Scott, Sir Walter, 11
Screens, 58–59, 180, 202, 237–238
Soulcoats, St. Mary, 257
Scunthorpe, 253
Secular uses of church buildings, 1
Sedding, E., architect, 194
Sedding, J. D., architect, 176, 194–
    196, 214, 261, 265, 268
Seddon, J. P., architect, 165 n., 241,
    242 n., 261
Selby Abbey, 254, 261
Semley, 264
Seven Lamps of Architecture, by
    Ruskin, 69, 136 f.
Seventeenth century, styles of Archi-
    tecture in, 6–8
Shaftesbury, Holy Trinity, 162
Shalford, 113
Shams in architecture, 54, 66, 68–69,
    83, 87, 116, 139–141, 159,
    163, 171, 189
Sharow, 262
Sharpe, E., architect, 258, 261
Shaw, J., architect, 262
Shaw, J., Junior, architect, 42, 262
  his suggestions for church-
    building, 42–43
Shaw, R. Norman, architect, 130,
    165 n., 176, 194, 210, 262,
    268
Sheen, East, 193
Sheffield, St. Andrew, Sharrow, 257
  St. George, 40
  St. John, Park, 41
  St. Paul, 3
  St. Marie (R.C.), 255
  Churches by T. J. Flockton in,
    254
Shelf, 256
Shellard, E. H., architect, 262
Shields, South, St. Mary, Tyne
    Dock, 254
Shenstone, 254
Shepherdswell (or Sibertswold), 113
Shere, 244
Shilbottle, 256
Sholing, 253
Shoreditch, St. James, 251
  St. Mark, Old Street, 113
  St. Michael, 156, 267
Short Critical History of Architecture,
    by H. H. Statham, 6, 120 n.
Shotley Bridge, 254
Shotton, 255
Shrewsbury, St. Chad, 4
Shrewsbury, Lord, 48
Sidcup, St. John, 259
Singleton, Great, 258
Sion College Library, 191

Skegness, St. Matthew, 254
Skelton, 155
Skelton-in-Cleveland, 257
Skidmore, Mr., metal-worker, 169
Skinner, Rev. J., 222
Skipton, 23
Skipworth, A. H., architect, 266
Skirlaw, Bishop's Chapel, 51
Slater, W., architect, 117, 242 n., 262
Sledmere, 225, 257
Slough, St. Mary, 261
Smannell, 263
Smeaton, 264
Smirke, Sir R., architect, 162, 262, 263, 266, 268
Smirke, S., architect, 253, 262
Smith, C. A. B., architect, 262
Smith, F., of Warwick, architect, 245
Smith, W. B., architect, 262
Soane, Sir J., architect, 35, 262, 265, 267
Soane Museum, 262, 264
Society for the Protection of Ancient Buildings, 238
Some Remarks, by Pugin, 61 n.
Souldern, 251
South, Dr. R., 237
Southampton, St. Augustine, Northam, 264
St. Lawrence, 264
St. Mark, 253
St. Mary, 263
Southborough, St. Peter, 252
Southend, All Saints', 156
Southsea, St. Matthew, 257
Southwark, Cathedral, 191
All Hallows, 214, 215, 226, 261, 267
Specimens of Ancient Sculpture and Painting, by J. Carter, 17
Specimens of Early French Architecture, by R. J. Johnson, 257
Specimens of Gothic Architecture, by Pugin and Willson, 38, 46
Speenhamland, 260
Speke, 206
Spitalfields, All Saints', 84
Christchurch, 9
St. Stephen, 159
Spofforth, 178 n.
Springbett, E. H., 161
Squirrell, Mr., architect, 263
Staines, St. Peter, 259
Staleybridge, St. Paul, 40
Stamford Hill, St. Ann, 252
Stanhope, R. Spencer, 214
Stanley, Rev. A. P., Dean of Westminster, 171
Stanmore, 253

Stapleton, 258
Statham, H. H., 6, 120
Stebbing, 259
Stephenson, D., architect, 253
Stepney, St. Benet, 159
St. Luke, 192
St. Paul, Bow Common, 225, 256
St. Philip, 267
English Martyrs, Tower Hill (R.C.), 259
Stevenage, Holy Trinity, 193
Stevens, Mr., architect, 266
Sticker, 146
Stockbridge, 253
Stockport, St. George, 258
Stockton, St. Mary (R.C.), 259
Stockwell, St. Michael, 260
Stoke Bishop, 258
Stoke D'Abernon, 229
Stoke Newington, All Saints', 254
St. Faith, 155, 267
St. Mary, 224, 261, 267
St. Matthias, 118, 121–122, 220, 225, 267
St. Olave, Woodberry Down, 159
Stones of Venice, by Ruskin, 135, 144
Stonyhurst, R.C. Church, 260
Stony Middleton (Derbys), 4
Stratford, Christchurch, 256
Stratton, 256
Strawberry Hill, 12–14
Streatham, St. Anselm, 264
Christchurch, 43, 84, 264, 267
Immanuel, 113
Street, A. E., architect, 109 n., 147, 148 n., 150 n., 151 n., 191
Street, G. E., architect, 109, 113, 114, 117, 120, 130, 131
his early life, 146
churches, 147–149
his opinions on Gothic, 149–150
planning of churches, 150–151
character, 151–152
Also 165 n., 172, 176, 183, 191, 192, 194, 199, 200, 208, 218, 237, 241, 242 n., 245, 254, 257, 259, 262–263, 266, 267, 268, 269
Stretton, 190, 252
Stride. L., architect, 252
Strood, St. Mary, 193
St. Nicholas, 262
Stuart and Revett, part in Greek Revival, 33
Studley Royal, 154
Styles of architecture, names of, 16–19, 87
suggestions of Church Building Society, 30

Styles of architecture (*contd.*)
  mixture in Commissioners'
    Churches, 32–33
  Gothic, 38–42
  Grecian, 33–37
  Norman for modern use, 42, 102,
    110, 112
  Lombardic, 42–43
  superiority of Second Pointed,
    78–79, 88, 96, 98, 105,
    108–109, 110, 129, 174, 179
  adoption of foreign Gothic, 128–
    159, 192, 199, 200, 209
  Ruskin's suggestions, 142
  return to English, 174, 176
  " Queen Anne," 175, 262
  less importance of, in later nine-
    teenth century, 175–176,
    184–185, 192
  Pearson's use of Early English,
    199 f.
  Bodley's use of fourteenth-cen-
    tury, 211
Sudbury (Suffolk), St. Peter, 251
Summerson, J., 36 n.
Sunbury, 246
Sunderland, St. Aidan, 254
  St. Paul, Hendon, 254
Sunningdale, 261
Surbiton, St. Andrew, 193
Sutton (Surrey), St. Nicholas, 258
Swanmore (Isle of Wight), 105
Swansea, St. James, 258
  St. Michael, 258
  St. Thomas, 258
Swinbrook, 238
Swindon, St. Barnabas, 261
Swinton, 263
Sydenham, St. Bartholomew, 263
  St. Matthew, 253
  St. Philip, 258
Sydney, St. Mary's R.C. Cathedral,
    263
Sykes, Sir Tatton, 225
Symbolism, 87–98, 102, 103, 134,
    149, 177, 180, 183, 212

Tait, Most Rev. A. C., 217, 246
Taplow, 259
Tapper, W., architect, 267
Tasmania, Carpenter's churches in,
    117
Tattershall, Mr., architect, 40
Taunton, St. James, 23
  St. John, 261
Tavistock, 253
Taylor, Sir R., architect, 4
Taylor, Mr., of Leeds, architect, 31
    269

Teddington, SS. Peter and Paul, 263
Tedstone Wafer, 226
Terbury, St. Michael, 264
Tetbury, 10
Teulon, S. S., architect, 157–158,
    242 n., 246, 263, 266, 269
Theology, 200 n.
Theydon Bois, 262
Thirkleby, 257
Thixendale, 225, 263
Thornaby, St. Luke, 256
Thornycroft, Hamo, 196
Thorpe, Rev. T., 75
Thwaites, 258
Tierney, Sir E., 113
Times, newspaper, 68, 167
Tinling, Miss R., afterwards Mrs.
    Sedding, 195
Tinsley, 263
Tite, W., M.P., architect, 134 n.,
    167, 265
Titsey, 198
Toft (Chesh.), 255
Tong (Yorks), 9
Tooting Graveney, All Saints', 215,
    257, 267
Topsham, 250
Torquay, St. John, 148, 263
  St. Mark, 260
  St. Mary Magdalene, Upton, 260
Torver, 258
Tottenham, Holy Trinity, 260
Trappes-Lomax, M., 62, 70, 259
*Treatise on Chancel Screens and
    Lofts*, by Pugin, 58
*Treatise on the Ecclesiastical Archi-
    tecture of England*, by Milner,
    15
Trent Park, 257
Trimen, A., architect and author,
    31–32, 74 n.
*True Principles of Pointed or Chris-
    tian Architecture*, by Pugin,
    53–55
Truefitt, G., architect, 263
Truro Cathedral, 199, 201, 203–205,
    210, 248, 260
Tubney, 259
Tue Brook, St. John, 209–210, 213,
    251
Tufnell Park, St. George, 263
Tulse Hill, Holy Trinity, 250
Tunbridge Wells, St. James, 159
  St. John, 255
Turner, Rev. Mr., 105
Turnham Green, Christchurch, *see*
    Chiswick.
*Twenty-three Reasons for Getting
    Rid of Church Pues*, 75

Twyford, St. Mary, 263
Tyldesley, St. George, 262
Tynemouth, 24

Uley, 263
Ullenhall, 261
Uplands, Stroud, All Saints', 257
Upton Cross, 193
Ushaw College Chapel (R.C.) 259
Uxbridge Moor, 23

Vallance, Aymer, 238
Vanburgh, Sir J., architect, 9
Vaughan, H., of Boston, architect, 210
Vaughan, Cardinal, 248
Vaults, 200–201
Vauxhall, St. Peter, 198–199, 201
   St. Anne (R.C.), 263
Vernham Dean, 250
Vestries, 82, 181, 188–189
Victoria, Queen, 8, 169, 251
Victoria Docks, The Ascension, 253
Viollet-le-Duc, M., architect, 130
Vitruvius, 6
Vobster, 113
Vulliamy, L., architect, 41, 263

Wadesmill (Thundridge), 113
Wadmore, J. F., architect, 263
Wagner, Rev. A. D., 226
Wailes, Mr., glass-painter, 114
Wakefield, Bridge Chapel, 164, 234 n.
Walcot, 24
Walesby, 257
Walker, Mr., architect, 259
Walker and Athron, architects, 269
Walker-on-Tyne, 254
Wallington, 252
Walmer, St. Mary, 193
   St. Saviour, 257
Walney, Isle of, 258
Walpole, Horace, 12
Walsall, St. Luke, 257
Walters, F. A., architect, 263
Walterstone, 23
Waltham Abbey, work of Burges at, 153
Walthamstow, St. Barnabas, 225
   St. Saviour, 254
Walton, Higher, 258
Walworth, St. Peter, 35, 262, 267
Wandsworth, All Saints', 258
   St. Anne, 258, 262, 267
   St. Mary, 258
Wansford (Yorks), 148, 263
Wanstead, Holy Trinity, 254
   St. Mary, 255
   Infant Orphan Asylum, 164

Wantage, 222
Warburton, Bishop, his opinions on Gothic, 14
Ward, J. S. M., 240, 241 n.
Ward, W. G., 48, 59
Wardell, W. W., architect, 263
Wareside, 222
Warrington, St. Luke, 213, 251
Warton, J. and T., 16, 17
Warwick, St. Nicholas, 10
Warwick Bridge, R.C. Church, 259
Washington Cathedral, 210
Waterford, 264
Waterhouse, A., architect, 165 n., 263
Watford, St. Andrew, 263
   Holy Rood (R.C.), 263
Watson, Joshua, 22, 24
Watts and Co., 213
Weale's Quarterly Papers, 72, 100, 101, 103
Weatherley, W. S., architect, 244
Weaverthorpe, 225
Webb, Sir Aston, architect, 263
Webb, Benjamin, 75, 87, 117, 118, 119, 137, 163, 242
Webb, Philip, architect, 176, 194, 214
Weedall, Rev. H., 48
Weightman, J. G., architect, 254, 255
Welby, Catherine, the Belle of Islington, afterwards Mrs. Pugin, 46, 47
Welch, E., architect, 255
Wellingborough, R.C. Church at, 258
Wellington College Chapel, 134
Wells Cathedral, 112
Welsh Bicknor, 226
Wenhaston, 238
Wentworth, 202–203
West, Rev. R. T., 218, 219
Westby, R.C. Church, 259
Westcott (Surrey), 113, 261
Weston-super-Mare, All Saints', 251
Westminster, Abbey, 13 n., 18, 101, 165, 170, 180, 205, 208, 227, 248, 251
   All Saints', Ennismore Gardens, 263
   St. Andrew, 261, 268
   St. George, Hanover Square, 178 n.
   Holy Trinity, Vauxhall Bridge Road, 198, 226, 268
   St. James-the-Less, 147, 199, 262, 268
   St. John, Great Marlborough Street, 193

Westminster (*contd.*)
St. John, Wilton Road, 192, 193, 268
St. Mark, North Audley Street, 36, 192, 246
St. Martin-in-the-Fields, 9, 35
St. Mary, Bourdon Street, 193
St. Mary, Graham Street, 264
St. Mary-le-Strand, 9
St. Matthew, 261, 268
St. Michael, Burleigh Street, 260
St. Michael, Chester Square, 253
St. Paul, Covent Garden, 255
St. Paul, Knightsbridge, 225, 251, 253
St. Peter, Eaton Square, 36, 192, 246, 255
St. Peter, Great Windmill Street, 252, 268
St. Stephen, Rochester Row, 112, 113, 116, 268
R.C. Cathedral, 96, 248, 250, 268
Proposed by Clutton, 253
SS. Anselm and Cecilia, Kingsway (R.C.), 263
St. Patrick, Soho (R.C.), 257
Church House, 191
church-building in, 26
Weybridge, 198
Weymouth, Christchurch, 159
St. John, 252
Whall, C. W., glass-painter, 196
Wheatley, 263
Whichcord, J., architect, 263
Whippingham, 112
Whipton, 250
Whitby, Abbey, 205
St. Hilda, 257
Whitchurch (Hants), 113
White, Rev. E. Milner, 200 n.
White of Selborne, 263
White, W., architect, 157, 242 n., 263–264, 265
Whitechapel, St. Mary Matfelon, 257, 268
Whitkirk, 251
Whitstable, St. Peter, 259
Whittingham, 229
Whitworth, St. Bartholomew, 252
Wibsey, 24
Widford, 190, 257
Wigan, All Saints', 258
St. Michael, 263
Wightwick, G., architect, 101, 102
Wilberforce, Rt. Rev. S., 160, 223, 240
Wild, J. W., architect, 43, 264
Wilkins, W., architect, 112
Wilkinson, Rt. Rev. G. H., 204

Willement, glass-painter, 247
Willesden, St. Andrew, 156
St. Gabriel, 262
William IV, 251
William George Ward and the Oxford Movement, 48 n., 60 n.
Williams, David, 119
Williams-Ellis, C. and A., architects, 152 n.
Williams, S. W., architect, 264
Willis, Brown, 17
Willis, Professor, 19
Willson, Mr., writer on Gothic, 38
Willson, T. J., architect, 258
Wilson, Rev. W. Carus, 27–28
Wilton, 107, 264
Wimbledon, All Saints', 190, 257
Holy Trinity, 257
St. John, 256
St. Luke, 256
St. Paul, 190, 257
Sacred Heart (R.C.), 263
Wimblington, 264
Wimborne, 237
Winchelsea, monument at, 51
Winchester, Cathedral, 17, 18, 170, 240, 251
Christchurch, 159
St. Peter (R.C.), 263
church-building in diocese, 223
Winmarleigh, 258
Windsor, Castle, 47, 251
St. George's Chapel, 14, 18, 51, 190
Holy Trinity, 251
Windyer, of Toronto, architect, 259
Wiseman, Cardinal, 64
Withers, R. J., architect, 242 n., 264
Withycombe Raleigh, 250
Witton, All Saints', 252
Woburn, 253
Woburn Sands, 253
Woking, Christchurch, 84
Wokingham, St. Paul, 264
Wolverhampton, St. Peter, 159
Wolverton (Bucks), 255
Wolverton (Hants), 244
Wood, J., of Bath, architect, 45
Woodborough, 264
Woodhead and Hurst, architects, 40, 255
Woodthorpe, Mr., architect, 244
Woodyer, H., architect, 114, 242 n., 264, 266
Woolhampton, 257
Woolton, Much, R.C. Church, 259
Woolwich, St. Michael, 123
Worcester Cathedral, 170
Wordsworth, Rt. Rev. Christopher, 24

Workhouses, by Scott, 162, 164
Workington, R.C. Church at, 259
Worksop, R.C. Church at, 255
Woronzow, Prince, 251
Worship, early nineteenth-century, according to Eastlake, 37
    suitability of early nineteenth-century churches to, 38
    dull, of Pugin in boyhood, 47
    debased in Church of Rome, 48–49
    revival in Church of England, 181–183, 197, 218–223
Worth, S., architect, 257
Worth, 238
Worthing, St. Andrew, 193
    St. George, 263
Wren, Sir Christopher, architect, 6, 101, 107, 115, 152, 177, 215 n.
    plans of churches, 4–5
    opinions on Gothic, 7
    use of Gothic, 8
Wren, Junior, author of *Parentalia*, 7
Wrightington, 258

Wyatt, B., architect, 255
Wyatt, J., architect, 12–13, 38, 65, 66, 71, 229, 234, 259
Wyatt, J. D., architect, 264
Wyatt, M., architect, 264
Wyatt, Sir M. Digby, architect, 152, 168, 264
Wyatt, T. H., architect, 107, 250, 260, 264
Wyesham, 261
Wyke (or Weeke) (Hants), 253
Wyke, St. Mary (Yorks), 256
Wykeham, William of, 87, 111

Yarmouth, Great, St. James, 261
    St. Peter, 260
    R.C. Church, 260
Yates, Rev. R., 20 n., 22
Yealmpton, 122
York, Cathedral, 14, 210
    St. Wilfrid (R.C.), 254
York, Duke of, 23
    Column, 255
York Town, 264
Yoxford, 24
Ystrad-Mynach, 258